Second Edition

NONVIOLENCE in
THEORY and PRACTICE

Second Edition

NONVIOLENCE in THEORY and PRACTICE

Robert L. Holmes
University of Rochester

Barry L. Gan
St. Bonaventure University

WAVELAND
PRESS, INC.
Long Grove, Illinois

For information about this book, contact:
Waveland Press, Inc.
4180 IL Route 83, Suite 101
Long Grove, IL 60047-9580
(847) 634-0081
info@waveland.com
www.waveland.com

Cover: Artwork by Inge K. Čimić

For Veronica
— Robert L. Holmes

For Maureen
— Barry L. Gan

Contents

PART FOUR
Pacifism   173

PART FIVE
The Practice of Nonviolence   233

PART SIX
Examples of Nonviolence   305

Preface to the Second Edition

In the fifteen years since this book was first published, the world has seen many changes, some violent, some nonviolent. The Gulf War, the NATO-led attacks on the former Yugoslavia, the U.S. invasions of Afghanistan and Iraq, and the Israeli-Palestinian conflict are the most notable examples of violence on a large scale over these past fifteen years. But the overthrow of Slobodan Milosevic, the emergence of international grassroots coalitions against the World Bank and the International Monetary Fund, and especially the break-up of the Soviet Union also were major events, and although violence played a role in each of these other stories, nonviolence arguably has played an even larger role.

This new edition provides fresh examples of the use of nonviolence in a number of these more recent historical developments. Specifically, we have added articles on nonviolence in the Middle East, Europe, Africa, and Tibet, as well as new articles addressing the theory and practice of nonviolence with respect to nature and animal rights. The second edition also features additions to the sections on the origins of nonviolence, nonviolence and women, pacifism, and the practice of nonviolence.

The readings have been arranged with a view to engaging those who are relatively new to the philosophy of nonviolence. We begin with a section on its origins, followed by a section that focuses on three principal philosophers of nonviolence. The next section emphasizes the role of women in the practice of nonviolence, followed by a discussion of pacifism. We conclude with a look at the various ways in which nonviolence is practiced, including specific examples drawn from different regions of the world. The readings could be organized differently with equal plausibility. One could, for example, have a separate section on civil disobedience. We have chosen to integrate that material with the other sections on the grounds that it has typically been through the engagement with concrete moral problems that civil disobedience has been practiced. For the most part (at least until recently) it also has been discussed in that context. On the other hand, we thought it important to highlight the often-neglected role of women and nonviolence by means of a separate section, even though most of the articles therein would fit quite well in the other sections. Further, one could opt for either an exclusively chronological or exclusively systematic presentation of these materials. We opted for a mix of the two, preserving as much of an historical orientation as possible while conforming to some of the more compelling systematic restraints. This explains, for example, why the article on the practice of civil disobedience by women in antiquity is included in the section on women and nonviolence rather than in the section on origins.

Readers will, we trust, explore all of these readings in the order that best fits their interests. Finally, we should note that many important writings could not be included. We hope readers will be led to delve more extensively into the works of Tolstoy, Gandhi, and King on the philosophy of nonviolence; the works of contemporary feminists such as Sara Ruddick, Arundhati Roy, and Starhawk, who are focusing increased attention on nonviolence; and the works of contemporary writers like Gene Sharp, Jack DuVall, and Peter Ackerman, who are at the forefront in analyzing the techniques of nonviolent action for social change and national defense.

In addition to thanking those people who helped with the first edition, we would also like to thank Laurie Prossnitz, our editor, for her very helpful suggestions and attention to detail; Bonnie Highsmith, for her work in securing the permissions; Maureen Bernas, for her occasional editorial advice; and Sue Martin, for her secretarial assistance.

—Robert L. Holmes and Barry L. Gan

Preface to the First Edition

Nonviolence has yet to emerge fully into the light of recognition in institutions of higher learning. One can learn about violence in its various forms: courses abound on the history of this or that war or revolution or, in colleges or universities with ROTC units, about military history, tactics, and strategy. In most major universities, one can even receive military training and instruction, for credit, given by military personnel holding professorships. But relatively few such institutions have courses in which students can learn about the alternative that nonviolence presents to the whole set of assumptions, attitudes, and values that are taken for granted in our history and culture.

This situation is changing slowly as new programs develop in peace studies, conflict resolution, and related areas; as feminism, which by its nature seeks to reorient our thinking in fundamental ways, gives more and more attention to nonviolence; and as institutes and resource centers dedicated to peace and nonviolence provide models of new ways to approach education in this area. Even so, many of these developments go only part way in challenging the whole way of thinking that has governed our attitudes about social, political, and international affairs; so in a sense the educational work has only begun.

The aim of this book is to provide a resource for people willing to take seriously the challenge of nonviolence. It is designed primarily for those with little or no background in either the history of nonviolence or its recent and contemporary expressions; but there are works here that should be of value to those who are experienced in both the theory and practice of nonviolence as well, if only because they are not widely known, and in one case have not been published before. Reading about nonviolence is not the only way to learn about it. It may not even be the best way. But it is one of the ways. And quite apart from whether one gravitates to nonviolence or ends up dismissing it as hopelessly naive, one cannot appreciate it without considering its many dimensions; and one cannot presume even to have begun a critical assessment of basic social, political, and cultural values without understanding it.

A few debts of gratitude: to Ken King for wise counsel at just the right moments; to John Ansbro for initiating the idea of such a collection; and to Barry Gan, Saint Bonaventure University; Nigel Young, Colgate University;

Adrienne Kaufmann, The American University; and Duane Campbell, California State University, Sacramento, for reviews of the initial proposal for this book.

Thanks also to Connie Slade for secretarial assistance and to Prasanta Bandyopadhyay and Abhaya Nayak for research assistance.

—Robert L. Holmes

General Introduction

On December 1, 1955, a 43-year-old seamstress boarded a bus in Montgomery, Alabama. She sat in the first row behind the white section. She was African American. When the front section filled she was asked to move to make room for more whites. She refused and was arrested.

On January 31, 1960, a college student took a seat at a lunch counter in Greensboro, North Carolina. He was refused service. He too was African American. The next day he and three friends sat in at a lunch counter in Woolworth's. They too were refused service.

Rosa Parks did not get her bus home that day, nor did Joseph McNeill get his lunch. But they sparked movements that were to transform the South and the nation.

Several things are significant about what they did.

First, they initially acted on their own. Although thousands soon rallied to their causes, they acted in individual witness of human dignity in the face of social injustice. Second, they engaged in civil disobedience: the law was on the side of segregation. Third, they acted nonviolently. This is the idea we want to explore.

What is nonviolence?

To answer this requires looking beyond a few specific acts on specific occasions; it requires considering how people would act under various kinds of circumstances, and why. Particularly relevant here are circumstances in which people are confronted with violence. Most of us are nonviolent most of the time; this is as true of those who approve of the use of violence in some circumstances as of those who do not. In fact, human interactions in general are nonviolent most of the time. It is when confronted with violence, threats, lawlessness, injustice, or oppression that most people think violence is justified.

This means that to understand nonviolence requires understanding something of the nature of violence. For a commitment to nonviolence, at the minimum, involves the renunciation of violence. But that renunciation may be qualified or unqualified.

It will be qualified, for example, if it involves only the renunciation of physical violence. Physical violence, which is what we most often have in mind when we speak about violence, is the use of physical force to cause harm, death, or destruction, as in rape, murder, or warfare. But some forms of mental or psychological harm are so severe as to warrant being called violence as well. People can be harmed mentally and emotionally in ways that are as bad as by physical violence. Verbal abuse of children can undermine their confidence and self-esteem; racism and sexism can do the same for whole groups. Although physical violence often attends the infliction of psychological violence, it need not do so. People can be done violence through brainwashing without being harmed physically. They can also be terrorized without being harmed physically (terrorism typically combines physical and psychological violence, using the first to cause the second). An unlimited commitment to nonviolence will renounce psychological as well as physical violence. This is the sort of commitment found in the Jains of ancient India, as well as in Mohandas Gandhi and Martin Luther King, Jr. Indeed, the Jains extended the renunciation of violence not only to words and deeds but to thoughts as well.

In addition to this negative aspect, the renunciation of violence, nonviolence typically has a positive aspect as well. It indicates what may justifiably be done when one encounters violence or wrongdoing (including oppression and injustice), either against oneself or against others. Here the commitment to nonviolence may assume the form of nonresistance, passive resistance, or nonviolent direct action (also called active or militant nonviolence).

Nonresistance, taken literally, means only that we should not resist violence and tells us nothing beyond that. Although Tolstoy sometimes seems to be saying this, few "nonviolentists" (as we may call advocates of nonviolence) understand the commitment in this way. Most of the time, even if they use the word "nonresistance," they have in mind something more, like passive resistance. And passive resistance is resistance; it is doing something. It is not passivity. Rosa Parks's act was an act of passive resistance. It was a refusal to comply with a directive, hence a refusal to acquiesce in the requirements of an unjust system. To have gotten up and relinquished her seat would have been passivity. Sometimes (from a moral standpoint) to refuse to perform a certain act is to be active, whereas to perform the act is to be passive.

On the other hand, when Joseph McNeill and his friends deliberately sat in at the Woolworth's lunch counter to protest segregation they engaged in nonviolent direct action. They did not wait for the injustice of the system to intrude on them the way it did with Rosa Parks. They set out to challenge the system where it stood, so to speak. They took the initiative.

So in addition to renouncing violence of either a physical or a psychological sort (or both), the nonviolentist must be prepared to offer some account of how one responds to the violence or wrongdoing of others. At this point further dimensions of nonviolence come into view. For how one responds to violence is an indicator of the scope and depth of one's commitment to renouncing violence.

A commitment to nonviolence will be unqualified if the nonviolentist renounces the use of violence in any circumstances whatsoever; it will be qualified otherwise. The Jains are unqualified nonviolentists. Gandhi, on the other hand, said that although nonviolence is always preferable, if the choice be between cowardice and violence, one might better use violence. Some pacifists likewise have only a qualified commitment to nonviolence; for pacifism, strictly, is the renunciation of (and opposition to) war, not all violence. Though many pacifists are nonviolentists as well, many are not. And some people subscribe to nonviolence only because they believe it is effective and do not rule out the use of violence in principle. Still others view nonviolence merely as a tactic, to be used in certain specific circumstances and not in others.

When nonviolence is practiced as a matter of principle, on the other hand, in the conviction that it is morally right in general and not just in this or that particular situation, it usually represents a philosophy and is embodied in a way of life. Sometimes it will be grounded in metaphysical views about the nature of reality, sometimes in a religious perspective. At other times its basis is exclusively moral.

In any case, does nonviolence work? This is perhaps the central question those who learn of nonviolence for the first time want to have answered.

The question is not as simple as it appears. To ask whether anything works requires specifying what it is intended to achieve. In the case of nonviolence, the goal may be differently defined, depending on whether one thinks of nonviolence merely as a tactic or as a philosophy or way of life.

Considered simply as a tactic, nonviolence sometimes works and sometimes does not. It carries with it no more guarantee of success than does the resort to violence. This does not mean that it may not work more often than violence; whether that is so is a matter for empirical study. It is just that it would be naive to suppose that the renunciation of violence automatically puts one in a privileged position with regard to the attainment of one's ends. It cannot even be assumed that nonviolence *per se* (meaning by this, the performance of actions that are only minimally nonviolent in that they do not use physical violence) is more moral than violence. As critics of nonviolence like Reinhold Niebuhr have pointed out, nonviolent actions can cause harm or suffering as much as violent actions. Strikes or boycotts can cause severe hardship—conceivably even death. Such "covert violence," as Niebuhr called it, has a questionable claim to moral superiority over violence. Even Gandhi acknowledged that sometimes destruction of people's property may harm them more than violence against them personally. One may cause harm even while refraining from violence. One may do psychological violence even while refraining from physical violence. And one may do violence to oneself even while refraining from physical or psychological violence to others.

Suppose, however, we are asking about the effectiveness of nonviolence as a matter of principle, and nonviolence of a sort that renounces both physical and psychological violence. Does it then work?

This requires specifying what ends or objectives nonviolence sets for itself. Nonviolence considered merely as a tactic will have different objectives according to the different circumstances in which it is tried, but principled nonviolence will normally have more basic ends in addition to such shorter-range objectives. Whether it "works" requires asking whether it furthers these aims as well.

If, for example, one of the ends of nonviolence is always to show respect for one's opponent in situations of conflict, one may succeed in doing this independently of whether one succeeds in achieving whatever other social or political objectives one may have. Or if (as seems clear) one of its aims is not to add to the amount of violence in the world, that, too, is achievable apart from success or failure at accomplishing other ends. Sometimes part of the aim of nonviolence is to effect certain changes in the thinking and character of those with whom one is in conflict; sometimes it is to effect certain changes in oneself as well. These, too, represent other yardsticks by which to measure whether it works.

In short, if one thinks of nonviolence as a way of life, then it works to the extent that one lives nonviolently and infuses everyday conduct with a nonviolent spirit. Effectiveness of this sort is not measurable in the same way as social and political changes. It cannot be quantified over a whole population. Nonetheless it is the relevant consideration in determining whether nonviolence is effective. Whether we are successful in bringing about certain consequences in our actions depends upon many circumstances beyond our control. It often depends also upon what others do. But whether we act nonviolently, considerately, and respectfully of others in all that we do is within our control. Nonviolence in that sense cannot fail to work if we resolve to see that it works.

In any event, to ask whether nonviolence works is to ask only part of what needs asking. What we really want to know is not merely, or perhaps even primarily, whether nonviolence works. We want to know whether it works better than violence. For whatever degree of success nonviolence has, if it works better than violence then it is the preferable course; if it does not, then arguably it is not.

This requires asking whether violence works. Since few have ever advocated violence as a matter of principle, its success or failure is usually viewed in terms of its effectiveness as a tactic. If our distinction between holding a commitment as a matter of principle as opposed to merely a tactic were applied to violence, most people would turn out to be "violentists" of a purely pragmatic sort. They do not advocate violence as a matter of principle or as a way of life. They advocate it only as a last resort, in circumstances in which they believe nothing else will achieve their objectives—and even then only when those objectives are unusually important.

Thus when an individual is assaulted, they believe, violence is justified in self-defense; when the nation is attacked, it is justified in national defense.

Viewed in this light, as a tactic to achieve specific objectives like defense or self-preservation, violence sometimes works and sometimes does not. Sometimes attackers are driven off; sometimes they are not. Sometimes aggressor nations are repelled; sometimes they are not.

But notice that all of these cases are two-sided. By hypothesis, both sides are using violence. And this means that for every case in which violence works on one side it fails on the other. Every time an attacker is driven off, violence has failed; but by the same token every time the attacker prevails the violent defense has failed. Similarly, every time an aggressive nation is defeated in war, violence has failed; but every time an aggressive nation is victorious, the violence of the defender has failed. In all such cases, violence fails precisely as often as it succeeds.

So for significant successes of violence we have to look to cases where it is used by one side only, and where that side achieves its objectives and could not have done so by other means. (Even when violence succeeds, that would constitute little argument for using it if other means could have been equally successful.)

At the interpersonal level there are clear cases of success of this sort: the mugger sometimes gets the money, the rapist sometimes gets his way. Matters are less clear at the international level. There violence is rarely used by one side only. Wars, for example, occur because both sides choose to fight (in this sense, paradoxically, wars are cooperative undertakings by the adversaries). Nations that are victims of aggression, of course, resort to violence because it is used against them first. But even aggressor nations usually use violence only because those they are aggressing against resist by means of violence; as the philosopher of war Carl von Clausewitz observed, most nations would far prefer to attain their objectives without having to fight. So while it certainly *may* happen that violence is used successfully at the international level without an offsetting failure, such successes are not particularly common; and victory in war does not represent such success.

But even if violence is used by one side only, and that side succeeds in achieving some objective by that means, is it clear that violence has worked? It has, to be sure, attained the particular objective in question. But is that all that is relevant?

I want to suggest another perspective from which to view the matter. This requires looking at the notion of means and ends.

For an action or practice to be effective, we have seen, requires that it succeed in achieving some end. Violence, by hypothesis, does just that in the sorts of cases we are now considering. But at what cost? In making these judgments we rarely factor into our assessments the extent to which the means we use to attain our ends transform the moral quality of the resultant state of affairs; we fail, that is, to see the extent to which means and ends are interrelated.

If you want a book on a shelf, the stool you stand on serves as a means. The end in this case is unaffected by the particular means you use: a chair would have done just as well, you possess the book either way, and all other things remain the same. In some cases, however, the means affect the very character of the end. Flour is part of the means by which you produce a loaf of bread. But if you use whole wheat rather than white flour that alters markedly the character of the end product. The same with colors when you mix paint.

In ethical matters the relation of means to ends is more akin to the bread-baking case than to that of book retrieving. The very character of the outcome is determined in part by the means used to achieve it. If we have got what we want by violence (and remember we are now talking about cases in which violence is not reciprocated), we will have brought into existence a certain amount of harm, pain, injury, death, or destruction; that is the nature of violence. This becomes a fact of the situation we have created. We may in addition have created a climate of fear, distrust, or hatred on the part of those against whom we have used the violence. We may also have contributed to the transformation of ourselves into insensitive or even cruel persons. These considerations should not be ignored. They are part of what we put into the attainment of our objectives. And they often lead to the eventual dissolution of what we most hoped to achieve. Revolutions, even when they overcome violent resistance, often end up breeding the same sorts of abuses their promoters hoped to eliminate, just as wars set the stage for new wars.

The point is that even after we have narrowed the range of cases in which violence succeeds to those in which it does not at the same time fail in obvious ways, there remains serious question whether violence really works, or works as well as is often unquestioningly assumed. And if we consider among our objectives the avoidance of harm or destruction, it is clear that violence not only does not work, it cannot work. By its very nature it precludes the attainment of such objectives.

This suggests that if we want to evaluate the effectiveness of nonviolence thoroughly, we need to begin looking at things in a different way. We need to think harder about what precisely constitutes the success or failure of both violence and nonviolence. The question is not merely whether nonviolence works; it is also whether violence works. And if they both sometimes work and sometimes do not, does nonviolence work better than violence? That requires deciding which ends or objectives (including moral ends as well as social and political objectives) are most important to us and which of them are most worthy of trying to live by.

The two questions posed here—What is nonviolence? Does it work?—are the primary concerns of the readings that follow, which are intended to represent some of the most considered attempts to explain what nonviolence is and to show some of the ways in which it has been or might be implemented. Nonviolence, despite its deep historical roots, is still in its infancy. It represents a revolutionary way of getting along in the world, a challenge to old ways of thinking in everything from personal interactions to international affairs. It has the potential to transform the entire world. Each person has the potential to help bring that about. But the first step is to understand it.

—Robert L. Holmes

Conscientious Objector

Edna St. Vincent Millay

I shall die, but that is all that I shall do for Death.

I hear him leading his horse out of the stall; I hear the clatter on the barn-floor.
He is in haste; he has business in Cuba, business in the Balkans, many calls to
 make this morning.
But I will not hold the bridle while he cinches the girth.
And he may mount by himself: I will not give him a leg up.

Though he flick my shoulders with his whip, I will not tell him which way
 the fox ran.
With his hoof on my breast, I will not tell him where the black boy hides in
 the swamp.
I shall die, but that is all that I shall do for Death; I am not on his pay-roll.

I will not tell him the whereabouts of my friends nor of my enemies either.
Though he promise me much, I will not map him the route to any man's door.

Am I a spy in the land of the living, that I should deliver men to Death?
Brother, the password and the plans of our city are safe with me; never
 through me
Shall you be overcome.

PART ONE

ORIGINS

Preview

The thinking on nonviolence encompasses thousands of years, vastly different cultures, and thousands of geographical miles. If it is true, as Gene Sharp has observed, that most of the work on the practical applications of nonviolence has occurred in the Western world, it is also true that most of the philosophical and religious thinking about it began in the Eastern world. Any considered treatment of nonviolence must give each its due.

Most people are familiar enough with the basic teachings of Jesus to understand why many would see in them a pronounced nonviolent orientation. This was how Christianity was understood by Christ's early followers, and this understanding did not change significantly until the time of Constantine in the fourth century AD. The selection by Lawrence Apsey highlights this orientation and the principal teachings of Jesus upon which it is based.

Less familiar, however, is the fact that nonviolence has roots in Judaism as well. Not that Judaism represents a nonviolent or pacifistic religion; but as Reuven Kimelman explains (and as discussed by Allan Solomonow in his piece in Part Six), there are clear strains of nonviolence to be found there, and a strong presumption against violence even where it is not prohibited.

Less familiar still is the nonviolent orientation of Islam. The article by Wasim Siddiqui notes that Islam requires individuals to strive or engage in a

1

struggle *(jihad)* to attain inner peace, thereby furthering peace in the larger society. He points out that, according to Islam, compassion and loving kindness are not only preconditions for peace between peoples but also the means to such peace.

Neither are Westerners generally familiar with the roots of nonviolence in early Eastern thought. Some of these writings have had a major influence on more recent writers in both the East and the West.

The *Bhagavad-Gita*, for example, had a major impact on Thoreau, and Thoreau influenced Tolstoy, Gandhi, and King. Indeed, the *Gita* was the single most influential work in the formation of Gandhi's thought, and it is said that he must have read it more than a thousand times. This cross-fertilization has not only deepened and enriched the understanding of nonviolence, but also has given intellectual embodiment to one of the recurrent themes in nonviolent philosophy—the unforeseeable consequences of our efforts. Just as Rosa Parks could not have predicted the events that would unfold as a result of her refusal to yield her seat on that bus in Montgomery, Alabama, so too the Jains in ancient India, Lao Tzu in ancient China, and the unknown author of the *Bhagavad-Gita* in India at about the time of the birth of Christianity could not have foreseen the influence their teachings would have upon so many. The links are not possible to trace in all cases. But it is perhaps less important to try to identify these links than to appreciate the way in which the intellectual, spiritual, and social realization of the power of nonviolence has surfaced and resurfaced repeatedly in the history of humankind.

Lao Tzu (c. 600 BC) often relies upon metaphors of what is female and what is childlike. The following selection, however, considers what is soft as opposed to what is hard. This contrasts not only with the masculine and warlike metaphors that have dominated much of Western thought since the time of the *Iliad* but also with the decidedly masculine orientation of some of the recent thinking about nonviolence as well (Gandhi, for example, at times extols the manliness of *satyagraha*, his nonviolent method of dealing with conflict). The *Gita's* counsel not to be preoccupied with the fruits of actions speaks to the concerns of many people who despair of being able to see the positive benefits of their individual actions. Had Rosa Parks acted only with advance assurance of a successful outcome, she probably would have done nothing. And most of us would do nothing in the face of bewilderingly complex social and world problems. People resort to violence no doubt in part because it holds promise of at least some immediate, calculable effect: the bomb explodes, the bullet kills. To allow ourselves to become caught up in the demand for results—a demand difficult to resist in the context of a highly competitive, success-oriented society—is to risk being seduced into thinking that violence ultimately holds the solutions to our problems. The way of nonviolence may in the end be of more lasting effect. It may be like the softness of water of which Lao Tzu writes (a theme picked up by Buddhist monk Thich Nhat Hanh in Part Five), which over time inexorably has its way against the hardest rock.

To believe this is to have faith, as Martin Luther King, Jr., put it, that "the universe is on the side of justice." This kind of faith is evident in both the *Dhammapada* and in the selections from *Apology* and *Crito* by Plato (427– 347 BC), all of which date from approximately the same point in history, the fourth century BC. The *Dhammapada* counsels patience, freedom from fear, and nonviolence. Plato's *Apology* and *Crito* urge respect for the rule of law, courage to seek the truth no matter the consequences, and a refusal to return injury for injury. Both the *Dhammapada* and the selections from Plato, like the *Qur'an* a millennium later, view the development of these qualities as necessary to the cultivation of good character, and they all see the development of a good character as striving to attain a good other than mere material fulfillment, as a willingness to plant without a guarantee of living to see the harvest.

Some of the following selections are writings *about* a philosophy rather than those *of* the original philosophers (though these writings contain ample quotations from the original). This is partly because the integration of the principal views of a position into a coherent whole is sometimes of more value for an introduction than a few disconnected and sketchy portions of the original. It is also, as in the cases of the *Gita* and the Talmud, partly to emphasize a particular reading of these works. The selection by Doris Hunter on the *Gita*, for example, shows the way in which that work was understood by Gandhi; this is important because it is through his understanding of it that so much of its influence in the twentieth century has been felt. It is also important to understand, however, that there are other interpretations of these works, some of which do not support nonviolence at all. Were the aim of this book to present the diversity of views about these various traditions it would include a balance of all these interpretations. As it is, the aim rather is to show the ways in which these works may be and have been read as contributing to the thinking about nonviolence.

Finally, Thoreau (1817–1862) serves as the bridge to the more recent writings in Part Two, not because he was a nonviolentist (he was not), but because his powerful essay has influenced so many people who see civil disobedience as an integral part of a nonviolent engagement with the institutionalized coercion and violence of the governments of modern nation-states.

NONVIOLENCE IN EASTERN PHILOSOPHY AND RELIGION

The Ethics of Jainism

I. C. Sharma

Historically Jainism is undoubtedly older than Buddhism. It is well known that the Jaina philosophy accepts and advocates nonviolence as the highest ideal of life, and as the means of attaining Mokṣa, or liberation. For these reasons Jainism may be regarded as the oldest philosophy based on nonviolence. The Jainas hold that their religion and philosophy are even older than Vedic thought. There is no doubt that Vardhmāna Mahāvīra cannot be regarded as the founder of the Jaina religion, for he was only a reformer or rejuvenator of Jainism. It is a fact that the Jaina Tīrthaṅkara Pārśvanātha was a historical person who lived at least 250 years prior to Mahāvīra, and that the parents of Mahāvīra were the followers of Pārśvanātha. Mahāvīra systematized the Jaina philosophy and established ethical principles based on nonviolence that are being followed by Jaina ascetics and laity to this day. . . .

It was the sight of suffering and death which actuated the Buddha to renounce the world and to search for truth. The case was similar with Aśoka the Great, whose name shines in the history of the world as an apostle of love and peace. Kant's unique doctrine of the categorical imperative, which makes morality unconditional and universal for mankind and leads to the discovery of the jewel of goodwill, is the result of his contemplation on sufferings and miseries to which mankind is subjected. The case was similar with Mahāvīra.

Source: *Ethical Philosophies of India* by I. C. Sharma, edited and revised by Stanley M. Daugert (Lincoln, NE: Johnsen Publishing Co., 1965). Reprinted by permission of Arun Jetli.

4

Strong diseases require strong remedies; even so the sufferings, disease, fear, famine, death and destruction which caused untold miseries could be stopped or prevented only by attaining Nirvāna, freedom from rebirth and transmigration. This strong feeling made Mahāvīra advocate an abrupt renunciation and the strictest possible ascetic life for the aspirant. Consequently he laid the foundation of a very elaborate moral code for ascetics, aiming at complete detachment, mental, physical and actual (pertaining to "action") from worldly affairs. Not only was it essential for the ascetic or nun to adopt non-violence; but also neither to do violence nor be instrumental in doing any kind of violence in any way. Similarly an ascetic is required not only to be true, but also to avoid telling lies and being instrumental in any falsehood or lie mentally, bodily and by action. In like manner the vow of non-stealing demands an ascetic neither to steal nor to be party to stealing directly or indirectly. The great vow of Brahmacarya demands of an ascetic to avoid all sexual intercourse and to avoid being instrumental in such acts. The fifth vow of nonpossession similarly demands that an ascetic neither possess any property nor give consent to be a cause for the possession of property by any individual. The Jaina Sūtras are very particular in emphasizing strict observance of these vows in spirit as well as in letter. The comprehensive instructions issued to the ascetics and nuns might appear to be trifling for a layman, but they are of vital importance to a Sādhu or a Sādhvī who sacrifices everything for the sake of attaining his or her cherished goal—liberation. . . .

Asceticism or Renunciation in Jaina Ethics

The special feature of Jaina ethics is its severely stringent character, because its goal is Mokṣa, which means the acquisition of infinite knowledge, infinite perception, infinite power and infinite bliss. The attainment of such a unique state cannot be accomplished without eschewing selfishness completely. According to the Jaina point of view, only an ascetic can follow the strict code of conduct because he gives up all worldly ties. In fact almost all schools of Indian philosophy accept principles of renunciation as a means of attaining the highest state. Detachment from all worldly objects is generally considered necessary for self-realization. Such longing, such yearning for renunciation is inspired by the intense desire of the soul to become infinite. This ascetic attitude expands the soul, frees the individual from narrow selfish desires, and leads him to adopt a life in which love and sympathy for all human beings predominate.

Asceticism means service and self-sacrifice. Service and self-devotion cannot be adopted by a weakling; on the contrary, only the brave and courageous soul can follow such a path. To a layman the life of renunciation might appear incomplete; but this so-called incomplete life is actually a life of perfection. The life of simplicity and truth is the highest life. Such a life was adopted by the great Chinese philosopher, Lao-Tze, who wrote that a simple life is a life of plainness, in which profit is discarded, cleverness abandoned, selfishness minimized and desires reduced. It is the life of "perfection," which seems to be incomplete, of "fullness which seems to be empty," of "absolute straightness, which seems to be crooked," of "skill, which seems to be clumsy," and of "eloquence which seems to stutter." It is the life of "producing and rearing things, without taking possession of them," of "doing work, but not taking pride in it," and of "ruling over things, but not dominating them." It is the life which is "as pointed as a spear, but does not pierce, as acute as a knife, but does not cut, as straight as an unbent line, but does not extend, and as bright as light, but does not dazzle."

It is this paradoxical nature of the ascetic life which cannot be easily understood by scholars who do not try to go deep into its spirit. The purpose of the life of an ascetic is the uplifting of humanity, and the ideal he adopts is the ideal of the attainment of full life. Such a goal is positive existence, not annihilation. There is no doubt that the ascetic scorns the so-called comforts of life, yet he aims at happiness. He seems disgusted with, or at least indifferent to everything around him, yet he is most concerned with the realization of the ultimate reality. Indian philosophy can be best understood with reference to the four noble truths of the Buddha, which may briefly be stated as follows: (1) There is suffering in the world, (2) there is a cause of suffering, (3) there can be an end to this suffering, and (4) there is a way to attain it.

Jainism is often called Śramanism, for Jains believe that only an ascetic can attain Mokṣa by following absolute nonviolence. Although it propounds moral principles even for householders, Jaina ethics is predominantly the ethics of asceticism. . . .

Ascetic Ethics

As we have already stated, according to Jainism nonviolence is the highest virtue. It lays down the five great vows or the principles of morality: (1) nonviolence (Ahiṁsā), (2) truth (Satya), (3) nonstealing (Asteya), (4) celibacy (Brahmacarya), and (5) nonpossession (Aparigraha). Jaina philosophy considers these five principles to be basic rules of the conduct for ascetics. Nonviolence means refraining from all injury and violence, whether such violence pertains to the subtlest invisible living beings or to animals or to human beings. Violence does not mean causing only physical injury, but it also includes mental and verbal injury. When a Jaina ascetic adopts nonviolence, he tries his best to follow it absolutely and not to cause injury to any living being, physically, mentally and verbally. Thus nonviolence requires three principles which are called the three Guptis. In other words, following the principles of nonviolence through mind, word and deed implies three Guptis, the Guptis of mental nonviolence, verbal nonviolence and physical nonviolence. Other Mahāvratas must also be adopted with reference to these three Guptis or implied rules. We should remember that the foundation of all the great vows is the great vow of nonviolence. All other moral rules are accepted only to maintain this great vow of nonviolence. Speaking truth is necessary because by telling lies against somebody we cause at least mental injury to him. A person would not be able to follow nonviolence by neglecting truth. By telling lies we commit verbal violence and injure the feelings of another person. In like manner stealing somebody's property, violating the third great vow, amounts to violence. A person whose property is stolen is mentally injured. Therefore, nonstealing as well is based on nonviolence. Hence it is evident that even Brahmacarya is based on nonviolence. Nonpossession means not to possess surplus property. A person who hoards wealth deprives poor and hungry persons of their wants. Surplus wealth could be used to provide food and clothing to the needy. Thus adopting the principle of nonpossession means following a nonviolent way of life.

The conduct of ascetics must be absolutely nonviolent. Therefore all the Jaina ascetics must adopt the following five Samitis, or co-rules, besides the five great vows and the three implied rules, or Guptis:

1. Iryā Samiti, or caution in avoiding injury to living beings while walking.

2. Bhāṣā Samiti, or control over speech to avoid verbal injury.

3. Eṣaṇā Samiti, or careful checking of food to assure that whatever food or drink has been given to him was not specially prepared for him.

4. Ādāna Nikṣepaṇā Samiti, or using necessary articles cautiously to avoid injury to subtle lives.

5. Parithāpāṇika Samiti, or disbursing or throwing away unnecessary articles with care and caution.

These five Samitis aid the ascetic in following the path of nonviolence and they also show that the life of an ascetic must be exemplary under all circumstances. This strictness of the ascetic code is very important, because it aims at eschewing both attachment and hatred. An ascetic can never attain Mokṣa until and unless he rises above the worldly antinomies and practices absolute nonviolence. Ordinarily, nonviolence means protecting the lives of animals, which is why most Jaina householders, or Śrāvakas, feed birds and nurse wounded birds and animals. Thus nonviolence is regarded as equivalent to compassion. But the Terāpanthī sect of the Jaina Śvetāmbara school gives a strange definition of nonviolence and distinguishes it from the protection of life. This definition must be dispassionately analysed since nonviolence is the supreme end of morality in Jainism. So far as the ethical code of ascetics is concerned, the explanation of nonviolence from the absolutistic point of view has special significance.

The explanation of absolute nonviolence is undoubtedly beyond the understanding of the common man. According to the viewpoint of absolute nonviolence, there is no difference between avoidable and unavoidable violence. Thus violence is violence under all circumstances whatever. If we once accept the existence of "subtle" lives, there is no reason that the violence to infinite subtle lives should not be regarded as immoral from the spiritual point of view, even if such a violence aims at the protection of human lives. Perhaps an intelligent person cannot adopt absolute nonviolence, because he cannot maintain his own life without killing subtle lives. But from the metaphysical point of view it would be equally erroneous to regard such "relative violence" to be "nonviolence." The Terāpaṅthīs hold that if a man is obliged by circumstances to practise relative violence, and if this course is supposed conducive to Mokṣa, a serious error occurs. They are of the opinion that there is a difference between spiritual life and practical life. Man should admit that he is weak and that he cannot at all times follow the spiritual morality. Absolute nonviolence, according to which violence to subtle as well as to gross life is equally immoral, can become the ideal only for the ascetic. This concept of nonviolence, according to the Terāpaṅtha, does not accept the difference between compassion to human beings and to subtle lives, though it recognizes the weakness of ordinary men who make the distinction. . . .

Ethics for Householders

Although Jainism does not consider it necessary for the aspirant to pass through the stages of a householder and of an anchorite (Vānaprastha), and instead advocates the direct adoption of an ascetic life with a view to attaining Mokṣa, it holds that a householder can lead the life of renunciation and prepare for asceticism partially by following the five great vows. All the schools and sects of Jainism agree that it is necessary for the householders, or Śrāvakas, to follow the Anuvratas, or atomic vows, to practise the life of renunciation. It is important to note that the adoption of the Anuvratas is in fact the training for ascetic life. Anuvrata means the minutest part, or atom, of the great vow (Mahāvrata). In other words, Anuvrata is a simple principle based on the great vows. For example, a householder adopts the following six atomic vows, thus partly applying the great vow of nonviolence:

1. I will not kill innocent moving animals voluntarily.
2. I will not commit suicide.
3. I will not commit abortion.
4. I will neither join an organization or party whose aim is violence and destruction, nor will I participate in such activities.
5. I will not consider any individual as an untouchable.
6. I will not behave cruelly towards anyone.

In the same manner the following Anuvratas can be derived from the great vow of truth:

1. Not using false weights and measures while selling and buying things.
2. Not passing false judgments intentionally.
3. Neither filing a false suit against anybody, nor giving false evidence in court.
4. Not giving out anyone's secret out of selfishness and jealousy.
5. Not refusing to return anything kept with a person as a deposit.
6. Not indulging in any kind of forgery.

One can follow the following Anuvratas, based on the great vow of non-stealing:

1. Not taking anything belonging to others with a view to stealing it.
2. Neither intentionally purchasing stolen goods nor aiding a thief in stealing.
3. Not dealing in the goods prohibited by law.
4. Not resorting to nefarious practices in business.
5. Not misappropriating the property or money belonging to a trust or an organization in the capacity of an office-holder of such an organization.

The following Anuvratas are based on the great vow of celibacy:

1. Neither committing adultery nor prostitution.
2. Not indulging in any kind of unnatural sexual intercourse.
3. Refraining from sexual intercourse for at least twenty days in a month.
4. Observing celibacy at least up to eighteen years.
5. Not marrying after the age of forty-five years.

The following Anuvratas may be adopted to follow the fifth great vow of nonpossession:

1. Not possessing anything more than one's normal quota.
2. Not accepting bribes and presents.
3. Neither offering nor accepting money for securing or giving votes.
4. Not prolonging the treatment of a patient out of greed.
5. Not demanding any amount of money in the matters of betrothal and marriage.

These atomic vows are apparently negative principles, yet even so their adoption can solve various moral and social problems. They may lead to self-purification and self-realization on the one hand, and build a strong character based on nonviolence, justice and courage on the other.

From *The Way of Lao Tzu*

31

Fine weapons are instruments of evil.
They are hated by men.
Therefore those who possess Tao turn away from them.
The good ruler when at home honors the left.
When at war he honors the right.
Weapons are instruments of evil, not the instruments of a good ruler.
When he uses them unavoidably, he regards calm restraint as the best principle.
Even when he is victorious, he does not regard it as praiseworthy.
For to praise victory is to delight in the slaughter of men.
He who delights in the slaughter of men will not succeed in the empire.

In auspicious affairs, the left is honored.
In inauspicious affairs, the right is honored.
The lieutenant general stands on the left.
The senior general stands on the right.
This is to say that the arrangement follows that of funeral ceremonies.
For the slaughter of the multitude, let us weep with sorrow and grief.
For a victory, let us observe the occasion with funeral ceremonies.

63

Act without action.
Do without ado.
Taste without tasting.
Whether it is big or small, many or few, repay hatred with virtue.
Prepare for the difficult while it is still easy.
Deal with the big while it is still small.

Source: From *The Way of Lao Tzu,* by Lao Tzu, translated by Wing-Tsit Chan.

Difficult undertakings have always started with what is easy.
And great undertakings have always started with what is small.
Therefore the sage never strives for the great,
And thereby the great is achieved.
He who makes rash promises surely lacks faith.
He who takes things too easily will surely encounter much difficulty.
For this reason even the sage regards things as difficult.
And therefore he encounters no difficulty.

67

All the world says that my Tao is great and does not seem to resemble (the
    ordinary).
It is precisely because it is great that it does not resemble (the ordinary).
If it did resemble, it would have been small for a long time.
I have three treasures. Guard and keep them:
    The first is deep love,
    The second is frugality,
    And the third is not to dare to be ahead of the world.
Because of deep love, one is courageous.
Because of frugality, one is generous.
Because of not daring to be ahead of the world, one becomes the leader of
    the world.
Now, to be courageous by forsaking deep love,
To be generous by forsaking frugality,
And to be ahead of the world by forsaking following behind—
This is fatal.

For deep love helps one to win in the case of attack,
And to be firm in the case of defense.
When Heaven is to save a person,
Heaven will protect him through deep love.

78

There is nothing softer and weaker than water,
And yet there is nothing better for attacking hard and strong things.
For this reason there is no substitute for it.
All the world knows that the weak overcomes the strong and the soft over-
    comes the hard.
But none can practice it.
Therefore the sage says:

He who suffers disgrace for his country
Is called the lord of the land.
He who takes upon himself the country's misfortunes
Becomes the king of the empire.
Straight words seem to be their opposite.

79

To patch up great hatred is surely to leave some hatred behind.
How can this be regarded as good?
Therefore the sage keeps the left-hand portion (obligation) of a contract
And does not blame the other party.
Virtuous people attend to their left-hand portions,
While those without virtue attend to other people's mistakes.

"The Way of Heaven has no favorites.
It is always with the good man."

80

Let there be a small country with few people.
Let there be ten times and a hundred times as many utensils
But let them not be used.
Let the people value their lives highly and not migrate far.
Even if there are ships and carriages, none will ride in them.
Even if there are arrows and weapons, none will display them.
Let the people again knot cords and use them (in place of writing).
Let them relish their food, beautify their clothing, be content with their
    homes, and delight in their customs.
Though neighboring communities overlook one another and the crowing of
    cocks and barking of dogs can be heard,
Yet the people there may grow old and die without ever visiting one another.

From *The Dhammapada*

Introduction: Chapters 9 and 10

Wrong actions are central to the concept of *papa*, "sin" or "evil," [which is the theme of verses 129–145 as well as earlier verses not reprinted here]. In Buddhism there is no one sitting in judgment to punish us for wrong actions, nor is there anyone to reward us for our good works. Instead, reward and punishment issue from the self-fulfilling law of karma, which permeates every aspect of the Buddha's teachings. Put simply, the law of karma states that as we sow, so shall we reap: everything we do, say, or even think has consequences, good or bad, and sooner or later those consequences must come back to us. Karma was already an ancient idea in India when the Buddha taught, and it can safely be said that his audience took for granted that the law of cause and effect governs not only physical events, but every event in human experience.

Like any physical law, the law of karma operates everywhere and at every moment. It is totally impersonal, requiring no agency other than ourselves. The Buddha taught that for an action to produce karma, it has to be accompanied by a conscious will, which presupposes the capacity of free choice. If a small child hits another child, there is probably no karmic residue, because he is still innocent and does not fully acquiesce in the action as an adult would have to; he may be playing happily with the same child minutes later. But when an adult says angry words to someone, the will is an accomplice, and the action will bear fruit (136). It is impossible to escape the karmic result of action no matter where we may try (127). The karma must return in kind, whether good or bad, even though it may take time for the right circumstances to come around (119–120).

According to the Buddha, a large part of our experience is simply the mechanical return of the karma our previous actions have accumulated. "Previous actions" here, of course, extends to previous lives. These ideas too were

Source: From *The Dhammapada*, translated by Eknath Easwaran, founder of the Blue Mountain Center of Meditation, © 1985; reprinted by permission of Nilgiri Press, P.O. Box 256, Tomales, CA, 94971, www.nilgiri.org.

an integral part of the Buddha's Hindu background, but no one else in Indian mysticism worked out their significance with greater breadth and precision. Dharma is a seamless web in which physical and mental events are inescapably intertwined, and even disasters or misfortunes may be a delayed karmic reaction to something we did in this life or in some previous life (137–140).

One aspect of the law of karma receives special attention in this chapter: that is the concept of *samskaras*, or karma-formed states. A samskara involves not just one action and its karmic return, but a mental inclination to act in a certain way. The reason the Buddha cautions us against repeating wrong actions—and recommends repeating good actions (117–118)—is that such habits cut a track in consciousness upon which future actions in similar circumstances are likely to run.

If we continue to commit a mistake—say, an outburst of anger—each repetition makes it easier to make the same mistake again, so that gradually anger becomes part of our character. That is very close to what the Buddha means by a samskara: a habit of thinking which karmically locks us into patterns of behavior over which we have less and less control with every succeeding repetition. With a samskara like anger, karma acts on the individual not just in his external environment, but also from within. An anger-prone person may get anger returned to him by other individuals, but he may also suffer karmic harm within: increased anxiety, risk of heart disease or other behavior-aggravated ailments, the turmoil of an unruly mind.

Because it is easiest to follow the worn path of stimulus and response, harmful samskaras are easy to form and to get trapped in. Actively asserting the responses that do *not* come naturally—love, forgiveness, patience, compassion in the face of hatred—is the only way to avoid gradually succumbing to evil (116): that is, to avoid becoming internally laced with harmful samskaras. In a very real way, we are what our samskaras are: as the network of choice-pathways in us, they constitute the karmic legacy of all our previous choices. Evil in Buddhism thus becomes a question of rightly understanding how a person becomes prone to harmful action and what courses of action can set his situation right.

The Buddha's emphasis is always on choice, and his prognosis is always hopeful. He shows us the power of evil habits, then reminds us that good habits are just as strong (121–122). If we do not try to shape our lives, the conditioning of our samskaras will shape them for us, little by little; but if we do try—again, little by little, in the numberless decisions of everyday life—then any one of us can become good, as a bucket is filled drop by drop.

10: Punishment

129   Everyone fears punishment; everyone fears death, just as you do.
      Therefore do not kill

130   or cause to kill. Everyone fears punishment; everyone loves life, as you
do. Therefore do not kill or cause to kill.

131   If, hoping to be happy, you strike at others who also seek happiness,
you will be happy
132   neither here nor hereafter. If, hoping to be happy, you do not strike at
others who are also seeking happiness, you will be happy here and
hereafter.

133   Speak quietly to everyone, and they too will be gentle in their speech.
Harsh words hurt,
134   and come back to the speaker. If your mind is still, like a broken gong,
you have entered nirvana, leaving all quarrels behind you.

135   As a cowherd with his staff drives cows to fresh fields, old age and
death lead all crea-
136   tures to new lives. The selfish, doing harm, do not know what is in store
for them. They are burned as if by fire by the results of their own deeds.

137   If one harms the innocent, suffering will
138   come in these ten ways. He may suffer grief, infirmity, painful accident,
serious illness,
139   loss of mind, legal prosecution, fearful accusation, family bereavement,
or financial
140   loss; or his house may burn down, and after death he may be thrown
into the fire of suffering.

141   Going about with matted hair, without food or bath, sleeping on the
ground smeared with dust, or sitting motionless—no amount of penance can help a person whose mind is
142   not purified. But one whose mind is serene and chaste, whose senses
are controlled and whose life is nonviolent—such a one is a true brahmin, a true monk, even if he wears fine clothes.

143   As a well-trained horse needs no whip, a well-trained mind needs no
prodding from
144   the world to be good. Be like a well-trained horse, swift and spirited,
and go beyond sorrow through faith, meditation, and energetic practice
of the dharma.

145   As an irrigator guides water to his fields, as an archer aims an arrow, as
a carpenter carves wood, the wise shape their lives.

19: The Person Established in Dharma

256– They are not following dharma who resort
257   to violence to achieve their purpose. But those who lead others through
      nonviolent means, knowing right and wrong, may be called guardians
      of the dharma.

258   One is not wise because he talks a good deal. They are wise who are
      patient, and free from hate and fear.

259   Dharma is not upheld by talking about it. Dharma is upheld by living in
      harmony with it, even if one is not learned.

260   Gray hair does not make an elder; one can
261   grow old and still be immature. A true elder is truthful, virtuous, gentle,
      self-controlled, and pure in mind.

262   Neither pleasant words nor a pretty face can make beautiful a person
      who is jealous, selfish,
263   or deceitful. Only those who have uprooted such impurities from their
      mind are fit to be called beautiful.

264   Shaving one's head cannot make a monk of one who is undisciplined,
      untruthful, and
265   driven by selfish desires. He is a real monk who has extinguished all
      selfish desires, large and small.

266   Begging alms does not make a bhikshu; one
267   must follow the dharma completely. He is a true bhikshu who is chaste
      and beyond the reach of good and evil, who passes through the world
      with detachment.

268– Observing silence cannot make a sage of one
269   who is ignorant and immature. He is wise who, holding the scales,
      chooses the good and avoids the bad.

270   One is not noble who injures living creatures. They are noble who hurt
      no one.

271– Not by rituals and resolutions, nor by much
272   learning, nor by celibacy, nor even by meditation can you find the
      supreme, immortal joy of nirvana until you have extinguished your
      self-will.

26: The Brahmin

. . .

399   Him I call a brahmin who fears neither prison nor death. He has the power of love no army can defeat.

400   Him I call a brahmin who is never angry, never goes astray from the path. He is pure and self-controlled. He has received his last body.

401   Him I call a brahmin who clings not to pleasure, no more than water to a lotus leaf or
402   mustard seed to the tip of a needle. For him no more sorrow will come. On him no more burden will fall.

403   Him I call a brahmin whose wisdom is profound and whose understanding deep, who by following the right path and avoiding the wrong has reached the highest goal.

404   Him I call a brahmin whose wants are few, who is detached from householders and homeless mendicants alike.

405   Him I call a brahmin who has put aside weapons and renounced violence toward all creatures. He neither kills nor helps others to kill.

406   Him I call a brahmin who is never hostile to those who are hostile toward him, who is detached among those who are selfish, and at peace among those at war.

407   Him I call a brahmin from whom passion and hatred, arrogance and deceit, have fallen away like mustard seed from the point of a needle.

408   Him I call a brahmin who is ever true, ever
409   kind. He never asks what life can give, only what he can give to life.

. . .

On the *Bhagavad-Gita*

Doris Hunter

Henry Canby in his biography of Thoreau writes, "It is not too much to say that Thoreau was made by two books, Emerson's *Essay on Nature* and the *Bhagavad-Gita*."[1] It is not too much, either, to believe that Ralph Waldo Emerson influenced the thinking of Thoreau but in what way did that ancient Hindu literature, the *Bhagavad-Gita*, with its background of violent civil war affect the mind of the Concord poet? The answer is found in the way Thoreau understood this literature. If this is the case, then it is necessary for us to be aware of some of these interpretations of the *Gita* and to see the relationship of these interpretations of the concept of *ahimsa* (nonviolence) which developed out of this literature.

The opening lines of the *Gita* present to us the spectacle of Arjuna, the great military leader, hesitating to kill his relatives in a civil war. Krishna, his charioteer who is really the Hindu God Vishnu, tells him to stop trembling, to pick up his bow and to do his duty as a warrior. Is this the message of the *Gita*—a lesson from God instructing men not to be cowards but to do their duty without fear? It is possible to answer "yes" after a superficial reading of the first two chapters. However, if you read the *Gita* more carefully and completely, you find that cowardice is not the essential issue concerning the warrior Arjuna or the God Krishna. Arjuna's reluctance to fight is a very serious matter because he has an obligation to perform this duty as a member of the warrior (Kshatriyas) caste in Hindu society. Being a member of this caste, Arjuna must fight to perform his caste duty in order to escape repeating that duty all over again in a next rebirth, or worse, to be reborn into a lower caste position. Is the meaning of the *Gita* then a divine command to do the caste duty so that the next rebirth brings to the faithful follower a more advanced spiritual stage in the long series of rebirths? Again, the answer may be "yes." Orthodox Hindu thought interprets the *Gita* precisely in this way—a divine summons to caste obligation. And yet you may ask, "Certainly Henry David Thoreau did not interpret the *Gita* in terms of caste duty and how that duty related to a series of rebirths?" Indeed, he did not. Thoreau along with Gandhi and other scholars from both East and West, found that this type of interpretation of the *Gita* omits its most important concern. The *Gita*, they believe, deals with the ultimate issue in man's life, how man is to *be* and to *act* in harmony with his real self. Arjuna exemplifies not only a man who fails to do his caste duty but also a man who is attached to his duty with a sense of a selfish ego-involvement. It is *my* duty, he believes, even though I choose not to do it. The *Gita*'s main task it to remove from Arjuna's mind— and all minds—this sense of ego-attachment, this sense of *mine!* Krishna knows from his endless incarnations that it is precisely this attitude of possession which causes a man to be selfish, jealous and violent. This is *my* right! This is *my* wife! This is *my* land! On the other hand, the way of Truth for man is the way of detachment (detached from all ego-desires and attached to the life of the spirit). A man committed to Truth is unselfish, open-minded and nonviolent. He has moved from *himsa* to *ahimsa*.

It is this type of interpretation of the *Gita* which appealed to both Gandhi and Thoreau. In *Walden*, Thoreau attempted to find his own unique life-style inspired by these principles described in the *Gita*. He sensed, in the power of "living deliberately" the influence of its spirit.

> I went to the woods because I wished to live deliberately, to front only the essential facts of life, and see if I could not learn what it had to teach, and not, when I came to die, discover that I had not lived. I did not wish to live what was not life, living is so dear; nor did I wish to practice resignation, unless it was quite necessary. I wanted to live deep and suck out all the marrow of life, to live so sturdily and Spartan-like as to put to rout all that was not life, to cut a broad swath and shave close, to drive life into a corner, and reduce it to its lowest terms, and, if it proved to be mean, why then to get the whole and genuine meanness of it, and publish its meanness to the world; or if it were sublime, to know it by experience, and be able to give a true account of it in my next excursion.[2]

Gandhi, in his own original response to the *Gita*, understood this literature as an allegory in which the battlefield is the soul, Arjuna is man's higher impulses struggling against evil, and Krishna is the Dweller within ever whispering in a pure heart.

> I venture to submit that the *Bhagavad Gita* is a gospel of non-co-operation between the forces of darkness and those of light. . . . I do not believe that the *Gita* teaches violence for doing good. It is pre-eminently a description of the duel that goes on in our own hearts. The divine author has used a historical incident for inculcating the lesson of doing one's duty even at the peril of one's life. It inculcates performance of duty irrespective of the consequences, for, we mortals, limited by our physical frames, are incapable of controlling actions save our own. The *Gita* distinguishes between the powers of light and darkness and demonstrates their incompatibility.[3]

If the essential meaning of the *Gita* is to teach us to "live deliberately" and to do our duty without fear, then how are we to learn this lesson? The entire text of the *Gita* is concerned with this question, but basically, we can understand its answer as a commitment to the belief that any sense of "mine" in regard to any aspect of life is an illusion! Perhaps by thinking about our physical bodies, we can begin to understand the meaning of this illusion. The body which sees, smells, tastes, feels, hears is not *real* but it is only a garment which will be thrown away when it is worn out.

> Worn-out garments
> Are shed by the body:
> Worn-out bodies
> Are shed by the dweller
> Within the body.
> New bodies are donned
> By the dweller, like garments.[4]

Your real self, which the *Gita* calls Atman (spirit), will continue to live and will eventually find another body for its physical expression. Thus the first lesson to learn is that your body is not the real you but that you are spirit *(Atman)*, deathless, indivisible and one with God *(Brahman-Atman)*.

> Know this Atman,
> Unborn, undying,
> Never ceasing,
> Never beginning,
> Deathless, birthless,
> Unchanging for ever.
> How can It die
> The death of the body?[5]

The importance of this lesson is to realize that the concerns of the body are secondary and that the concerns of the spirit *(Atman)* are primary. The *Gita* states that only a man who has this perspective on life can live without attachment to *his* body, *his* family, *his* home, *his* nation. However, it takes a life-time of rigorous discipline for a believer to acquire this sense of detachment. In fact, many Hindus believe in the theory of reincarnation because they know it takes many rebirths (many lives) in order for the spirit to fulfill this ideal and not to allow itself to be seduced by the lower concerns of the body and its possessions.

The *Gita* points out that there are several ways to discipline your life away from the illusion of attachment. There is the way of action *(Karma Yoga)*, the way of love *(Bhakti Yoga)*, the way of knowledge *(Jnana Yoga)* and the way of psychological exercises *(Raja Yoga)*. The first way, yoga of action *(Karma)*, is the most relevant to our study of nonviolence since it is the man of action (such as Gandhi, Thoreau, Martin Luther King) who has the greatest impact upon our understanding of what is involved in a commitment to nonviolence.

Gandhi, who called the *Gita* "Mother" because it nourished his spirit, took the way of Karma Yoga as his personal discipline. Temperamentally, he was a man of action rather than a man of wisdom (scholar) or a man of devotion (priest) although both wisdom and devotion were essential aspects of his life. The section of the *Gita* cited previously was his favorite section. He memorized it and used it as a constant reminder of the ideal he should meet in his attempt to use the means *(ahimsa)* to attain the end (Truth). This section specifically described the one discipline Gandhi and all its adherents need to develop—selflessness in action.

> You have the right to work, but for the work's sake only. You have no right to the fruits of work. Desire for the fruits of work must never be your motive in working.

The ideal of Karma Yoga, therefore, is to take action for a just cause without thought of any personal advantage. This does not mean that the man of action is indifferent to the results of his just action or that he refuses to act out of frustration (this was Arjuna's problem). The *Gita* commands such a man to act and to act in the way of Truth *but* he cannot brood over the results. Gandhi described the reason for this demand: "He who is ever brooding over results often loses nerve in the performance of his duty. He becomes impatient and then gives vent to anger and begins to do unworthy things; he jumps from action to action, never remaining faithful to any. He who broods over results is like a man given to objects of senses; he is ever distracted, he says goodbye to all scruples, everything is right in his estimation and he therefore resorts to means fair and foul to attain his end."[6] To renounce attachment to the "fruits" of action is to discover, Gandhi believed, the ideal of desirelessness. To the Hindu devotee of Karma Yoga this type of renunciation gives to a man that inner peace and poise necessary to achieve real lasting results, even material results, untainted by ugly means.

In this way the *Gita* becomes the inspiration for a life committed to nonviolence *(ahimsa)*. If you are able through discipline to detach yourself from the results of your action, an action which you believe is right, then you are able to perform this action again no matter how distorted the truth of this action or the motive behind this action becomes because of the misunderstanding of other people who are judging its validity by the consequences alone. It is very difficult to understand the motive behind someone's action. How difficult it is then for us to expect other people to understand completely our intentions and to understand our actions by the way the results of those actions work out in public life. We become angry when our truth is misunderstood and abused by other people. However, the *Gita* points out that this attitude occurs when we are attached to the consequences of our "just" action with a selfish concern. Consequences are sensory reflections of truth and as sense-objects, they present to different people a limited view of truth.

> Thinking about sense-objects
> Will attach you to sense-objects;
> Grow attached, and you become addicted;
> Thwart your addiction, it turns to anger;
> Confuse your mind, you forget the lesson of experience;

Forget experience, you lose discrimination;
Lose discrimination, and you miss life's only purpose.[7]

If we have no selfish involvement in our actions, if we don't make a one-to-one relationship between the consequences of our action and Truth, if we believe Truth still survives even when it appears to be destroyed in the outcome of our actions, then there will be no opportunity for us to feel angry or violent. From the perspective of the *Gita*, the power of Truth makes even the thought of anger and violence unthinkable. The only alternative possible for a man who holds this perspective is an inward and outward life committed to nonviolence *(ahimsa)* as the essential way to Truth.

He knows bliss in the Atman
And wants nothing else.
Cravings torment the heart:
He renounces cravings.
I call him illumined.
Not shaken by adversity,
Not hankering after happiness:
Free from fear, free from anger,
Free from the things of desire.
I call him a seer, and illumined.
The bonds of his flesh are broken.
He is lucky, and does not rejoice:
He is unlucky, and does not weep.
I call him illumined.[8]

Notes

[1] Henry Canby, *Thoreau* (Boston: Beacon Press, 1939), 97.

[2] Henry David Thoreau, *Walden* (New York: Holt, Rinehart and Winston, Inc., 1961), 74.

[3] Mohandas K. Gandhi, *Gita the Mother* (Lahore, India: Free India Publications), 172, 155, 160.

[4] *The Song of God, Bhagavad-Gita,* translated by Swami Prabhavananda and Christopher Isherwood (New York: Mentor Religious Classics, New American Library, 1944), 37.

[5] *Gita*, loc. cit.

[6] Gandhi, *Gita the Mother,* 10.

[7] *Gita*, 42.

[8] *Gita*, 41–42.

JUDAISM, CHRISTIANITY, AND ISLAM

Nonviolence in the Talmud

Reuven Kimelman

The doctrine of nonviolence affirms that our humanity unites us more than our conflicts divide us. It seeks a unique mode of response to conflict, realizing that not by force shall man prevail. To find such a mode of response we will investigate, in the main, the Palestinian Talmudic sources from the middle third through the early fourth century. The key figures in our discussion will be the Aggadists of the second, third, and fourth generation of Amoraim. This period is particularly suited for our purpose, for while religious persecution was on the wane political oppression was gaining ascendancy. We should thus find most helpful the approach of those teachers who looked askance at violent resolution of conflict. Our investigation will be in three parts: I) Response to enmity; II) Response to intent to inflict injury; III) Response to persecution.

I

One of the serious issues of our time is how man should respond to conflict. We are told to love our neighbor (*Lev.* 19:18), but how are we to react to our enemy? May we individually return evil for evil, or is that beyond human

Source: *Roots of Jewish Nonviolence,* edited by Allan Solomonow (Nyack: Jewish Peace Fellowship, 1985). Reprinted by permission of the Jewish Peace Fellowship. Footnotes have been edited.

23

calculation? The *Book of Proverbs* warns against saying, "I will do so to him as he has done to me; I will pay the man back for what he has done" (24:29). If tit for tat is discouraged, then what is the alternative? The Midrash offers an approach:[1]

> "If a man returns evil for good, evil will not depart from his house" (*Prov.* 17:13). R. Simeon b. Abba said: Not only he who returns evil for good, but even he who returns evil for evil, "evil will not depart from his house." R. Alexandri commented on the verse, "He who returns evil for good": Now the Torah said: "If you see the ass of one who hates you lying under its burden, you shall refrain from leaving him with it, you shall lift it up" (*Ex.* 23:5); of such Scripture says, "He who returns evil for good, evil shall not depart."

According to these two second-generation Palestinian Amoraim, one may not only not return evil for good, as the verse says, but one may not even return evil for evil. And according to R. Alexandri, one must even repay good for evil, as the verse states, "If you see the ass of one who hates you lying under his burden . . . help him to lift it up."[2] . . .

It is in the third century that we find this approach supplemented with concrete illustrations which dramatize the inner workings of a method. The author is the same Palestinian Rabbi who declared above that to avoid evil one must return good.

> R. Alexandri said: Two donkey-drivers who were walking by the way hated each other. One of their donkeys sat down. His companion saw it, and passed on. When he had passed, he thought: It is written in the Torah, "If you see the ass of one who hates you . . . you shall surely help him to lift it up." Immediately he returned and loaded with him. He [the former] began to say to himself: So-and-so is thus my friend and I did not know. Both entered an inn and ate and drank. Who is responsible for their making peace? The fact that the latter had looked into the Torah. Accordingly, it is written: "Thou hast established righteousness" (*Psa.* 99:4).[3]

The inner dynamics are produced here by responding in such a manner as to unleash the flow of good will which has been damned by blocks of hate. (This thought has been well expressed in a contemporary book on nonviolence:[4] "If through love of your enemy you can create in him respect or admiration for you, this provides the best possible means by which your new idea or suggestion to him will become an auto-suggestion within him, and it will also help to nourish that auto-suggestion.")

Another *midrash*[5] explains this interaction even more explicitly:

> When your enemy sees that you came and you helped him, he will say to himself, "I thought that he is my enemy. God forbid! If he was my enemy he would not have helped me, but if he is my friend, then I am his enemy in vain. I will go and pacify him." He went to him and made peace. Accordingly, it says, "And all her paths are peace" (*Prov.* 3:17).

The two operative insights here are that human responses are results of the situation, and that hate must not be allowed to remain and grow. Instead, it must be transmuted by a constructive act channeling that energy into promoting positive relations. This *midrash* underscores the fact that it is insufficient to have been freed from hate; one must seek to free one's opponent from it. Otherwise, if one "hates another the other will hate him. As the *Book of Proverbs* points out, 'As in water face answers face, so the heart of man to man' (27:19). It follows that the hate will grow, and hence it is appropriate to curb the initial response."

This insight is caught by another *midrash*[6] through a play on the wording of the verse in *Exodus* (23:5), Instead of reading *azov ta'azov* as "you shall surely help," it exploits the more common understanding of the root-verb *azv* which is "discard" and thereby renders it as "you shall surely discard"—and then adds the implied object, "the hate." Only by such discarding can anger, resentment, hatred, and revenge be diverted from entering "the process of reciprocal imitative violence mount[ing] higher and enter[ing] into more and more of the personalities of the combatants."[7]

So far the Midrash offers a two-point program for reconciliation. First, control your urge to hate. Second, act in such a manner that your enemy will become your friend. The *Mishna Avot*[8] captures this program in capsule form, claiming, "Who is a hero? He who controls his urge." And the Talmudic commentary adds, "Who is a hero among heroes? He who controls his urge, and he who makes of his enemy his friend."[9] . . .

II

How far does the prohibition to kill extend? The following *midrashim* illustrate incidents where the right to kill in self-defense gave little comfort.

> "Then Jacob was greatly afraid and was distressed" (*Gen.* 32:8). R. Judah b. R. Ilai said: Are not fear and distress identical? The meaning, however, is that "he was afraid" lest he should be slain, "and was distressed" lest he should slay. For he thought: If he prevails against me, will he not slay me, while if I am stronger than he, will I not slay him? That is the meaning of "He was afraid"—lest he should be slain; "And was distressed"—lest he should slay.[10]

According to one commentator the reason is as follows: "Since it is not good for the righteous to punish (*Prov.* 17:26), and as the proverb of the ancients says, 'Out of the wicked comes forth wickedness (but my hand shall not be against you)' (1 *Sam.* 24:13), accordingly it is not right for Jacob to spill blood, even of the wicked."[11] The author of this alleged response of Jacob's is R. Judah b. R. Ilai, who may be identified with the R. Judah in the previous *midrash*, and thus his horror at violence remains constant. Moreover, he was well-known as a *hasid* (pious one) and naturally attributed the standard of the pious to the patriarch. The other possibility is that the R. Judah of the previous *midrash* is matched with a different R. Nehemiah. Thus, both would turn out to be fourth-generation Palestinian Amoraim, confirming the position that it was the second- to fourth-generation Palestinian Aggadists who most fully developed a theory of nonviolence. (The above *midrash* is also quoted by R. Pinchas HaCohen b. Hama, a fourth-generation Palestinian Amora.)

The following *midrash* follows the path of nonviolence one step further.

> "Then Jacob was greatly afraid." Did you think that Jacob really feared Esau, that he could not overcome him? It is not so. Rather, why did he fear him? That he would not stumble into the shedding of blood. Jacob thought, "Anyway you want, if I kill him I will transgress [the command] 'Thou shalt not murder.'"[12]

This is the ultimate, that killing in self-defense is called murder.

The second incident where violence as an alternative was transcended is the encounter between Saul and David. Saul had been pursuing David in an effort to kill this rival. David was hiding in a cave. The story continues:

> And Saul went in [the cave] to relieve himself. Now David and his men were sitting in the innermost parts of the cave. And the men of David said to him, "Here is the day of which the Lord said to you, 'Behold, I will give your enemy into your hand, and you shall do to him as it shall seem good to you.'" Then David arose and stealthily cut off the skirt of Saul's robe. And afterward David's heart smote him . . . (I *Sam.* 24:3–5).

What happened at that moment when David could have prevailed over his mortal enemy? What does it mean that "his heart smote him"? Answers a third-generation Palestinian Amora:

> R. Samuel b. Nahmani said: His urge appeared and said, "If you fell into his hand he would have no mercy for you and would kill you. And from the Torah it is permissible to kill him, for he is a pursuer." Accordingly, he [David] leaped and swore twice, "By God, I won't kill him!"[13]

According to another Amora, not only did David not want to kill, he dreaded being faced with the possibility. "R. Isaac said: 'Just as David prayed that he not fall in the hand of Saul, so did he pray that Saul would not fall into his hand.'"[14]

The decisive element is not only that David does not respond with violence, but the fact that he had the means of solving the crisis violently and refuses to use them. This point is underscored by Gandhi: "Nonviolence is not a cover for cowardice, but it is the supreme virtue of the brave. . . . Cowardice is wholly inconsistent with nonviolence. . . . Nonviolence presupposes the ability to strike."

Nevertheless, how does one react to a potential murderer when one is not in a superior position? The real issue is how to act to insure that nobody is killed. We will present three possible approaches that the *midrash* has Jacob take.

> The sages taught:[15] For five reasons Jacob sent messengers to Esau . . . to determine whether or not his anger had subsided . . . and to remove his

envy and enmity with softspoken words, as it says, "A soft answer turns away wrath" (*Prov.* 15:1).

The second approach[16] also has Jacob refuse to rely on might.

> Why did he send messengers to him? . . . He [Jacob] informed him [Esau], "If you are prepared for peace, I am with you; and if for war, I am ready for you. I have stalwarts and strong men, for I make a request of the Holy One . . . and He fulfills it," as it says, "He will fulfill the desires of them that fear him" (*Psa.* 145:19). For that reason David came to utter praise and glory to God who helped him when he fled from Saul . . . In reference to that incident was it said, "Some trust in chariots, and some in horses, but we will make mention of the name of the Lord our God" (*Psa.* 20:8).

According to a contemporary commentator, the difference between Jacob and David was that "David fought his enemies with the same means that they fought him, i.e. with chariots and horses. With Jacob, however, the verse was fulfilled. Esau confronted him with four hundred men, yet Jacob mentioned the name of God: 'And Jacob said, O God of my father Abraham and God of my father Isaac . . .' And with that the matter was closed; Esau yielded and made peace with Jacob."[17]

While the first approach has Jacob strive to remove the cause of aggression to prevent any conflict, the second has him operating from a position of relative strength. But what was the purpose of such might? On this there is disagreement between two third-century Palestinian Amoraim, one condoning violence and one not. R. Judah b. Simon said: [Jacob declared] "I have the strength to engage him in prayer." R. Levi said: [He declared] "I have the strength to engage him in battle."

A third approach suggests how to treat an aggressor whose enmity is still burning as he advances. This idea first appears in the first generation of Amoraim in the words of R. Hunia and receives its more developed form from the great fourth-generation Aggadist, R. Berahia, both Palestinians.

> "And Jacob settled down" (*Gen.* 37:1). R. Hunia said: This may be compared to a man who saw a pack of dogs and being afraid of them he sat down among them. Similarly, when Jacob saw Esau and his chiefs he was afraid of them and so he settled [sat] down among them.[18]

This is explained as follows: Jacob "feared his enemies that encircled him. In order that they not strive with him, Jacob sat down there, so that they would say that he considers them friends who would not struggle with him." This reasoning, that by an act of nonviolence one shows that one is not a threat to the well-being of the assailant, thereby allowing his aggression to subside, is made even more explicit in the later version:[19]

> R. Berahia said . . . [A man] saw dogs holding him. He thought: Who would be able to withstand all these? What did he do? He sat before them and soothed their anger. . . . Thus Jacob sat before them [Esau and his chiefs], and they did not harm him.

"Such are the tactics of the subtle, that they appear as trusting the amity of the wicked, so they should not be harmed: which would not be if they fled. And one should be careful that he does not appear as lacking trust, for he is his opponent."[20]

The underlying assumption of these "sit-ins" was expressed by Isaiah: "In sitting still and rest you shall be saved; in quietness and in confidence shall be your strength" (30:15ff.). It is this attitude which will allow a man to "take more care that he not injure others than that he not be injured." The hope is that such a show of faith-force, which demonstrates also concern for the welfare of the opponent, will so stir him that non-injury will result.

To what lengths this method goes and what a potential victim can do actively is dealt with in the following *midrash* on two verses in *Proverbs* by a second-generation Palestinian Amora. The verses are: "If your enemy is hungry, give him bread to eat; and if he is thirsty, give him water to drink; for you will heap coals of fire on his head, and the Lord will reward you" (25:21–22):

> "If your enemy is hungry," R. Hama b. Hanina says: Even though he rose early *(hishkeem)* to kill you and came hungry and thirsty to your home, feed him and give him to drink. Why? "For you will heap coals of fire on his head, and the Lord will reward *(yeshalem)* you." Do not read "reward" *(yeshalem)* but "he will cause him to be at peace" *(yashlemeno)* with you.

"Thus nonviolent resistance acts as a sort of moral jiu jitsu. The nonviolence and good will of the victim act like the lack of physical opposition by the user of physical jiu jitsu, to cause the attacker to lose his moral balance. He suddenly and unexpectedly loses the moral support which the usual violent resistance of most victims would render him."[21] The best way to take this radical nonviolent position is to quote the response of another radical of nonviolence. "When asked if it was lawful to overcome force with force, Erasmus answered . . . 'If your enemy is hungry, give him to eat. . . . In so doing, you will heap coals of fire upon his head, that is to say, you will kindle the fire of love in him.'"

This tactic, that mutual regard and acts of love can have a transforming effect, was an old tradition in Israel.

> Our Rabbis taught: What was Esther's reason for inviting Haman? . . . R. Joshua said: She learned to do so from her father's house, as it says, "If your enemy is hungry, give him bread to eat, etc." (*Proverbs* 25:21–22)[22]

The insight again is that the means one chooses to respond to an assailant will largely determine his reaction. Thus, "nonviolent resistance is a sort of moral manipulative activity in which the factors used and operated upon are largely psychological."[23] "When a man's ways please the Lord he makes even his enemies to be at peace with him" (*Prov.* 16:7).

It would be wrong to think that this method is soft on evil. It is rather a stratagem that so abhors evil that it refuses to use evil to attain anything. This is based on the profound insight that the means employed determine the end achieved, for means are actually ends *in potentia*. Accordingly, the good can only be achieved through the good. Or poetically put:

> Point not the goal until you plot the course
> For ends and means to man are entangled so
> That different means quite different aims enforce.
> Conceive the means as end in embryo.[24]

III

Essential to any ethic of nonviolence is the idea of self-suffering. This does not automatically imply any asceticism nor any search for suffering; rather, it is a conviction of the practitioner of nonviolence that if physical suffering is to be inflicted he would rather be the inflicted rather than the inflicter. Similarly, he holds that he can retain his humanity better in being persecuted than by being persecutor. Accordingly, he is faced with a real challenge when he chooses to oppose an oppressive regime. What avenues are open, and what can be considered proper means? The issue became glaringly real when Talmudic Palestine had to deal with the frequent outbreak of rebellion throughout almost all of Roman rule.

The following *midrash*[25] dealing with this problem is attached to the Priestly Blessing for peace. It grapples with the issue of how to promote ultimate peace:

> "Thus you shall bless the people of Israel [so that]. . . . The Lord will grant peace" (*Num.* 6:22ff.). This bears on what is written in Scripture, "Do not envy a man of violence and do not choose any of his ways" (*Prov.* 3:31). The "man of violence" refers to the wicked Esau. . . . And the reason why it says, "do not envy" is because it is manifest to the Holy One . . . that Israel [is] destined to be enslaved beneath the power of Edom [Rome] and will be oppressed and crushed in their midst, and that Israel will at some time raise angry protest against this, as Malachi asserts, "You have said, 'It is vain to serve God. What is the good of our keeping his charge, etc. (*Mal.* 3:14); henceforth we deem the arrogant blessed; evildoers not only prosper, but when they put God to the test they escape'" (ibid. 15). Accordingly the Holy Spirit, speaking through Solomon, said, "Do not envy a man of violence!" Envy not the peace enjoyed by the wicked Esau! "And do not choose any of his ways," i.e., you must not do according to their deeds.

What is the blessing of peace worthy of Israel? That he not choose the way of violence even to overthrow his oppressors. Moreover, it is prohibited "to desire to be like him, to do violence to men; [accordingly] do not choose any of his ways, for that will bring you to sin as he does."[26] There can be no violence without sin. The *midrash* continues:

> . . . Moreover, it says, "Then once more you shall distinguish between the righteous and the wicked, between one who serves God and one who

does not serve him" (*Mal.* 3:18). . . . The wicked—Esau; the righteous—Israel, about whom it is written, "Your people shall all be righteous; they shall possess the land forever" (*Isa.* 60:21).

It follows that the sign that Israel is righteous and worships God is that it rejects the use of violence. And it is through such virtue that it will be found worthy to possess the land.

In order constantly to endure suffering without retaliation one must have a strong trust in a God who cares and will help in the ultimate victory. As Martin Luther King, Jr. confessed: "Perhaps the suffering, frustration and agonizing moments which I have had to undergo occasionally as a result of my involvement in a difficult struggle have drawn me closer to God . . . I am convinced that the universe is under the control of a loving purpose and that in the struggle for righteousness man has cosmic companionship." And as Gandhi testified: "Truth and nonviolence are not possible without a living belief in God . . . I am unable to account for my life without belief in this all-embracing living light. . . . [Thus] my greatest weapon is mute prayer."

This theory rests also on the faith that God is always on the side of the persecuted even though he be pursued for his wickedness. As the *midrash* says:[27]

> "And God seeks that which is pursued" (*Ecc.* 3:15). R. Huna in the name of R. Joseph explained: Always "God seeks that which is pursued." You find a righteous man pursues a righteous man, "and God seeks that which is pursued"; where a wicked man pursues a righteous man, "and God seeks that which is pursued"; where a wicked man pursues a wicked man, "and God seeks that which is pursued"; where a righteous man pursues a wicked man, "and God seeks that which is pursued." Whatever the case, "God seeks that which is pursued." R. Judah b. Simon in the name of R. Jose b. R. Nehorai said: The Holy One . . . demands satisfaction for the pursued at the hands of the pursuers . . . Therefore God chose Abel . . . Noah . . . Abraham . . . Isaac . . . Jacob . . . Joseph . . . Moses . . . David . . . Saul . . . and Israel.

Once it is realized that God sides always with the persecuted, it becomes impossible for even righteous indignation to be a motive for inflicting suffering. In fact, by virtue of persecuting, one removes himself from God. "As it is written, 'God befriends the persecuted and repudiates the persecutors.'"[28] Furthermore, if a man once persecuted his fellow-man he loses all prerogatives of special pleading if he should in the future be persecuted. Only he whose hands are clean may request that another be handed over.

> R. Samuel b. Nahmani said: We possess an Aggadic tradition that Esau will not fall except into the hands of the children of Rachel. Why? For if the tribes come to try Esau saying, "Why did you persecute your brother?"—he will say to them, "Why did you persecute Joseph, your brother? You are no better than me." But when he comes to Joseph, he [Joseph] says to him, "Why did you persecute your brother?" And he [Esau] will not be able to answer him. "If you will say [continues Joseph] that he did you evil, also my brothers paid me evil, and I repaid them with good." Immediately, he quiets.[29]

In these last two third-century *midrashim*, it could never be claimed that the end justifies the means. As long as there is no distinction in the means there is no distinction in the moral right to victory. One can claim no moral superiority as long as the same tactics are employed, even though there may be two disparate goals. By their means shall you judge them. . . .

We have seen that alongside the normative legal tradition there existed, in this period, a concomitant undercurrent which may be considered the standard of the *hasid*. The *hasid* was not one who stood on his legal rights, but always sought a solution which would find favor in the eyes of God. He was a self-sufferer who avoided the remotest possibility of doing harm. He sought good and shunned evil. Quick to forgive, he was pacific in human relationships, basing his life on what he had learned. Valuing life above possessions, he never arrogated anything to himself. Above all he sought to prevent injury and acted lovingly to his fellowman.

The prototype of the *hasid* was David. According to R. Judah, "He was benevolent to all, saying: 'Even to a murderer as well as to the slain, to a pursuer as well as to the pursued, I show kindness to a righteous man.' That is what is written: 'But as for me, in Thy mercy do I trust; my heart shall rejoice in Thy salvation. I will sing unto the Lord because He has dealt bountifully with me!' (*Psa.* 13:6)."[30] This sentiment is ascribed to David in light of his cry, "How long shall my enemy be exalted over me?" (ibid. 13:3). Unless one can truly say, "In Thy mercy do I trust," it would seem an almost insuperable task to maintain one's composure consistently against one's enemies. This relationship is implicit in the famous lines from *Lamentations*: "Let him give his cheek to the smiter, and be filled with insults. For the Lord will not cast off forever" (3:30–31).

Notes

[1] *Bereshith Rabbah* 38, 3 (henceforth *B. R.*); *Yalkut Shimoni II*, No. 956 (henceforth *Y. S.*).

[2] *Deuteronomy* 22:4.

[3] *Tanhuma Yashan, Mishpatim I; T. S., Exodus* 23, No. 68; *Exodus Rabbah* 30, 1.

[4] Richard Gregg, *The Power of Non-Violence* (New York 1966), 50.

[5] *Midrash Aggadah, Exodus* 23:5.

[6] *Midrash Lekah Tov, Exodus* 23.5, see *Targum Onkelos, ad loc.*

[7] Gregg, op. cit., p. 54; see *Menorat Hama'or* (ed. Enelow), Vol. 4, p. 320.

[8] *Avot* 4, 1.

[9] *Avot de Rabbi Natan* 23.

[10] *B. R.* 76, 2.

[11] *Yefeh Toar*, quoted by the *Etz Yosef* on *Tanhuma, Vayishlah* 4; see *Hilkhot Teshuvah* 2, 10.

[12] *Ginze Schecter*, p. 60.

[13] *Tanhuma, B'ha'alotkha* 10.

[14] *Y. S. II*, No. 888; see *Midrash Tehilim* 7, 13: "Rabbi Tarfon said: David said at that moment, 'Although Saul pursues me, my song shall not leave my lips (lit. mouth).'"

[15] *Midrash Ha'beur* (manuscript) in *T. S., Genesis* 32, No. 11; see *Midrash Lekah Tov* ad loc. See also *Berakhot* 17a: "a pearl in the mouth of Abbaye . . ." With J. Schecter's explanation in *Sefer Mishle with Rabbinic Comments*, p. 94, showing how Abbaye's changes in the proverb increase its efficiency. Cf. *B. R.* 75, 11: Jacob sent messengers to see whether Esau would repent.

[16] *B. R.* 75, 11.

[17] Ibid., ed. Mirkin, p. 174. See *Midrash Hagadol, Bereshith,* p. 550.

[18] Ibid., 84, 5. Instead of translating *vayeshev* as "dwelt" (Soncino and R. S. V.), it is rendered as "settled down," for the *midrash* is playing on the primary meaning of the word, which is "sit down."

[19] *Midrash Hagadol, Bereshith,* p. 621.

[20] *T. S. Genesis* 37, No. 3.

[21] Gregg, op. cit., p. 44.

[22] *Megillah* 15b; in *Ein Yaakov; Midrash Lekah Tov* to *Esther* 5:4.

[23] Gregg, op. cit., p. 57.

[24] J. V. Bondurant, *Conquest of Violence* (Los Angeles 1967), p. xiii, quoted from Arthur Koestler, *Darkness at Noon,* p. 31. Similarly, Gandhi claimed: "In *Satyagraha* the cause has to be just and clear as well as the means." (*Satyagraha*, truth-force or soul-force, is the technique for effecting social and political change based on truth, nonviolence and self-suffering.)

[25] *Bamidbar Rabbah* 11, 1; see *Y. S. I*, No. 227; cf. end of *Shmoth Rabbah* 30, 1, for God's concern for legality.

[26] Ralbag, *Proverbs* 3:31; see *T. S., Exodus* 2, No. 112; 102; 120.

[27] *Vayikra Rabbah* 27, 5.

[28] *Pesikta Rabati* 193b; *Vayikra Rabbah* 27, 5; variants line 5 (ed. Margoloth), p. 631. See *Sefer Hahinukh, Mitzvah* No. 600; cf. *Bamidbar Rabbah* 14, 4, for illustrations that God saves the weak from the strong.

[29] *Y. S. II*, No. 51.

[30] *Koheleth, Rabbah* 7, 1.

How Transforming Power Has Been Used in the Past by Early Christians

Lawrence S. Apsey

Perhaps the most frequent argument against Transforming Power as a practical solution of current conflicts is that it will not work against a godless dictatorship or a pagan nation. Gandhi's success against a Christian nation with a strong moral conscience is said to be no indication that similar methods could prevail against a nation like Communist China, the Soviet Union, or South Africa.

This argument ignores the lessons of history. The Roman Empire during the first three centuries of Christianity equaled modern dictatorships in ruthlessness, paganism and violence. Nevertheless, during this period, Christianity, by its witness of love and sacrifice, grew from a tiny Jewish sect to become a religion professed by the majority in the most populous areas of mankind.[1] In the words of K. S. Latourette, a leading historian of the period, "Never in so short a time has any other religious faith or, for that matter, any other set of ideas, religious, political or economic, without the aid of physical force or of social or cultural prestige, achieved so commanding a position in such an important culture."[2]

During this period, Christians refused service in the army;[3] and there is no direct evidence that they ever used force against the bloodthirsty persecutions to which they were subjected.[4] While paying lip service to the mythology of the ancients, most people in the Empire at the time of Jesus recognized no responsibility to a divine power beyond themselves, and their rulers spared no cruelty in the ten major persecutions which were launched against the Christians. Under Nero, Christians were torn by dogs or nailed to crosses and set on fire to serve at night as living torches.[5] Under Valerian, the death penalty was enforced for meeting in church and entering cemeteries. Christian leaders were exiled for not doing homage to the pagan gods. Clerics were

Source: *Transforming Power for Peace*, by Lawrence S. Apsey, James Bristol, and Karen Eppler (Philadelphia: Religious Education Committee of Friends General Conference, 1986). Reprinted by permission of Lawrence S. Apsey.

put to death, others deprived of property, enslaved or burned at the stake.[6] Christians were happy, without resistance by force, to share the martyrdom of Jesus;[7] and this had a tremendous effect in converting those who witnessed their suffering.[8] The Christians disregarded the restrictive laws and continued to witness to the power of the Spirit regardless of the consequences. The truth, as they saw it, was much more precious than life; and they never ceased to act publicly and privately in proclaiming their beliefs.

At last, even the Emperor was converted. He had a waking vision of a cross bearing the inscription "Conquer by this"[9] and it is one of the greatest tragedies of history that he was unable to interpret this vision in the light of the teachings of Jesus. Had he been sensitive to the tenderness of the divine love, Constantine would have understood his vision to mean that he should conquer by love, courage and self-sacrifice (Transforming Power) even as the Christians had conquered his Empire. Instead, he interpreted it as a guarantee of victory by the same violence that had failed against the Christians—provided only that he would profess Christianity and adopt the cross as his symbol. This was a prostitution of the message of Jesus and a prelude to centuries of the propagation of Christianity by the sword. It is small wonder that today non-Christians conceive of Christianity as one of the most bloodthirsty of religions. Not only is Constantine's interpretation of his vision accountable for the propagation of Christianity by the sword which resulted in the Crusades of the Middle Ages; but in our day the so-called Christian nations have, in the name of Christ, engaged in wars of unprecedented cruelty, destroying combatants and non-combatants alike, until at the present moment they are preparing for an Armageddon which threatens to make the world unfit for habitation.

Behind this Armageddon, is there a possibility of the Millennium, the establishment of the Kingdom of Peace? Can we recapture the power of love-witnessing by which Christianity conquered the Roman world without violence?

Modern Transforming Power, it is argued, cannot accomplish the results of early Christianity because it is not a religion. If faith and practice in the teachings of Jesus, the Apostles and the Ten Commandments is a religion, however, then Transforming Power is a religion, for its basic principles are the same. Is it religion to believe that as children of a divine Father we are all brothers and sisters, to love our neighbors as ourselves? Here are the principles we are discussing embedded in the teachings of the New Testament:

> "You have heard that it was said to the men of old, 'you shall not kill; and whoever kills, shall be liable to judgment.' But I say to you that everyone who is angry with his brother shall be liable to judgment; whoever insults his brother shall be liable to the council, and whoever says 'you fool!' shall be liable to the hell of fire."[10]

> "All who take the sword will perish by the sword."[11]

> "You have heard it said, 'An eye for an eye and a tooth for a tooth.' But I say to you, Do not resist one who is evil. But if anyone strike you on the right cheek, turn to him the other also and if anyone would sue you and

take your coat, let him have your cloak as well; and if anyone force you to go one mile, go with him two miles."[12]

"You have heard that it was said, 'You shall love your neighbor and hate your enemy.' But, I say to you, love your enemies and pray for those who persecute you."[13]

"If your enemy is hungry, feed him; if he is thirsty, give him drink; for by so doing you will heap burning coals on his head. Do not be overcome by evil, but overcome evil with good."[14]

This is Transforming Power and while it was practiced by most Christians it was the power of Christianity. In its revival lies the greatest hope of overcoming the threat of universal destruction and of establishing a just and lasting peace.

Notes

[1] K. S. Latourette, *A History of the Expansion of Christianity*, Vol. 1, "The First Five Centuries" (New York: Harper & Bros., 1937), 369.
[2] Ibid., 112.
[3] Ibid., 268.
[4] Ibid., 274.
[5] Ibid., 137–38.
[6] Ibid., 152.
[7] Ibid., 162.
[8] Ibid., 156.
[9] Ibid., 158.
[10] Matt. 5:21–22.
[11] Matt. 26:52.
[12] Matt. 5:38–41.
[13] Matt. 5:43–44.
[14] Romans 12: 20–21.

Nonviolence in Islam

Wasim Siddiqui

Since recorded history, the human race has yearned for world peace. The major religious faiths have urged their followers to strive toward the attainment of this goal. Yet, even in our present day civilization, might is still right, and the poor and weak are still brutally ruled and suppressed. The pursuits of wealth, power and fame have been the dominant endeavors of the human race. Submission to God, awareness of spiritual principles, and promotion of higher ethical values have been continuously supplanted within the individual and society by greed, self-promotion, lust, false pride, and power—each of which has been proven to be counter-productive to the pursuit of peace. Why has the human race failed to achieve universal peace? We have built lofty institutions, churches, synagogues, temples and mosques. Yet we have remained distant from the spirit and teachings of God. From Adam to Muhammad, prophets of all races and traditions have taught that worldly pursuits need not be the goal of humans, that God is the source of fulfillment of our every need. Yet the human race has demonstrated a collective ignorance of this promise of God. The simple truths that have been revealed to the human race again and again by the prophets of God all point to the fact that God exists as a Creator, as an essential part of every human being, and as the infinite provider of all our material and spiritual needs. God is the origin and exemplar of peace within each major religion.

For a Muslim, Islam, Christianity, and Judaism are but three forms of one religion. In its original purity, this was the religion and faith of Abraham, Al-Islam, which means the absolute self-surrender to the Will of God. [All references to the Qur'an are from Abdullah Yusuf Ali, *Ba Holy Qur'an*, U.S. ed. (New York: Tahrike Tarsile Qur'an, 1987).]

> The same religion has He established for you as that which He enjoined on Noah, which We have sent by inspiration to thee. And that which We enjoined on Abraham, Moses and Jesus namely, that ye should remain steadfast in religion and make no divisions therein. (*Qur'an* XLII.13)

Source: From *Nonviolence in Hawaii's Spiritual Traditions*, edited by Glenn D. Paige and Sarah Gilliatt. Center for Global Nonviolence Planning Project. Reprinted with permission of Matsunaga Institute for Peace.

Say ye, We believe in God and the revelation given to us, and to Abraham, Ismail, Issac, Jacob and the Tribes, and that given to Moses and Jesus and that given to (all) Prophets from their Lord: We make no difference between one and another of them; and we bow to God. (*Qur'an* II.136)

O ye Apostles! Enjoy (all) things good and pure, and work righteousness; for I am well acquainted with (all) that ye do. And verily this brotherhood is one and I am your lord and Cherisher; therefore fear Me (and no other). (*Qur'an* XXIII.51, 52)

One of the distinguishing features of Islam is the relationship between humans and their Creator which is free from any intermediaries. Each human being has the ability and responsibility to communicate directly with God through their own individual consciousness.

When my servant ask thee concerning Me, I am indeed close (to them), I listen to the prayer of every supplicant when he calleth on Me: let them also, with a will, listen to My call and believe in Me that they walk in the right way. (*Qur'an* 11.186)

There is not a secret consultation between three, but He makes thee fourth among them, nor between five but He makes the sixth, nor between fewer nor more, but He is in their midst, wheresoever they be. (*Qur'an* L. VIII.7)

And your Lord says, "Call on Me, I will answer your prayer!" (*Qur'an* IL.60)

For my Lord is (always) near, ready to answer. (*Qur'an* XI.61)

For God is nearer to him than (his) jugular vein. (*Qur'an* L.16)

The Islamic concept of peace is derived from the unity of all existence: inanimate, plant, and animal. All activities of the cosmos are encompassed within the inner workings of the human mind. There is a unity of all energy whether it is the physical striving for necessities or the spiritual craving for elation. Islam believes that there is one faith for humankind and that this faith entails complete surrender to the Creator in both secular and spiritual matters. This idea is inherent in our mental and emotional processes. In the Islamic faith, peace is the foundation for the principle of harmony—harmony in the universe, in the natural laws of life and in the origin of human beings. Islam also maintains that God is an essential part of every person's consciousness. As such, God is ever aware of each individual's prayers and needs. By learning to follow the Will of God as it is revealed within individual consciousness, every human being may discover their material and spiritual needs abundantly filled with peace as the reward. Islam believes that it is imperative that the individual human being be at peace with himself or herself before the goal of universal peace may be realized. Therefore, Islam, through its teachings in the *Qur'an* and *Hadith*, aims to implant peace within the individual's innermost conscience.

By focusing upon the individual first, Islam acknowledges the unique-
ness of each person's instincts and ambitions as being individual expressions
and creations of God. The term *jihad* literally means effort or endeavor. In
religious connotation, it applies to the whole effort of the individual Muslim
to realize the sovereignty of God within their inner conscience. "The greatest
Jihad is that against a man's own lust" *(Hadith: Sayings of Prophet Muhammad)*. This *jihad* takes place within the individual's own heart and mind until
an awareness develops that there truly exists only one Will within individual
conscience, and that is the sweet and pleasurable Will of God. The term *jihad*
is also applicable to patience under persecution, to active charity, and indeed
to every form of human endeavor which aims at self-improvement and
greater awareness of God. For instance, the term *"Al-Jihad ul-Akbar"* (the
greatest *jihad*) is applied by Prophet Muhammad to the effort of the student
to become learned and the effort of the learned to spread knowledge. "The
ink of the scholar is more holy than the blood of the martyr" *(Hadith: Sayings
of Prophet Muhammad)*. Thus, in Islam, the needs, interests, ideals, and goals
of society and humanity at large are realized first at the individual level.

In striving to inculcate such a living relationship with God, the teachings
of Islam transform individual character. The transformed person, although
outwardly associating with people, places and things, is nevertheless
inwardly with God. In the midst of a crowd, the transformed person dwells in
the spiritual retreat of the Divine Secret. This person, though perhaps running
here and there in pursuit of material goals and experiencing events both bitter
and sweet, pleasant and unpleasant, beautiful and ugly, has yet a heart that is
free. Such an individual exists in a world of tranquility in which the Face of
God is seen everywhere he or she looks. The teachings of Islam strive to
inculcate a positive peace that will exalt and enrich life. Every aspect of life,
from birth to marriage to death is meant to be experienced to build character
and strengthen faith in God and love for humanity. Everything and everyone
that one touches or sees is to be treated with reverence as a beloved creation
of God. Hence, conscientious Muslims, those dedicated to unveiling the Will
of God for their personal lives, extend their spiritual life into every aspect of
their material life. So, irrespective of wherever they are or whatever they are
doing, such people are always close to God.

A true Muslim seeks to follow the Will of God as it is revealed within
individual consciousness. Through obedience to the Will of God, prayer and
meditation, individuals realize their closeness to God and become aware of
God's mercy and compassion. Obedience to the "inner-voice," prayer and
meditation become a way of life as the individual experiences more and more
of the love and Grace of God in his or her life. The knowledge that their individual consciousness will reveal the Will of God for their lives gives great
inner strength to individuals to pursue righteous paths without fear of obstacles such as conflict with people who claim to have personal power, wealth
and influence that is not God-given. With a living faith that Allah (God) is
always in one's thoughts (consciousness) and actions, and that Allah is able

to guide and provide abundance, the individual attains inner peace and contributes to the external peace of societies.

Islam emphasizes the character of the individual. Individuals are the nucleus of society. They embody the Spirit of God which is incorporated into their own consciousness. When they are attentive to this consciousness, the Spirit of God is manifested through their conduct. Islam sees the individual as the nucleus of the family and the family as the nucleus of society. Through its teachings, Islam strives to transform the individual into a peace-loving person both in thought and action. Islam believes that peace in the individual's inner mind creates peace at home which leads to peace within the society. To encourage this, besides broader spiritual guidance, Islam has outlined specific codes of conduct and laws for individual members of the family. The rights and duties of spouses, children, parents, and extended family members are all considered. For instance, the Islamic code of life strongly prohibits the use of alcohol, drugs, and sensual allurements. These acts are considered to have serious adverse effects on the peace and harmony of the family. When one has a realization of personal peace and an awareness of a personal relationship with God, then one will act in accordance with one's God-given purpose and there would be no need to compete for a limited resource since God would provide for each person uniquely according to the Will which was given them to fulfill. Such a society would be based upon peace, since each individual would be revealing and contributing to the wholeness of God.

In conclusion, Islam promotes peace in society by emphasizing to individuals their role as the recipients of God's grace and the custodians of the earth. Islam reminds us that we were all individual expressions of God created from one Soul. The spiritual principle of equality that makes no distinction between black and white, man and woman, noble and humble, rich and poor, strong and weak, educated and uneducated, is strictly emphasized. Islam strongly encourages compassion, tolerance and love toward all human beings. In Islam, the path to be followed in life has been designed in such a way that man's social and material life is like a cradle in which the spiritual life is nurtured. The balance of the individual's human experience and spiritual development fosters the growth of God-awareness and initiates an inner peace which is active, not passive. God-awareness grows into an obedience to the Will of God which, in turn, fosters the creation of inner peace. This peace grows as the individual recognizes the oneness and omnipotence of God and realizes that God's justice is the basis for achieving social equilibrium and cooperation. Thus, in Islam, world peace may be attained through the evolution of the passions and desires of individual consciousness into an inner harmony of obedience to God's Will. This creates an awareness that the family is the support and expression of each individual member's God-spirit which leads to the creation of a vital, harmonious peace among societies and nations.

Suggested Reading

Author's Note: The author gratefully acknowledges the invaluable contributions of Susan M. Lofton to the writing and editing of this paper and would like to suggest the following books for the interested reader of Islam:

Khan, Fateh Ullah. *God, Universe and Man, The Holy Qur'an and the Hereafter.* Lahore, Pakistan: Wajidalis, 1982.

Kotb, Sayed. *Social Justice in Islam.* New York: Octagon Books, 1970.

Qutb, Syed. *In the Shade of Al-Qur'an.* Bangladesh: Islamic Cultural Center, 1981.

Rahman, Fazlur. *Islam.* Chicago: University of Chicago Press, 1979.

SECULAR ORIGINS
CHALLENGES TO INJUSTICE AND GOVERNMENT POWER

From *Apology* and *Crito*

Plato

Civil Disobedience for the Good of the State

From Plato's *Apology, 28e–30.*

Strange, indeed, would be my conduct, O men of Athens, if I who, when I was ordered by the generals whom you chose to command me at Potidaea and Amphipolis and Delium, remained where they placed me, like any other man, facing death; if, I say, now, when, as I conceive and imagine, God orders me to fulfil the philosopher's mission of searching into myself and other men, I were to desert my post through fear of death, or any other fear; that would indeed be strange, and I might justly be arraigned in court for denying the existence of the gods, if I disobeyed the oracle because I was afraid of death: then I should be fancying that I was wise when I was not wise. For this fear of death is indeed the pretence of wisdom, and not real wisdom, being the appearance of knowing the unknown; since no one knows whether death, which they in their fear apprehend to be the greatest evil, may not be the greatest good. Is there not here conceit of knowledge, which is a disgraceful sort of ignorance? And this is the point in which, as I think, I am superior to men in general, and in which I might perhaps fancy myself wiser than other men—that whereas I know but little of the world below, I do not

Source: From the translation by Benjamin Jowett.

41

suppose that I know: but I do know that injustice and disobedience to a better, whether God or man, is evil and dishonorable, and I will never fear or avoid a possible good rather than a certain evil. And therefore if you let me go now, and reject the counsels of Anytus, who said that if I were not put to death I ought not to have been prosecuted, and that if I escape now, your sons will all be utterly ruined by listening to my words—if you say to me, Socrates, this time we will not mind Anytus, and will let you off, but upon one condition, that you are not to inquire and speculate in this way any more, and that if you are caught doing this again you shall die;—if this was the condition on which you let me go, I should reply: Men of Athens, I honor and love you; but I shall obey God rather than you, and while I have life and strength I shall never cease from the practice and teaching of philosophy, exhorting anyone whom I meet after my manner, and convincing him, saying: O my friend, why do you who are a citizen of the great and mighty and wise city of Athens, care so much about laying up the greatest amount of money and honor and reputation, and so little about wisdom and truth and the greatest improvement of the soul, which you never regard or heed at all? Are you not ashamed of this? And if the person with whom I am arguing says: Yes, but I do care; I do not depart or let him go at once; I interrogate and examine and cross-examine him, and if I think that he has no virtue, but only says that he has, I reproach him with undervaluing the greater, and overvaluing the less. And this I should say to everyone whom I meet, young and old, citizen and alien, but especially to the citizens, inasmuch as they are my brethren. For this is the command of God, as I would have you know; and I believe that to this day no greater good has ever happened in the state than my service to the God. For I do nothing but go about persuading you all, old and young alike, not to take thought for your persons and your properties, but first and chiefly to care about the greatest improvement of the soul. I tell you that virtue is not given by money, but that from virtue come money and every other good of man, public as well as private. This is my teaching, and if this is the doctrine which corrupts the youth, my influence is ruinous indeed. But if anyone says that this is not my teaching, he is speaking an untruth. Wherefore, O men of Athens, I say to you, do as Anytus bids or not as Anytus bids, and either acquit me or not; but whatever you do, know that I shall never alter my ways, not even if I have to die many times.

Do No Harm

From Plato's *Crito, 48d–49e.*

Soc. Let us consider the matter together, and do you either refute me if you can, and I will be convinced; or else cease, my dear friend, from repeating to me that I ought to escape against the wishes of the Athenians: for I am extremely desirous to be persuaded by you, but not against my own better judgment. And now please to consider my first position, and do your best to answer me.

Cr. I will do my best.

Soc. Are we to say that we are never intentionally to do wrong, or that in one way we ought and in another way we ought not to do wrong, or is doing wrong always evil and dishonorable, as I was just now saying, and as has been already acknowledged by us? Are all our former admissions which were made within a few days to be thrown away? And have we, at our age, been earnestly discoursing with one another all our life long only to discover that we are no better than children? Or are we to rest assured, in spite of the opinion of the many, and in spite of consequences whether better or worse, of the truth of what was then said, that injustice is always an evil and dishonor to him who acts unjustly? Shall we affirm that?

Cr. Yes.

Soc. Then we must do no wrong?

Cr. Certainly not.

Soc. Nor when injured injure in return, as the many imagine; for we must injure no one at all?

Cr. Clearly not.

Soc. Again, Crito, may we do evil?

Cr. Surely not, Socrates.

Soc. And what of doing evil in return for evil, which is the morality of the many—is that just or not?

Cr. Not just.

Soc. For doing evil to another is the same as injuring him?

Cr. Very true.

Soc. Then we ought not to retaliate or render evil for evil to anyone, whatever evil we may have suffered from him. But I would have you consider, Crito, whether you really mean what you are saying. For this opinion has never been held, and never will be held, by any considerable number of persons; and those who are agreed and those who are not agreed upon this point have no common ground, and can only despise one another, when they see how widely they differ. Tell me, then, whether you agree with and assent to my first principle, that neither injury nor retaliation nor warding off evil by evil is ever right. And shall that be the premise of our agreement? Or do you decline and dissent from this? For this has been of old and is still my opinion; but, if you are of another opinion, let me hear what you have to say. If, however, you remain of the same mind as formerly, I will proceed to the next step.

Cr. You may proceed, for I have not changed my mind.

Respect for Law

From Plato's *Crito, 49e–54e* (end).

Soc. But if this is true, what is the application? In leaving the prison against the will of the Athenians, do I wrong any? or rather do I not wrong those whom I ought least to wrong? Do I not desert the principles which were acknowledged by us to be just? What do you say?

Cr. I cannot tell, Socrates, for I do not know.

Soc. Then consider the matter in this way: Imagine that I am about to play truant (you may call the proceeding by any name which you like), and the laws and the government come and interrogate me: "Tell us, Socrates," they say; "what are you about? are you going by an act of yours to overturn us—the laws and the whole State, as far as in you lies? Do you imagine that a State can subsist and not be overthrown, in which the decisions of law have no power, but are set aside and over-thrown by individuals?" What will be our answer, Crito, to these and the like words? Anyone, and especially a clever rhetorician, will have a good deal to urge about the evil of setting aside the law which requires a sentence to be carried out; and we might reply, "Yes; but the State has injured us and given an unjust sentence." Suppose I say that?

Cr. Very good, Socrates.

Soc. "And was that our agreement with you?" the law would say, "or were you to abide by the sentence of the State?" And if I were to express astonishment at their saying this, the law would probably add: "Answer, Socrates, instead of opening your eyes: you are in the habit of asking and answering questions. Tell us what complaint you have to make against us which justifies you in attempting to destroy us and the State? In the first place did we not bring you into existence? Your father married your mother by our aid and begat you. Say whether you have any objection to urge against those of us who regulate marriage?" None, I should reply. "Or against those of us who regulate the system of nurture and education of children in which you were trained? Were not the laws, who have the charge of this, right in commanding your father to train you in music and gymnastic?" Right, I should reply. "Well, then, since you were brought into the world and nurtured and educated by us, can you deny in the first place that you are our child and slave, as your fathers were before you? And if this is true you are not on equal terms with us; nor can you think that you have a right to do to us what we are doing to you. Would you have any right to strike or revile or do any other evil to a father or to your master, if you had one, when you have been struck or reviled by him, or received some other evil at his hands?—you would not say this? And because we think right to destroy you, do you think that you have any right to destroy us in return, and your country as far as in you lies? And will you, O professor of true virtue, say that you are justified in this? Has a philosopher like you failed to discover that our country is more to be valued and higher and holier far than mother or father or any ancestor, and more to be regarded in the eyes of the gods and of men of understanding? also to be soothed, and gently and reverently entreated when angry, even more than a father, and if not persuaded, obeyed? And when we are punished by her, whether with imprisonment or stripes, the punishment is to be endured in silence; and if she leads us to wounds or death in battle, thither we follow as is right; neither may anyone yield or retreat or leave his rank, but whether in battle or in a court of law, or in any other place, he must do what his city and his country order him; or he must change their view of what is just: and if he may do no violence to his father or mother, much less may he do violence to his country." What answer shall we make to this, Crito? Do the laws speak truly, or do they not?

Cr.   I think that they do.

Soc. Then the laws will say: "Consider, Socrates, if this is true, that in your present attempt you are going to do us wrong. For, after having brought you into the world, and nurtured and educated you, and given you and every other citizen a share in every good that we had to give, we further proclaim and give the right to every Athenian, that if he does not like us when he has come of age and has seen the ways of the city, and made our acquaintance, he may go where he pleases and take his goods with him; and none of us laws will forbid him or interfere with him. Any of you who does not like us and the city, and who wants to go to a colony or to any other city, may go where he likes, and take his goods with him. But he who has experience of the manner in which we order justice and administer the State, and still remains, has entered into an implied contract that he will do as we command him. And he who disobeys us is, as we maintain, thrice wrong: first, because in disobeying us he is disobeying his parents; secondly, because we are the authors of his education; thirdly, because he has made an agreement with us that he will duly obey our commands; and he neither obeys them nor convinces us that our commands are wrong; and we do not rudely impose them, but give him the alternative of obeying or convincing us; that is what we offer and he does neither. These are the sort of accusations to which, as we were saying, you, Socrates, will be exposed if you accomplish your intentions; you, above all other Athenians." Suppose I ask, why is this? they will justly retort upon me that I above all other men have acknowledged the agreement. "There is clear proof," they will say, "Socrates, that we and the city were not displeasing to you. Of all Athenians you have been the most constant resident in the city, which, as you never leave, you may be supposed to love. For you never went out of the city either to see the games, except once when you went to the Isthmus, or to any other place unless when you were on military service; nor did you travel as other men do. Nor had you any curiosity to know other States or their laws: your affections did not go beyond us and our State; we were your especial favorites, and you acquiesced in our government of you; and this is the State in which you begat your children, which is a proof of your satisfaction. Moreover, you might, if you had liked, have fixed the penalty at banishment in the course of the trial—the State which refuses to let you go now would have let you go then. But you pretended that you preferred death to exile, and that you were not grieved at death. And now you have forgotten these fine sentiments, and pay no respect to us, the laws, of whom you are the destroyer; and are doing what only a miserable slave would do, running away and turning your back upon the compacts and agreements which you made as a citizen. And first of all answer this very question: Are we right in saying that you agreed to be governed according to us in deed, and not in word only? Is that true or not?" How shall we answer that, Crito? Must we not agree?

Cr.   There is no help, Socrates.

Soc.   Then will they not say: "You, Socrates, are breaking the covenants and agreements which you made with us at your leisure, not in any haste or under any compulsion or deception, but having had seventy years to think of them, during which time you were at liberty to leave the city, if we were not to your mind, or if our covenants appeared to you to be unfair. You had your choice, and might have gone either to Lacedaemon or Crete, which you often praise for their good government, or to some other Hellenic or foreign State. Whereas you, above all other Athenians, seemed to be so fond of the State, or, in other words, of us her laws (for who would like a State that has no laws?), that you never stirred out of her: the halt, the blind, the maimed, were not more stationary in her than you were. And now you run away and forsake your agreements. Not so, Socrates, if you will take our advice; do not make yourself ridiculous by escaping out of the city.

"For just consider, if you transgress and err in this sort of way, what good will you do, either to yourself or to your friends? That your friends will be driven into exile and deprived of citizenship, or will lose their property, is tolerably certain; and you yourself, if you fly to one of the neighboring cities, as, for example, Thebes or Megara, both of which are well-governed cities, will come to them as an enemy, Socrates, and their government will be against you, and all patriotic citizens will cast an evil eye upon you as a subverter of the laws, and you will confirm in the minds of the judges the justice of their own condemnation of you. For he who is a corrupter of the laws is more than likely to be corrupter of the young and foolish portion of mankind. Will you then flee from well-ordered cities and virtuous men? and is existence worth having on these terms? Or will you go to them without shame, and talk to them, Socrates? And what will you say to them? What you say here about virtue and justice and institutions and laws being the best things among men? Would that be decent of you? Surely not. But if you go away from well-governed States to Crito's friends in Thessaly, where there is great disorder and license, they will be charmed to have the tale of your escape from prison, set off with ludicrous particulars of the manner in which you were wrapped in a goatskin or some other disguise, and metamorphosed as the fashion of runaways is—that is very likely; but will there be no one to remind you that in your old age you violated the most sacred laws from a miserable desire of a little more life? Perhaps not, if you keep them in a good temper; but if they are out of temper you will hear many degrading things; you will live, but how?—as the flatterer of all men, and the servant of all men; and doing what?—eating and drinking in Thessaly, having gone abroad in order that you may get a dinner. And where will be your fine sentiments about justice and virtue then? Say that you wish to live for the sake of your children, that you may bring them up and educate them—will you take them into Thessaly and deprive them of Athenian citizenship? Is that the benefit which you would confer upon them? Or are you under the impression that they will be better cared for and educated here if you are still alive, although absent from them; for that your friends will take care of them? Do you fancy that if you are an inhabitant of Thessaly they will take care of them, and if you are an inhabitant of the other world they will not take care of them? Nay; but if they who call themselves friends are truly friends, they surely will.

"Listen, then, Socrates, to us who have brought you up. Think not of life and children first, and of justice afterwards, but of justice first, that you may be justified before the princes of the world below. For neither will you nor any that belong to you be happier or holier or juster in this life, or happier in another, if you do as Crito bids. Now you depart in innocence, a sufferer and not a doer of evil; a victim, not of the laws, but of men. But if you go forth, returning evil for evil, and injury for injury, breaking the covenants and agreements which you have made with us, and wronging those whom you ought least to wrong, that is to say, yourself, your friends, your country, and us, we shall be angry with you while you live, and our brethren, the laws in the world below, will receive you as an enemy; for they will know that you have done your best to destroy us. Listen, then, to us and not to Crito."

This is the voice which I seem to hear murmuring in my ears, like the sound of the flute in the ears of the mystic; that voice, I say, is humming in my ears, and prevents me from hearing any other. And I know that anything more which you will say will be in vain. Yet speak, if you have anything to say.

Cr. I have nothing to say, Socrates.

Soc. Then let me follow the intimations of the will of God.

Civil Disobedience

Henry David Thoreau

I heartily accept the motto—"That government is best which governs least"; and I should like to see it acted up to more rapidly and systematically. Carried out, it finally amounts to this, which also I believe—"That government is best which governs not at all"; and when men are prepared for it, that will be the kind of government which they will have. Government is at best but an expedient; but most governments are usually, and all governments are sometimes, inexpedient. The objections which have been brought against a standing army, and they are many and weighty, and deserve to prevail, may also at last be brought against a standing government. The standing army is only an arm of the standing government. The government itself, which is only the mode which the people have chosen to execute their will, is equally liable to be abused and perverted before the people can act through it. Witness the present Mexican war, the work of comparatively a few individuals using the standing government as their tool; for, in the outset, the people would not have consented to this measure.

This American government—what is it but a tradition, though a recent one, endeavoring to transmit itself unimpaired to posterity, but each instant losing some of its integrity? It has not the vitality and force of a single living man; for a single man can bend it to his will. It is a sort of wooden gun to the people themselves. But it is not the less necessary for this; for the people must have some complicated machinery or other, and hear its din, to satisfy that idea of government which they have. Governments show thus how successfully men can be imposed on, even impose on themselves, for their own advantage. It is excellent, we must all allow. Yet this government never of itself furthered any enterprise, but by the alacrity with which it got out of its way. *It* does not keep the country free. *It* does not settle the West. *It* does not educate. The character inherent in the American people has done all that has been accomplished; and it would have done somewhat more, if the government had not sometimes got in its way. For government is an expedient by which men would fain succeed in letting one another alone; and, as has been said, when it is most expedient, the governed are most let alone by it. Trade

Source: Henry David Thoreau, *Civil Disobedience: Theory and Practice.*

and commerce, if they were not made of India-rubber, would never manage to bounce over the obstacles which legislators are continually putting in their way; and, if one were to judge these men wholly by the effects of their actions and not partly by their intentions, they would deserve to be classed and punished with those mischievous persons who put obstructions on the railroads.

But, to speak practically and as a citizen, unlike those who call themselves no-government men, I ask for, not at once no government, but *at once* a better government. Let every man make known what kind of government would command his respect, and that will be one step toward obtaining it.

After all, the practical reason why, when the power is once in the hands of the people, a majority are permitted, and for a long period continue, to rule, is not because they are most likely to be in the right, nor because this seems fairest to the minority, but because they are physically the strongest. But a government in which the majority rule in all cases cannot be based on justice, even as far as men understand it. Can there not be a government in which majorities do not virtually decide right and wrong, but conscience?— in which majorities decide only those questions to which the rule of expediency is applicable? Must the citizen ever for a moment, or in the least degree, resign his conscience to the legislator? Why has every man a conscience, then? I think that we should be men first, and subjects afterward. It is not desirable to cultivate a respect for the law, so much as for the right. The only obligation which I have a right to assume, is to do at any time what I think right. It is truly enough said, that a corporation has no conscience; but a corporation of conscientious men is a corporation *with* a conscience. Law never made men a whit more just; and, by means of their respect for it, even the well-disposed are daily made the agents of injustice. A common and natural result of an undue respect for law is, that you may see a file of soldiers, colonel, captain, corporal, privates, powder-monkeys, and all, marching in admirable order over hill and dale to the wars, against their wills, ay, against their common sense and consciences, which makes it very steep marching indeed, and produces a palpitation of the heart. They have no doubt that it is a damnable business in which they are concerned; they are all peaceably inclined. Now, what are they? Men at all? or small movable forts and magazines, at the service of some unscrupulous man in power? Visit the Navy-Yard, and behold a marine, such a man as an American government can make, or such as it can make a man with its black arts—a mere shadow and reminiscence of humanity, a man laid out alive and standing, and already, as one may say, buried under arms with funeral accompaniments, though it may be—

> "Not a drum was heard, not a funeral note,
> As his corpse to the rampart we hurried;
> Not a soldier discharged his farewell shot
> O'er the grave where our hero we buried."

The mass of men serve the state thus, not as men mainly, but as machines, with their bodies. They are the standing army, and the militia, jailers, constables, posse comitatus, & c. In most cases there is no free exercise whatever of the judgment or of the moral sense; but they put themselves on a level with wood and earth and stones; and wooden men can perhaps be manufactured that will serve the purpose as well. Such command no more respect than men of straw or a lump of dirt. They have the same sort of worth only as horses and dogs. Yet such as these even are commonly esteemed good citizens. Others—as most legislators, politicians, lawyers, ministers, and officeholders—serve the state chiefly with their heads; and, as they rarely make any moral distinctions, they are as likely to serve the Devil, without *intending* it, as God. A very few, as heroes, patriots, martyrs, reformers in the great sense, and *men*, serve the state with the consciences also, and so necessarily resist it for the most part; and they are commonly treated as enemies by it. A wise man will only be useful as a man, and will not submit to be "clay," and "stop a hole to keep the wind away," but leave that office to his dust at least:

> "I am too high-born to be propertied,
> To be a secondary at control,
> Or useful serving-man and instrument
> To any sovereign state throughout the world."

He who gives himself entirely to his fellowmen appears to them useless and selfish; but he who gives himself partially to them is pronounced a benefactor and philanthropist.

How does it become a man to behave toward this American government to-day? I answer, that he cannot without disgrace be associated with it. I cannot for an instant recognize the political organization as *my* government which is the *slave's* government also.

All men recognize the right of revolution; that is, the right to refuse allegiance to, and to resist, the government, when its tyranny or its inefficiency are great and unendurable. But almost all say that such is not the case now. But such was the case, they think, in the Revolution of '75. If one were to tell me that this was a bad government because it taxed certain foreign commodities brought to its ports, it is most probable that I should not make an ado about it, for I can do without them. All machines have their friction; and possibly this does enough good to counterbalance the evil. At any rate, it is a great evil to make a stir about it. But when the friction comes to have its machine, and oppression and robbery are organized, I say, let us not have such a machine any longer. In other words, when a sixth of the population of a nation which has undertaken to be the refuge of liberty are slaves, and a whole country is unjustly overrun and conquered by a foreign army, and subjected to military law, I think that it is not too soon for honest men to rebel and revolutionize. What makes this duty the more urgent is the fact, that the country so overrun is not our own, but ours is the invading army.

Paley, a common authority with many on moral questions, in his chapter on the "Duty of Submission to Civil Government," resolves all civil obligation into expediency; and he proceeds to say, "that so long as the interest of the whole society requires it, that is, so long as the established government cannot be resisted or changed without public inconveniency, it is the will of God that the established government be obeyed, and no longer. . . . This principle being admitted, the justice of every particular case of resistance is reduced to a computation of the quantity of the danger and grievance on the one side, and of the probability and expense of redressing it on the other." Of this, he says, every man shall judge for himself. But Paley appears never to have contemplated those cases to which the rule of expediency does not apply, in which a people, as well as an individual, must do justice, cost what it may. If I have unjustly wrested a plank from a drowning man, I must restore it to him though I drown myself. This, according to Paley, would be inconvenient. But he that would save his life, in such a case, shall lose it. This people must cease to hold slaves, and to make war on Mexico, though it cost them their existence as a people.

In their practice, nations agree with Paley; but does any one think that Massachusetts does exactly what is right at the present crisis?

> "A drab of state, a cloth-o'-silver slut,
> To have her train borne up, and her soul trail in the dirt."

Practically speaking, the opponents to a reform in Massachusetts are not a hundred thousand politicians at the South, but a hundred thousand merchants and farmers here, who are more interested in commerce and agriculture than they are in humanity, and are not prepared to do justice to the slave and to Mexico, *cost what it may.* I quarrel not with far-off foes, but with those who, near at home, co-operate with, and do the bidding of those far away, and without whom the latter would be harmless. We are accustomed to say, that the mass of men are unprepared; but improvement is slow, because the few are not materially wiser or better than the many. It is not so important that many should be as good as you, as that there be some absolute goodness somewhere; for that will leaven the whole lump. There are thousands who are *in opinion* opposed to slavery and to the war, who yet in effect do nothing to put an end to them; who, esteeming themselves children of Washington and Franklin, sit down with their hands in their pockets, and say that they know not what to do, and do nothing; who even postpone the question of freedom to the question of free-trade, and quietly read the prices-current along with the latest advices from Mexico, after dinner, and, it may be, fall asleep over them both. What is the price-current of an honest man and patriot to-day? They hesitate, and they regret, and sometimes they petition; but they do nothing in earnest and with effect. They will wait, well disposed, for others to remedy the evil, that they may no longer have it to regret. At most, they give only a cheap vote, and a feeble countenance and Godspeed, to the right, as it goes by them. There are nine hundred and ninety-nine patrons of virtue to one virtuous man. But it is easier to deal with the real possessor of a thing than with the temporary guardian of it.

All voting is a sort of gaming, like checkers or backgammon, with a slight moral tinge to it, a playing with right and wrong, with moral questions;

and betting naturally accompanies it. The character of the voters is not staked. I cast my vote, perchance, as I think right; but I am not vitally concerned that that right should prevail. I am willing to leave it to the majority. Its obligation, therefore, never exceeds that of expediency. Even voting *for the right* is *doing* nothing for it. It is only expressing to men feebly your desire that it should prevail. A wise man will not leave the right to the mercy of chance, nor wish it to prevail through the power of the majority. There is but little virtue in the action of masses of men. When the majority shall at length vote for the abolition of slavery, it will be because they are indifferent to slavery, or because there is but little slavery left to be abolished by their vote. *They* will then be the only slaves. Only *his* vote can hasten the abolition of slavery who asserts his own freedom by his vote.

I hear of a convention to be held at Baltimore, or elsewhere, for the selection of a candidate for the Presidency, made up chiefly of editors, and men who are politicians by profession; but I think, what is it to any independent, intelligent, and respectable man what decision they may come to? Shall we not have the advantage of his wisdom and honesty, nevertheless? Can we not count upon some independent votes? Are there not many individuals in the country who do not attend conventions? But no: I find that the respectable man, so called, has immediately drifted from his position, and despairs of his country, when his country has more reason to despair of him. He forthwith adopts one of the candidates thus selected as the only *available* one, thus proving that he is himself *available* for any purposes of the demagogue. His vote is of no more worth than that of any unprincipled foreigner or hireling native, who may have been bought. O for a man who is a man, and, as my neighbor says, has a bone in his back which you cannot pass your hand through! Our statistics are at fault: the population has been returned too large. How many *men* are there to a square thousand miles in this country? Hardly one. Does not America offer any inducement for men to settle here? The American has dwindled into an Odd Fellow—one who may be known by the development of his organ of gregariousness, and a manifest lack of intellect and cheerful self-reliance; whose first and chief concern, on coming into the world, is to see that the Almshouses are in good repair; and, before yet he has lawfully donned the virile garb, to collect a fund for the support of the widows and orphans that may be; who, in short, ventures to live only by the aid of the Mutual Insurance Company, which has promised to bury him decently.

It is not a man's duty, as a matter of course, to devote himself to the eradication of any, even the most enormous wrong; he may still properly have other concerns to engage him; but it is his duty, at least, to wash his hands of it, and, if he gives it no thought longer, not to give it practically his support. If I devote myself to other pursuits and contemplations, I must first see, at least, that I do not pursue them sitting upon another man's shoulders. I must get off him first, that he may pursue his contemplations too. See what gross inconsistency is tolerated. I have heard some of my townsmen say, "I should like to have them order me out to help put down an insurrection of the slaves, or to march to Mexico—see if I would go"; and yet these very men have each, directly by their allegiance, and so indirectly, at least, by their money, furnished a substitute. The soldier is applauded who refuses to serve in an unjust war by those who do not refuse to sustain the unjust government which makes the war; is applauded by those whose own act and authority he disregards and sets at naught; as if the State were penitent to that degree that it hired one to scourge it while it sinned, but not to that degree that it left off sinning for a moment. Thus, under the name of Order and Civil Government, we are all made at last to pay homage to and support our own meanness. After the first blush of sin comes its indifference; and from immoral it becomes, as it were, *un*moral, and not quite unnecessary to that life which we have made.

The broadest and most prevalent error requires the most disinterested virtue to sustain it. The slight reproach to which the virtue of patriotism is commonly liable, the noble are most likely to incur. Those who, while they disapprove of the character and measures of a government, yield to it their allegiance and support, are undoubtedly its most conscientious supporters, and so frequently the most serious obstacles to reform. Some are petitioning the State to dissolve the Union, to disregard the requisitions of the President. Why do they not dissolve it themselves—the union between themselves and the State—and refuse to pay their quota into its treasury? Do not they stand in the same relation to the State, that the State does to the Union? And have not the same reasons prevented the State from resisting the Union, which have prevented them from resisting the State?

How can a man be satisfied to entertain an opinion merely, and enjoy *it?* Is there any enjoyment in it, if his opinion is that he is aggrieved? If you are cheated out of a single dollar by your neighbor, you do not rest satisfied with knowing that you are cheated, or with saying that you are cheated, or even with petitioning him to pay you your due; but you take effectual steps at once to obtain the full amount, and see that you are never cheated again. Action from principle, the perception and the performance of right, changes things and relations; it is essentially revolutionary, and does not consist wholly with anything which was. It not only divides states and churches, it divides families; ay, it divides the *individual*, separating the diabolical in him from the divine.

Unjust laws exist: shall we be content to obey them, or shall we endeavor to amend them, and obey them until we have succeeded, or shall we transgress them at once? Men generally, under such a government as this, think that they ought to wait until they have persuaded the majority to alter them. They think that, if they should resist, the remedy would be worse than the evil. But it is the fault of the government itself that the remedy is worse than the evil. *It* makes it worse. Why is it not more apt to anticipate and provide for reform? Why does it not cherish its wise minority? Why does it cry and resist before it is hurt? Why does it not encourage its citizens to be on the alert to point out its faults, and *do* better than it would have them? Why does it always crucify Christ, and excommunicate Copernicus and Luther, and pronounce Washington and Franklin rebels?

One would think, that a deliberate and practical denial of its authority was the only offence never contemplated by government; else, why has it not assigned its definite, its suitable and proportionate penalty? If a man who has no property refuses but once to earn nine shillings for the State, he is put in prison for a period unlimited by any law that I know, and determined only by the discretion of those who placed him there; but if he should steal ninety times nine shillings from the State, he is soon permitted to go at large again.

If the injustice is part of the necessary friction of the machine of government, let it go, let it go: perchance it will wear smooth—certainly the machine will wear out. If the injustice has a spring, or a pulley, or a rope, or a crank, exclusively for itself, then perhaps you may consider whether the remedy will not be worse than the evil; but if it is of such a nature that it requires you to be the agent of injustice to another, then, I say, break the law. Let your life be a counter friction to stop the machine. What I have to do is to see, at any rate, that I do not lend myself to the wrong which I condemn.

As for adopting the ways which the State has provided for remedying the evil, I know not of such ways. They take too much time, and a man's life will be gone. I have other affairs to attend to. I came into this world, not chiefly to make this a good place to live in, but to live in it, be it good or bad. A man has not everything to do, but something; and because he cannot do *everything*, it is not necessary that he should do *something* wrong. It is not my business to be petitioning the Governor or the Legislature any more than it is theirs to petition me; and, if they should not hear my petition, what should I do then? But in this case the State has provided no way: its very Constitution is the evil. This may seem to be harsh and stubborn and unconciliatory; but it is to treat with the utmost kindness and consideration the only spirit that can appreciate or deserves it. So is all change for the better, like birth and death, which convulse the body.

I do not hesitate to say, that those who call themselves Abolitionists should at once effectually withdraw their support, both in person and property, from the government of Massachusetts, and not wait till they constitute a majority of one, before they suffer the right to prevail through them. I think that it is enough if they have God on their side, without waiting for that other one. Moreover, any man more right than his neighbors constitutes a majority of one already.

I meet this American government, or its representative, the State government, directly, and face to face, once a year—no more—in the person of its tax-gatherer; this is the only mode in which a man situated as I am necessarily meets it; and it then says distinctly, Recognize me; and the simplest, the most effectual, and, in the present posture of affairs, the indispensablest mode of treating with it on this head, of expressing your little satisfaction with and love for it, is to deny it then. My civil neighbor, the tax-gatherer, is the very man I have to deal with—for it is, after all, with men and not with parchment that I quarrel—and he has voluntarily chosen to be an agent of the government. How shall he ever know well what he is and does as an officer of the government, or as a man, until he is obliged to consider whether he shall treat me, his neighbor, for whom he has respect, as a neighbor and well-disposed man, or as a maniac and disturber of the peace, and see if he can get over this obstruction to his neighborliness without a ruder and more impetuous thought or speech corresponding with his action. I know this well, that if one thousand, if one hundred, if ten men whom I could name—if ten *honest* men only—ay, if *one* HONEST man, in this State of Massachusetts, *ceasing to hold slaves*, were actually to withdraw from this copartnership, and be locked up in the county jail therefore, it would be the abolition of slavery in America. For it matters not how small the beginning may seem to be: what is once well done is done forever. But we love better to talk about it: that we say is our mission. Reform keeps many scores of newspapers in its service, but not one man. If my esteemed neighbor, the State's ambassador, who will devote his days to the settlement of the question of human rights in the Council Chamber, instead of being threatened with the prisons of Carolina, were to sit down the prisoner of Massachusetts, that State which is so anxious to foist the sin of slavery upon her sister—though at present she can discover only an act of inhospitality to be the ground of a quarrel with her—the Legislature would not wholly waive the subject the following winter.

Under a government which imprisons any unjustly, the true place for a just man is also a prison. The proper place to-day, the only place which Massachusetts has provided for her freer and less desponding spirits, is in her prisons, to be put out and locked out of the State by her own act, as they have already put themselves out by their principles. It is there that the fugitive slave, and the Mexican prisoner on parole, and the Indian come to plead the wrongs of his race, should find them; on that separate, but more free and honorable ground, where the State places those who are not *with* her, but *against* her—the only house in a slave State in which a free man can abide with honor. If any think that their influence would be lost there, and their voices no longer afflict the ear of the State, that they would not be as an enemy within its walls, they do not know by how much truth is stronger than error, nor how much more eloquently and effectively he can combat injustice who has experienced a little in his own person. Cast your whole vote, not a strip of paper merely, but your whole influence. A minority is powerless while it conforms to the majority; it is not even a minority then; but it is irresistible when it clogs by its whole weight. If the alternative is to keep all just men in prison, or give up war and slavery, the State will not hesitate which to choose. If a thousand men were not to pay their tax-bills this year, that would not be a violent and bloody measure, as it would be to pay them, and enable the State to commit violence and shed innocent blood. This is, in fact, the definition of a peaceable revolution, if any such is possible. If the tax-gatherer, or any other public officer, asks me, as one has done, "But what shall I do?" my answer is, "If you really wish to do anything, resign your office." When the subject has refused allegiance, and the officer has resigned his office, then the revolution is accomplished. But even suppose blood should flow. Is there not a sort of blood shed when the conscience is wounded? Through this wound a man's real manhood and immortality flow out, and he bleeds to an everlasting death. I see this blood flowing now.

I have contemplated the imprisonment of the offender, rather than the seizure of his goods—though both will serve the same purpose—because they who assert the purest right, and consequently are most dangerous to a corrupt State, commonly have not spent much time in accumulating property. To such the State renders comparatively small service, and a slight tax is wont to appear exorbitant, particularly if they are obliged to earn it by special labor with their hands. If there were one who lived wholly without the use of money, the State itself would hesitate to demand it of him. But the rich man—not to make any invidious comparison—is always sold to the institution which makes him rich. Absolutely speaking, the more money, the less virtue; for money comes between a man and his objects, and obtains them for him; and it was certainly no great virtue to obtain it. It puts to rest many questions which he would otherwise be taxed to answer; while the only new question which it puts is the hard but superfluous one, how to spend it. Thus his moral ground is taken from under his feet. The opportunities of living are diminished in proportion as what are called the "means" are increased. The best thing a man can do: for his culture when he is rich is to endeavor to carry out those schemes which he entertained when he was poor. Christ answered the Herodians according to their condition. "Show me the tribute-money," said he—and one took a penny out of his pocket; if you use money which has the image of Caesar on it, and which he has made current and valuable, that is, *if you are men of the State*, and gladly enjoy the advantages of Caesar's government, then pay him back some of his own when he demands it; "Render therefore to Caesar that which is Caesar's, and to God those things which are God's"—leaving them no wiser than before as to which was which; for they did not wish to know.

When I converse with the freest of my neighbors, I perceive that, whatever they may say about the magnitude and seriousness of the question, and their regard for the public tranquility, the long and the short of the matter is, that they cannot spare the protection of the existing government, and they dread the consequences to their property and families of disobedience to it. For my own part, I should not like to think that I ever rely on the protection of the State. But, if I deny the authority of the State when it presents its tax-bill, it will soon take and waste all my property, and so harass me and my children without end. This is hard. This makes it impossible for a man to live honestly, and at the same time comfortably, in outward respects. It will not be worth the while to accumulate property; that would be sure to go again. You must hire or squat somewhere, and raise but a small crop, and eat that soon. You must live within yourself, and depend upon yourself always tucked up and ready for a start, and not have many affairs. A man may grow rich in Turkey even, if he will be in all respects a good subject of the Turkish government. Confucius said: "If a state is governed by the principles of reason, poverty and misery are subjects of shame; if a state is not governed by the principles of reason, riches and honors are the subjects of shame." No: until I want the protection of Massachusetts to be extended to me in some distant Southern port, where my liberty is endangered, or until I am bent solely on building up an estate at home by peaceful enterprise, I can afford to refuse allegiance to Massachusetts, and her right to my property and life. It costs me less in every sense to incur the penalty of disobedience to the State, than it would to obey. I should feel as if I were worth less in that case.

Some years ago, the State met me in behalf of the Church, and commanded me to pay a certain sum toward the support of a clergyman whose preaching my father attended, but never I myself. "Pay," it said, "or be locked up in the jail." I declined to pay. But, unfortunately, another man saw fit to pay it. I did not see why the schoolmaster should be taxed to support the priest, and not the priest the schoolmaster; for I was not the State's schoolmaster, but I supported myself by voluntary subscription. I did not see why the lyceum should not present its tax-bill, and have the State to back its demand, as well as the Church. However, at the request of the selectmen, I condescended to make some such statement as this in writing: "Know all men by these presents, that I, Henry Thoreau, do not wish to be regarded as a member of any incorporated society which I have not joined." This I gave to the town clerk; and he has it. The State, having thus learned that I did not wish to be regarded as a member of that church, has never made a like demand on me since; though it said that it must adhere to its original presumption that time. If I had known how to name them, I should then have signed off in detail from all the societies which I never signed on to; but I did not know where to find a complete list.

I have paid no poll-tax for six years. I was put into a jail once on this account, for one night; and, as I stood considering the walls of solid stone, two or three feet thick, the door of wood and iron, a foot thick, and the iron grating which strained the light, I could not help being struck with the foolishness of that institution which treated me as if I were mere flesh and blood and bones, to be locked up. I wondered that it should have concluded at length that this was the best use it could put me to, and had never thought to avail itself of my services in some way. I saw that, if there was a wall of stone between me and my townsmen, there was a still more difficult one to climb or break through, before they could get to be as free as I was. I did not for a moment feel confined, and the walls seemed a great waste of stone and mortar. I felt as if I alone of all my townsmen had paid my tax. They plainly did not know how to treat me, but behaved like persons who are underbred. In every threat and in every compliment there was a blunder; for they thought that my chief desire was to stand the other side of that stone wall. I could not but smile to see how industriously they locked the door on my meditations, which followed them out again without let or hindrance, and *they* were really all that was dangerous. As they could not reach me, they had resolved to punish my body; just as boys, if they cannot come at some person against whom they have a spite, will abuse his dog. I saw that the State was half-witted, that it was timid as a lone woman with her silver spoons, and that it did not know its friends from its foes, and I lost all my remaining respect for it, and pitied it.

Thus the State never intentionally confronts a man's sense, intellectual or moral, but only his body, his senses. It is not armed with superior wit or honesty, but with superior physical strength. I was not born to be forced. I will breathe after my own fashion. Let us see who is the strongest. What force has a multitude? They can only force me who obey a higher law than I. They force me to become like themselves. I do not hear of *men* being *forced* to live this way or that by masses of men. What sort of life were that to live? When I meet a government which says to me, "Your money or your life," why should I be in haste to give it my money? It may be in a great strait, and not know what to do: I cannot help that. It must help itself; do as I do. It is not worth the while to snivel about it. I am not responsible for the successful working of the machinery of society. I am not the son of the engineer. I perceive that, when an acorn and a chestnut fall side by side, the one does not remain inert to make way for the other, but both obey their own laws, and spring and grow and flourish as best they can, till one, perchance, overshadows and destroys the other. If a plant cannot live according to its nature, it dies; and so a man.

The night in prison was novel and interesting enough. The prisoners in their shirtsleeves were enjoying a chat and the evening air in the doorway, when I entered. But the jailer said, "Come, boys, it is time to lock up"; and so they dispersed, and I heard the sound of their steps returning into the hollow apartments. My roommate was introduced to me by the jailer, as "a first-rate fellow and a clever man." When the door was locked, he showed me where to hang my hat, and how he managed matters there. The rooms were whitewashed once a month; and this one, at least, was the whitest, most simply furnished, and probably the neatest apartment in the town. He naturally wanted to know where I came from, and what brought me there; and, when I had told him, I asked him in my turn how he came there, presuming him to be an honest man, of course; and, as the world goes, I believe he was. "Why," said he, "they accuse me of burning a barn; but I never did it." As near as I could discover, he had probably gone to bed in a barn when drunk, and smoked his pipe there; and so a barn was burnt. He had the reputation of being a clever man, had been there some three months waiting for his trial to come on, and would have to wait as much longer; but he was quite domesticated and contented, since he got his board for nothing, and thought that he was well treated.

He occupied one window, and I the other; and I saw, that, if one stayed there long, his principal business would be to look out the window. I had soon read all the tracts that were left there, and examined where former prisoners had broken out, and where a grate had been sawed off, and heard the history of the various occupants of that room; for I found that even here there was a history and a gossip which never circulated beyond the walls of the jail. Probably this is the only house in the town where verses are composed, which are afterward printed in a circular form, but not published. I was shown quite a long list of verses which were composed by some young men who had been detected in an attempt to escape, who avenged themselves by singing them.

I pumped my fellow-prisoner as dry as I could, for fear I should never see him again; but at length he showed me which was my bed, and left me to blow out the lamp.

It was like traveling into a far country, such as I had never expected to behold, to lie there for one night. It seemed to me that I never had heard the town-clock strike before, nor the evening sounds of the village; for we slept with the windows open, which were inside the grating. It was to see my native village in the light of the Middle Ages, and our Concord was turned into a Rhine stream, and visions of knights and castles passed before me. They were the voices of old burghers that I heard in the streets. I was an involuntary spectator and auditor of whatever was done and said in the kitchen of the adjacent village-inn—a wholly new and rare experience to me. It was a closer view of my native town. I was fairly inside of it. I never had seen its institutions before. This is one of its peculiar institutions; for it is a shire town. I began to comprehend what its inhabitants were about.

In the morning, our breakfasts were put through the hole in the door, in small oblong-square tin pans, made to fit, and holding a pint of chocolate, with brown bread, and an iron spoon. When they called for the vessels again, I was green enough to return what bread I had left; but my comrade seized it, and said that I should lay that up for lunch or dinner. Soon after he was let out to work at haying in a neighboring field, whither he went every day, and would not be back till noon; so he bade me good-day, saying that he doubted if he should see me again.

When I came out of prison—for some one interfered, and paid that tax—I did not perceive that great changes had taken place on the common, such as he observed who went in a youth, and emerged a tottering and grayheaded man; and yet a change had to my eyes come over the scene—the town, and State, and country—greater than any that mere time could effect. I saw yet more distinctly the State in which I lived. I saw to what extent the people among whom I lived could be trusted as good neighbors and friends; that their friendship was for summer weather only; that they did not greatly propose to do right; that they were a distinct race from me by their prejudices and superstitions, as the Chinamen and Malays are; that, in their sacrifices to humanity, they ran no risks, not even to their property; that, after all, they were not so noble but they treated the thief as he had treated them, and hoped, by a certain outward observance and a few prayers, and by walking in a particular straight though useless path from time to time, to save their souls. This may be to judge my neighbors harshly; for I believe that many of them are not aware that they have such an institution as the jail in their village.

It was formerly the custom in our village, when a poor debtor came out of jail, for his acquaintances to salute him, looking through their fingers, which were crossed to represent the grating of a jail window, "How do ye do?" My neighbors did not thus salute me, but first looked at me, and then at one another, as if I had returned from a long journey. I was put into jail as I was going to the shoemaker's to get a shoe which was mended. When I was let out the next morning, I proceeded to finish my errand, and having put on my mended shoe, joined a huckleberry party, who were impatient to put themselves under my conduct; and in half an hour—for the horse was soon tackled—was in the midst of a huckleberry field, on one of our highest hills, two miles off, and then the State was nowhere to be seen.

This is the whole history of "My Prisons."

I have never declined paying the highway tax, because I am as desirous of being a good neighbor as I am of being a bad subject; and, as for supporting schools, I am doing my part to educate my fellow-countrymen now. It is for no particular item in the tax-bill that I refuse to pay it. I simply wish to refuse allegiance to the State, to withdraw and stand aloof from it effectually. I do not care to trace the course of my dollar, if I could, till it buys a man or a musket to shoot one with—the dollar is innocent—but I am concerned to trace the effects of my allegiance. In fact, I quietly declare war with the State, after my fashion, though I will still make what use and get what advantage of her I can, as is usual in such cases.

If others pay the tax which is demanded of me, from a sympathy with the State, they do but what they have already done in their own case, or rather they abet injustice to a greater extent than the State requires. If they pay the tax from a mistaken interest in the individual taxed, to save his property, or prevent his going to jail, it is because they have not considered wisely how far they let their private feelings interfere with the public good.

This, then, is my position at present. But one cannot be too much on his guard in such a case, lest his action be biased by obstinacy, or an undue regard for the opinions of men. Let him see that he does only what belongs to himself and to the hour.

I think sometimes, Why, this people mean well; they are only ignorant; they would do better if they knew how: why give your neighbors this pain to treat you as they are not inclined to? But I think again, this is no reason why I should do as they do, or permit others to suffer much greater pain of a different kind. Again, I sometimes say to myself, When many millions of men, without heat, without ill will, without personal feeling of any kind, demand of you a few shillings only, without the possibility, such is their constitution, of retracting or altering their present demand, and without the possibility, on your side, of appeal to any other millions, why expose yourself to this overwhelming brute force? You do not resist cold and hunger, the winds and the waves, thus obstinately; you quietly submit to a thousand similar necessities. You do not put your head into the fire. But just in proportion as I regard this as not wholly a brute force, but partly a human force, and consider that I have relations to those millions as to so many millions of men, and not of mere brute or inanimate things, I see that appeal is possible, first and instantaneously, from them to the Maker of them, and secondly, from them to themselves. But, if I put my head deliberately into the fire, there is no appeal to fire or to the Maker of fire, and I have only myself to blame. If I could convince myself that I have any right to be satisfied with men as they are, and to treat them accordingly, and not according, in some respects, to my requisitions and expectations of what they and I ought to be, then, like a good Mussulman and fatalist, I should endeavor to be satisfied with things as they are, and say it is the will of God. And, above all, there is this difference between resisting this and a purely brute or natural force, that I can resist this with some effect; but I cannot expect, like Orpheus, to change the nature of the rocks and trees and beasts.

I do not wish to quarrel with any man or nation. I do not wish to split hairs, to make fine distinctions, or set myself up as better than my neighbors. I seek rather, I may say, even an excuse for conforming to the laws of the land. I am but too ready to conform to them. Indeed, I have reason to suspect myself on this head; and each year, as the tax-gatherer comes round, I find myself disposed to review the acts and position of the general and State governments, and the spirit of the people, to discover a pretext for conformity.

> "We must affect our country as our parents;
> And if at any time we alienate
> Our love or industry from doing it honor,
> We must respect effects and teach the soul
> Matter of conscience and religion,
> And not desire of rule or benefit."

I believe that the State will soon be able to take all my work of this sort out of my hands, and then I shall be no better a patriot than my fellow-countrymen. Seen from a lower point of view, the Constitution, with all its faults, is very good; the law and the courts are very respectable; even this State and this American government are, in many respects, very admirable and rare things, to be thankful for, such as a great many have described them; but seen from a point of view a little higher, they are what I have described them; seen from a higher still, and the highest, who shall say what they are, or that they are worth looking at or thinking of at all?

However, the government does not concern me much, and I shall bestow the fewest possible thoughts on it. It is not many moments that I live under a government, even in this world. If a man is thought-free, fancy-free, imagination-free, that which *is not* never for a long time appearing *to be* to him, unwise rulers or reformers cannot fatally interrupt him.

I know that most men think differently from myself; but those whose lives are by profession devoted to the study of these or kindred subjects, content me as little as any. Statesmen and legislators, standing so completely within the institution, never distinctly and nakedly behold it. They speak of moving society, but have no resting-place without it. They may be men of a certain experience and discrimination, and have no doubt invented ingenious and even useful systems, for which we sincerely thank them; but all their wit and usefulness lie within certain not very wide limits. They are wont to forget that the world is not governed by policy and expediency. Webster never goes behind government, and so cannot speak with authority about it. His words are wisdom to those legislators who contemplate no essential reform in the existing government; but for thinkers, and those who legislate for all time, he never once glances at the subject. I know of those whose serene and wise speculations on this theme would soon reveal the limits of his mind's range and hospitality. Yet, compared with the cheap professions of most reformers, and the still cheaper wisdom and eloquence of politicians in general, his are almost the only sensible and valuable words, and we thank Heaven for him. Comparatively, he is always strong, original, and, above all, practical. Still his quality is not wisdom, but prudence. The lawyer's truth is not Truth, but consistency, or a consistent expediency. Truth is always in harmony with herself, and is not concerned chiefly to reveal the justice that may consist with wrong-doing. He well deserves to be called, as he has been called, the Defender of the Constitution. There are really no blows to be given by him but defensive ones. He is not a leader, but a follower. His leaders are the men of '87. "I have never made an effort," he says, "and never propose to make an effort; I have never countenanced an effort, and never mean to countenance an effort, to disturb the arrangement as originally made, by which the various States came into the Union." Still thinking of the sanction which the Constitution gives to slavery, he says, "Because it was a part of the original compact—let it stand." Notwithstanding his special acuteness and ability, he is unable to take a fact out of its merely political relations, and behold it as it lies absolutely to be disposed of by the intellect—what, for instance, it behooves a man to do here in America today with regard to slavery, but ventures, or is driven, to make some such desperate answer as the following, while professing to speak absolutely, and as a private man—from which what new and singular code of social duties might be inferred? "The manner," says he, "in which the governments of those States where slavery exists are to regulate it, is for their own consideration, under their responsibility to their constituents, to the general laws of propriety, humanity, and justice, and to God. Associations formed elsewhere, springing from a feeling of humanity, or any other cause, have nothing whatever to do with it. They have never received any encouragement from me, and they never will."

They who know of no purer sources of truth, who have traced up its stream no higher, stand, and wisely stand, by the Bible and the Constitution, and drink at it there with reverence and humility; But they who behold where it comes trickling into this lake or that pool, gird up their loins once more, and continue their pilgrimage towards its fountainhead.

No man with a genius for legislation has appeared in America. They are rare in the history of the world. There are orators, politicians, and eloquent men, by the thousand; but the speaker has not yet opened his mouth to speak, who is capable of settling the much-vexed questions of the day. We love eloquence for its own sake, and not for any truth which it may utter, or any heroism it may inspire. Our legislators have not yet learned the comparative value of free-trade and of freedom, of union, and of rectitude, to a nation. They have no genius or talent for comparatively humble questions of taxation and finance, commerce and manufactures and agriculture. If we were left solely to the wordy wit of legislators in Congress for our guidance, uncorrected by the seasonable experience and the effectual complaints of the people, America would not long retain her rank among the nations. For eighteen hundred years, though perchance I have no right to say it, the New Testament has been written, yet where is the legislator who has wisdom and practical talent enough to avail himself of the light which it sheds on the science of legislation?

The authority of government, even such as I am willing to submit to—for I will cheerfully obey those who know and can do better than I, and in many things even those who neither know nor can do so well—is still an impure one: to be strictly just, it must have the sanction and consent of the governed. It can have no pure right over my person and property but what I concede to it. The progress from an absolute to a limited monarchy, from a limited monarchy to a democracy, is a progress toward a true respect for the individual. Even the Chinese philosopher was wise enough to regard the individual as the basis of the empire. Is a democracy, such as we know it, the last improvement possible in government? Is it not possible to take a step further toward recognizing and organizing the rights of man? There will never be a really free and enlightened State, until the State comes to recognize the individual as a higher and independent power, from which all its own power and authority are derived, and treats him accordingly. I please myself with imagining a State at last which can afford to be just to all men, and to treat the individual with respect as a neighbor; which even would not think it inconsistent with its own repose, if a few were to live aloof from it, not meddling with it, nor embraced by it, who fulfilled all the duties of neighbors and fellow-men. A State which bore this kind of fruit, and suffered it to drop off as fast as it ripened, would prepare the way for a still more perfect and glorious State, which also I have imagined, but not yet anywhere seen.

PART TWO

THREE MODERN PHILOSOPHERS OF NONVIOLENCE
TOLSTOY, GANDHI, AND KING

Preview

Just as some of the major contributors to life of the mind and spirit—thinking here of Confucius, Buddha, Lao Tzu, and Socrates—appeared in different areas of the ancient world at roughly the same time, so in the modern world three of the principal figures in the development of nonviolence lived in close temporal proximity to one another: Leo Tolstoy (1828–1910) in the late nineteenth and early twentieth century, Mohandas K. Gandhi (1869–1948) (known honorifically as "Mahatma," meaning "great-souled" or "wise") in the nineteenth and twentieth centuries, and Martin Luther King, Jr. (1929–1968) in the twentieth century.

Tolstoy's and Gandhi's lives overlapped, and the two corresponded for a time. Gandhi's and King's lives also overlapped, though Gandhi died when King was still a young man and before the work for which he is most remembered began. All were deeply religious (Tolstoy and King were Christians, Gandhi a Hindu who showed strong Christian influences), all were influenced by Thoreau, and all were absorbed in the social and political injustices of their day.

Tolstoy was born into privilege in czarist Russia and is remembered mainly for his novels. In his later years, however, he devoted his energies increasingly to philosophical and religious writing. Although by comparison with his literary works these writings have been largely ignored, they constitute some of the most powerful writings the Western world has produced. St. Augustine in the fifth century AD provided the rationale for Christian participation in war. No one should read Augustine without reading Tolstoy. For in Tolstoy one finds a relentless argument to the conclusion that, whether one agrees with Christ's teachings or not, it is virtually impossible to render those teachings intelligible in any way other than as counseling nonviolence and nonresistance to evil. So strong was Tolstoy's conviction of this, and his determination in his later years to live in accordance with it, that he became known as the thirteenth apostle.

Tolstoy pursued this understanding of Christianity to what he saw as its logical conclusion: the rejection not only of the organized violence of war but also of the institutionalized violence of government itself, which makes war possible. This renunciation of war is relatively easy for nonviolentists to accept, since most of them are pacifists. But the second of these renunciations is a challenge to nonviolentists and pacifists alike. For one must at some point ask whether the abolition of war and the widespread adoption of nonviolence are possible without the radical restructuring and perhaps even the dismantling of the modern nation-state.

In the selection we have chosen here, Tolstoy is making a philosophical point: that meaning to life must be sought in self-transcendence, not in the absorption with personal happiness or gain, or even in promoting the happiness and material gain of others. He hereby in effect rejects both ethical egoism and utilitarianism as bases for the conduct of life. Only a life in accordance with what God has ordained for us has true meaning. And such a life requires loving one another, living according to the golden rule, and perfecting ourselves in this love.

Neither Gandhi nor King followed Tolstoy's lead into anarchism, though Gandhi moved decidedly in that direction. He emphasized the importance of small, self-reliant communities in which a simplicity of life would be achievable that would counterbalance the rush to modernization and industrialization. Gandhi also, as noted in the introduction, held a more qualified opposition to violence than Tolstoy, allowing that nonviolence should never be practiced out of weakness or cowardice, and that, as inferior as it is to nonviolence, violence is preferable to cowardice.

It is the Gandhian emphasis upon truth that we want to take particular note of here, however. His conception of Satyagraha, as the second selection makes clear, stands for truth-force. Gandhi thought of himself as engaged in an experiment with truth.

Contemporary philosophy tends to think of truth as a property of propositions and of science as the exemplary method by which its presence is confirmed. But there are other, much earlier conceptions. Ancient Indian thought, once again, associated truth with reality itself, an association that the American idealist Josiah Royce found implicit in the metaphysics of ordinary thought. Gandhi employs the notion in a way that has both a metaphysical and an epistemological dimension. He speaks as though in the practical realm of personal and social interactions there is an objective reality that constitutes the truth. However, it is a truth that the various parties to a conflict only partially grasp. The aim of Satyagraha is to discover this truth; it is not to try to force your own particular outlook upon others, to try to prevail at any cost.

The conditions that make for success in prevailing over others may have little to do with truth. To get at the truth requires approaching conflict in a spirit of openness to the possibility that your own convictions about what is right may represent a partial and imperfect grasp of the truth, and that your opponent may have perceived parts of it that have eluded you. A commitment to truth—and truth, Gandhi says, is God—requires that you approach conflict in such a way as to enable both you and your opponent to progress toward greater awareness of the truth that is in the situation. We must be mindful always of our limitations in sensitivity and awareness. Experience will teach us whether the way of nonviolence is best.

Part of this experiment must be a willingness to suffer. Gandhi perceived this as helping to cultivate the necessary discipline of the Satyagraha and to help transform an opponent by confronting him with the reality, in human terms, of his violence or oppression. It is as though there are some situations that can be remedied only at the cost of a certain amount of suffering. Violentists seek always to impose this cost on others. Nonviolentists, of the sort Gandhi conceives of in his notion of Satyagraha, take this cost upon themselves. Only in this way can one maximize the conditions by which both sides can progress toward understanding the truth. Joan Bondurant, one of the leading exponents of the Gandhian philosophy, details two of Gandhi's nonviolent campaigns in the selection "Satyagraha in Action."

King likewise stressed the willingness to suffer as part of a commitment to nonviolence. He also, in his own thinking, exemplified a somewhat similar approach to truth. In his book *Stride Toward Freedom* (1958) he explains how his quest for understanding led him to study Marxism, and how he eventually came to the conclusion that, although both Marxism and capitalism have hold of a part of the truth, the fuller truth lies somewhere between the two:

> Insofar as Marx posited a metaphysical materialism, an ethical relativism, and a strangulating totalitarianism, I responded with an unambiguous "no"; but insofar as he pointed to weaknesses of traditional capitalism, contributed to the growth of a definite self-consciousness in the masses, and challenged the social conscience of the Christian churches, I responded with a definite "yes." (p. 77)

It was the freedom, the recognition of the worth of the individual, and the spiritual values that were allowed to flourish that King saw as representing the truth in the socioeconomic system that has developed as part of capitalism. True, the evolution of King's own thinking in this regard probably owed more to Hegel than to Gandhi (with Hegel's notion of a dialectical synthesis of thesis and antithesis), but it nonetheless gave expression to very much the same process of seeking and distilling out the truth in antithetical positions that is central to Gandhi's Satyagraha.

In addition to the willingness to suffer, King cites five principal points in the commitment to nonviolence. First, like Gandhi he says that nonviolence is not for cowards; it requires courage and discipline. Second, it seeks friendship and reconciliation rather than the defeat or humiliation of an opponent. Third, it is "evil that the nonviolent resister seeks to defeat, not the persons victimized by evil." Fourth, again in the spirit of Gandhi, and of the Jains before him, nonviolence must avoid "not only external physical violence but also internal violence of spirit"; that is, it must renounce both physical and what we have called psychological violence. Finally, one must have faith, as we noted earlier, in the future, and faith that the universe is on the side of justice.

These points combine with a recognition of the interpenetration of means and ends, so that evil means may not be used to further good ends and good means may not be used to further evil ends, and with a commitment to love in the Christian sense of *agape*, which means an "understanding, redeeming good will for all men. It is an overflowing love which is purely spontaneous, unmotivated, groundless, and creative. . . . It is the love of God operating in the human heart." This love of God is manifest in the early civil rights actions described so well in Lawrence Apsey's selection on transforming power.

Particularly noteworthy is the third of these points. For King recognizes that violence not only victimizes those it is used against, it victimizes its users as well. Indeed, the users of violence may often be the principal victims. Those against whom violence is done suffer pain, injury, injustice, or even death. But violentists risk what may be the greater harm, moral corruption. Violence, even when used only against those who use it against others, does not undo this corruption; it leaves it intact and simply tries to overwhelm the wrongdoer by dint of sheer force. Nonviolence, on the other hand, shows a concern for evildoers as well as for those they afflict. Both are victims of violence, though in different ways. If love in the sense that is central to Tolstoy, Gandhi, and King has any central meaning, it is this.

NONRESISTANCE TO EVIL

Letter to Ernest Howard Crosby

Leo Tolstoy

Fifty years ago Lloyd Garrison's Declaration of Nonresistance only estranged people from him; and Ballou's fifty years' labor in the same direction was constantly met by a conspiracy of silence. I now read with great pleasure, in the *Voice*, admirable thoughts by American writers on this question of nonresistance. I need only demur to the notion expressed by Mr. Bemis. It is an old but unfounded libel upon Christ to suppose that the expulsion of the cattle from the temple indicates that Jesus beat people with a whip, and advised His disciples to behave in a like manner. The opinions expressed by these writers, especially by Heber Newton and George D. Herron, are quite correct; but unfortunately they do not reply to the problem which Christ put to men, but to another, which has been substituted for it by those chief and most dangerous opponents of Christianity, the so-called "orthodox" ecclesiastical authorities.

Mr. Higginson says: "I do not believe nonresistance admissible as a universal rule." Heber Newton says that people's opinion as to the practical result of the application of Christ's teaching will depend on the extent of people's belief in His authority. Carlos Martyn considers the transition stage in which we live not suited for the application of the doctrine of nonresistance. George D. Herron holds that to obey the law of nonresistance we must learn to apply it to life. Mrs. Livermore, thinking that the law of nonresis-

Source: *Writings on Civil Disobedience and Nonviolence*, by Leo Tolstoy (Philadelphia: New Society Publishers, 1987). Reprinted by permission of New Society Publishers.

tance can be fully obeyed only in the future, says the same. All these views refer to the question, "What would happen if people were all obliged to obey the law of nonresistance?"

But, in the first place, it is impossible to oblige every one to accept the law of nonresistance. Secondly, if it were possible to do so, such compulsion would in itself be a direct negation of the very principle set up. Oblige all men to refrain from violence? Who then should enforce the decision? Thirdly, and this is the chief point, the question, as put by Christ, is not at all, "Can nonresistance become a general law for humanity?" but, "How must each man act to fulfil his allotted task, to save his soul, and to do the will of God, three things which are really one and the same thing?"

Christian teaching does not lay down laws for everybody, and does not say to people, "You all, for fear of punishment, must obey such and such rules, and then you will all be happy"; but it explains to each individual his position in relation to the world, and gives him to see what results, for him individually, inevitably flow from that relation. Christianity says to mankind (and to each man separately), that a man's personal life can have no rational meaning if he counts it as belonging to himself or as having for its aim worldly happiness for himself or for other people. This is so, because the happiness he seeks is unattainable—(1) for the reason that, all beings striving after worldly advantages, the gain of one is the loss of others, and it is most probable that each individual will incur much superfluous suffering in the course of his vain effort to seize unattainable blessings; (2) because, even if a man gains worldly advantages, the more he obtains the less he is satisfied, and the more he hankers after fresh ones; (3) and chiefly because the longer a man lives the more irresistible becomes the approach of old age, sickness, death, destroying all possibility of worldly advantages. So that if a man considers his life to be his own, to be spent in seeking worldly happiness for himself as well as for others, then that life can have no rational explanation for him. Life takes a rational meaning only when one understands that, to consider our life our own, or to see its aim in worldly happiness for ourselves or for other people, is a delusion; that a man's life does not belong to him who has received it, but to Him who has given it; and therefore its object should be, not the attainment of worldly happiness, either for one's self or for other individuals, but solely to fulfil the will of Him, the Creator of this life.

This conception alone gives life a rational meaning, and makes life's aim (which is to fulfil the will of God) attainable. And, most important of all, only when enlightened by this conception does man see clearly the right direction for his own activity. Man is then no longer destined to suffer and to despair, as was inevitable under the former conception. "The universe and I in it," says a man of this conception to himself, "exist by the will of God. I cannot know the whole of the universe, for in immensity it transcends my comprehension; nor can I know my own position in it; but I do know with certainty what God, who has sent me into this world, infinite in time and space, and therefore incomprehensible to me, demands from me. This is revealed to me

(1) by the collective wisdom of the best men who have gone before me, i.e. by tradition; (2) by my own reason; and (3) by my heart, i.e. by the highest aspirations of my nature.

Tradition—the collective wisdom of my greatest forerunners—tells me that I should do unto others as I would that they should do unto me. My reason shows me that only by all men acting thus is the highest happiness for all men attainable. Only when I yield myself to that intuition of love which demands obedience to this law is my own heart happy and at rest. And not only can I then know how to act, but I can and do discern that work, to cooperate in which my activity was designed and is required. I cannot fathom God's whole design, for the sake of which the universe exists and lives; but the divine work which is being accomplished in this world, and in which I participate by living, is comprehensible to me.

This work is the annihilation of discord and strife among men, and among all creatures; and the establishment of the highest unity, concord, and love. It is the fulfilment of the promises of the Hebrew prophets, who foretold a time when all men should be taught by truth, when spears should be turned into reaping-hooks, swords be beaten to plowshares, and the lion lie down with the lamb. So that a man of Christian intelligence not only knows what he has to do, but he also understands the work he is doing. He has to act so as to cooperate toward the establishment of the kingdom of God on earth. For this, a man must obey his intuition of God's will, i.e. he must act lovingly toward others, as he would that others should act toward him. Thus the intuitive demands of man's soul coincide with the external aim of life which he sees before him.

Man in this world, according to Christian teaching, is God's laborer. A laborer does not know his master's whole design, but he does know the immediate object which he is set to work at. He receives definite instructions what to do, and especially what not to do, lest he hinder the attainment of the very ends toward which his labor must tend. For the rest he has full liberty given him. And therefore, for a man who has grasped the Christian conception of life, the meaning of his life is perfectly plain and reasonable; nor can he have a moment's hesitation as to how he should act, or what he should do to fulfil the object for which he lives.

And yet, in spite of such a twofold indication, clear and indubitable to a man of Christian understanding of what is the real aim and meaning of human life, and of what men should do and should not do, we find people (and people calling themselves Christians) who decide that in such and such circumstances men ought to abandon God's law and reason's guidance, and act in opposition to them; because, according to their conception, the effects of actions performed in submission to God's law may be detrimental or inconvenient.

According to the law, contained alike in tradition, in our reason, and in our hearts, man should always do unto others as he would that they should do unto him; he should always cooperate in the development of love and union among created beings. But on the contrary, in the judgment of these people who look ahead, as long as it is premature, in their opinion, to obey this law, man should do violence, imprison or kill people, and thereby evoke anger and venom instead of loving union in the hearts of men. It is as if a bricklayer, set to do a particular task, and knowing that he was cooperating with others to build a house, after receiving clear and precise instructions from the master himself how to build a certain wall, should receive from some fellow brick-layers (who like himself knew neither the plan of the house nor what would fit in with it) orders to cease building his wall, and instead rather to pull down a wall which other workmen had erected.

Astonishing delusion! A being who breathes one day and vanishes the next receives one definite, indubitable law to guide him through the brief term of his life; but instead of obeying that law he prefers to fancy that he knows what is necessary, advantageous, and well-timed for men, for all the world—this world which continually shifts and evolves; and for the sake of some advantage (which each man pictures after his own fancy) he decides that he and other people should temporarily abandon the indubitable law given to one and to all, and should act, not as they would that others should act toward them, bringing love into the world, but instead do violence, imprison, kill, and bring into the world enmity whenever it seems profitable to do so. And he decides to act thus, though he knows that the most horrible cruelties, martyrdoms, and murders—from the inquisitions, and the murders, and horrors of all the revolutions, down to the violences of contemporary anarchists, and their slaughter by the established authorities—have only occurred because people will imagine that they know what is necessary for mankind and for the world. But are there not always, at any given moment, two opposite parties, each of which declares that it is necessary to use force against the other—the "law and order" party against the "anarchist"; the "anarchist" against the "law and order" men; English against Americans, and Americans against English, and English against Germans; and so forth in all possible combinations and rearrangements?

A man enlightened by Christianity sees that he has no reason to abandon the law of God, given to enable him to walk with sure foot through life, in order to follow the chance, inconstant, and often contradictory demands of men. But besides this, if he has lived a Christian life for some time, and has developed in himself a Christian moral sensibility, he literally cannot act as people demand of him. Not this reason only, but his feeling also, makes it impossible. To many people of our society it would be impossible to torture or kill a baby, even if they were told that by doing so they could save hun-dreds of people. And in the same way a man, when he has developed a Chris-tian sensibility of heart, finds a whole series of actions that are impossible for him. For instance, a Christian who is obliged to take part in judicial proceed-ings in which a man may be sentenced to death, or who is obliged to take part in evictions, or in debating a proposal leading to war, or to participate in preparations for war (not to mention war itself), is in a position parallel to that of a kindly man called on to torture or to kill a baby. It is not reason alone that forbids him to do what is demanded of him; he feels instinctively that he cannot do it. For certain actions are morally impossible, just as others are physically impossible. As a man cannot lift a mountain, and as a kindly man cannot kill an infant, so a man living the Christian life cannot take part in deeds of violence. Of what value then to him are arguments about the imaginary advantages of doing what is morally impossible for him to do?

But how is a man to act when he sees clearly an evil in following the law of love and its corollary law of nonresistance? How (to use the stock example) is a man to act when he sees a criminal killing or outraging a child, and he can only save the child by killing the criminal? When such a case is put, it is generally assumed that the only possible reply is that one should kill the assailant to save the child. But this answer is given so quickly and decidedly only because we are all so accustomed to the use of violence, not only to save a child, but even to prevent a neighboring government altering its frontier at the expense of ours, or to prevent someone from smuggling lace across that frontier, or even to defend our garden fruit from a passer-by. It is assumed that to save the child the assailant should be killed.

But it is only necessary to consider the question, "On what grounds ought a man, whether he be or be not a Christian, to act so?" in order to come to the conclusion that such action has no reasonable foundation, and only seems to us necessary because up to two thousand years ago such conduct was considered right, and a habit of acting so had been formed. Why should a non-Christian, not acknowledging God, and not regarding the fulfilment of His will as the aim of life, decide to kill the criminal in order to defend the child? By killing the former he kills for certain; whereas he cannot know positively whether the criminal would have killed the child or not. But letting that pass, who shall say whether the child's life was more needed, was better, than the other's life? Surely, if the non-Christian knows not God, and does not see life's meaning to be in the performance of His will, the only rule for his actions must be a reckoning, a conception, of which is more profitable for him and for all men, a continuation of the criminal's life or of the child's. To decide that, he needs to know what would become of the child whom he saves, and what, had he not killed him, would have been the future of the assailant. And as he cannot know this, the non-Christian has no sufficient rational ground for killing a robber to save a child.

If a man be a Christian, and consequently acknowledges God, and sees the meaning of life in fulfilling His will, then, however ferocious the assailant, however innocent and lovely the child, he has even less ground to abandon the God-given law, and to do to the criminal as the criminal wishes to do to the child. He may plead with the assailant, may interpose his own body between the assailant and the victim; but there is one thing he cannot do—he cannot deliberately abandon the law he has received from God, the fulfilment of which alone gives meaning to his life. Very probably bad education, or his animal nature, may cause a man, Christian or non-Christian, to kill an assailant, not to save a child, but even to save himself or to save his purse. But it does not follow that he is right in acting thus, or that he should accustom himself or others to think such conduct right. What it does show is that, notwithstanding a coating of education and of Christianity, the habits of the stone age are yet so strong in man that he still commits actions long since condemned by his reasonable conscience.

I see a criminal killing a child, and I can save the child by killing the assailant—therefore, in certain cases, violence must be used to resist evil. A man's life is in danger, and can be saved only by my telling a lie—therefore, in certain cases, one must lie. A man is starving, and I can only save him by stealing—therefore, in certain cases, one must steal. I lately read a story by Coppee, in which an orderly kills his officer, whose life was insured, and thereby saves the honor and the family of the officer, the moral being that, in certain cases, one must kill. Such devices, and the deductions from them, only prove that there are men who know that it is not well to steal, to lie, or to kill, but who are still so unwilling that people should cease to do these things that they use all their mental powers to invent excuses for such conduct. There is no moral law concerning which one might not devise a case in which it is difficult to decide which is more moral, to disobey the law or to obey it? But all such devices fail to prove that the laws, "Thou shalt not lie, steal, or kill," are invalid.

It is thus with the law of nonresistance. People know it is wrong to use violence, but they are so anxious to continue to live a life secured by "the strong arm of the law," that, instead of devoting their intellects to the elucidation of the evils which have flowed, and are still flowing, from admitting that man has a right to use violence to his fellow-men, they prefer to exert their mental powers in defense of that error. *"Fais ce que dois, advienne que pourra"*—"Do what's right, come what may"—is an expression of profound wisdom. We each can know indubitably what we ought to do, but what results will follow from our actions we none of us either do or can know. Therefore it follows that, besides feeling the call of duty, we are further driven to act as duty bids us by the consideration that we have no other guidance, but are totally ignorant of what will result from our action.

Christian teaching indicates what a man should do to perform the will of Him who sent him into life; and discussion as to what results we anticipate from such or such human actions have nothing to do with Christianity, but are just an example of the error which Christianity eliminates. None of us has ever yet met the imaginary criminal with the imaginary child, but all the horrors which fill the annals of history and of our own times came, and come, from this one thing, namely, that people will believe they really foresee speculative future results of actions.

The case is this. People once lived an animal life, and violated or killed whom they thought well to violate or to kill. They even ate one another, and public opinion approved of it. Thousands of years ago, as far back as the times of Moses, a day came when people had realized that to violate or kill one another is bad. But there were people for whom the reign of force was advantageous, and these did not approve of the change, but assured themselves and others that to do deeds of violence and to kill people is not always bad, but that there are circumstances when it is necessary and even moral. And violence and slaughter, though not so frequent or so cruel as before, continued, only with this difference, that those who committed or commended such acts excused themselves by pleading that they did it for the benefit of humanity.

It was just this sophistical justification of violence that Christ denounced. When two enemies fight, each may think his own conduct justified by the circumstances. Excuses can be made for every use of violence, and no infallible standard has ever been discovered by which to measure the worth of these excuses. Therefore Christ taught us to disbelieve in any excuse for violence, and (contrary to what had been taught by them of old times) never to use violence. One would have thought that those who have professed Christianity would be indefatigable in exposing deception in this matter; for in such exposure lay one of the chief manifestations of Christianity. What really happened was just the reverse. People who profited by violence, and who did not wish to give up their advantages, took on themselves a monopoly of Christian preaching, and declared that, as cases can be found in which nonresistance causes more harm than the use of violence (the imaginary criminal killing the imaginary child), therefore Christ's doctrine of nonresistance need not always be followed; and that one may deviate from His teaching to defend one's life or the life of others; or to defend one's country, to save society from lunatics or criminals, and in many other cases.

The decision of the question in what cases Christ's teaching should be set aside was left to the very people who employed violence. So that it ended by Christ's teaching on the subject of not resisting evil by violence being completely annulled. And what was worst of all was that the very people Christ denounced came to consider themselves the sole preachers and expositors of His doctrines. But the light shines through the darkness, and Christ's teaching is again exposing the pseudoteachers of Christianity. We may think about rearranging the world to suit our own taste—no one can prevent that; and we may try to do what seems to us pleasant or profitable, and with that object treat our fellow creatures with violence on the pretext that we are doing good. But so acting we cannot pretend that we follow Christ's teaching, for Christ denounced just this deception. Truth sooner or later reappears, and the false teachers are shown up, which is just what is happening today.

Only let the question of man's life be rightly put, as Christ put it, and not as it has been perversely put by the Church, and the whole structure of falsehood which the Church has built over Christ's teaching will collapse of itself. The real question is not whether it will be good or bad for a certain human society that people should follow the law of love and the consequent law of nonresistance. But it is this: Do you, who today live and tomorrow will die, you who are indeed tending deathward every moment, do you wish now, immediately and entirely, to obey the law of Him who sent you into life, and who clearly showed you His will, alike in tradition and in your mind and heart; or do you prefer to resist His will? And as soon as the question is put thus, only one reply is possible: I wish now, this moment, without delay or hesitation, to the very utmost of my strength, neither waiting for one or counting the cost, to do that which alone is clearly demanded by Him who sent me into the world; and on no account, and under no conditions, do I wish to, or can I, act otherwise—for herein lies my only possibility of a rational and unharassed life.

FROM PASSIVE RESISTANCE TO DIRECT ACTION

On Satyagraha

Mohandas K. Gandhi

Before one can be fit for the practice of civil disobedience one must have rendered a willing and respectful obedience to the State laws. For the most part we obey such laws for fear of the penalty for their breach, and this holds good particularly in respect of such laws as do not involve a moral principle. For instance, an honest, respectable man will not suddenly take to stealing whether there is a law against stealing or not, but this very man will not feel any remorse for failure to observe the rule about carrying headlights on bicycles after dark. Indeed, it is doubtful whether he would even accept advice kindly about being more careful in this respect. But he would observe any obligatory rule of this kind, if only to escape the inconvenience of facing a prosecution for a breach of the rule. Such compliance is not, however, the willing and spontaneous obedience that is required of a Satyagrahi. A Satyagrahi obeys the laws of society intelligently and of his own free will, because he considers it to be his sacred duty to do so. It is only when a person has thus obeyed the laws of society scrupulously that he is in a position to judge as to which particular rules are good and just and which unjust and iniquitous. Only then does the right accrue to him of the civil disobedience of certain laws in well-defined circumstances.

Source: The introductory paragraph comes from *Non-Violent Resistance*, by M. K. Gandhi. (Dover Publications, 2001 republication of work originally published by the Navajivan Trust, 1951.) The remaining selections: © Navajivan Trust 1986/1987. Reprinted from *The Moral and Political Writings of Mahatma Gandhi*, edited by Ragharan Iyer, vol. 2 (1986) and vol. 3 (1987) by permission of Oxford University Press.

Soul-Force and *Tapasya*

[About 2 September 1917]

The force denoted by the term "passive resistance" and translated into Hindi as *nishkriya pratirodha* is not very accurately described either by the original English phrase or by its Hindi rendering. Its correct description is "*satyagraha.*" *Satyagraha* was born in South Africa in 1908. There was no word in any Indian language denoting the power which our countrymen in South Africa invoked for the redress of their grievances. There was an English equivalent, namely, "passive resistance," and we carried on with it. However, the need for a word to describe this unique power came to be increasingly felt, and it was decided to award a prize to anyone who could think of an appropriate term. A Gujarati-speaking gentleman submitted the word "*satyagraha,*" and it was adjudged the best.

"Passive resistance" conveyed the idea of the Suffragette Movement in England. Burning of houses by these women was called "passive resistance" and so also their fasting in prison. All such acts might very well be "passive resistance" but they were not "*satyagraha.*" It is said of "passive resistance" that it is the weapon of the weak, but the power which is the subject of this article can be used only by the strong. This power is not "passive" resistance; indeed it calls for intense activity. The movement in South Africa was not passive but active. The Indians of South Africa believed that Truth was their object, that Truth ever triumphs, and with this definiteness of purpose they persistently held on to Truth. They put up with all the suffering that this persistence implied. With the conviction that Truth is not to be renounced even unto death, they shed the fear of death. In the cause of Truth, the prison was a palace to them and its doors the gateway to freedom.

Satyagraha is not physical force. A *satyagrahi* does not inflict pain on the adversary; he does not seek his destruction. A *satyagrahi* never resorts to firearms. In the use of *satyagraha*, there is no ill-will whatever.

Satyagraha is pure soul-force. Truth is the very substance of the soul. That is why this force is called *satyagraha*. The soul is informed with knowledge. In it burns the flame of love. If someone gives us pain through ignorance, we shall win him through love. "Nonviolence is the supreme *dharma*" [*Ahimsa paramo Dharma*] is the proof of this power of love. Nonviolence is a dormant state. In the waking state, it is love. Ruled by love, the world goes on. In English there is a saying, "Might is Right." Then there is the doctrine of the survival of the fittest. Both these ideas are contradictory to the above principle. Neither is wholly true. If ill-will were the chief motive-force, the world would have been destroyed long ago; and neither would I have had the opportunity to write this article nor would the hopes of the readers be fulfilled. We are alive solely because of love. We are all ourselves the proof of this. Deluded by modern western civilization, we have forgotten our ancient civilization and worship the might of arms.

We forget the principle of nonviolence, which is the essence of all religions. The doctrine of arms stands for irreligion. It is due to the sway of that doctrine that a sanguinary war is raging in Europe.

In India also we find worship of arms. We see it even in that great work of Tulsidas. But it is seen in all the books that soul-force is the supreme power.

Rama stands for the soul and Ravan for the non-soul. The immense physical might of Ravana is as nothing compared to the soul-force of Rama. Ravana's ten heads are as straw to Rama. Rama is a *yogi*, he has conquered self and pride. He is "placid equally in affluence and adversity," he has "neither attachment, nor greed nor the intoxication of status." This represents the ultimate in *satyagraha*. The banner of *satyagraha* can again fly in the Indian sky and it is our duty to raise it. If we take recourse to *satyagraha*, we can conquer our conquerors the English, make them bow before our tremendous soul-force, and the issue will be of benefit to the whole world.

It is certain that India cannot rival Britain or Europe in force of arms. The British worship the war-god and they can all of them become, as they are becoming, bearers of arms. The hundreds of millions in India can never carry arms. They have made the religion of nonviolence their own. It is impossible for the *varnashrama* system to disappear from India.

The way of *varnashrama* is a necessary law of nature. India, by making a judicious use of it, derives much benefit. Even the Muslims and the English in India observe this system to some extent. Outside of India, too, people follow it without being aware of it. So long as this institution of *varnashrama* exists in India, everyone cannot bear arms here. The highest place in India is assigned to the *brahmana dharma*—which is soul-force. Even the armed warrior does obeisance to the *Brahmin*. So long as this custom prevails, it is vain for us to aspire for equality with the West in force of arms.

It is our Kamadhenu.[1] It brings good both to the *satyagrahi* and his adversary It is ever victorious. For instance, Harishchandra was a *satyagrahi*, Prahlad was a *satyagrahi*, Mirabai was a *satyagrahi*. Daniel, Socrates and those Arabs who hurled themselves on the fire of the French artillery were all *satyagrahas*. We see from these examples that a *satyagrahi* does not fear for his body, he does not give up what he thinks is Truth; the word "defeat" is not to be found in his dictionary, he does not wish for the destruction of his antagonist, he does not vent anger on him; but has only compassion for him.

A *satyagrahi* does not wait for others, but throws himself into the fray, relying entirely on his own resources. He trusts that when the time comes, others will do likewise. His practice is his precept. Like air, *satyagraha* is all-pervading. It is infectious, which means that all people—big and small, men and women—can become *satyagrahas*. No one is kept out from the army of *satyagrahis*. A *satyagrahi* cannot perpetrate tyranny on anyone; he is not subdued through application of physical force; he does not strike at anyone. Just as anyone can resort to *satyagraha*, it can be resorted to in almost any situation.

People demand historical evidence in support of *satyagraha*. History is for the most part a record of armed activities. Natural activities find very little mention in it. Only uncommon activities strike us with wonder. *Satyagraha* has been used always and in all situations. The father and the son, the man and the wife are perpetually resorting to *satyagraha*, one towards the other. When a father gets angry and punishes the son, the son does not hit back with a weapon, he conquers his father's anger by submitting to him. The son refuses to be subdued by the unjust rule of his father but he puts up with the punishment that he may incur through disobeying the unjust father. We can similarly free ourselves of the unjust rule of the Government by defying the unjust rule and accepting the punishments that go with it. We do not bear malice towards the Government. When we set its fears at rest, when we do not desire to make armed assaults on the administrators, nor to unseat them from power, but only to get rid of their injustice, they will at once be subdued to our will.

The question is asked why we should call any rule unjust. In saying so, we ourselves assume the function of a judge. It is true. But in this world, we always have to act as judges for ourselves. That is why the *satyagrahi* does not strike his adversary with arms. If he has Truth on his side, he will win, and if his thought is faulty, he will suffer the consequences of his fault.

What is the good, they ask, of only one person opposing injustice; for he will be punished and destroyed, he will languish in prison or meet an untimely end through hanging. The objection is not valid. History shows that all reforms have begun with one person. Fruit is hard to come by without *tapasya*. The suffering that has to be undergone in *satyagraha* is *tapasya* in its purest form. Only when the *tapasya* is capable of bearing fruit do we have the fruit. This establishes the fact that when there is insufficient *tapasya*, the fruit is delayed. The *tapasya* of Jesus Christ, boundless though it was, was not sufficient for Europe's need. Europe has disapproved Christ. Through ignorance, it has disregarded Christ's pure way of life. Many Christs will have to offer themselves as sacrifice at the terrible altar of Europe, and only then will realization dawn on that continent. But Jesus will always be the first among these. He has been the sower of the seed and his will therefore be the credit for raising the harvest. . . .

Nonviolence and Nonretaliation

Mansehra,
[8 November 1938]

It has become the fashion these days to say that society cannot be organized or run on nonviolent lines. I join issue on that point. In a family, when a father slaps his delinquent child, the latter does not think of retaliating. He obeys his father not because of the deterrent effect of the slap but because of the offended love which he senses behind it. That in my opinion is an epitome of the way in which society is or should be governed. What is true of family must be true of society which is but a larger family. It is man's imagination that divides the world into warring groups of enemies and friends. In the ultimate resort it is the power of love that acts even in the midst of the clash and sustains the world. . . .

Nonviolence of the Strong and of the Weak

Hence I ask you, is our nonviolence the nonviolence of the coward, the weak, the helpless, the timid? In that case, it is of no value. A weakling is a born saint. A weak person is obliged to become a saint. But we are soldiers of nonviolence, who, if the occasion demands, will lay down their lives for it. Our nonviolence is not a mere policy of the coward. But I doubt this. I am afraid that the nonviolence we boast of might really be only a policy. It is true that, to some extent, nonviolence works even in the hands of the weak. And, in this manner, this weapon has been useful to us. But, if one makes use of nonviolence in order to disguise one's weakness or through helplessness, it makes a coward of one. Such a person is defeated on both the fronts. Such a one cannot live like a man and the Devil he surely cannot become. It is a thousand times better that we die trying to acquire the strength of the arm. Using physical force with courage is far superior to cowardice. At least we would have attempted to act like men. That was the way of our forefathers. That is because some people hold the view that the ancestors of the human race were animals. I do not wish to enter into the controversy whether Darwin's theory is tenable or not. However, from one standpoint we must all have originally been animals. And I am ready to believe that we are evolved from the animal into the human state. That is why physical strength is called brute force.

We are born with such strength, hence if we used it we could be, to say the least, courageous. But we are born as human beings in order that we may realize God who dwells within our hearts. This is the basic distinction between us and the beasts. . . .

Man is by nature nonviolent. But he does not owe his origin to nonviolence. We fulfil our human life when we see the *atman*, and when we do so we pass the test. Now is the time for our test. God-realization means seeing Him in all beings. Or, in other words, we should learn to become one with every creature. This is man's privilege and that distinguishes him from the beasts. This can happen only when we voluntarily give up the use of physical force and when we develop the nonviolence which lies dormant in our hearts. It can be awakened only through real strength. . . .

Nonviolence is an active principle of the highest order. It is soul-force or the power of the godhead within us. Imperfect man cannot grasp the whole of that Essence—he would not be able to bear its full blaze—but even an infinitesimal fraction of it, when it becomes active within us, can work wonders.

The sun in the heavens fills the whole universe with its life-giving warmth. But if one went too near it, it would consume him to ashes. Even so is it with godhead. We become godlike to the extent we realize nonviolence; but we can never become wholly God. Nonviolence is like radium in its action. An infinitesimal quantity of it imbedded in a malignant growth, acts continuously, silently, and ceaselessly till it has transformed the whole mass of the diseased tissue into a healthy one. Similarly, even a tiny grain of true nonviolence acts in a silent, subtle, unseen way and leavens the whole society.

It is self-acting. The soul persists even after death, its existence does not depend on the physical body. Similarly, nonviolence or soul-force too, does not need physical aids for its propagation or effect. It acts independently of them. It transcends time and space.

It follows, therefore, that if nonviolence becomes successfully established in one place, its influence will spread everywhere. So long as a single dacoity takes place in Utmanzai, I will say that our nonviolence is not genuine.

The basic principle on which the practice of nonviolence rests is that what holds good in respect of yourself holds good equally in respect of the whole universe. All mankind in essence are alike. . . .

Nonviolence and Bravery

Just as one must learn the art of killing in the training for violence, so one must learn the art of dying in the training for nonviolence. Violence does not mean emancipation from fear, but discovering the means of combating the cause of fear. Nonviolence, on the other hand, has no cause for fear. The votary of nonviolence has to cultivate the capacity for sacrifice of the highest type in order to be free from fear. He recks not if he should lose his land, his wealth, his life. He who has not overcome all fear cannot practice *ahimsa* to perfection. The votary of *ahimsa* has only one fear, that is of God. He who seeks refuge in God ought to have a glimpse of the *atman* that transcends the body; and the moment one has a glimpse of the Imperishable *atman* one sheds the love of the perishable body. Training in nonviolence is thus diametrically opposed to training in violence. Violence is needed for the protection of things external, nonviolence is needed for the protection of the *atman*, for the protection of one's honour.

This nonviolence cannot be learnt by staying at home. It needs enterprise. In order to test ourselves we should learn to dare danger and death, mortify the flesh and acquire the capacity to endure all manner of hardships. He who trembles or takes to his heels the moment he sees two people fighting is not nonviolent, but a coward. A nonviolent person will lay down his life in preventing such quarrels. The bravery of the nonviolent is vastly superior to that of the violent. The badge of the violent is his weapon—spear, or sword, or rifle. God is the shield of the nonviolent.

This is not a course of training for one intending to learn nonviolence. But it is easy to evolve one from the principles I have laid down.

It will be evident from the foregoing that there is no comparison between the two types of bravery. The one is limited, the other is limitless. There is no such thing as out-daring or out-fighting nonviolence. Nonviolence is invincible. There need be no doubt that this nonviolence can be achieved. . . .

The Acid Test

Indeed the acid test of nonviolence is that one thinks, speaks and acts nonviolently, even when there is the gravest provocation to be violent. There is no merit in being nonviolent to the good and the gentle. Nonviolence is the mightiest force in the world capable of resisting the greatest imaginable temptation. Jesus knew "the generation of vipers," minced no words in describing them, but pleaded for mercy for them before the Judgment Throne, "for they knew not what they were doing."

I gave the company chapter and verse in support of the statements I made. I regard myself as a friend of the missionaries. I enjoy happy relations with many of them. But my friendships have never been blind to the limitations of my friends or the systems or methods they have supported.

False notions of propriety or fear of wounding susceptibilities often deter people from saying what they mean and ultimately land them on the shores of hypocrisy. But if nonviolence of thought is to be evolved in individuals or societies or nations, truth has to be told, however harsh or unpopular it may appear to be for the moment. And mere nonviolent action without the thought behind it is of little value. It can never be infectious. It is almost like a whited sepulchre. Thought is the power and the life behind it. We hardly know that thought is infinitely greater than action or words. When there is correspondence between thought, word and deed, either is a limitation of the first. And the third is a limitation of the second. Needless to say that here I am referring to the living thought which awaits translation into speech and action. Thoughts without potency are airy nothings and end in smoke. . . .

The way of peace is the way of truth. Truthfulness is even more important than peacefulness. Indeed, lying is the mother of violence. A truthful man cannot long remain violent. He will perceive in the course of his search that he has no need to be violent and he will further discover that so long as there is the slightest trace of violence in him, he will fail to find the truth he is searching.

There is no half way between truth and nonviolence on the one hand and untruth and violence on the other. We may never be strong enough to be entirely nonviolent in thought, word and deed. But we must keep nonviolence as our goal and make steady progress towards it. The attainment of freedom, whether for a man, a nation or the world, must be in exact proportion to the attainment of nonviolence by each. Let those, therefore, who believe in nonviolence as the only method of achieving real freedom, keep the lamp of non-violence burning bright in the midst of the present impenetrable gloom. The truth of a few will count, the untruth of millions will vanish even like chaff before a whiff of wind.

Notes

[1] Mythical cow that yielded whatever one wished.

Satyagraha in Action

Joan Bondurant

The Vykom Temple Road Satyagraha[1]

Dates, Duration, and Locale

1. Spring 1924 to autumn 1925.
2. Pursued over sixteen months.
3. The village Vykom, State of Travancore, at the southern tip of India.

Objectives

1. *Immediate:* To remove the prohibition upon the use by untouchables of roadways passing the temple. This was a serious disability inasmuch as it required untouchables to take a long, circuitous route to reach their dwellings.
2. *Long-range:* A step towards ridding Hinduism of the "blot" of untouchability.

Satyagraha Participants and Leadership

1. *Character of leadership:* Among the initiators of the movement was a Syrian Christian. However, opinion favored Hindu leaders because of the reform objective. Local Hindus took up the prominent leadership roles. Gandhi, who kept in touch with the campaign from the beginning, was not its leader and was not in Travancore until late in the movement, when he was instrumental in securing a concession from the State government.
2. *Character of participants:* Hindus, both untouchables and caste (including orthodox) Hindus provided the majority of participants. Sikhs from the Punjab offered direct support by opening a kitchen to feed satyagrahis, but upon Gandhi's recommendation, they were

Source: Bondurant, Joan V., *Conquest of Violence.* © 1958 Princeton University Press, 1986 renewed PUP. Reprinted by permission of Princeton University Press.

replaced by local Hindus so that orthodox Hindu opponents might not be offended.

3. *Number of participants:* Active satyagrahis residing in the camp established for the volunteers was about 50. Many others cooperated, with estimates of total participants varying from 600 to "thousands."

Participants and Leadership of the Opposition

1. *Orthodox Hindus.* An occasional untouchable was numbered among the opposition, but the majority were high caste Hindus, especially Brahmans. An orthodox Hindu society, the Savarna Mahajana Sabha, supported the Brahman position throughout the struggle.

2. *Police* of the State of Travancore.

3. *Members of the Travancore Legislative Council.* The majority on the Council supported the orthodox position.

Organization and Constructive Program

1. *Camp headquarters:* A satyagraha ashram (camp) was established early in the campaign.

2. *Constructive activity:* Daily maintenance and camp routine were made an integral part of the movement, with *satyagrahis* assigned either maintenance duties or direct action duties. A high degree of self-sufficiency was attained. Hand-spinning, building of a school, and other constructive efforts were continued during the movement.

Preparation for Action

1. *Prayer:* A religious tone was given the movement, with prayer meetings an important part of ashram life.

2. *Instruction in satyagraha:* Participants in the campaign engaged in discussion of the principles underlying satyagraha. Emphasis was laid upon understanding the viewpoint of their orthodox opponents, and upon winning them over through persuasion.

Preliminary Action

1. *Negotiation:* Among the efforts made to negotiate a settlement was a deputation to State authorities.

2. *Agitation:* Efforts were made to attract public attention to the disabilities of the Vykom untouchables.

Action

First phase:

1. Procession of untouchables and caste Hindus taken along the forbidden road. Refusal to retaliate when attacked and beaten by Brahmans.

2. Submission to arrest. A second procession along the road led to the arrest of satyagrahi leaders.

3. Replacement of leaders. Upon the arrest of satyagrahis, others came forward to fill their places.

4. Submission of secondary leadership to arrest.

Second phase:

1. Opposition to police barricade. Upon the erection by police of a barricade on the road, caste Hindus alongside untouchables took up positions opposite the police and held them day after day.

2. Action during monsoon. When the monsoon flooded the road and the police occupied their positions in boats, satyagrahis continued to stand three-hour shifts, in some instances even up to shoulders in water.

Third phase:

1. Persuasion of State authorities. Gandhi, visiting Travancore for the first time during the movement in April 1925, persuaded the authorities to remove the barricade.

2. Announcement of intention not to take advantage of removal of barricade. Satyagrahis refrained from entering the road even though the barricade and police cordon had been removed. They announced they would not enter upon the road until the Brahmans were fully persuaded, and the government declared acceptance of untouchable use of the road.

3. Persuasion of Brahman opponents. Through persistent reasoning supported by prayer, the opposition was won over.

Reaction of Opponents

1. *Violence* against satyagrahis by personal physical attack.

2. *Imprisonment* of satyagrahis following arrest.

3. *Cessation of arrests* when prisons became overcrowded.

4. *Erection of barricade.* Police built and manned barricade on the roadway upon an order to prevent entry.

5. *Support by State Legislative Council.* Majority of the State Council upheld police action.

6. *Social ostracism* of satyagraha organizers. Ostracism, accompanied by threats of depriving participants of family property and barring them from other family privileges, was especially serious.

7. *Removal of barricades.* Following Gandhi's talks (in April 1925) with State authorities, police were ordered to remove the barricades which they had manned daily.

8. *Confusion over satyagraha reaction.* Brahmans, who had expected them to re-enter the roadway as soon as police cordon and barricade

were removed, were thrown off balance when satyagrahis refrained from entering the road.

9. *Capitulation.* In the autumn of 1925, the Brahmans declared: "We cannot any longer resist the prayers that have been made to us, and we are ready to receive the untouchables."

Results

1. *Roads opened to all comers.* The immediate objective of the satyagraha had been fully achieved.

2. *Brahman areas elsewhere opened.* In other parts of India this campaign had repercussions, with the opening to untouchables of areas and temples formerly closed to them.

3. *Conditions of untouchables improved.* Through an extension of the constructive program, the general condition of untouchables was improved.

4. *Long-range results:* The campaign constituted a major turning point in the fight against untouchability. . . .

The Bardoli Campaign of Peasants Against the Government of Bombay[2]

Dates, Duration, and Locale

1. Officially began 12 February 1928; concluded 4 August 1928.

2. Movement continued for six months.

3. Action took place in Bardoli *taluka* in Surat district, Bombay Presidency.

Objectives

1. The *immediate*, single objective of the direct action: To persuade the government to launch an impartial enquiry into the enhancement of the land revenue assessment in Bardoli.

2. *Nature of the basic grievance:* Through arbitrary machinery of the Revenue Department, the Bombay government had, in 1927, enhanced the assessment in Bardoli *taluka* by a nominal 22 per cent which, when applied, amounted in some cases to as much as 60 per cent enhancement. (Jurisdiction of the civil courts in matters of revenue assessment had been excluded by a special Act of the Legislature.)

3. *Claims of the Bardoli peasants:*
   a. The rate of enhancement was unjust.
   b. The rate had been established without full and appropriate investigation.

c. The tax official's report was inaccurate.

d. An increase in the tax was unwarranted.

4. *Further implications of the movement:* Though this campaign was limited to the local objective, it was explained by Gandhi that similar conditions existed in other parts of India and that the Bardoli experience would exercise a wide influence. The duty to resist arbitrary unjust levies was a universal duty. "Whatever awakens people to a sense of their wrongs," Gandhi wrote in *Young India* (8 March 1928), "and whatever gives them strength for disciplined and peaceful resistance and habituates them to corporate suffering brings us nearer Swaraj."

Satyagraha Participants and Leadership

1. *Commander of the campaign:* Sardar Vallabhbhai Patel, who was invited by the people to come to Bardoli to lead them in a struggle for redress of their grievances.

2. *Secondary leadership:* Constructive workers including two Muslims who had worked with Gandhi in South Africa. From outside the district also came several women including Parsi from Bombay City.

3. *The role of Gandhi:* Gandhi supported the campaign through his writings in *Young India.* He visited Bardoli six months after satyagraha had been launched and then placed himself under Sardar Patel's command.

4. *Active satyagrahis* ("volunteers"): Numbered about 250 and included Hindus of all and no castes, Muslims, a few Parsis. Several thousand *Kaliparaj* (aboriginals) cooperated with the movement. Women freely participated and led some of the central action.

5. *Sympathizers and cooperators.* Most of the people of the *taluka* (total population was 87,000) ultimately cooperated. Initial reluctance on the part of moneylenders, village headmen, subordinate officials, but later many of these joined the campaign, the officials resigning their positions.

Participants and Leadership of the Opposition

1. *Officials* of the Revenue Department.

2. *Police* of the district re-enforced by contingents of Pathans (Muslims of the North West Frontier Province) brought from Bombay City (described as "strong-arm" men).

3. *The Governor of Bombay* who declared the issue to be: "whether the writ of His Majesty the King-Emperor is to run in a portion of His Majesty's dominions, or whether the edict of some unofficial body of individuals is to be obeyed. That issue . . . is one which Government is prepared to meet with all the power which Government possesses."

Organization and Constructive Program

1. *Nucleus organization:* The four centers of constructive work already established in the *taluka*.

2. *Expanded organization:* With Bardoli village as headquarters, a total of 16 satyagraha camps were established at various villages within the *taluka*.

3. *Publicity office:* From headquarters, a daily news bulletin was issued, as were occasional pamphlets and speeches of Sardar Patel. Initially 5,000 copies were printed at Surat (center of the district) and distributed through the satyagraha organization free of charge to peasants of Bardoli. Later an increase in copies to 14,000 made possible circulation of this publicity to other villages and towns in the province. Paid subscriptions were received from outside the district.

4. *Direction of the campaign:* Instructions to volunteers emanated from headquarters and were carried by satyagrahi messengers.

5. *Constructive work:* Spinning and social welfare activities were continued throughout the campaign, with an emphasis upon the entire khadi program. The wearing of *khadi* was required of satyagrahis and it served as a sort of uniform.

Preparation for Action

1. *Educating the people* in the meaning of the struggle: Speeches by leaders emphasized the need for discipline and preparation to undergo hardship and austerity. Government reaction was expected to be harsh and to include imprisonment and land confiscation.

2. *Using mass media of communication:* Songs about the satyagraha were composed and taught. Mass meetings were held where prayers were recited, satyagraha songs sung, and excerpts from Gandhi's autobiography read.

3. *Eliciting response from villagers:* Signatures were collected to the satyagraha pledge. Efforts were made to convert headmen to the cause by persuading them they should become spokesmen for their respective villages, rather than agents of the government. News bulletins from neighboring *talukas* expressing sympathy and encouragement were circulated.

4. *Anticipating opposition:* Protests were recorded from those refusing to sign the satyagraha pledge. (Later, those who had refused were subjected to social boycott, but care was taken not to deprive them of necessities.) Peasants were prepared to refuse to cultivate lands for any outside purchasers of land which might be forfeited.

Preliminary Action

1. *Opposition to the Revenue Department report* for the *taluka* was expressed from mid-1926. The local Congress Party organization published a critical report to show that peasants could not sustain the enhanced assessments.

2. *Petitioning:* A Committee organized by the Congress waited upon the Revenue Member of the State government early in 1927.

3. *Conference held* in Bardoli, September 1927, unanimously resolved to withhold payment of the enhanced portion of the assessment.

4. *Patel invited to lead satyagraha* following a government order (5 January 1928) to collectors to proceed with collections. Patel examined the entire situation, then accepted presidency of the conference of peasants which met 4 February.

5. *Patel initiated correspondence with the government.* Upon the reply that the government was "not prepared to make any concession," a resolution was adopted (12 February) setting forth the demand for an enquiry and the refusal of the peasants to pay the assessment until the government either accepted the amount of the old assessment as full payment or until an impartial tribunal was appointed to investigate the entire situation.

Action

1. *Noncooperation:* Peasants met revenue collectors with closed doors, or, receiving them, read extracts aloud from Patel's speeches and tried by argument to persuade them that they could not collect the revenue. When police re-enforcements broke down doors and carried away equipment, peasants began to dismantle carts and other equipment, hiding the parts in different places

2. *Technical trespass:* Women volunteers built huts and camped on attached lands. Peasants continued regular sowing despite the change in legal status of land.

3. *Submission to arrest:* Volunteers followed officials everywhere, camping on roads outside official bungalows. When arrested, they were replaced by others "until authorities tired of the process."

4. *Resignation of offices:* Petty village officials were persuaded to resign in protest. Several elected members of the Bombay Legislative Council resigned seats in sympathy.

5. *Protest at the national level:* The President of the Central Legislative Assembly placed the facts before the Viceroy and contributed heavily to satyagraha funds, pledging monthly financial support.

6. *Treatment of the opponents:* Collectors were supplied all needs "at market rates." Continued emphasis upon nonviolence and lack of resentment was urged by Patel, who explained that they could "melt

even the stony heart of an autocratic Commissioner." The quit-rent, which was not subject to enhancement, was paid in full. Leaders urged that the Pathan "strong-arm" police and Muslim officials especially be treated as friends.

7. *Social boycott:* Exercised with restraint. Those discovered seceding from the group were urged to pay "sooner rather than later," whereupon some, instead of paying the revenue, contributed to the satyagraha fund.

8. *Rejection of violent tactics:* Suggestions of erecting barricades along the roads or of puncturing tires were firmly rejected.

9. *Nonpossession used as a tool:* All conveniences were discarded, even brass vessels, with the objective ". . . we will see that Government will have nothing on which they can lay their hands."

10. *Revision of demands:* In July Patel was invited to confer with the Governor. The government insisted upon full payment before agreeing to an enquiry, which might then be conducted by a Revenue officer, possibly together with a Judicial officer. Patel accepted the principle of an official enquiry provided it be judicial in nature and that representatives of the people be invited to give evidence. Additional demands were presented:

    a. Satyagrahi prisoners to be discharged.

    b. Restoration of all forfeited lands.

    c. Payment at market price for confiscated movable property.

    d. Remission of all dismissals and other punishments arising from the struggle.

    Patel reasserted the intention of the satyagrahis to arrive at a solution honorable both to the government and the people.

11. *Agreement reached:* On 4 August, a formula was agreed upon which would meet the satyagrahis' full basic demands yet save face for the government.

Reaction of Opponents

1. *Land seizure:* Widescale attachment of land in payment of revenue. Forfeiture notices reported well above 1,500.

2. *Attachment of movable property:* Police, supported by Pathan reenforcements, forcibly seized personal property, including utensils, cots, carts, buffaloes.

3. *Arrests:* Widescale arrest for obstructing performance of official duties and for criminal trespass.

4. *Violence:* Repeated instances of police violence resulting in personal injury.

5. *Misrepresentation of facts:* Attempts to cajole peasants into paying assessment by saying that a prominent citizen of the village had paid. One case reported of Collector paying the amount himself and pressing the receipt upon a villager in order to use him as an example.

6. *Propaganda against organizers of satyagraha:* Accounts circulated that villagers were terrorized by outside organizers into withholding payment.

7. *Announcement of exemption from delay penalty:* Attempt to obtain payment during later months of campaign by promising exemption from fine if paid within given time.

8. *Issue of counter-propaganda:* The State Information Bureau supplied leaflets, which were distributed under the direction of the District Collector.

9. *Use of minority groups:* Introduction of Muslims as officials and police to split peasants on the basis of religious community; pressure on Parsis and Banias (moneylenders). Banias advised to keep currency notes on hand so that they might be attached, which would, in effect, amount to full payment.

10. *Concessions:* As the campaign proceeded, Pathans were removed from the police forces. Some villages were regrouped with the effect that rates of enhancement were reduced. The demand for an enquiry was finally agreed to upon the undertaking by satyagrahis that conditions of payment would be fulfilled. The wording of the agreement allowed the government to save face.

Results

1. *Enquiry Committee* (known as the Broomfield Committee) was appointed, thus fulfilling the initial single demand of the satyagraha. This Committee investigated conditions in Bardoli and the neighboring *taluka*, Chorasi, from November 1928 to March 1929. Representatives of the villagers were freely heard. The Committee reported that the people "though naturally not lacking in complaints, were entirely lacking in hostility. . . ."

2. *Forfeited lands restored* to their original owners. The District Collector, who had declared that sold lands would never be restored, was replaced by a new Collector who accomplished the restoration of lands.

3. *All satyagrahis taken prisoner were released.*

4. *Subordinate officials who had resigned during the movement were reinstated.*

5. *Assessment revised:* The Enquiry Committee finally recommended an enhancement not to exceed 6¼ per cent. In the final assessment settlement, factors which the Committee had declared itself incompetent to

rule upon were taken into consideration at the insistence of the peasants with the result that virtually no enhancement of revenue was
assessed in Bardoli.

6. *Closer cooperation was established between Hindus and Muslims,*
   moneylenders and peasants, and between other sections of the community. Indeed, the effect extended well beyond Bardoli. As Nehru
   observed, "the real success of their campaign . . . lay in the effect it
   produced amongst the peasantry all over India. Bardoli became a sign
   and a symbol of hope and strength and victory to the Indian peasant."

Notes

[1] The data used in this outline have been abstracted from the following sources: C. F.
Andrews, *Mahatma Gandhi's Ideas* (New York: Macmillan, 1930). Andrews was present
during this struggle and therefore writes as an eyewitness. R. R. Diwakar, *Satyagraha: Its
Technique and History* (Bombay: Hind Kitabs, 1946), p. 115; Richard B. Gregg, *The Power
of Non-Violence* (rev. ed., London: George Routledge and Sons, Ltd., 1938): Files of *Young
India* during the period of the movement; Correspondence exchanged between the author
and the following: The Hon. R. R. Diwakar, Richard R. Keithahn, and Pyarelal (Nayyar).

[2] The data for this outline have been abstracted from the following sources: Mahadev Desai,
The Story of Bardoli: Being a History of the Bardoli Satyagraha of 1928 and Its Sequel
(Ahmedabad: Navajivan, 1929). This intimate record of the Bardoli campaign is credited by
Indian authorities with primary authenticity. Mahadev Desai acted as one of three representatives for the peasants at the time of the Broomfield Committee enquiry which followed the
satyagraha. The appendix to this work includes the following documents which supply fur-
ther critical data: Notification of the Government of Bombay (May 21, 1928) to the occu-
pants of land in Bardoli *taluka* and Valod *mahal*; The reply of Sir Leslie Wilson to K. M.
Munshi (May 29, 1928); Speech of the Governor of Bombay in the Legislative Council (July
23, 1928). Gregg, op. cit.; G. N. Dhawan, *The Political Philosophy of Mahatma Gandhi*
(Bombay: The Popular Book Depot, 1946); Diwakar, op. cit.; B. Pattabhi Sitaramayya, *The
History of the Indian National Congress: (1885–1935)* (Madras: Working Committee of the
Congress, 1935); *The Indian Year Book, 1929*, Sir Stanley Reed, S. T. Sheppard, eds. (Bom-
bay: Bennett, Coleman, 1929); *The Indian Quarterly Register*, Nripendra Nath Mitra, ed.
(Calcutta: Annual Register Office, 1930?), Vol. II, July–December, 1928, Vol. I, January–
June, 1929; *Jawaharlal Nehru: An Autobiography* (London: John Lane, The Bodley Head,
reprint with add. chapter, 1942). See also, *Times of India* for the period March to August
1928 for pro-government and anti-satyagraha opinion on the Bardoli dispute.

ACTIVE NONVIOLENCE

How Transforming Power Was Used in Modern Times—Against Race Prejudice in America

Lawrence S. Apsey

On December 1, 1955, Mrs. Rosa Parks, a black seamstress, was riding home from work on a bus in Montgomery, Alabama. Weary from the day's work, she was sitting in the first seat behind the section reserved for whites. The bus filled up. More white passengers boarded and the bus operator, as required by the segregation laws, ordered her to give her seat to a white man. Quietly, she refused and was thereafter arrested.[1] As news of this incident spread through the black community in Montgomery, the feeling grew that the time had come to protest and it was decided to boycott the buses. The boycott was organized by the civic leaders of the black community in the churches and under the guidance of the ministers. The Montgomery Improvement Association was organized to conduct the struggle and the Rev. Martin Luther King, Jr., was elected president.[2]

At the first mass meeting, King said that while the White Citizens Councils and the Ku Klux Klan were "protesting for the perpetuation of injustice in the community, we are protesting for the birth of justice; . . . in our protest

Source: *Transforming Power for Peace*, by Lawrence S. Apsey, James Bristol, and Karen Eppler (Philadelphia: Religious Education Committee of Friends General Conference, 1986). Reprinted by permission of Lawrence S. Apsey.

there will be no cross burnings. No white person will be taken from his home by a hooded Negro mob and brutally murdered. There will be no threats and intimidation. . . . Our method will be that of persuasion, not coercion . . . we must hear the words of Jesus echoing across the centuries: 'Love your enemies, bless them that curse you, and pray for them that despitefully use you' . . . as Booker T. Washington said, 'Let no man pull you so low as to make you hate him.'" The meeting unanimously passed a resolution calling on the blacks not to resume riding the buses until (1) courteous treatment by the drivers was guaranteed, (2) passengers were seated on a first-come, first-served basis, blacks seating from the back toward the front and whites vice versa, and (3) black bus operators were employed on predominantly black routes.[3]

The boycott was nearly 100% effective from the start. Handbills were circulated and black taxi companies agreed to transport blacks for the price of the bus fare.[4] Opposition measures were increased as the boycott was prolonged. The police commissioner ordered the black cab companies to charge the legal minimum fare of 45¢. Volunteer car pools took the place of cabs.[5] Contributions poured in from all over the world.[6] Meetings were held twice a week for several months, then reduced to once a week. At these meetings King told the people about Gandhi and his philosophy.[7] "The tension in this city is not between white people and Negro people," he said, "the tension is, at bottom, between justice and injustice. . . . We are out to defeat injustice and not white persons who may be unjust."[8] The people responded with amazing ardor.

The authorities held conferences with the blacks, but refused to yield to their demands. The whites spread false rumors about the black leaders.[9] They announced a settlement which had not occurred in the hopes of tricking the blacks back onto the buses.[10] Then they started a "get-tough" policy, consisting of a series of arrests for minor and imaginary traffic violations. King himself was arrested but released when a large crowd collected in front of the jail.[11] A campaign of threatening telephone calls, letters and postcards was intensified. Finally, King's house was bombed. Fortunately, there were no injuries. An angry crowd gathered. Some of the blacks were armed. "If you have weapons, take them home," King told them. "We must meet violence with nonviolence. . . . We must love our white brothers no matter what they do to us."[12]

Two nights later a stick of dynamite was thrown on the lawn of E. D. Nixon.[13] A law against boycotts was discovered, under which more than 100 blacks were indicted, including King.[14] The blacks went voluntarily to the sheriff's office to be arrested. At the trial they testified as to the abuses they had received on the buses. According to the testimony, one man had been shot and killed by a policeman for refusing to leave a bus until he got his fare back. Another, who was blind, had been dragged along the ground when the driver slammed the door on his leg and started the bus; still another had been driven off a bus at the point of a pistol because he did not have the right

En la parte superior

change. Despite the testimony, King was convicted of participating in an illegal boycott and fined $500.[15]

The blacks filed a suit in the Federal Court asking an end to bus segregation on the grounds that it was contrary to the Fourteenth Amendment of the Federal Constitution. The suit was successful, but the City appealed to the Supreme Court.[16] In the meantime, the liability insurance on the cars in the pool was cancelled, but the blacks got new insurance from Lloyd's of London. The City then filed a petition in the State Court to enjoin the operation of the car pools. During the hearing, the news arrived that the Supreme Court had affirmed the order of the Federal Court declaring bus segregation unconstitutional. Nevertheless, the State Court enjoined the motor pool. At a mass meeting, the blacks decided to call off the protest but to refrain from riding the buses until the Supreme Court's mandate reached Alabama.

That night the Ku Klux Klan rode through the black community—the usual signal for blacks to retire and put out their lights. This time the blacks came out on their porches with the lights on and fearlessly watched the ride. A few waved. After several blocks the Klansmen disappeared.[17] They had lost their power to terrify. One cold night a black boy was even seen warming his hands at a burning cross.[18]

A strenuous effort was made to train the blacks how to behave when integrated bus service was resumed. A mimeographed list of 17 suggestions was circulated. Typical of these was the following: "If cursed, do not curse back. If pushed, do not push back. If struck, do not strike back, but evidence love and good will at all times."[19]

On resumption of service, after a few days of peaceful compliance there was a reign of terror. Buses were fired on. A teen-age black girl was beaten by four or five white men. One black woman was shot. The Ku Klux Klan rode again. The houses of two black ministers and four black churches were bombed. The damage to churches was $70,000. All buses were ordered off the streets. The People's Service Station and Cab Stand and the house of a black hospital worker were bombed. Finally, the City began to investigate in earnest. Seven white men were arrested and five indicted. Two signed confessions but were nevertheless acquitted;[20] and the others were set free in an amnesty that cancelled the cases against the blacks arrested under the anti-boycott law.[21] This prosecution, however, effectively stopped the disturbance and desegregation on the buses became an accomplished fact.[22]

The situation was summed up by Martin Luther King in the following words:

> The Negro, once a helpless child, has now grown up politically, culturally and economically. Many white men fear retaliation. The job of the Negro is to show them that they have nothing to fear, that the Negro understands and forgives and is ready to forget the past. He must convince the white man that all he seeks is justice *for both himself and the white man*. A mass movement exercising nonviolence is an object lesson in power under discipline, a demonstration to the white community that

if such a movement attained a degree of strength, it would use its power creatively and not vengefully.[23]

The successful use of nonviolence in Montgomery, Alabama, marked the beginning of this mass movement. During the next thirteen years the civil rights movement would grow to encompass a great variety of nonviolent strategies, to include blacks and whites, to confront the racial oppression in the North as well as in the South.

On February 1st, 1960, four black students in Greensboro, North Carolina, decided that they had wasted too much time talking about injustice. The time had come to do something about it. Of course they knew about Martin Luther King, but when they decided to demand service at Woolworth's "Whites Only" lunch counter they were not thinking about King or even nonviolence. On that first day they were simply trying to dramatize the inequity of segregation. The four entered Woolworth's, and sat down at the lunch counter. The waitress refused to serve them and the students refused to leave. The next day over twenty-five students occupied all the seats at Woolworth's. The sit-in movement grew rapidly. At its height there were over ten thousand people sitting-in at every segregated restaurant and lunch counter in Greensboro. Unwilling to serve blacks and unable to serve whites, management relented and within a year all of Greensboro's theaters and restaurants were desegregated.

By this time nonviolence had become a central part of the sit-in ideology. As Franklin McCain, one of the original students, explained,

> We wanted to make it clear to everybody, that it was a movement that was seeking justice more than anything else and not a movement to start a war. . . . We knew that probably the most powerful and potent weapon that people have literally no defense for is love.[24]

From Greensboro, sit-ins spread all over the South, hitting supermarkets, movie theaters, and any place that practiced segregation. As the presidential elections approached, the sit-ins took on national importance. Martin Luther King participated in the sit-in movement in Atlanta. After King asked to be served at a segregated lunch counter, Dekalb County revoked his probation for a driver's license infraction. For this trivial offense King was placed in a maximum security prison for four months of hard labor. Robert Kennedy asked the judge to reconsider and John Kennedy called Coretta King to express his sympathy. Small things, but significant two weeks before the election. Many claim that Kennedy's victory depended on the support he won from the black population.

The Congress of Racial Equality (CORE) attempted to expand the localized sit-ins into a national movement. With this as his goal, James Farmer led the first Freedom Ride: a bus trip from Washington, D.C., to Jackson, Mississippi, in which the passengers, white and black, consciously violated the segregation laws at every station stop on their journey southward. In theory the Freedom Rides were not much different from the sit-in movement. In practice, however, they were the beginning of a new phase of the civil rights movement.

The violence of the Ku Klux Klan in Montgomery had been sporadic and ineffective in its attempt to intimidate the boycotting blacks. The sit-in movement was met by white stubbornness and anger, but very little violence. Black victories in these campaigns roused white southerners, and as CORE prepared for the ride, southern mobs prepared to meet them. All through May 1961, Freedom Riders boarded buses in Washington. Every few days the buses were ambushed. A white mob in Anniston, Alabama, set fire to one bus. The riders were brought to the local hospital, but the doctors there refused to treat them. The same day another bus of Freedom Riders was attacked in Birmingham. The police of that city promised the KKK that they would allow the mob to beat the riders for fifteen minutes before intervening. In Montgomery this scene of white violence was repeated. The public was so outraged by these stories of white violence that President Kennedy ordered the National Guard to protect the Freedom Riders for the remainder of their journey.[25]

White reaction to the Freedom Rides marked the beginning of an era of white violence and black courage. Television coverage of white cruelty convinced America that the oppression of black Americans was real. Even more dramatic than the mobs which attacked the Freedom Riders was the violence with which southern police met black nonviolent protestors. In Birmingham, Alabama, the movement began as merely another protest against segregation. On April 12th, 1963, Dr. King led a protest march through downtown Birmingham. His arrest produced what has become the most famous document of the civil rights movement: "Letter from Birmingham Jail." In this letter, King explained the principles of nonviolence, and the conditions which made black nonviolent direct action necessary. The police brutality which King experienced inside the jail was only a forewarning of the violence to come. The Southern Christian Leadership Conference (SCLC), led by Dr. King, organized a Children's Crusade in which children would lead the marchers. Police commissioner Eugene "Bull" Connor led his men in attacking the demonstrators. Fire hoses, police dogs, clubbings, were used against men, women and children. Television footage of a huge dog leaping on a little black girl outraged the American public. Birmingham's economic leaders agreed to desegregate the city. The release of this plan marked a major success for the movement and the beginning of retaliatory violence, including the fatal shooting of Medgar Evers and the infamous bombing of the 16th Street Baptist Church in which four black children were killed.

The campaign to desegregate had been largely successful. SCLC and the more radical Student Nonviolent Coordinating Committee (SNCC) decided that the next step should be to insure black voting rights. A march to dramatize the voting rights drive was organized. The demonstrators were to walk from Selma to Montgomery. The marchers, predominantly black, set out. March 7th, 1965, was to become the symbol of police brutality and oppression: "Bloody Sunday." The blacks crossed the bridge leaving Selma. On the other side stood Alabama State Troopers and Jim Clark's police force. The blacks knelt to pray for themselves, and, in the spirit of Transforming Power, for their oppressors. Major Cloud ordered his troops to advance. With tear gas, clubs and horses the troopers turned the quiet rows of praying people into a scene of panic and terror. President Johnson, outraged at this cruelty, submitted a Voting Rights Bill to Congress. Two weeks later Martin Luther King led a march of black people and white people from all over America from Selma to Montgomery where the movement began. The National Guard protected the marchers during their four day journey. This final march was no longer part of a struggle, it was a march of triumph. On August 6th, 1965, President Johnson put his signature on the Voting Rights Act and made it law.

The assassination of Dr. Martin Luther King shocked America. He was a man who used Transforming Power to successfully overcome segregation and voting discrimination. Blacks in America are still not equal citizens, however. The "dream" which Dr. King preached at the March on Washington has still to be fulfilled in the hearts of a large segment of the American public.

Notes

[1] Martin Luther King, Jr., *Stride Toward Freedom* (New York: Harper & Brothers, 1958) cit. Ch. 2, f.n. 5, 43.

[2] Ibid., 56–57.

[3] Ibid., 62–64.

[4] Ibid., 44–49.

[5] Ibid., 76.

[6] Ibid., 80.

[7] Ibid., 85.

[8] Ibid., 103.

[9] Ibid., 122.

[10] Ibid., 124.

[11] Ibid., 126–30.

[12] Ibid., 132–38.

[13] Ibid., 140.

[14] Ibid., 142.

[15] Ibid., 146–49.

[16] Ibid., 151–53.

[17] Ibid., 157–62.

[18] Ibid., 175.

[19] Ibid., 163–65.

[20] Ibid., 174–80.

[21] Ibid., 183.

[22] Ibid., 180.

[23] Ibid., 215.

[24] Howell Raines, *My Soul is Rested* (New York: Bantam Books, 1977), p. 79.

[25] James Peck, *Freedom Ride* (New York: Grove Press, 1962).

Letter from Birmingham Jail*

Martin Luther King, Jr.

April 16, 1963

My Dear Fellow Clergymen:

While confined here in the Birmingham city jail, I came across your recent statement calling my present activities "unwise and untimely." Seldom do I pause to answer criticism of my work and ideas. If I sought to answer all the criticisms that cross my desk, my secretaries would have little time for anything other than such correspondence in the course of the day, and I would have no time for constructive work. But since I feel that you are men of genuine good will and that your criticisms are sincerely set forth, I want to try to answer your statement in what I hope will be patient and reasonable terms.

I think I should indicate why I am here in Birmingham, since you have been influenced by the view which argues against "outsiders coming in." I have the honor of serving as president of the Southern Christian Leadership Conference, an organization operating in every southern state, with headquarters in Atlanta, Georgia. We have some eighty-five affiliated organizations across the South, and one of them is the Alabama Christian Movement for Human Rights. Frequently we share staff, educational and financial resources with our affiliates. Several months ago the affiliate here in Birmingham asked us to be on call to engage in a nonviolent direct-action program if such were deemed necessary. We readily consented, and when the hour came we lived up to our promise. So I, along with several members of

---

*Author's Note: This response to a published statement by eight fellow clergymen from Alabama (Bishop C. C. J. Carpenter, Bishop Joseph A. Durick, Rabbi Hilton L. Grafman, Bishop Paul Hardin, Bishop Holan B. Harmon, the Reverend George M. Murray, the Reverend Edward V. Ramage and the Reverend Earl Stallings) was composed under somewhat constricting circumstances. Begun on the margins of the newspaper in which the statement appeared while I was in jail, the letter was continued on scraps of writing paper supplied by a friendly Negro trusty, and concluded on a pad my attorneys were eventually permitted to leave me. Although the text remains in substance unaltered, I have indulged in the author's prerogative of polishing it for publication.

my staff, am here because I was invited here. I am here because I have organizational ties here.

But more basically, I am in Birmingham because injustice is here. Just as the prophets of the eighth century B.C. left their villages and carried their "thus saith the Lord" far beyond the boundaries of their home towns, and just as the Apostle Paul left his village of Tarsus and carried the gospel of Jesus Christ to the far corners of the Greco-Roman world, so am I compelled to carry the gospel of freedom beyond my own home town. Like Paul, I must constantly respond to the Macedonian call for aid.

Moreover, I am cognizant of the interrelatedness of all communities and states. I cannot sit idly by in Atlanta and not be concerned about what happens in Birmingham. Injustice anywhere is a threat to justice everywhere. We are caught in an inescapable network of mutuality, tied in a single garment of destiny. Whatever affects one directly, affects all indirectly. Never again can we afford to live with the narrow, provincial "outside agitator" idea. Anyone who lives inside the United States can never be considered an outsider anywhere within its bounds.

You deplore the demonstrations taking place in Birmingham. But your statement, I am sorry to say, fails to express a similar concern for the conditions that brought about the demonstrations. I am sure that none of you would want to rest content with the superficial kind of social analysis that deals merely with effects and does not grapple with underlying causes. It is unfortunate that demonstrations are taking place in Birmingham, but it is even more unfortunate that the city's white power structure left the Negro community with no alternative.

In any nonviolent campaign there are four basic steps: collection of the facts to determine whether injustices exist; negotiation; self-purification; and direct action. We have gone through all these steps in Birmingham. There can be no gainsaying the fact that racial injustice engulfs this community. Birmingham is probably the most thoroughly segregated city in the United States. Its ugly record of brutality is widely known. Negroes have experienced grossly unjust treatment in the courts. There have been more unsolved bombings of Negro homes and churches in Birmingham than in any other city in the nation. These are the hard, brutal facts of the case. On the basis of these conditions, Negro leaders sought to negotiate with the city fathers. But the latter consistently refused to engage in good-faith negotiation.

Then, last September, came the opportunity to talk with leaders of Birmingham's economic community. In the course of the negotiations, certain promises were made by the merchants—for example, to remove the stores' humiliating racial signs. On the basis of these promises, the Reverend Fred Shuttlesworth and the leaders of the Alabama Christian Movement for Human Rights agreed to a moratorium on all demonstrations. As the weeks and months went by, we realized that we were the victims of a broken promise. A few signs, briefly removed, returned; the others remained.

As in so many past experiences, our hopes had been blasted, and the shadow of deep disappointment settled upon us. We had no alternative except to prepare for direct action, whereby we would present our very bodies as a means of laying our case before the conscience of the local and the national community. Mindful of the difficulties involved, we decided to undertake a process of self-purification. We began a series of workshops on nonviolence, and we repeatedly asked ourselves: "Are you able to accept blows without retaliating?" "Are you able to endure the ordeal of jail?" We decided to schedule our direct-action program for the Easter season, realizing that except for Christmas, this is the main shopping period of the year. Knowing that a strong economic-withdrawal program would be the by-product of direct action, we felt that this would be the best time to bring pressure to bear on the merchants for the needed change.

Then it occurred to us that Birmingham's mayoralty election was coming up in March, and we speedily decided to postpone action until after election day. When we discovered that the Commissioner of Public Safety, Eugene "Bull" Connor, had piled up enough votes to be in the run-off, we decided again to postpone action until the day after the run-off so that the demonstrations could not be used to cloud the issues. Like many others, we waited to see Mr. Connor defeated, and to this end we endured postponement after postponement. Having aided in this community need, we felt that our direct-action program could be delayed no longer.

You may well ask: "Why direct action? Why sit-ins, marches and so forth? Isn't negotiation a better path?" You are quite right in calling for negotiation. Indeed, this is the very purpose of direct action. Nonviolent direct action seeks to create such a crisis and foster such a tension that a community which has constantly refused to negotiate is forced to confront the issue. It seeks so to dramatize the issue that it can no longer be ignored. My citing the creation of tension as part of the work of the nonviolent-resister may sound rather shocking. But I must confess that I am not afraid of the word "tension." I have earnestly opposed violent tension, but there is a type of constructive, nonviolent tension which is necessary for growth. Just as Socrates felt that it was necessary to create a tension in the mind so that individuals could rise from the bondage of myths and half-truths to the unfettered realm of creative analysis and objective appraisal, so must we see the need for non-violent gadflies to create the kind of tension in society that will help men rise from the dark depths of prejudice and racism to the majestic heights of understanding and brotherhood.

The purpose of our direct-action program is to create a situation so crisis-packed that it will inevitably open the door to negotiation. I therefore concur with you in your call for negotiation. Too long has our beloved Southland been bogged down in a tragic effort to live in monologue rather than dialogue.

One of the basic points in your statement is that the action that I and my associates have taken in Birmingham is untimely. Some have asked: "Why didn't you give the new city administration time to act?" The only answer that I can give to this query is that the new Birmingham administration must be prodded about as much as the outgoing one, before it will act. We are sadly mistaken if we feel that the election of Albert Boutwell as mayor will bring the millennium to Birmingham. While Mr. Boutwell is a much more gentle person than Mr. Connor, they are both segregationists, dedicated to maintenance of the status quo. I have hope that Mr. Boutwell will be reasonable enough to see the futility of massive resistance to desegregation. But he will not see this without pressure from devotees of civil rights. My friends, I must say to you that we have not made a single gain in civil rights without determined legal and nonviolent pressure. Lamentably, it is an historical fact that privileged groups seldom give up their privileges voluntarily. Individuals may see the moral light and voluntarily give up their unjust posture; but, as Reinhold Niebuhr has reminded us, groups tend to be more immoral than individuals.

We know through painful experience that freedom is never voluntarily given by the oppressor; it must be demanded by the oppressed. Frankly, I have yet to engage in a direct-action campaign that was "well timed" in the view of those who have not suffered unduly from the disease of segregation. For years now I have heard the word "Wait!" It rings in the ear of every Negro with piercing familiarity. This "Wait" has almost always meant "Never." We must come to see, with one of our distinguished jurists, that "justice too long delayed is justice denied."

We have waited for more than 340 years for our constitutional and God-given rights. The nations of Asia and Africa are moving with jetlike speed toward gaining political independence, but we still creep at horse-and-buggy pace toward gaining a cup of coffee at a lunch counter. Perhaps it is easy for those who have never felt the stinging darts of segregation to say, "Wait." But when you have seen vicious mobs lynch your mothers and fathers at will and drown your sisters and brothers at whim; when you have seen hate-filled policemen curse, kick and even kill your black brothers and sisters; when you see the vast majority of your twenty million Negro brothers smothering in an airtight cage of poverty in the midst of an affluent society; when you suddenly find your tongue twisted and your speech stammering as you seek to explain to your six-year-old daughter why she can't go to the public amusement park that has just been advertised on television, and see tears welling up in her eyes when she is told that Funtown is closed to colored children, and see ominous clouds of inferiority beginning to form in her little mental sky, and see her beginning to distort her personality by developing an unconscious bitterness toward white people; when you have to concoct an answer for a five-year-old son who is asking: "Daddy, why do white people treat colored people so mean?"; when you take a cross-country drive and find it necessary to sleep night after night in the uncomfortable corners of your automobile because no motel will accept you; when you are humiliated day in and day out by nagging signs reading "white" and "colored"; when your first name becomes "nigger," your middle name becomes "boy" (however old you are) and your last name becomes "John," and your wife and mother are never given the respected title "Mrs."; when you are harried by day and haunted by night by the fact that you are a Negro, living constantly at tiptoe stance, never quite knowing what to expect next, and are plagued with inner fears and outer resentments; when you are forever fighting a degenerating sense of "nobodiness"—then you will understand why we find it difficult to wait. There comes a time when the cup of endurance runs over, and men are no longer willing to be plunged into the abyss of despair. I hope, sirs, you can understand our legitimate and unavoidable impatience.

You express a great deal of anxiety over our willingness to break laws. This is certainly a legitimate concern. Since we so diligently urge people to obey the Supreme Court's decision of 1954 outlawing segregation in the public schools, at first glance it may seem rather paradoxical for us consciously to break laws. One may well ask: "How can you advocate breaking some laws and obeying others?" The answer lies in the fact that there are two types of laws: just and unjust. I would be the first to advocate obeying just laws. One has not only a legal but a moral responsibility to obey just laws. Conversely, one has a moral responsibility to disobey unjust laws. I would agree with St. Augustine that "an unjust law is no law at all."

Now, what is the difference between the two? How does one determine whether a law is just or unjust? A just law is a man-made code that squares with the moral law or the law of God. An unjust law is a code that is out of harmony with the moral law. To put it in the terms of St. Thomas Aquinas: An unjust law is a human law that is not rooted in eternal law and natural law. Any law that uplifts human personality is just. Any law that degrades human personality is unjust. All segregation statutes are unjust because segregation distorts the soul and damages the personality. It gives the segregator a false sense of superiority and the segregated a false sense of inferiority. Segregation, to use the terminology of the Jewish philosopher Martin Buber, substitutes an "I–it" relationship for an "I–thou" relationship and ends up relegating persons to the status of things. Hence segregation is not only politically, economically and sociologically unsound, it is morally wrong and sinful. Paul Tillich has said that sin is separation. Is not segregation an existential expression of man's tragic separation, his awful estrangement, his terrible sinfulness? Thus it is that I can urge men to obey the 1954 decision of the Supreme Court, for it is morally right; and I can urge them to disobey segregation ordinances, for they are morally wrong.

Let us consider a more concrete example of just and unjust laws. An unjust law is a code that a numerical or power majority group compels a minority group to obey but does not make binding on itself. This is *difference* made legal. By the same token, a just law is a code that a majority compels a minority to follow and that it is willing to follow itself. This is *sameness* made legal.

Let me give another explanation. A law is unjust if it is inflicted on a minority that, as a result of being denied the right to vote, had no part in enacting or devising the law. Who can say that the legislature of Alabama which set up that state's segregation laws was democratically elected? Throughout Alabama all sorts of devious methods are used to prevent

Negroes from becoming registered voters, and there are some counties in which, even though Negroes constitute a majority of the population, not a single Negro is registered. Can any law enacted under such circumstances be considered democratically structured?

Sometimes a law is just on its face and unjust in its application. For instance, I have been arrested on a charge of parading without a permit. Now, there is nothing wrong in having an ordinance which requires a permit for a parade. But such an ordinance becomes unjust when it is used to maintain segregation and to deny citizens the First-Amendment privilege of peaceful assembly and protest.

I hope you are able to see the distinction I am trying to point out. In no sense do I advocate evading or defying the law, as would the rabid segregationist. That would lead to anarchy. One who breaks an unjust law must do so openly, lovingly, and with a willingness to accept the penalty. I submit that an individual who breaks a law that conscience tells him is unjust, and who willingly accepts the penalty of imprisonment in order to arouse the conscience of the community over its injustice, is in reality expressing the highest respect for law.

Of course, there is nothing new about this kind of civil disobedience. It was evidenced sublimely in the refusal of Shadrach, Meshach and Abednego to obey the laws of Nebuchadnezzar, on the ground that a higher moral law was at stake. It was practiced superbly by the early Christians, who were willing to face hungry lions and the excruciating pain of chopping blocks rather than submit to certain unjust laws of the Roman Empire. To a degree, academic freedom is a reality today because Socrates practiced civil disobedience. In our own nation, the Boston Tea Party represented a massive act of civil disobedience.

We should never forget that everything Adolf Hitler did in Germany was "legal" and everything the Hungarian freedom fighters did in Hungary was "illegal." It was "illegal" to aid and comfort a Jew in Hitler's Germany. Even so, I am sure that, had I lived in Germany at the time, I would have aided and comforted my Jewish brothers. If today I lived in a Communist country where certain principles dear to the Christian faith are suppressed, I would openly advocate disobeying that country's antireligious laws.

I must make two honest confessions to you, my Christian and Jewish brothers. First, I must confess that over the past few years I have been gravely disappointed with the white moderate. I have almost reached the regrettable conclusion that the Negro's great stumbling block in his stride toward freedom is not the White Citizen's Counciler or the Ku Klux Klanner, but the white moderate, who is more devoted to "order" than to justice; who prefers a negative peace which is the absence of tension to a positive peace which is the presence of justice; who constantly says: "I agree with you in the goal you seek, but I cannot agree with your methods of direct action"; who paternalistically believes he can set the timetable for another man's freedom; who lives by a mythical concept of time and who constantly advises the

Negro to wait for a "more convenient season." Shallow understanding from people of good will is more frustrating than absolute misunderstanding from people of ill will. Lukewarm acceptance is much more bewildering than outright rejection.

I had hoped that the white moderate would understand that law and order exist for the purpose of establishing justice and that when they fail in this purpose they become the dangerously structured dams that block the flow of social progress. I had hoped that the white moderate would understand that the present tension in the South is a necessary phase of the transition from an obnoxious negative peace, in which the Negro passively accepted his unjust plight, to a substantive and positive peace, in which all men will respect the dignity and worth of human personality. Actually, we who engage in nonviolent direct action are not the creators of tension. We merely bring to the surface the hidden tension that is already alive. We bring it out in the open, where it can be seen and dealt with. Like a boil that can never be cured so long as it is covered up but must be opened with all its ugliness to the natural medicines of air and light, injustice must be exposed, with all the tension its exposure creates, to the light of human conscience and the air of national opinion before it can be cured.

In your statement you assert that our actions, even though peaceful, must be condemned because they precipitate violence. But is this a logical assertion? Isn't this like condemning a robbed man because his possession of money precipitated the evil act of robbery? Isn't this like condemning Socrates because his unswerving commitment to truth and his philosophical inquiries precipitated the act by the misguided populace in which they made him drink hemlock? Isn't this like condemning Jesus because his unique God-consciousness and never-ceasing devotion to God's will precipitated the evil act of crucifixion? We must come to see that, as the federal courts have consistently affirmed, it is wrong to urge an individual to cease his efforts to gain his basic constitutional rights because the quest may precipitate violence. Society must protect the robbed and punish the robber.

I had also hoped that the white moderate would reject the myth concerning time in relation to the struggle for freedom. I have just received a letter from a white brother in Texas. He writes: "All Christians know that the colored people will receive equal rights eventually, but it is possible that you are in too great a religious hurry. It has taken Christianity almost two thousand years to accomplish what it has. The teachings of Christ take time to come to earth." Such an attitude stems from a tragic misconception of time, from the strangely irrational notion that there is something in the very flow of time that will inevitably cure all ills. Actually, time itself is neutral; it can be used either destructively or constructively. More and more I feel that the people of ill will have used time much more effectively than have the people of good will. We will have to repent in this generation not merely for the hateful words and actions of the bad people but for the appalling silence of the good people. Human progress never rolls in on wheels of inevitability; it comes through the tireless efforts of men willing to be coworkers with God, and without this hard work, time itself becomes an ally of the forces of social stagnation. We must use time creatively, in the knowledge that the time is always ripe to do right. Now is the time to make real the promise of democracy and transform our pending national elegy into a creative psalm of brotherhood. Now is the time to lift our national policy from the quicksand of racial injustice to the solid rock of human dignity.

You speak of our activity in Birmingham as extreme. At first I was rather disappointed that fellow clergymen would see my nonviolent efforts as those of an extremist. I began thinking about the fact that I stand in the middle of two opposing forces in the Negro community. One is a force of complacency, made up in part of Negroes who, as a result of long years of oppression, are so drained of self-respect and a sense of "somebodiness" that they have adjusted to segregation; and in part of a few middle-class Negroes who, because of a degree of academic and economic security and because in some ways they profit by segregation, have become insensitive to the problems of the masses. The other force is one of bitterness and hatred, and it comes perilously close to advocating violence. It is expressed in the various black nationalist groups that are springing up across the nation, the largest and best-known being Elijah Muhammad's Muslim movement. Nourished by the Negro's frustration over the continued existence of racial discrimination, this movement is made up of people who have lost faith in America, who have absolutely repudiated Christianity, and who have concluded that the white man is an incorrigible "devil."

I have tried to stand between these two forces, saying that we need emulate neither the "do-nothingism" of the complacent nor the hatred and despair of the black nationalist. For there is the more excellent way of love and nonviolent protest. I am grateful to God that, through the influence of the Negro church, the way of nonviolence became an integral part of our struggle.

If this philosophy had not emerged, by now many streets of the South would, I am convinced, be flowing with blood. And I am further convinced that if our white brothers dismiss as "rabble-rousers" and "outside agitators" those of us who employ nonviolent direct action, and if they refuse to support our nonviolent efforts, millions of Negroes will, out of frustration and despair, seek solace and security in black-nationalist ideologies—a development that would inevitably lead to a frightening racial nightmare.

Oppressed people cannot remain oppressed forever. The yearning for freedom eventually manifests itself, and that is what has happened to the American Negro. Something within has reminded him of his birthright of freedom, and something without has reminded him that it can be gained. Consciously or unconsciously, he has been caught up by the *Zeitgeist*, and with his black brothers of Africa and his brown and yellow brothers of Asia, South America and the Caribbean, the United States Negro is moving with a sense of great urgency toward the promised land of racial justice. If one recognizes this vital urge that has engulfed the Negro community, one should readily understand why public demonstrations are taking place. The Negro has many pent-up resentments and latent frustrations, and he must release them. So let him march; let him make prayer pilgrimages to the city hall; let him go on freedom rides—and try to understand why he must do so. If his repressed emotions are not released in nonviolent ways, they will seek expression through violence; this is not a threat but a fact of history. So I have not said to my people: "Get rid of your discontent." Rather, I have tried to say that this normal and healthy discontent can be channeled into the creative outlet of nonviolent direct action. And now this approach is being termed extremist.

But though I was initially disappointed at being categorized as an extremist, as I continued to think about the matter I gradually gained a measure of satisfaction from the label. Was not Jesus an extremist for love: "Love your enemies, bless them that curse you, do good to them that hate you, and pray for them which despitefully use you, and persecute you." Was not Amos an extremist for justice: "Let justice roll down like waters and righteousness like an ever-flowing stream." Was not Paul an extremist for the Christian gospel: "I bear in my body the marks of the Lord Jesus." Was not Martin Luther an extremist: "Here I stand; I cannot do otherwise, so help me God." And John Bunyan: "I will stay in jail to the end of my days before I make a butchery of my conscience." And Abraham Lincoln: "This nation cannot survive half slave and half free." And Thomas Jefferson: "We hold these truths to be self-evident, that all men are created equal. . . ." So the question is not whether we will be extremists, but what kind of extremists we will be. Will we be extremists for hate or for love? Will we be extremists for the preservation of injustice or for the extension of justice? In that dramatic scene on Calvary's hill three men were crucified. We must never forget that all three were crucified for the same crime—the crime of extremism. Two were extremists for immorality, and thus fell below their environment. The other, Jesus Christ, was an extremist for love, truth and goodness, and thereby rose above his environment. Perhaps the South, the nation and the world are in dire need of creative extremists.

I had hoped that the white moderate would see this need. Perhaps I was too optimistic; perhaps I expected too much. I suppose I should have realized that few members of the oppressor race can understand the deep groans and passionate yearnings of the oppressed race, and still fewer have the vision to see that injustice must be rooted out by strong, persistent and determined action. I am thankful, however, that some of our white brothers in the South have grasped the meaning of this social revolution and committed themselves to it. They are still all too few in quantity, but they are big in quality. Some—such as Ralph McGill, Lillian Smith, Harry Golden, James McBride Dabbs, Ann Braden and Sarah Patton Boyle—have written about our struggle in eloquent and prophetic terms. Others have marched with us down nameless streets of the South. They have languished in filthy, roach-infested jails, suffering the abuse and brutality of policemen who view them as "dirty niggerlovers." Unlike so many of their moderate brothers and sisters, they have recognized the urgency of the moment and sensed the need for powerful "action" antidotes to combat the disease of segregation.

Let me take note of my other major disappointment. I have been so greatly disappointed with the white church and its leadership. Of course, there are some notable exceptions. I am not unmindful of the fact that each of you has taken some significant stands on this issue. I commend you, Reverend Stallings, for your Christian stand on this past Sunday, in welcoming Negroes to your worship service on a nonsegregated basis. I commend the Catholic leaders of this state for integrating Spring Hill College several years ago.

But despite these notable exceptions, I must honestly reiterate that I have been disappointed with the church. I do not say this as one of those negative critics who can always find something wrong with the church. I say this as a minister of the gospel, who loves the church; who was nurtured in its bosom; who has been sustained by its spiritual blessings and who will remain true to it as long as the cord of life shall lengthen.

When I was suddenly catapulted into the leadership of the bus protest in Montgomery, Alabama, a few years ago, I felt we would be supported by the white church. I felt that the white ministers, priests and rabbis of the South would be among our strongest allies. Instead, some have been outright opponents, refusing to understand the freedom movement and misrepresenting its leaders; all too many others have been more cautious than courageous and have remained silent behind the anesthetizing security of stained-glass windows.

In spite of my shattered dreams, I came to Birmingham with the hope that the white religious leadership of this community would see the justice of our cause and, with deep moral concern, would serve as the channel through which our just grievances could reach the power structure. I had hoped that each of you would understand. But again I have been disappointed.

I have heard numerous southern religious leaders admonish their worshipers to comply with a desegregation decision because it is the law, but I have longed to hear white ministers declare: "Follow this decree because integration is morally right and because the Negro is your brother." In the midst of blatant injustices inflicted upon the Negro, I have watched white churchmen stand on the sideline and mouth pious irrelevancies and sanctimonious trivialities. In the midst of a mighty struggle to rid our nation of racial and economic injustice, I have heard many ministers say: "Those are social issues, with which the gospel has no real concern." And I have watched many churches commit themselves to a completely otherworldly religion which makes a strange, un-Biblical distinction between body and soul, between the sacred and the secular.

I have traveled the length and breadth of Alabama, Mississippi and all the other southern states. On sweltering summer days and crisp autumn mornings I have looked at the South's beautiful churches with their lofty spires pointing heavenward. I have beheld the impressive outlines of her massive religious-education buildings. Over and over I have found myself asking: "What kind of people worship here? Who is their God? Where were their voices when the lips of Governor Barnett dripped with words of interposition and nullification? Where were they when Governor Wallace gave a clarion call for defiance and hatred? Where were their voices of support when bruised and weary Negro men and women decided to rise from the dark dungeons of complacency to the bright hills of creative protest?"

Yes, these questions are still in my mind. In deep disappointment I have wept over the laxity of the church. But be assured that my tears have been tears of love. There can be no deep disappointment where there is not deep love. Yes, I love the church. How could I do otherwise? I am in the rather unique position of being the son, the grandson and the great-grandson of preachers. Yes, I see the church as the body of Christ. But, oh! How we have blemished and scarred that body through social neglect and through fear of being nonconformists.

There was a time when the church was very powerful—in the time when the early Christians rejoiced at being deemed worthy to suffer for what they believed. In those days the church was not merely a thermometer that recorded the ideas and principles of popular opinion; it was a thermostat that transformed the mores of society. Whenever the early Christians entered a town, the people in power became disturbed and immediately sought to convict the Christians for being "disturbers of the peace" and "outside agitators." But the Christians pressed on, in the conviction that they were "a colony of heaven," called to obey God rather than man. Small in number, they were big in commitment. They were too God-intoxicated to be "astronomically intimidated." By their effort and example they brought an end to such ancient evils as infanticide and gladiatorial contests.

Things are different now. So often the contemporary church is a weak, ineffectual voice with an uncertain sound. So often it is an archdefender of the status quo. Far from being disturbed by the presence of the church, the power structure of the average community is consoled by the church's silent—and often even vocal—sanction of things as they are.

But the judgment of God is upon the church as never before. If today's church does not recapture the sacrificial spirit of the early church, it will lose its authenticity, forfeit the loyalty of millions, and be dismissed as an irrelevant social club with no meaning for the twentieth century. Every day I meet young people whose disappointment with the church has turned into outright disgust.

Perhaps I have once again been too optimistic. Is organized religion too inextricably bound to the status quo to save our nation and the world? Perhaps I must turn my faith to the inner spiritual church, the church within the church, as the true *ekklesia* and the hope of the world. But again I am thankful to God that some noble souls from the ranks of organized religion have broken loose from the paralyzing chains of conformity and joined us as active partners in the struggle for freedom. They have left their secure congregations and walked the streets of Albany, Georgia, with us. They have gone down the highways of the South on tortuous rides for freedom. Yes, they have gone to jail with us. Some have been dismissed from their churches, have lost the support of their bishops and fellow ministers. But they have acted in the faith that right defeated is stronger than evil triumphant. Their witness has been the spiritual salt that has preserved the true meaning of the gospel in these troubled times. They have carved a tunnel of hope through the dark mountain of disappointment.

I hope the church as a whole will meet the challenge of this decisive hour. But even if the church does not come to the aid of justice, I have no despair about the future. I have no fear about the outcome of our struggle in Birmingham, even if our motives are at present misunderstood. We will reach the goal of freedom in Birmingham and all over the nation, because the goal of America is freedom. Abused and scorned though we may be, our destiny is tied up with America's destiny. Before the pilgrims landed at Plymouth, we were here. Before the pen of Jefferson etched the majestic words of the Declaration of Independence across the pages of history, we were here. For more than two centuries our forebears labored in this country without wages; they made cotton king; they built the homes of their masters while suffering gross injustice and shameful humiliation—and yet out of a bottomless vitality they continued to thrive and develop. If the inexpressible cruelties of slavery could not stop us, the opposition we now face will surely fail. We will win our freedom because the sacred heritage of our nation and the eternal will of God are embodied in our echoing demands.

Before closing I feel impelled to mention one other point in your statement that has troubled me profoundly. You warmly commended the Birmingham police force for keeping "order" and "preventing violence." I doubt that you would have so warmly commended the police force if you had seen its dogs sinking their teeth into unarmed, nonviolent Negroes. I doubt that you would so quickly commend the policemen if you were to observe their ugly and inhumane treatment of Negroes here in the city jail; if you were to watch them push and curse old Negro women and young Negro girls; if you were to see them slap and kick old Negro men and young boys; if you were to observe them, as they did on two occasions, refuse to give us food because we wanted to sing our grace together. I cannot join you in your praise of the Birmingham police department.

It is true that the police have exercised a degree of discipline in handling the demonstrators. In this sense they have conducted themselves rather "nonviolently" in public. But for what purpose? To preserve the evil system of segregation. Over the past few years I have consistently preached that nonviolence demands that the means we use must be as pure as the ends we seek. I have tried to make clear that it is wrong to use immoral means to attain moral ends. But now I must affirm that it is just as wrong, or perhaps even more so, to use moral means to preserve immoral ends. Perhaps Mr. Connor and his policemen have been rather nonviolent in public, as was Chief Pritchett in Albany, Georgia, but they have used the moral means of nonviolence to maintain the immoral end of racial injustice. As T. S. Eliot has said: "The last temptation is the greatest treason: To do the right deed for the wrong reason."

I wish you had commended the Negro sit-inners and demonstrators of Birmingham for their sublime courage, their willingness to suffer and their amazing discipline in the midst of great provocation. One day the South will recognize its real heroes. They will be the James Merediths, with the noble sense of purpose that enables them to face jeering and hostile mobs, and with the agonizing loneliness that characterizes the life of the pioneer. They will be old, oppressed, battered Negro women, symbolized in a seventy-two-year-old woman in Montgomery, Alabama, who rose up with a sense of dignity and with her people decided not to ride segregated buses, and who responded with ungrammatical profundity to one who inquired about her weariness: "My feets is tired, but my soul is at rest." They will be the young high school and college students, the young ministers of the gospel and a host of their elders, courageously and nonviolently sitting in at lunch counters and willingly going to jail for conscience' sake. One day the South will know that when these disinherited children of God sat down at lunch counters, they were in reality standing up for what is best in the American dream and for the most sacred values in our Judaeo-Christian heritage, thereby bringing our nation back to those great wells of democracy which were dug deep by the founding fathers in their formulation of the Constitution and the Declaration of Independence.

Never before have I written so long a letter. I'm afraid it is much too long to take your precious time. I can assure you that it would have been much shorter if I had been writing from a comfortable desk, but what else can one do when he is alone in a narrow jail cell, other than write long letters, think long thoughts and pray long prayers?

If I have said anything in this letter that overstates the truth and indicates an unreasonable impatience, I beg you to forgive me. If I have said anything that understates the truth and indicates my having a patience that allows me to settle for anything less than brotherhood, I beg God to forgive me.

I hope this letter finds you strong in the faith. I also hope that circumstances will soon make it possible for me to meet each of you, not as an integrationist or a civil-rights leader but as a fellow clergyman and a Christian brother. Let us all hope that the dark clouds of racial prejudice will soon pass away and the deep fog of misunderstanding will be lifted from our fear-drenched communities, and in some not too distant tomorrow the radiant stars of love and brotherhood will shine over our great nation with all their scintillating beauty.

> Yours for the cause of
> Peace and Brotherhood,
> Martin Luther King, Jr.

PART THREE

WOMEN AND NONVIOLENCE

Preview

A Soviet academic, talking with a group of American scholars shortly after the full impact of *glasnost* (openness) had become felt in Moscow academic circles, remarked that Soviet professors were now having to become students. The past, which had for so long been carefully guarded and only selectively revealed in accordance with the wishes of the Soviet leadership, had suddenly opened up, and professors were having to learn anew a history they had thought they understood.

Something not unlike that has happened in the United States with regard to the accomplishments of women. Owing to the movement for women's liberation, an awakening is gradually taking place in regard to the role of women, both in the history of this country and throughout history in general.

The problem here, however, is not like the case of the Soviet Union; it has not been that of officially restricted freedom of speech, expression, and inquiry. In principle, people have had the freedom to explore and learn about the role of women in any way they chose. The constraints have been those of attitudes and ignorance rather than the whims of censors, but the limits they impose are perhaps more effective. If an individual, group, or agency is known to restrict freedom of expression and inquiry, there will always be some who will oppose such obvious curtailment of basic rights. But when the right is there and expressly enshrined in a constitution and continually flaunted in the rhetoric of officials and politicians, the attitudes that prevent its exercise become even more insidious than heavy-handed government censorship. Under totalitarian regimes people know things are bad and know who is responsible. In societies that practice discrimination people often do not even realize how bad things are, and so it never occurs to them to ask who is responsible.

So we need to begin to learn anew certain areas of our moral, cultural, and intellectual heritage and to recognize the centrality of women to so much of it.

One obstacle to doing this in the area of nonviolence is the predictable fact that one of the effects of the subordination of women has been that works by them constitute a disproportionately small portion of the writings on nonviolence. Tolstoy had the leisure time to devote to writing, and he also had women—his wife primarily, and a daughter—to spend endless hours transcribing what he wrote. Gandhi was able to study in England and earn a law degree and travel to South Africa, opportunities that were open to him as a man and that figured incalculably in the development of his commitment to nonviolence. Although he says that he learned nonviolence from his wife, we today hear of him, not her. Even Martin Luther King, Jr., though growing up under the inestimable burden of being African American in a society steeped in racial prejudice, was relatively privileged by comparison with other African Americans and especially by comparison with African American women. Even though it was women who were preeminently responsible for the success of the Montgomery bus boycott that began the civil rights movement, it is primarily King whom we associate with that success.

A second obstacle is the fact that, because women were confined to the home and to roles as wives and mothers, much of the caring and loving to which they were devoted (qualities ingredient in the deepest commitments to nonviolence, whether or not they ever evolve into such a commitment) has escaped the notice of history. History is written in broad brush strokes. It is the measurable, quantifiable events that command attention, particularly wars and revolutions. Even much of the study of society today is of that sort. This means that quiet strength, courage, and compassion—qualities that many people display in their personal lives in ways that are known only to a few friends or family—usually do not get recorded. When these are the primary moral excellences allowed expression in the lives of a whole group of people, the accomplishments of those people will almost certainly go unheralded.

Phillip Hallie, in a moving account of the nonviolent action by the citizens of a small French village to save Jewish children and adults from the Nazis during World War II, beams a small ray of recognition into the courageous lives of a few people that history would otherwise have largely ignored. And, not surprisingly, it is women whom one sees playing a central role:

The struggle in Le Chambon began and ended in the privacy of people's homes. Decisions that were turning points in that struggle took place in kitchens, and not with male leaders as the only decision-makers, but often with women centrally involved. A kitchen is a private, intimate place; in it there are no uniforms, no buttons or badges symbolizing public duty of public support. In the kitchen of a modest home only a few people are involved. In Le Chambon only the lives of a few thousand people were changed, compared to the scores of millions of human lives directly affected by the larger events of World War II. (Hallie 1979:8–9)

The role of women in nonviolence almost certainly has not been less than that of men. It may even have been more. But it is one that almost certainly will in large measure never be known, which makes its inclusion here all the more important.

The selections that follow begin with an account by David Daube of women confronting established power and male supremacy in the literature of the ancient world. While theirs are primarily acts of civil disobedience rather than commitments to nonviolence per se, they nonetheless symbolize nonviolent ways of responding to injustice or dealing with conflict. The depiction of the fictional Antigone belongs beside that of the historical Socrates as a representation of the strength of individual conviction confronting established authority. In her essay on nonviolence and women, Margaret Hope Bacon, a Quaker and author of several books including *The Way Opens: The Story of Quaker Women in America*, depicts the visible but neglected role of women, particularly Lucretia Mott, in the moral awakening of America in the nineteenth century.

In Barbara Deming (1917–1984) we encounter militant nonviolence geared to the crises of Vietnam and the nuclear age. She was in the forefront of the antiwar movement and an editor of, and frequent contributor to, the radical magazine *Liberation*. She traveled to Vietnam with A. J. Muste in 1966 only to be deported by the Saigon government for her protest activities. As a lesbian, she was committed to the liberation of women, not only socially and politically but sexually as well.

Liane Ellison Norman, a Quaker and founder of the Pittsburgh Peace Institute, draws a portrait of Molly Rush, a wife and mother whose clear vision, unencumbered by complex arguments and statistics about throw-weight and payloads, led her to perform civil disobedience with seven other people in protest against the nuclear arms race. The "plowshares eight," as they were called, included Father Daniel Berrigan, Phillip Berrigan, Dean Hammer, Father Carl Kabat, Elmer Maas, Sister Anne Montgomery, and John Schuchardt. This group entered a General Electric plant in Pennsylvania and took hammers to the nose cones of the nuclear warheads being produced there. It was Rush's understanding of her role as a mother that directed her to do this. And while her action led her out of the home and into prison, it is Norman's account, like that of Phillip Hallie and the people of Le Chambon, that preserves for us this story of courage and commitment.

Finally, Sara Ruddick paints a picture of the nature of nonviolence by examining the ways in which mothers ideally address conflict in their lives. She considers four ideals of nonviolence in particular, and her examination makes clear that nonviolence is practiced in a world where the perfect is not always possible. People do the best they can under the circumstances, and maternal nonviolence can teach us much about how to implement ideals in a less-than-perfect world.

In Part Four, we will see how such ideals have been applied to the issue of war.

Reference

Hallie, Phillip. 1979. *Lest Innocent Blood Be Shed*. New York: Harper Colophon.

The Women of the Bible and Greece

David Daube

1

I ought to begin by saying what I mean by civil disobedience of women in antiquity. I guess I may dispense with a definition of women, though I admit that ever since the recent litigation, Corbett vs. Corbett, alias Ashley, in London, I am no longer so certain of my standing in this matter. By antiquity I mean the Jewish-Greek-Hellenistic-Roman world up to the end of Justinian in the sixth century.

It is more difficult to define civil disobedience. I am not concerned with any unfriendly response like a refusal to be taken out, but only with such behaviour as contravenes the law, or at any rate, deep-rooted custom. Furthermore, I exclude purely selfish actions performed in the hope of remaining undetected; for example, theft of a purse inadvertently left behind in the lecture room. I shall confine myself to offences committed openly, maybe by way of demonstration, in a higher cause or a cause thought to be higher. In this sense it would be civil disobedience, say, if a utopian socialist working-woman entered an elegant shop where purses were sold, declared that she had a better claim to one of them than wealthy idlers, and then simply seized the most attractive specimen from the display. Possibly, too, if a lady-colleague

Source: *Civil Disobedience in Antiquity*, by David Daube (Edinburgh: Edinburgh University Press, 1972). Reprinted by permission of Edinburgh Press. Footnotes have been edited.

of mine, in order to emphasize equal rights, took my right hand and kissed it in Austrian fashion. Helen of Troy committed adultery, but she did it for pleasure, so she does not qualify for this afternoon's discussion. We may contrast with her Ibsen's Nora who, for the sake of her own liberation as well as that of her fellow-sufferers, leaves her husband and children, her doll's home, and embarks on a lonely road. There are, of course, borderline cases. Often it will be easier to class an incident if civil is replaced by civic: civic disobedience brings out more clearly that the act is carried out in the name of society (or a part of it) at large.

I am aware that on psychological probing the distinction between vulgar and principled conduct often dissolves. A person may believe or pretend to act from high-mindedness and in reality be quite egotistic. Or he may look an egotist and even proclaim himself one, yet really have the public good at heart. But I shall, on the whole, take the simplistic approach which ancients as well as moderns use in judging these matters—otherwise this survey would just not be possible. Whatever the science of the soul may bring to light, some interest may attach to how the cases in question were in fact dealt with in former times.

As I understand it, civil disobedience presupposes absence of violence; and from this point of view civic would be less appropriate, it sounds less proper, less "civilised"—civic resistance, I feel, should cover violent action. No doubt a case might be made for treating civil disobedience as no less inclusive. In fact, I shall later on illustrate at some length the precariousness, if we want to trace the history of a conflict, of separating peaceful and violent behaviour. Moreover, let me make it clear that I can think of circumstances in which I would blame no one for resorting to force. Xenophon was optimistic when, in trying to whitewash the memory of Socrates and dissociate him from wild characters like Alcibiades, he asserted that whatever was attainable by violent means at great cost "was attainable through persuading, without danger and in friendship."[1] Still, the means employed do matter; so as far as this series is concerned, permit me to confine civil disobedience to nonviolence.

Here again we run into complications and border-line possibilities. On the second of February of this year,[2] at the Hastings College of the Law at San Francisco, while Professor Camera was holding a class, some two dozen lady students entered and clamoured in chorus for his dismissal because he had expressed doubts as to the effectiveness of female attorneys in criminal trials. No violence occurred throughout this incident. But suppose he had expected the trouble and had barricaded the door by means of a table, perhaps with some flower-pots on it, and the students had overthrown the obstacle. Would this have turned the affair into a violent one? Or suppose the ladies had been boxing champions and had surrounded him with threatening gestures. In this particular case it would not have been so serious because Professor Camera is a great footballer. But I have been at demonstrations which, though in the end they passed without bloodshed, yet in spirit and potentiality were anything but gentle.

For the purpose of this course, it may be best to assume nonviolence wherever there is no serious danger to life, limb or object of value. Medea, who slaughtered before Jason's eyes the children she had borne to him, was obviously violent. If you collect mortars, machine-guns, bombs, with a view to intimidating the government, I subsume it under violence, even before any of these weapons have gone off. On the other hand the English suffragette movement at the turn of the century I deem nonviolent, although when it went on people thought very differently: you have a look at the press of the time. The worst that happened was a few broken windows, and Miss Pankhurst ended up as a Conservative Member of Parliament. *Tempora mutantur:* what counts as terrorism in one epoch, stratum of society or situation, counts as innocence itself in another. That the boundary is indeterminate cannot be helped. The Mafia has oscillated from its inception between banditry *à la* Robin Hood and downright criminality, and between nonviolent and violent crime.

One more point concerning definition. It is common in definitions of civil disobedience to require that the perpetrator be willing to undergo the punishment prescribed by law. I daresay the model in the minds of the proponents of this doctrine is Socrates, who willingly drank the hemlock tendered to him. I shall discuss his trial in the lecture on philosophers. For the moment I would say that I do not concur. I shall not quibble—scholars are free to formulate their premises, and I can see a good deal of sense in this stipulation. However, I do not subscribe to it; and a person who, having performed his act of defiance, attempts the very best defence in court, maybe exploits procedural loopholes, or even one who runs away to a neighbouring country, may still, for the purpose of my lectures, be civilly disobedient. He may not, but he may.

I suspect that a motive—not the only one, but still a motive—behind the restriction of the term to the takers-of-the-consequences has to do with the honourable overtone nowadays attaching to it in a wide section of the public. Those who avoid or evade punishment are to be debarred from this honourable category, with effects which are obviously welcome to the authorities. If you joyfully or at least resignedly accept the legal penalty, you indicate your basic recognition of the regime in power.

Precisely the likely existence of this motive in the advocates of the dominant appraisal is a motive for me to decline it and do without the requirement. I am not persuaded that current notions of honourable conduct are thoroughly justifiable. The question is complicated and a proper exploration would lead too far afield. The orthodox attitude has affinity with the admiration we are invited to have for the "good loser"—a concept manifestly coined by the lucky winner: he has an enormous interest in the other party putting a cheerful face on the outcome, an interest at once material and concerning his psychic well-being. More generally, it is the entire structure called "the rules of the game" which the prevalent definition seems to support. But again, they are biased. Of course, substantively the same ideals are formulated differently in different cultures and periods: it is mainly in modern England that they are of a sporting nature. (English society has been outstandingly successful in achieving compliance with them.) However expressed, it is remarkable what a huge influence they are throughout history, in all walks of life public and private. However, I cannot dwell on these ramifications.

To recapitulate, this afternoon's subject will be those women of antiquity who, from avowed conviction yet without the employment of destructive means, flouted the prevalent order.

2

The oldest record in world literature of the spurning of a governmental decree occurs in the Second Book of Moses.[3] Pharaoh ordered the Hebrew midwives to kill all male newborn immediately on delivery. "But the midwives feared God and did not do as the king of Egypt commanded them, but saved the men children alive." In passing: this oldest instance of conscientious disobedience concerns a case of genocide.[4] In our context, however, what interests is the absence of violence; the appeal to a higher duty, very clearly expressed—"they feared God and did not as the king commanded them"—and taken up over a thousand years later by Peter and John when they were threatened because they preached the risen Jesus[5] (though, for this case, we must consider also the parallel of Socrates, "men of Athens, I shall obey the god rather than you"[6]); and, above all, the female sex of the resisters. A woman is the main figure also in the Greek prototype of civil disobedience: Antigone, who, despite King Creon's strict prohibition, buried her brother who had perished as a traitor. Remember that at that time a corpse left unburied was supposed to find no rest. (I say "at that time," though the belief retains much of its vitality in ours—if to some extent underground.) Again no violence, again appeal to a higher authority: "Nor did I deem," she affirms in Sophocles' tragedy,[7] "that thou, a mortal man, couldst override the immutable, unwritten laws of heaven."

That both cases involve heroines is not accidental, and if this has hitherto been neglected, it proves only that the male, scholarly world had no eyes for it. Women are largely outside the power structure; indeed, on the whole they belong to the oppressed ones of this earth. "The stronger rules; we must obey this law and others even more grievous," thus counsels Ismene, Antigone's weaker sister.[8] Enmity to tyranny, or better, the ability to manage without falling in with it, to jog along unaffected by it, not bothering about it, is their typical response. It has been said of *A Doll's House*[9] that "it is not a feminist play. Ibsen was preoccupied with the struggle between society and the individual, and he chose a woman as his protagonist because he knew that, on the whole, women were more likely to take a personal view of life than men." Feminist or not, Ibsen is conscious of the trait I am pointing to; so is his biographer from whom I have quoted; so, indeed, is King Creon, only he does not like it.

"She ruins states," Sophocles represents him as complaining,[10] "she dissipates the host, while discipline preserves the ordered ranks; therefore we must maintain authority and yield no title to a woman's will." When we consider, furthermore, that women have neither the training nor the weapons for physical power struggle, the appropriateness of nonviolent resistance becomes even clearer.

The two narratives of the midwives and Antigone are totally independent of one another; not a trace of mutual influence. The common insight they offer is all the weightier. Perhaps I should here insert that I may leave it open whether the events are historical, legendary, or partly this and partly that. They do provide evidence of the role which antiquity attributed to women.

My interpretation is supported by another common feature of the two incidents so widely separated in time, space and cultural background. The actions defying the despot are elementary loving offices: assistance at birth and burial. Women are more closely in touch with becoming and dying than men, hence are more inclined to furtherance and saving of life and humanity and less to destruction and cruelty. "My nature," exclaims Antigone "is for mutual love, not hate."[11] How motherly the poet imagines her loyalty to her brother to be, and how close it is, therefore, to the attitude of the midwives, is shown by the description of her sorrow as she discovers that the soil she had placed on her dead brother has been removed again. "There stood this maid, a piercing cry she uttered, sad and shrill, as when the mother bird beholds her nest robbed of its nestlings." Terrible that, precisely for this caring, the king orders her to be dragged to her death, young, unwedded and childless. His reply to her creed I have just quoted, "My nature is for mutual love, not hate," is: "Die, then, and love the dead, if love thou must; no woman shall be master while I live."[12] Senseless male pride drives him to decisions which in the end result in his being left in tomb-like desolation.

Antigone is famous, the midwives are not. I am hardly mistaken in assuming that, prior to this lecture, of ten persons in this hall familiar with Antigone, one only remembered the midwives. The reason is that while Antigone stood by her deed, the midwives denied theirs. "The king of Egypt called for the midwives and said unto them, Why have you done this thing and have saved the men-children alive? And the midwives replied, Because the Hebrew women are not as the Egyptian ones; they are lively and are delivered before the midwives visit them."[13] So they told the king a fib, they had nothing to do with the birth of these children at all. The arrested Antigone, when asked by Creon: "Wast thou acquainted with the interdict?" answers arrogantly: "I knew, all knew; how should I fail to know?"[14] This is the posture our teachers recommended to our fantasy. Had she answered instead: "I beg your pardon, I had not heard of it," not much would have happened to her and you would remember her as little as you remember the midwives. Strictly speaking, the latter did not practice civil disobedience according to the definition I laid down at the beginning. That, you may recall, requires openness, publicity. On the other hand, they did not enjoy the protection of absolute, safe secrecy: their conduct was of course widely known, at least among their fellow Jewesses, so that they had constantly to reckon with detection and execution—for they could not hope for mercy. We might compare those Mexican priests who, in the years following 1926, conducted schools contrary to the constitution.

How are we to explain this difference—Antigone's insistence on being called to account, the shrewd escape of the midwives? Antigone knows that her confrontation, even though it may mean her ruin, will not be in vain. Not only does retribution quickly catch up with the tyrant in that his own son, Antigone's fiancé, and his wife both commit suicide. Not only does he recognize and repent his overweening mistake, if too late. What is of decisive importance is that her unflinching firmness shakes the entire foundation of arbitrary government. To this day her voice is feared by any usurper whose position is in the least endangered.

There are additional factors: her membership of the nobility—pride is a traditional aristocratic virtue—and indeed her personal character. She is both extraordinarily ambitious and desirous of dying. She is a murderee; she does want to be a victim (a wish which does not prevent her from, in the end, being profoundly aware of the questionability and terror of the way she has chosen). "How sweet to die," she says: and immured in a rock-hewn chamber to perish there, she hastens her death by hanging herself. I would not have allowed her to drive me, though I am fond of lifts. These qualities are hardly surprising in one who definitely came from a broken family: her father was Oedipus, her mother Jocasta, Oedipus' mother and wife. . . . Here also lies the explanation of her indifference to the disaster her conduct inflicts on innocent bystanders, so to speak—her fiancé, for example. It is a general rule: the more high-minded, the more inconsiderate.

By contrast, there is not the remotest chance of breaching the absolutism of the Pharaohnic regime. Nor are the midwives representatives of an elevated stratum where concealment is despicable; they belong to the common folk. Above all, if they confessed, they would deprive themselves of all possibility of further saving activity.[15] Their lie enables them to carry on their good work unmolested—a consideration which has no place in the case of Antigone. As Ecclesiastes has it (or shall I say, Judy Collins?):[16] "To everything there is a season—a time to rend and a time to sew, a time to keep silence and a time to speak." Whoever is forced to live under a regime of terror, and also whoever wishes to understand those under such a regime, might learn a good deal from the antithesis of Antigone and the midwives. . . .

5

I come now to the *Lysistrata*, a comedy by Aristophanes, which equals Shakespeare's *Tempest* in profundity and excels it in ambiguity, or perhaps in unambiguity. As the war between Athens and Sparta goes on endlessly and senselessly, the women of the two cities conspire to abstain from intercourse both with husbands and friends until peace is concluded. (At Birmingham in England, wives of striking motor car workers have recently been reported to have shut out their husbands from the bedrooms in order to make them disgruntled and return to the factories—not quite the same thing.) Moreover, the Athenian women occupy the Parthenon, a temple where the public treasury with the war chest is housed, a kind of Fort Knox: the first sit-in in history.

In this revolt, too, exactly as in the cases of the midwives and Antigone, the intention is to protect and rescue human values and to call a halt to barbarous devastation. The dialectic of the situation brings it about that the women prove their love precisely by barring its joys during the war which, while conducive to facile amatory diversion, tramples on the genuine article in three ways: the married women are left behind by their soldiering husbands, the unmarried ones grow up for a lonely existence, and—worst misuse—the sons born and brought up in sweet devotion are being sent to their death.[17] The participants in the action, it should be noted, are all married. Their motherliness prompts them to feel particularly for the young girls condemned to remain single.

The word *sozo*, to save, to bring salvation, which in Greek religiosity often alludes to redemption, occurs quite a few times. The aim, reached only in the play, alas, not in reality, is to free the men—and be it against their stupid will—from the killing they are entangled in,[18] and to unite them in fertile friendship. Significantly, the name of the Spartan female leader, Lampito, has the same meaning as that of one of the midwives, Shiphra, "the shining one"; and I trust the militant wing of Women's Lib will not be offended by the fact that in all three cases, the midwives, Antigone, and Lysistrata, the women fight for members of the male sex: for the male newborn, for the slain brother, for the soldiers at the front. Aeschylus, highly admired by Aristophanes, had mentioned as an objection to wars like the Trojan, which had been caused by the abduction of Helen, that "men die for the sake of women." Unmistakably behind such a critique lurks a higher ranking of man in comparison with woman. In Aristophanes' comedy, however, the women insist on more rights and on being heard precisely because they can no longer bear the insane slaughter of men by men. Women here try to cause wars to cease.

As their main enemies they regard dried-up old fogies and politicians, both hostile to true, genuine life; the former without a spark, the latter greedy for office and positions. They share Plato's view that lust for wealth and luxury, avarice, is the cause of wars: "What, is the war for the sake of the silver, then?"—"Yes; and all other disputes that there are. Why is Peisander forever embroiling us? Why do the rest of our officers feel always a pleasure in strife and disturbances? Simply to gain an occasion to steal."[19] The laws produced by these men cannot but be harsh and bitter. The magistrate who opposes the rebels is swathed by them in wreaths and funeral ribbons: that is how they see the ruling clique, mouldering corpses. They look on themselves as equal to men in intelligence and as superior to them in judgement and discrimination between essence and surface lustre. There are certainly values for which one might even go to battle; for example, one might defend Greece against the Persians. The women themselves successfully ward off the police who try to eject them from the Parthenon. "What did you expect, you fool," they tease the magistrate who led the attack on them, "was it unknown to you that we women, too, can be raging?"[20] But men fight for crude objects and indeed for the sake of fighting; they love to show themselves in uniform and to boast— not only to the enemy but even to their most innocent fellow-citizens: "Troth, 'tis a mighty ridiculous jest, watching them haggle for shrimps in the market-place, grimly accoutred with shield and with crest. Lately I witnessed a captain of cavalry, proudly the while on a charger he sat, buying an omelet, stowing it all in his cavalry hat. Comes a Thracian irregular, shaking his dart and his target to boot; off runs the shop-girl, appalled at the sight of him, down he sits soldierly, gobbles her fruit."[21]

The insurrection has two fronts, a private one, in so far as the individual Athenian or Spartan woman must somehow deal with her husband or friend, and a public one, where it is a question of maintaining occupation of the temple and, ultimately, of enforcing a basic change for the better in the relations between the two cities. As far as the private front is concerned, the women must look as seductive as possible so that their refusal should hurt all the more. They also agree that if a man uses force to get his lady into the bedroom, she should hold fast to the door and any suitable piece of furniture; but if he starts beating her up she may yield, yet so ill-humouredly that he will derive little pleasure from the transaction. An extremely effective way to make clear to a passionate husband what he loses by the strike is shown in a scene which I would not dare to describe to my respectable audience. I must be content with the hint that, compared with what this poor lovelorn chap is being put through, the tortures of Tantalus who, standing in water up to his chin, is eternally thirsty because, as soon as he bends down to drink, the water disappears, and who is eternally starving because the branches full of fruit which touch his forehead are swept away by a wind as soon as he tries to reach them, are mere child's play.

In passing—it is significant that the idea of homosexual activity as a way out does not occur. In fact, except for a brief aside making fun of a rich pederast, that area is not mentioned at all throughout the play. On the whole, homosexuality was confined to a relatively small upper stratum of society, and even there it played the role of champagne, not of *vin ordinaire*. After all, a strike of women would cause much hardship even at North Beach in San Francisco.

On the public front, while things are not entirely peaceful, they are not much worse than in the suffragette years, or in the Berkeley of 1964 when the parties were not yet divided by a wide gulf. *Lysistrata* is a comedy in which there may be neither corpses nor even serious injuries. The women seize the Parthenon by means of a stratagem: some elderly ladies assemble there on the pretence to offer a sacrifice, then they admit all the others, and now the doors are barricaded, so there is no more money for the war. A number of enraged citizens of advanced years (the young ones are at the front) come along with burning oak beams and fire pots in order to smoke out the occupants—a kind of tear gas attack—and if necessary even to drive them out by setting fire to the building. The smoke hurts mainly the attackers, and the fire is prevented by excellent planning and co-operation of the defenders. The men now stand there drenched with water, when at last a magistrate appears with his police. There is a scuffle, but the magistrate's assistants, badly led and not very numerous, have the worst of it. . . . The entire affair is depicted by Aristophanes most convincingly, right into details like the sudden rumour among the citizens that the lady rebels are instigated by men and indeed, by external agents, by Spartans; also the final recognition, after mutual affection and common sense have proved victorious, that it would be a good thing if statesmen conducted their business and negotiations, not when they are sober and therefore petty and suspicious, but when they are a little turned-on.

Some twenty years after the *Lysistrata*, Aristophanes wrote *The Female Parliament*. The theme here is that the women are fed up with the male mismanagement of the city. They disguise themselves as men and early in the morning, long before the bulk of the real men get up, appear in the legislative assembly; they move that the government be handed over to the women and, of course, the motion is carried. The entire city is now being reorganized as one large household, a happy commune, in which there is neither private property nor private marriage. Meals are in common and free, everything is at the disposal of everybody, and there is complete promiscuity—except, indeed, that slavery remains: that was just too anchored an institution and too necessary in the eyes of the free for civilized existence. The constitution is indeed utopian, but again the women are found on the side of life, general joy and advance. Special arrangements are laid down to insure that the freedom in sexual matters will not disadvantage ugly men and women. For example, a presentable young guy, before he spends a night with the lady of his choice, has to be gallant to one not a beauty queen who chooses him. An amusing scene (it would be brutal if performed before a female public, but in Aristophanes' time women did not as a rule attend comedies) reveals the poet's understanding for the ageing woman who is in a harder situation than the ageing man.

In his recent publication *A Certain World*,[22] W. H. Auden suggests that males are so ridiculously jealous of one another that with modern machinery at their disposal this is now a real threat to the survival of the human race. "Today our phallic toys have become too dangerous to be tolerated: I see little hope for a peaceful world until men are excluded from the realm of foreign policy altogether and all decisions concerning international relations are reserved for women, preferably married ones." Auden, a great poet and an excellent classical scholar, is alive to the desperately serious nucleus in Aristophanes' comedy. As for his special confidence in married women, who know what loving means, what children mean, what sorrow means, the conspirators in the *Lysistrata*, we saw, all belong to this category. In *The Female Parliament*, owing to the abolition of binding unions, the distinction between married and unmarried loses its importance. Homosexuality is of as little relevance in the latter comedy as in the former.

Notes

[1] *Memorabilia* 1. 2. 10.

[2] See *San Francisco Chronicle*, 3 Feb. 1971, p. 3.

[3] Exodus 1:15 ff.

[4] "Any of the following acts committed with intent to destroy, in whole or in part, a national, ethical, racial or religious group, as such: (a) Killing members of the group . . . (d) Imposing measures intended to prevent births within the group." Article II of the Convention of 9 Dec. 1948, on the Prevention and Punishment of the Crime of Genocide, *United Nations Treaty Series*, 78, 1961, p. 280.

[5] Acts 4:19, 5:29: "Whether it be right to hearken unto you more than God, judge you. . . . We ought to obey God rather than men."

[6] Plato, *Apology* 17.29 D; cp. 28.37 E.

[7] Sophocles, *Antigone* 453f. Translation by Storr, *Sophocles* (Loeb Classical Library), I, 1912, p. 349.

[8] *Antigone* 63f. (Storr, p. 319: "The stronger rules; we must obey his orders, these or worse.")

[9] See Roberts, *Encyclopaedia Britannica*, 12, 1953, p. 38.

[10] *Antigone* 674ff. (Storr, p. 367). Cp. "No woman shall be master while I live," 525 (Storr, p. 355); "Son, be warned and let no woman fool away thy wits," 648f. (Storr, p. 365); "O heart corrupt, a woman's minion thou," 746 (Storr, p. 373); "A woman's servant thou, do not cajole me," 756. (Storr, p. 373: "Play not the spaniel, thou a woman's slave").

[11] *Antigone* 523 (Storr, p. 355). Cp. "To die and rest—two lovers side by side," 73 (Storr, p. 321: "To die, to rest—sister and brother linked in love's embrace").

[12] *Antigone* 524 f. (Storr, p. 355).

[13] Exodus 1.18f. According to a rabbinic suggestion we ought to render not "they are lively," but "they are animals": Exodus Rabba I ad loc.

[14] *Antigone* 448 f. (Storr, p. 349).

[15] The Egyptian king's bitter determination comes out in the edict which he issues now that his plan to use the midwives has failed: the entire population is now commanded to drown any male Hebrew new-born. Exodus 1.22.

[16] 3.1, 7.

[17] *Lysistrata* 589ff.

[18] "Whether you like it or not, we'll deliver you"—"That were a terrible shame, by Demeter"—"Friend, we must save you"—"But how if I wish it not?"—"That will but make our resolve the completer," 499ff. Translation by Rogers, *Aristophanes* (Loeb Classical Library), 3, 1946, pp. 49f.

[19] 489ff. (Rogers, p. 49).

[20] 463ff. (Rogers, p. 45: "What did the fool expect? Think you we women feel no thirst for glory?"). Lysistrata is speaking; and one of the things she says is "Did you believe you would be coming only upon some slave maids?" (Rogers: "Was it to fight with slaves you came?"). Some of her preaching is reminiscent of the prophets: there is to be brotherhood between citizens and sojourners, mother city and colonies, rich and poor, 579ff. Yet slavery continues unchanged.

[21] 559ff. (Rogers, pp. 57f.).

[22] I quote from McCabe's column in *San Francisco Chronicle*, 8 October 1971, p. 51.

Nonviolence and Women

Margaret Hope Bacon

While the connections can be traced deep into human history, neither feminism nor nonviolence were expressed in specific social activism until the nineteenth century. With the organization of the New England Non-Resistance Society in the Fall of 1838 and the publication of a newspaper, *The Non-Resistant*, a movement to spread the ideas and to use the methods of nonviolence in the struggle for justice was begun. Less than ten years later, in July of 1848, the women's rights movement was launched with the "Seneca Falls Declaration of the Rights of Women."

The proximity of the birthdates of these two movements is no accident. Both grew out of the abolitionist struggle against slavery, and both were the product of a new group, the radical reformers, who believed that Christian principles must be translated into action and who saw the struggle for peace and for justice as one and the same. As Lydia Maria Child, a novelist and founding member of the Non-Resistance Society wrote:

"Abolition principles and nonresistance seem to me identical . . . the former is a mere unit of the latter. I never saw any truth more clearly insomuch that it seems strange to me that any comprehensive mind can embrace one and not the other."

Not all abolitionists agreed, however, and not all nonresisters understood and accepted the equal importance of the Woman Question. The one person who gave leadership to and embodied all three issues was Lucretia Mott, a small Quaker minister with a mighty spiritual stature.

When she died in 1880, the *New York Times* called Lucretia Mott "One of the greatest fighters of the world." She fought most of her long life for the slaves; for an end to racial discrimination; for the rights of women, Native Americans, workers; for freedom of thought and religion. To her the impulse to struggle for justice and to use the methods of "moral suasion" in that struggle were identical. When people suggested to her that she drop one cause to concentrate upon another she was perplexed. The Inner Light demanded that she oppose injustice wherever she encountered it and to oppose it always with the weapons of love.

Source: *Reweaving the Web of Life: Feminism and Nonviolence*, edited by Pam McAllister (Philadelphia: New Society Publishers, 1982). Reprinted by permission of New Society Publishers.

Born Lucretia Coffin on the island of Nantucket, Lucretia came from a long line of strong, self-reliant women who drew upon the Quaker belief in the equality of the sexes and their position as the wives of seafarers responsible for the maintenance of shops and farms while their husbands were at sea for the formation of their characters. Lucretia grew up with a hot temper and a warm heart; early stories of the capture of slaves and their transportation to the Caribbean upset her and converted her to the antislavery position. Later, at boarding school in New York State, she learned that women teachers were paid less than half the salaries that men commanded and determined that she must do something also about the rights of women.

At eighteen Lucretia married a fellow teacher, James Mott, in Philadelphia, and here she spent the rest of her life. Although she was soon busy with a family of six children, she was independent and active, teaching school for some years after she was married, struggling against the growing conservatism in the Religious Society of Friends, and pushing the movement against the use of the products of slavery, an early form of boycott.

In 1833, when Lucretia was forty, William Lloyd Garrison came to Philadelphia to organize the American Antislavery Society which pledged to "use no carnal weapons for deliverance of those in bondage." The Society was made up of men only, as was the social custom of the day, but four days later Lucretia helped to organize the Philadelphia Female Antislavery Society. This group can be regarded today as the first active political organization of women, the launching pad for the women's rights movement and the marriage of nonviolence and feminism.

The women of the Antislavery Society circulated petitions, organized meetings, distributed literature and raised money. As they uncovered their own abilities, they began to question the rule that they could not speak before public meetings in which men were present or participate in all male organizations. Two women from South Carolina, Angelina and Sara Grimke, having joined the Society, began to attract "mixed" audiences when they spoke against the slavery they had known in childhood. As a result, "The Woman Question" was hotly debated within clerical and antislavery circles.

The controversy came to a climax in May of 1838 when the First Annual Convention of Antislavery Women met in Philadelphia in newly dedicated Pennsylvania Hall. A mob formed around the building, angry that Black and white women were meeting together and angrier yet when it was decided to permit women to address a mixed male and female or "promiscuous" audience. On the night of May 17th the mob, with the tacit permission of the mayor and his police, burned the new structure to the ground. They then prepared to attack the home of the Motts, nearby, until a friend shouting, "On to the Motts," led them in the wrong direction.

Although Lucretia Mott had been raised as a Quaker pacifist and was an advocate of the boycott, the events of the burning of Pennsylvania Hall began her lifelong practice of personal nonviolence. On the afternoon before the burning of the hall, she had shepherded the women to safety by asking them to walk with linked arms, one Black woman with one white woman, and to ignore provocations. On the night of the fire, she and James and their guests decided to await the arrival of the mob at their house as calmly as possible. The next day the women conducted their meeting in a nearby school room, pledged themselves to increase, not decrease, their practice of holding integrated gatherings and to struggle harder for equal rights for women within the antislavery societies.

When the women's convention met in Philadelphia the following year, Lucretia had a series of animated conferences with the mayor who wanted to provide police protection and who urged her to prevent Black and white women from walking together in the streets. Lucretia insisted that the women needed no such advice and were prepared to protect themselves. Some months later, travelling in Delaware with an elderly abolitionist, Daniel Neall, she offered herself to a tar and feather mob who had captured her companion. "Take me, since I am the chief offender," she insisted. "I ask no favor for my sex." Embarrassed by her persistence, the mob gave Neall only a token brush with the tar.

When the New England Non-Resistance Society was formed in the fall of 1838, Lucretia was unable to be present. Her good Boston friend, Maria Chapman, Lydia Maria Child, Anne Weston, and Abby Kelley of Worcester, Massachusetts, all members of the abolitionist crusade, were there instead. The next year, however, Lucretia played a leading role in the convention, arguing that nonresistance principles should be applied in the classroom and in raising children as well as in public life. This was regarded as too Utopian by some of the most ardent male nonresisters. Few, if any of them, had homes based on equality of responsibility as did the Motts, and consequently probably did not see the implications of nonresistance for the Victorian relationships between husband and wife, father and child.

Lucretia herself practiced both nonviolence and democracy in her home life. All the Motts, everyone, male or female, had his or her chore so that housework did not fall too heavily on any one member. Her marriage to James was a unique one of mutual support. She frequently urged newly-wed couples to follow her example. Her motto, often repeated at weddings, was "In the true marriage relationship, the independence of husband and wife is equal, their dependence mutual, and their obligations reciprocal."

The antislavery movement at this time was split over the issue of nonresistance as well as the Woman Question. Some conservative abolitionists, particularly clergymen, objected to the inclusion of these "divisive" issues in the antislavery crusade. There was a series of schisms climaxing in May of 1840, when Abby Kelley was placed on a business committee and half of the American Antislavery Society walked out to form a New Organization.

At the time of this meeting, Lucretia Mott was on the high seas on her way to London, England to represent the Pennsylvania Antislavery Society at the World Antislavery Convention. She and her followers had succeeded in obtaining equal rights in the Pennsylvania Society eighteen months earlier, and the New England Antislavery Society was also sending women. Having gotten rid of their conservative members through the schism, the old American Antislavery Society proceeded to name her their representative in absentia. When she reached London, therefore, she had dual sponsorship. She was nevertheless denied a seat; the British had not yet faced the Woman Question, and members of the New Organization from the United States were present to spread rumors about her as a heretic.

Lucretia fought vigorously against this exclusion and yet maintained such poise and good temper that she won many admirers. Among these was Anne Knight, a young British woman who later started a women's rights movement in that country, and Elizabeth Cady Stanton, present as the twenty-year-old bride of Henry Stanton, a New Organization delegate to the convention. Elizabeth Cady Stanton had believed in the strength and power of women all her life but she had never before seen her ideals acted out as they were by Lucretia Mott. She pledged herself then and there, she said later in her autobiographical notes, to do something about women's rights. On the last day of the convention the two took a walk and promised each other to hold a convention upon their return to the United States.

The convention was long in coming. Elizabeth Cady Stanton promptly became pregnant, and the next years were devoted to a string of baby boys and interesting social life on the outskirts of Boston. Lucretia meanwhile returned to do battle on a whole series of issues. She lectured vigorously against slavery, making a trip into the South, addressing Congressmen, and meeting with the President to express her feelings; and she became involved in an across-the-sea women to women exchange during the crisis between the United States and Great Britain over the Oregon territory, 54-40-Or Fight. She was also struggling within the Society of Friends for equal rights for women in the business of the church, and for a time she had to defend herself against efforts to have her disowned from the Society because of her radical views.

Finally, however, in July of 1848, while Lucretia was visiting her sister in upstate New York, she and Stanton met at a tea party and decided to have a convention that very next week. Hastily called, the Seneca Falls Convention was a success, winning advocates and critics as well. At the Convention, and for many years thereafter, Lucretia was recognized as the guiding spirit of women's rights, giving counsel and direction to the younger women. As the Woman Question became more and more controversial and angry mobs circled the national conventions, she was often called upon to chair the meetings in order to use her unique presence to keep order. She still had her sharp tongue, but she combined it with a warm spirit and was able to use wit and sarcasm delicately to put hecklers into place without offending them.

In her speeches at the women's conventions Lucretia frequently referred to the links between women's rights, nonresistance and peace. She often said it was actually human rights, not just women's rights, that they must try to achieve: "It has sometimes been said that if women were associated with men in their efforts, there would be not as much immorality as now exists in Congress, for instance, and other places. But we ought, I think, to claim no more for woman than for man; we ought to put woman on a par with man, not invest her with power, or call for her superiority over her brother. If we do, she is just as likely to become a tyrant as man is, as with Catherine the Second. It is always unsafe to invest man with power over his fellow being. 'Call no man master . . .' is a true doctrine. But be sure that there would be a better rule than now; the elements which belong to woman as such and to man as such, would be beautifully and harmoniously blended. It is to be hoped that there would be less war, injustice, and intolerance in the world than now."

During the turbulent 1850s she continued to practice nonviolence, helping with several slave rescues and making a daring trip into the South to preach against slavery. While many of her abolitionist colleagues were beginning to question nonresistance, and to support John Brown and his followers in their idea of encouraging an armed slave revolt, she remained faithful to the superiority of moral weapons. Following the tragic events at Harpers Ferry she wrote movingly of her belief in the power of nonresistance: "For it is not John Brown the soldier we praise, it is John Brown the moral hero; John Brown the noble confessor and patient martyr we honor, and whom we think it proper to honor in his day when men are carried away by the corrupt and proslavery clamour against him. Our weapons were drawn only from the armory of Truth; they were those of faith and love. They were those of moral indignation, strongly expressed against any wrong. Robert Purvis has said that I was 'The most belligerent Non-Resistant he ever saw.' I accept the character he gives me; and I glory in it. I have no idea because I am a Non-Resister of submitting tamely to injustice inflicted either on me or on the slave. I will oppose it with all the moral power with which I am endowed. I am no advocate of passivity. Quakerism as I understand it does not mean quietism. The early Friends were agitators, disturbers of the peace, and were more obnoxious in their day to charges which are now so freely made than we are."

During the Civil War she remained a pacifist, supporting conscientious objectors and arguing that the struggle should be pursued with moral force alone, while she lamented that the best and the bravest were dying on the battlefields. Following the war she devoted much of her energy to the cause of peace, serving as the spirited President of the Pennsylvania Peace Society for many years. At the same time she tried to make peace between warring branches of the women's rights movement while she continued to support women's admission to the professions and schools of higher education.

Far less well known, but at times more radical than Lucretia, was Abby Kelley who married a fellow radical, Stephen S. Foster. Abby attended the women's rights meetings, but made the abolition of slavery her first priority. In her marriage to Stephen, however, she practiced a complete sharing of household duties and a system where one partner took care of the farm and their only child, Alla, while the other travelled and spoke against slavery. She was not always well liked, but she was often admired as "The Woman of the Age." Both Stephen and Abby were devoted to nonresistance, and both practiced it dramatically. One weekend when they were arrested in Ohio for distributing antislavery literature on the Sabbath, Abby went limp and had to be carried by several sheriff's deputies to jail and later to the courthouse where she absolutely refused to cooperate until the Fosters' case was won by a young antislavery lawyer and the two were set free.

Later, after the Civil War, when the drive for suffrage for women began in earnest, Abby and Stephen decided to refuse to pay taxes on their farm in Worcester since it was taxation without representation for Abby. Everyone was impressed that the Fosters, who loved their farm deeply, were willing to continually risk it for principle.

Civil disobedience, such as Abby committed, became a favorite technique in the long post Civil War battle for suffrage led by the Quaker feminist and pacifist, Susan B. Anthony. In 1872 Susan, with a group of sixteen women, voted illegally in an election in Rochester. Susan was convicted in a court of law for this action and fined $100. She refused to pay the fine and was never prosecuted for this refusal. Her courtroom statement was, "May it please Your Honor, I shall never pay a dollar of your unjust penalty . . . and I shall earnestly and persistently continue to urge all women to the practical recognition of the old revolutionary maxim, that 'Resistance to tyranny is obedience to God.'" Elsewhere other women conducted vigils and demonstrations at polling places. Four years later, in 1876, members of the National Women's Suffrage Association interrupted proceedings during the Centennial Celebration at Independence Hall in Philadelphia to present the startled delegates with a revised version of the Declaration of the Rights of Women.

The majority of the suffragists in the late nineteenth century were concerned with other reforms affecting women; temperance, protection for working women and children and elimination of military training from the schools. Although some Black women were involved in the movement, there was a tendency to move away from the earlier close alliance of Blacks and women and to make the women's movement a middle class white phenomenon. This became more pronounced as the drive for suffrage lingered on into the twentieth century and women began to narrow their focus to suffrage alone.

The growing conservatism of the suffrage movement was challenged at the time of World War I by Alice Paul, a Philadelphia Quaker who had participated in the British suffrage movement under the leadership of the Pankhurst women and came back to the United States to introduce more militant methods into the faltering campaign. She was opposed to the war, and, as the United States entered it, she organized pickets outside the White House, protesting a battle for democracy abroad while there was so little democracy at home. When the police began to arrest the picketers for "disturbing traffic," she taught them to refuse food in jail and to resist force feeding. The resulting news stories brought women flocking to Washington from all over the country and helped in the final passage of the Nineteenth Amendment.

Alice Paul recognized that suffrage was only one of a number of feminist issues, and decided to concentrate her attention next on the passage of an Equal Rights Amendment. She remembered that Lucretia Mott, who had been a lifetime hero of hers, had been the first president of the American Equal Rights Association at a time after the Civil War when it was thought possible to combine the interests of Blacks and women. She decided to name the ERA, as introduced into Congress in 1923, the Lucretia Mott Amendment.

Thus, ninety years after the Philadelphia Female Antislavery Society was formed, the central core of ideas—feminism, nonviolence, and social justice which Mott represented to her contemporaries—were present at the inauguration of a new phase of the struggle. Not all feminists in the nineteenth or the twentieth century have seen the correlations or shared the central vision, but all can attest that their challenge to male supremacy seems to challenge the whole system of society. Mott said it for her colleagues in 1853: "Any great change must expect opposition, because it strikes at the very foundation of privilege." Understood in its broadest sense, nonviolence can be a powerful tool in the feminist struggle for social change and justice.

WOMEN AND MILITANT NONVIOLENCE IN THE NUCLEAR AGE

On Revolution and Equilibrium

Barbara Deming

> What we want to do is to go forward all the time . . . in the company of all men. But can we escape becoming dizzy?
>
> —Frantz Fanon in *The Wretched of the Earth*

"Do you want to remain pure? Is that it?" a black man asked me, during an argument about nonviolence. It is not possible to act at all and to remain pure; and that is not what I want, when I commit myself to the nonviolent discipline. There are people who are struggling to change conditions that they find intolerable, trying to find new lives; in the words of Frantz Fanon in *The Wretched of the Earth*, they want "to set afoot a new man." That is what I want, too; and I have no wish to be assigned, as it were, separate quarters from those who are struggling in a way different from mine—segregated from my companions rather as, several years ago in Birmingham at the end of a demonstration, I found myself segregated in the very much cleaner and airier white section of the jail. I stand with all who say of present conditions that

Source: *Revolution and Equilibrium*, by Barbara Deming (New York: Grossman Publishers, 1971). Reprinted by permission of the Barbara Deming estate.

they do not allow men to be fully human and so they must be changed—all who not only say this but are ready to act.

At a recent conference about the directions the American Left should take, a socialist challenged me: "Can you call degrading the violence used by the oppressed to throw off oppression?" When one is confronted with what Russell Johnson calls accurately "the violence of the *status quo*"—conditions which are damaging, even murderous, to very many who must live within them—it is degrading for all to allow such conditions to persist. And if the individuals who can find the courage to bring about change see no way in which it can be done without employing violence on their own part—a very much lesser violence, they feel, than the violence to which they will put an end—I do not feel that I can judge them. The judgments I make are not judgments upon men but upon the means open to us—upon the promise these means of action hold or withhold. The living question is: What are the best means for changing our lives—for really changing them?

The very men who speak of the necessity of violence, if change is to be accomplished, are the first, often, to acknowledge the toll it exacts among those who use it—as well as those it is used against. Frantz Fanon has a chapter in *The Wretched of the Earth* entitled "Colonial War and Mental Disorders" and in it he writes, "We are forever pursued by our actions." After describing, among other painful disorders, those suffered by an Algerian terrorist—who made friends among the French after the war and then wondered with anguish whether any of the men he had killed had been men like these—he comments, "It was what might be called an attack of vertigo." Then he asks a poignant question: "But can we escape becoming dizzy? And who can affirm that vertigo does not haunt the whole of existence?"

"Vertigo"—here is a word, I think, much more relevant to the subject of revolutionary action than the word "purity." No, it is not that I want to remain pure; it is that I want to escape becoming dizzy. And here is exactly the argument of my essay: we can escape it. Not absolutely, of course; but we can escape vertigo in the drastic sense. It is my stubborn faith that if, as revolutionaries, we will wage battle without violence, we can remain very much more in control—of our own selves, of the responses to us which our adversaries make, of the battle as it proceeds, and of the future we hope will issue from it.

The future—by whom will it be built? By all those whom the struggle has touched and marked. And so the question of how it marks them is not irrelevant. The future will be built even, in part, by those who have fought on the losing side. If it is a colonial struggle, of course, a good many of the adversaries can be expected to leave at the end of a successful revolution; but if it is a civil struggle, those who have been defeated, too, will at least help to make the new society what it is. How will the struggle have touched them? How will it have touched the victors?

Carl Oglesby, in *Containment and Change*, quotes a Brazilian guerilla: "We are in dead earnest. At stake is the humanity of man." Then he asks,

"How can ordinary men be at once warm enough to want what revolutionaries say they want [humanity], cold enough to do without remorse what they are capable of doing [cutting throats], and poised enough in the turbulence of their lives to keep the aspiration and the act both integrated and distinct? How is it that one of these passions does not invade and devour the other?" Yes—the question is one of equilibrium. How does one manage to keep it?

Oglesby would seem to answer that, generally speaking, one cannot expect the rebel to have the poise he describes. "He is an irresponsible man whose irresponsibility has been decreed by others. . . . He has no real views about the future . . . is not by *type* a Lenin, a Mao, a Castro. . . . His motivating vision of change is at root a vision of something absent—not of something that *will* be there . . . a missing landlord, a missing mine owner, a missing sheriff. . . ." Ultimately, says Oglesby, he must *become* responsible. But how? It is in the midst of the struggle that he must at least begin to be, isn't it? And so the very means by which we struggle, and their tendency either to give us poise or to leave us dizzy, is surely, again, relevant.

I think of the words with which Fanon opens the final chapter of *The Wretched of the Earth*: "Come then, comrades; it would be as well to decide at once to change our ways." I quote Fanon often—because he is eloquent, but also because he is quoted repeatedly these days by those who plead the need for violence. It is my conviction that he can be quoted as well to plead for nonviolence. It is true that he declares: "From birth it is clear . . . that this narrow world, strewn with prohibitions, can only be called in question by absolute violence." But I ask all those who are readers of Fanon to make an experiment: Every time you find the word "violence" in his pages, substitute for it the phrase "radical and uncompromising action." I contend that with the exception of a very few passages this substitution can be made, and that the action he calls for could just as well be nonviolent action.

He writes, for example: "Violence alone, violence committed by the people, violence organized and educated by its leaders, makes it possible for the masses to understand social truths and gives the key to them. Without that struggle, without that knowledge of the practice of action, there's nothing but a fancy-dress parade . . . a few reforms at the top . . . and down there at the bottom an undivided mass . . . endlessly marking time." "Knowledge of the practice of action"—*that* is what Fanon sees to be absolutely necessary, to develop in the masses of people an understanding of social truths, accomplish that "work of clarification," "demystification," "enlightening of consciousness" which is the recurring and the deepest theme of his book. This action could be nonviolent action; it could very much better be nonviolent action— if only that action is bold enough.

Here is Fanon as he argues the necessity for "mere rebellion"—which Oglesby has described—to become true revolution: "Racialism and hatred and resentment—'a legitimate desire for revenge'—cannot sustain a war of liberation. Those lightning flashes of consciousness which fling the body into stormy paths or which throw it into an almost pathological trance where the face of the other beckons me on to giddiness, where any blood calls for the blood of the other . . . that intense emotion of the first few hours falls to pieces if it is left to feed on its own substance. . . . You'll never overthrow the terrible enemy machine, and you won't change human beings if you forget to raise the standard of consciousness of the rank-and-file."

The task involves the enlightening of consciousness. But violence "beckons me on to giddiness." I repeat Fanon's words: "It would be as well to decide at once to change our ways." Another man with whom I was arguing the other day declared to me, "You can't turn the clock back now to nonviolence!" Turn the clock back? The clock has been turned to violence all down through history. Resort to violence hardly marks a move forward. It is nonviolence which is in the process of invention, if only people would not stop short in that experiment. Fanon again: "If we want humanity to advance a step further, if we want to bring it up to a different level than that which Europe has shown it, then we must invent and we must make discoveries." It is for that spirit of invention that I plead. And again I would like to ask something of all readers of Fanon. Turn to that last chapter of *The Wretched of the Earth* and read it again. Is he not groping here visibly for a way that departs from violence?

He writes, "We today can do everything, so long as we do not imitate Europe." And earlier in the book he has reported, "The argument the native chooses has been furnished by the settler. . . . The native now affirms that the colonialist understands nothing but force." He writes, "We must leave our dreams. . . ." And earlier he has written, "The native is an oppressed person whose permanent dream is to become the persecutor." He writes, "Leave this Europe where they are never done talking of Man, yet murder men everywhere they find them, at the corner of every one of their own streets, in all the corners of the globe. . . . Europe has . . . set her face against all solicitude and all tenderness. . . . So, my brother, how is it that we do not understand that we have better things to do than to follow that same Europe. . . . When I search for Man in the technique and the style of Europe, I see only a succession of negations of man, and an avalanche of murders. . . . Let us combine our muscles and our brains in a new direction. Let us try to create the whole man, whom Europe has been incapable of bringing to triumphant birth. All the elements of a solution . . . have, at different times, existed in European thought. But the action of European men has not carried out the mission which fell to them. We must try to set afoot a new man." And he writes, "It is simply a very concrete question of not dragging men toward mutilation. . . . The pretext of catching up must not be used to push men around, to tear him away from himself or from his privacy, to break and kill him. No, we do not want to catch up with anyone. What we want to do is to go forward all the time, night and day, in the company of Man, in the company of all men."

But how in the company of all men if we are willing to kill? In the passages I have quoted does Fanon not warn us again and again against murder, warn us that murder cannot possibly bring to birth the new man—that it was precisely Europe's propensity for murder that kept her from carrying out the mission we now inherit? What really but radical nonviolence is he here straining to be able to imagine? We must "vomit up" the values of Europe, he has written. Is it not above all the value that Europe and America have put upon violence that we must vomit up? He writes, "It is simply a very concrete question of not dragging men toward mutilation." Yes, very concrete, I urge, because it comes down to the means by which we struggle, comes down to a choice of *which* "practice of action" we are going to study.

At this point suddenly I can hear in my head many voices interrupting me. They all say: "Who among us likes violence? But nonviolence has been tried." It has *not* been tried. We have hardly begun to try it. The people who dismiss it now as irrelevant do not understand what it could be. And, again, they especially do not understand the very much greater control over events that they could find if they would put this "practice of action," rather than violence, to a real test.

What most people are saying just now of course is that nonviolence gives us no control at all over events. "After years of this," says Stokely Carmichael, "we are at almost the same point." Floyd McKissick expresses the same disillusion: all the nonviolent campaigns have accomplished essentially nothing for black people. They have served to integrate a token few into American society. Even those few cannot be said to have been absorbed into the mainstream; they still are not allowed to forget the color of their skins. And the great majority of black people are actually worse off than before. He declares, with reason, "We are concerned about the aspirations of the 90 per cent down there"—those of whom Fanon spoke, the many "endlessly marking time."

I won't try to pretend that progress has been made that has not been made. Though I would add to the picture these two men and others paint that there is one sense in which things hardly can be said to be at the same point still. If one speaks of psychological forces that will make a difference—the determination of black people not to accept their situation any longer, the determination of some white people not to accept it either, and a consciousness on the part of other white people that changes are bound to come now, doubts about their ability to prevent them—in these terms all has been in constant motion. And these terms—Fanon for one would stress—are hardly unimportant. Literally, yes, one can speak of gains that seem to mock those who have nearly exhausted themselves in the struggle for them. But I think one has to ask certain questions. Have gains been slight because nonviolent tactics were the wrong tactics to employ—or did many of those leading the battle underestimate the difficulties of the terrain before them? Did they lack at the start a sufficiently radical vision? Can those who have now turned from reliance upon nonviolence say surely that resort to violence over those same years would have brought greater gains?

There are those who are implying this now. One observer who implies it strongly is Andrew Kopkind, writing in *The New York Review of Books* in

August about the uprisings in the ghettos. He writes, "Martin Luther King and the 'leaders' who appealed for nonviolence, CORE, the black politicians, the old S.N.C.C. *are all* beside the point. Where the point is is in the streets. . . . The insurrections of July have done what everyone in America for thirty years has thought impossible; mass action has convulsed the society and brought smooth government to a halt." He itemizes with awe: they caused tanks to rumble through the heart of the nation's biggest cities, brought out soldiers by the thousands, destroyed billions of dollars worth of property. This violence (or as Dave Dellinger better names it, this counterviolence of the victimized) certainly called out the troops. One thing violence can be counted on to do is bring the antagonist forth in battle dress. The question that hasn't been answered yet is: Did this gain the rebels an advantage? It gained them many casualties. The powers-that-be paid their price, too, as Kopkind points out. But it is one thing to be able to state the price the antagonist paid, another to be able to count your own real gains. Kopkind gives us the heady sense of an encounter really joined at last, of battle lines drawn. But in the days of Birmingham, too, people had the excited sense of an engagement entered. Kopkind himself grants, "It is at once obvious that the period of greatest danger is just beginning."

I have slighted, however, one point that he is making, and a very central point: "Poor blacks," he writes, "have stolen the center stage from the liberal elites . . . their actions indict the very legitimacy of [the] government." Yes, this is a fact not to overlook: the people of the ghettos have thrown down a challenge to government that is radical. But Kopkind is writing about two things: the offering of radical challenge and resort to violence. And he writes clearly as though he assumes that such a challenge can only be offered violently. It is with this assumption that I argue.

It is an assumption many share. Carl Oglesby seems to share it. In *Containment and Change* he criticizes "the politics of the appeal to higher power . . . the same thing as prayer . . . a main assumption of which is that [the higher power] is not bad, only misinformed." He appears to see all nonviolent action as covered by this definition. "This way of thinking brought the peasants and priests to their massacre at Kremlin Square in 1905. . . . It rationalized the 1963 March on Washington for Jobs and Freedom. The Freedom Rides, the nonviolent sit-ins, and the various Deep South marches were rooted in the same belief: that there was indeed a higher power which was responsive and decent. . . . The Vietnam war demonstrations are no different. . . . The main idea has always been to persuade higher authority . . . to do something. Far from calling higher authority into question, these demonstrations actually dramatize and even exaggerate its power."

He goes on then to describe how the "whimsical" hopes that are entertained about the powerful evaporate: "Sometimes mass-based secular prayer has resulted in change. But more often it has only shown the victim-petitioner that the problem is graver and change harder to get than [he] had imagined. . . . It turns out that the powerful know perfectly well who their victims are . . . and that they have no intention of changing anything. This recognition is momentous, no doubt the spiritual low point of the emergent revolutionary's education. He finds that the enemy is not a few men but a whole system whose agents saturate the society. . . . He is diverted by a most realistic despair. But this despair contains within itself the omen of that final reconstitution of the spirit which will prepare [him] . . . for the shift to insurgency, rebellion, revolution. . . . At the heart of his despair lies the new certainty that there will be no change which he does not produce by himself."

With this description I do not argue at all. It is a very accurate description of the education those protesting in this country have been receiving. May more and more read the lesson. I argue with the contention that nonviolent action can only be prayerful action—must by its nature remain naive. Too often in the past it has confined itself to petition, but there is no need for it to do so—especially now that so many have learned "change [is] harder to get than they had imagined." As Kopkind writes, "All that has come until now is prologue." But this does not mean that our alternatives have suddenly been reduced. There have always been those in the nonviolent movement who called for radical action. The pressure that nonviolent moves could put upon those who are opposing change, the power that could be exerted this way, has yet to be tested.

I have introduced the word "power" deliberately. When the slogan "Black Power" was first taken up, the statements immediately issued, both for and against it, all seemed to imply that "power" was a word inconsistent with a faith in nonviolence. This was of course the position taken by Stokely Carmichael: "We had to work for power because this country does not function by morality, love and nonviolence, but by power. For too many years, black Americans marched and had their heads broken and got shot. They were saying to the country, 'Look, you guys are supposed to be nice guys and we are only going to do what we are supposed to do. Why . . . don't you give us what we ask?' . . . We demonstrated from a position of weakness. We cannot be expected any longer to march and have our heads broken in order to say to whites: Come on, you're nice guys. For you are not nice guys. We have found you out."

Carmichael gives us: the humble appeal to conscience on the one hand, the resort to power on the other. If the choice were really this, anyone who wanted change would certainly have to abandon nonviolent action. For as Bradford Lyttle comments in a paper on Black Power, no, most people are not nice guys. "It isn't necessary to be hit over the head to learn this. . . . Some Christians call the un-niceness of people 'original sin.' It's Freud's 'ego.' Naturalist Konrad Lorenz studies it as aggressiveness and argues convincingly that it's instinctive with men. Whatever the un-niceness may be, it is part of all of us, and our job is to minimize it."

The trouble is that advocates of nonviolence themselves often write in terms that seem to corroborate the picture Carmichael paints. When they actually engage in direct action, they pay great attention to other than moral pressures that can be and have to be placed on those with whom they are struggling. But on paper they tend again and again to stress only the appeal that can be made to conscience. Bradford, in his paper on Black Power, notes: "Carmichael's vision isn't limited to Negroes. Machiavelli had it: . . . 'A man who wishes to make a profession of goodness in everything must necessarily come to grief among so many who are not good. Therefore it is necessary . . . to learn how not to be good.'" Then he pleads that to put one's faith in coercive power is tragic, and his argument is: "Throughout history, those who have most deeply touched the hearts of hardened men have been the ones who chose not to defend themselves with violence." He, too, seems here to pose a narrow choice: resort to power (learning how not to be good) or appeal to conscience (learning, Carmichael would put it, to do only what we are supposed to do).

But the choice is very much wider than this (as Bradford of course knows); and the distinctions that seem to have been set up here are unreal. To resort to power one need not be violent,[1] and to speak to conscience one need not be meek. The most effective action both resorts to power *and* engages conscience. Nonviolent action does not have to beg others to "be nice." It can in effect force them to consult their consciences—or to pretend to have them. Nor does it have to petition those in power to do something about a situation. It can face the authorities with a new fact and say: Accept this new situation which *we* have created.

If people doubt that there is power in nonviolence, I am afraid that it is due in part to the fact that those of us who believe in it have yet to find for ourselves an adequate vocabulary. The leaflets we pass out tend to speak too easily about love and truth—and suggest that we hope to move men solely by being loving and truthful. The words do describe our method in a kind of shorthand. But who can read the shorthand? It is easy enough to recommend "love." How many, even among those who like to use the word, can literally feel love for a harsh opponent—not merely pretending to while concealing from themselves their own deepest feelings? What is possible is to act toward another human being on the assumption that all men's lives are of value, that there is something about any man to be loved, whether one can *feel* love for him or not.[2] It happens that, if one does act on this assumption, it gives one much greater poise in the situation. It is easy enough to speak about truth; but we had better spell out how, in battle, we rely upon the truth. It is not simply that we pay our antagonist the human courtesy of not lying to him. We insist upon telling him truths he doesn't want to hear—telling what seems to us the truth about the injustice he commits. Words are not enough here. Gandhi's term for nonviolent action was "satyagraha"—which can be translated as "clinging to the truth." What is needed is this—to *cling* to the truth as one sees it. And one has to cling with one's entire weight. One doesn't simply say, "I have a right to sit here," but acts out that truth—and sits here. One doesn't just say, "If we are customers in this store, it's wrong that we're never hired here," but refuses to be a customer any longer. One doesn't just say, "I don't believe in this war," but refuses to put on a uniform. One doesn't just say, "The use of napalm is atrocious," but refuses to pay for it by refusing to pay one's taxes. And so on and so on. One brings what economic weight one has to bear, what political, social, psychological, what physical weight. There is a good deal more involved here than a moral appeal. It should be acknowledged both by those who argue against nonviolence and those who argue for it that we, too, rely upon force.

If greater gains have not been won by nonviolent action it is because most of those trying it have, quite as Oglesby charges, expected too much from "the powerful"; and so, I would add, they have stopped short of really exercising their peculiar powers—those powers one discovers when one refuses any longer simply to do another's will. They have stopped far too short not only of widespread nonviolent disruption but of that form of noncooperation which is assertive, constructive—that confronts those who are "running everything" with independent activity, particularly independent economic activity. There is leverage for change here that has scarcely begun to be applied.

To refuse one's cooperation is to exert force. One can, in fact, exert so very much force in this way that many people will always be quick to call noncooperators violent. How, then, does one distinguish nonviolent from violent action? It is not that it abstains from force, to rely simply upon moral pressure. It resorts even to what can only be called physical force—when, for example, we sit down and refuse to move, and we force others to cope somehow with all these bodies. The distinction to make is simply that those committed to a nonviolent discipline refuse to injure the antagonist. Of course if nonviolent action is as bold as it must be in any real battle for change, some at least of those resisting the change are bound to *feel* that injury has been done them. For they feel it as injury to be shaken out of the accustomed pattern of their lives. The distinction remains a real one. Perhaps there is another way it could be put. The man who acts violently forces another to do *his* will—in Fanon's words, he tears the other away from himself, pushes him around, often willing to break him, kill him. The man who acts nonviolently insists upon acting out his *own* will, refuses to act out another's—but in this way, only, exerts force upon the other, not tearing him away from himself but tearing from him only that which is not properly his own, the strength which has been loaned to him by all those who have been giving him obedience.

But the distinction I have just made is a little too neat. In almost any serious nonviolent struggle, one has to resort to obstructive action. When we block access to buildings, block traffic, block shipments, it can be charged that we go a little further than refusing obedience and impose upon the freedom of action of others. There is some justice to the charge. I nevertheless think it appropriate to speak of nonviolent obstruction, and I would revert to my original description as the definitive one: the person committed to nonviolent action refuses to injure the antagonist. It is quite possible to frustrate another's action without doing him injury.[3] And some freedoms are basic freedoms, some are not. To impose upon another man's freedom to kill, or his freedom to help to kill, to recruit to kill, is not to violate his person in a fundamental way.[4]

But I can imagine the impatience of some of my readers with these various scruples. What, they might say, has this to do with fighting battles—battles which are in dead earnest? How can we hope to put any real pressure upon an adversary for whom we show such concern?

This is the heart of my argument: We can put *more* pressure on the antagonist for whom we show human concern. It is precisely solicitude for his person *in combination with* a stubborn interference with his actions that can give us a very special degree of control (precisely in our acting both with love, if you will—in the sense that we respect his human rights—and truthfulness, in the sense that we act out fully our objections to his violating *our* rights). We put upon him two pressures—the pressure of our defiance of him and the pressure of our respect for his life—and it happens that in combination these two pressures are uniquely effective.

One effect gained is to "raise the level of consciousness" for those engaged in the struggle—those on both sides. Because the human rights of the adversary are respected, though his actions, his official policies are not, the focus of attention becomes those actions, those policies, and their true nature. The issue cannot be avoided. The antagonist cannot take the interference with his actions personally, because his person is not threatened, and he is forced to begin to acknowledge the reality of the grievance against him. And those in rebellion—committed to the discipline of respect for all men's lives, and enabled by this discipline to avoid that "trance" Fanon describes, "where the face of the other beckons me on to giddiness," is enabled to see more and more clearly that (as Oglesby says) "the enemy is not a few men but a whole system," and to study that system.

The more the real issues are dramatized, and the struggle raised above the personal, the more control those in nonviolent rebellion begin to gain over their adversary. For they are able at one and the same time to disrupt everything for him, making it impossible for him to operate within the system as usual, and to temper his response to this, making it impossible for him simply to strike back without thought and with all his strength. They have as it were two hands upon him—the one calming him, making him ask questions, as the other makes him move.

In any violent struggle one can expect the violence to escalate. It does so automatically, neither side being really able to regulate the process at will. The classic acknowledgment of this fact was made by President Kennedy when he saluted Premier Khrushchev for withdrawing nuclear missiles from Cuba. "I welcome this message," he said, because "developments were approaching a point where events could have become unmanageable." In nonviolent struggle, the violence used against one may mount for a while (indeed, if one is bold in one's rebellion, it is bound to do so), but the escalation is no longer automatic; with the refusal of one side to retaliate, the mainspring of the automation has been snapped and one can count on reaching a point where de-escalation begins. One can count, that is, in the long run, on receiving far fewer casualties.

Nothing is more certain than this and yet, curiously, nothing is less obvious. A very common view is that nonviolent struggle is suicidal. This is, for example, Andrew Kopkind's view: "Turn-the-other-cheek was always a personal standard, not a general rule: people can commit suicide but peoples cannot. Morality, like politics, starts at the barrel of a gun." (A surprising sentence, but by morality he means, no doubt, the assertion of one's rights.) The contention that nonviolent struggle is suicidal hardly stands up under examination. Which rebels suffered more casualties—those who, under Gandhi, managed to throw the British out of India or the so-called Mau Mau who struggled by violence to throw the British out of Kenya? The British were certainly not "nice guys" in their response to the Gandhians. They, and the Indian troops who obeyed their orders, beat thousands of unarmed people, shot and killed hundreds. In the Amritsar Massacre, for example, they fired into an unarmed crowd that was trapped in a spot where no one could escape and killed 379 people, wounding many more. There was a limit, nevertheless, to the violence they could justify to themselves—or felt they could justify to the world. Watching any nonviolent struggle, it is always startling to learn how long it can take the antagonist to set such limits; but he finally does feel constrained to set them—especially if his actions are well publicized. In Kenya, where the British could cite as provocation the violence used against them, they hardly felt constrained to set any limits at all on their actions, and they adopted tactics very similar to those the Americans are using today against the Vietnamese. In that struggle for independence, many thousands of Africans fighting in the forest and many thousands of their supporters and sympathizers on the reserves were killed. Many were also tortured.[5]

One can, as I say, be certain if one adopts the discipline of nonviolence that in the long run one will receive fewer casualties. And yet very few people are able to see that this is so. It is worth examining the reasons why the obvious remains unacknowledged. Several things, I think, blind people to the plain truth.

First, something seems wrong to most people engaged in struggle when they see more people hurt on their own side than on the other side. They are used to reading this as an indication of defeat, and a complete mental readjustment is required of them. Within the new terms of struggle, victory has nothing to do with their being able to give more punishment then they take (quite the reverse); victory has nothing to do with their being able to punish the other at all; it has to do simply with being able, finally, to make the other move. Again, the real issue is kept in focus. Vengeance is not the point; change is. But the trouble is that in most men's minds the thought of victory and the thought of punishing the enemy coincide. If they are suffering casualties and the enemy is not, they fail to recognize that they are suffering *fewer* casualties than they would be if they turned to violence.

Actually, something seems wrong to many people, I think, when—in nonviolent struggle—they receive any casualties at all. They feel that if they are not hurting anybody, then they shouldn't get hurt themselves. (They shouldn't.

But it is not only in nonviolent battle that the innocent suffer.) It is an intriguing psychological fact that when the ghetto uprisings provoked the government into bringing out troops and tanks—and killing many black people, most of them onlookers—observers like Kopkind decided that the action had been remarkably effective, citing as proof precisely the violence of the governments' response. But when James Meredith was shot, just for example, any number of observers editorialized: "See, nonviolence doesn't work." Those who have this reaction overlook the fact that nonviolent battle is still battle, and in battle of whatever kind, people do get hurt. If personal safety had been Meredith's main concern, he could, as the saying goes, have stayed at home.

Battle of any kind provokes a violent response—because those who have power are not going to give it up voluntarily. But there is simply no question that—in any long run—violent battle provokes a more violent response and brings greater casualties. Men tend not to think in long-run terms, of course; they tend to think in terms of isolated moments. There will always be such moments that one can cite, in which a particular man might have been safer if he had been armed. If Meredith had been carrying a loaded pistol, he might well have shot his assailant before the man shot him. (He might also well have been ambushed by still more men.) Whatever one can say about overall statistics, some men will always *feel* safer when armed—each able to imagine himself the one among many who would always shoot first.

To recognize that men have greater, not less control in the situation when they have committed themselves to nonviolence requires a drastic readjustment of vision. And this means taking both a long-range view of the field and a very much cooler, more objective one. Nonviolence can inhibit the ability of the antagonist to hit back. (If the genius of guerilla warfare is to make it impossible for the other side really to exploit its superior brute force, nonviolence can be said to carry this even further.) And there is another sense in which it gives one greater leverage—enabling one both to put pressure upon the antagonist and to modulate this response to that pressure. In violent battle the effort is to demoralize the enemy, to so frighten him that he will surrender. The risk is that desperation and resentment will make him go on resisting when it is no longer even in his own interest. He has been driven beyond reason. In nonviolent struggle the effort is of quite a different nature. One doesn't try to frighten the other. One tries to undo him—tries, in the current idiom, to "blow his mind"—only in the sense that one tries to shake him out of former attitudes and force him to appraise the situation now in a way that takes into consideration your needs as well as his. One is able to do this— able in a real sense to change his mind (rather than to drive him out of it)— precisely because one reassures him about his personal safety all the time that one keeps disrupting the order of things that he has known to date. When— under your constant pressure—it becomes to his own interest to adapt himself to change, he is able to do so. Fear for himself does not prevent him. In this sense a liberation movement that is nonviolent sets the oppressor free as well as the oppressed. . . .

What has very clearly worked, in the evolution of animals, to preserve and advance the life of each species, has been a particular *balance* of two instincts. The one, as it were, asserts the individual's right to exist. This is the so-called evil instinct. Lorenz names it "aggression." But just as I would substitute another word for Fanon's "violence," I would substitute another word here—and rename "aggression" "self-assertion." The second instinct restrains the first when it endangers another's right to exist. In human terms, the first amounts to respecting one's own person, the second to respecting the person of the other. Lorenz points out, by the way, that the only animals capable of love are those that are "aggressive." One can, it seems, *only* love another "as one loves oneself."

This life-saving balance—this equilibrium between self-assertion and respect for others—has evolved among animals on the physiological plane. In human beings it can be gained only on the plane of consciousness. And the plea this essay makes is precisely that we make the disciplined effort to gain it—all those of us who hope really to change men's lives, who, in Fanon's words, "want humanity to advance a step further," want to "set afoot a new man." My plea is that the key to a revolution that would "go forward all the time . . . in the company of Man, in the company of all men," lies in discovering within ourselves this poise. But it calls equally for the strengthening of *two* impulses—calls both for assertion (for speaking, for acting out "aggressively" the truth, as we see it, of what our rights are) and for restraint toward others (for the acting out of love for them, which is to say of respect for their human rights). May those who say that they believe in nonviolence learn to challenge more boldly those institutions of violence that constrict and cripple our humanity. And may those who have questioned nonviolence come to see that one's rights to life and happiness can only be claimed as inalienable if one grants, in action, that they belong to all men.

Notes

[1] Although those in the Movement who issued critical statements against use of the slogan "Black Power" seemed almost always to imply that "power" was an improper word, I couldn't help noticing that just that word had a way of slipping into their own publicity releases—an S.C.L.C. release, for example, repudiating the slogan but speaking the next moment of the "political power" they sought through pushing voter registration.

[2] Sometimes, if one disciplines oneself to act upon this assumption, the feeling itself of love for one's enemy enters one, taking one by surprise—a kind of grace. Some readers may ask: Why should one want to feel love for one's enemy? But I note that Fanon in *Black Skin, White Masks* writes, "I, the man of color, want only this: . . . That it be possible for me to discover and to love man, wherever he may be."

[3] It is possible, but not always simple. When we stage an act of massive obstruction in a city, for example, there is always the risk that we will prevent some emergency call from being answered—prevent a doctor's car from getting through, perhaps. One has obviously to anticipate such situations and be ready to improvise answers to the human problems raised.

[4] I am uneasy, however, at the way Carl Davidson of S.D.S. words his defense of obstruction. He writes in *New Left Notes* of November 13, 1967: "The institutions our resistance has desanctified and delegitimized, as a result of our action against their oppression of others, have lost all authority and hence all respect. As such, they have only raw coercive power.

Since they are without legitimacy in our eyes, they are without rights. Insofar as individuals, such as recruiters, continue to remain in association with those institutions, they run the risk of being given the same treatment. . . . We can assert the Nuremberg decisions and other past criteria of war crimes as the criteria by which we, in conscience, decide whether or not an institution and individuals associated with that institution have lost their legitimacy and their rights." *Can* one give individuals the same treatment that one gives institutions—and deny them *all* respect? If he means that we need not grant individuals the right to oppress others, I am in agreement. But if he means that when we can identify an individual as an oppressor, then we need not treat him as though he had *any* human rights—he alarms me. This formulation would seem to me to lead into grim territory.

[5] See *Mau Mau from Within* by Barnett and Njama.

Molly Rush and the Plowshares Eight

Liane Ellison Norman

"Why me?" Molly wrote to her husband and children on the lined stationery of Berks County jail. It was the question each member of her family asked over and over: "Why *her?*"

"Because I know," Molly went on by way of answer. "Because I love you."

"I have no idea what any of the products actually consist of or what they are for," said Cox. "My job is strictly security."

Patrolman Simmons, the security guard who started out as a janitor, said his job was "to protect General Electric property. I didn't ask them what the property was. My job is checking people coming in."

One of the toolmakers explained, "All I know is we make hardware. My responsibilities are to design and fabricate special tooling that fabricates that particular product."

The financial analyst, who—using purchase orders and vouchers—later computed the dollar value of the damage that the eight had done, said, "I call it a product, the hardware that we ship. That is all I know it as."

Another toolmaker insisted, "I work on tooling only. I am a toolmaker. I don't work on hardware at all." He said he had no idea whether the hardware was designed to be outfitted with a thermonuclear bomb. "If it does or not, I don't know. It don't carry it in G.E."

Still another toolmaker said, "I don't know what you mean by nuclear warhead. I have never seen a nuclear warhead."

Robert Hartmann, manager of Shop Operations, acknowledged, in his somewhat grand way, "I know what a reentry vehicle is," and he named it with some pride, the Mark 12 A, but he declined to know its use. "I have no idea whether it is first-strike capability or not. I have no idea what the so-called payload could be or would be."

The *Philadelphia Inquirer* advertised for engineers. "Break State of the Art Barriers with G.E. Re-Entry Systems Division," said the ad. "You'll have all the freedom and responsibility you'd like. Plenty of room to move up. Close to convenient public transportation, with free parking for those who drive. Give us a chance to make history together." The ad did not say the state of *which* art's barriers were to be broken, nor in what respect employees would be free and responsible, nor how history was to be made. General Electric did not seem eager for future employees to know what they would be employed to make, nor did the employees themselves seem eager to know what they made.

It wasn't so much that when Molly said "Because I know," she was privy to special information, but that what others chose not to know or knew only in a distant way, she felt with the sense of vivid reality that would not permit her to dismiss it. "Gut level," she said, smiling and laying her hand across the belly that had six times grown large with child.

These people, Molly said, "come to work every day and disconnect themselves from what they do so they won't know what they're doing." She and the other seven, who came to be known as the Plowshares Eight, meant to disrupt the daily calm, the workaday disconnections of the people who drove the swift roads that separated them from their homes and families and communities to earn their living at General Electric. Their daily work was unreality, Molly thought—unlocking doors; checking workers' badges and bundles; patrolling to ensure the customary tedium; taking the permitted breaks; making tools to make hardware, equipment, products; packing, shipping, and tagging them; toting up the dollars and cents. "We wanted to get to the reality, to the truth that these things are for human destruction." In this ordinary building, at the busy crossroads where the old inn of lapsed hospitality and forgotten history stood neglected, "They're building genocide."

For the two funnels, that looked like four-foot ice-cream cones upended, were the outer casings of a pair of Mark 12 A nuclear warheads.

Each began as a finely tooled, glistening aluminum shell, which was then coated with the hard black material so that—when they were fired outside of the earth's atmosphere by an intercontinental ballistic missile, a Minuteman III or an MX missile—the warhead would not burn up in the friction of reentry into the earth's atmosphere. This coating was the material on the black cone, which rang like a bell when it was hit, and which made the aluminum "shell" into the "shield and shell."

At a later stage of manufacture, each warhead would be fitted with a miniature electronic guidance system which would direct it with great accuracy to its own target. Each warhead would have, as far as could be determined, a fifty-fifty chance of hitting within six hundred feet of that target. Three or more such warheads, each with its own guidance system, would be fitted into the "shroud" manufactured, according to a General Electric floorplan, in a room not far from the Non-Destructive Test Area.

The last stage of the warhead's manufacture would take place in Amarillo, Texas, a town famous for its slaughterhouses. There at the Pantex plant, a thermonuclear bomb of at least 350 kilotons would be fitted into each shield and shell. A kiloton is the explosive equivalent of a thousand tons of dynamite: the atomic bomb dropped on Hiroshima in 1945 was twelve and a half kilotons.

It was the precision, coupled with the explosive power of these warheads that most worried and outraged Molly Rush and her seven companions, who therefore brought their hammers and their blood into General Electric on that autumn day. The warheads would be, when they were finished, first-strike weapons. They were constructed with such precision and explosive power in order to be able to "kill" enemy missile silos before the weapons those silos held could be launched. But though the targets which the warheads were intended to destroy were other weapons, millions of people, or "soft targets" as they are called in military jargon, would be killed, too, not to mention "collateral damage"—the destruction of communities and their homes, churches, schools, museums, grocery stores, croplands, roads, bridges, historic monuments, and family Bibles, listing generations of births and deaths.

The killing part of such weapons—designed to be shot out into space, to reenter the earth's atmosphere, to find targets programmed into their circuits ahead of time, and to explode with such force—would be huge and invulnerable, Molly had thought.

Both she and Sister Anne Montgomery, the slender nun who had kept Cox from the phone for a few seconds, were surprised by the fragility of what the employees referred to as "hardware," "material," or "equipment."

Molly had been sure that "these things would be absolutely impregnable." She had imagined herself "hammering on this thing and not making a dent." She remembered feeling flakes of aluminum fly up around her face as she hammered, and she later discovered tiny bruises under her chin where they had hit. That a small woman, only five feet two inches tall, hammering with an ordinary household hammer, could render these two warheads forever useless "exploded so many myths in my mind!" Molly exclaimed. She hoped that the destructibility of the warhead casings and her own unarmed capacity to destroy them had exploded some of the same myths in the minds of General Electric employees.

When Chester Drobek, greatly perturbed by the events in Building Number 9, had escorted Molly and her seven companions to the back lobby, she had looked back at the wreckage they had made and had been pleased. It was "an incredible scene," she said, the dented gold and the scratched black cones, the dribbled blood, all vivid under the bright industrial lighting in the large, blank room. And then again, when the police took her back in the wheelchair to be identified, "I got this picture of the whole scene." It had been roped off, like a reconstructed room in an historic house, the beaten objects, the blood, the ruined papers. "But it hadn't been touched. Employees were clustered around in doorways and hallways, absolutely awestruck looks on their faces, absolutely astonished, I don't know what word to use—white faces, and," she groped for the word, "shock, profound shock." After that glimpse, "We were taken back to the police station."

Molly had thought about the employees at General Electric long and hard beforehand. "Every day many people go to work, building these weapons that are going to kill their children and my kids," she said, wonder in her voice.

The employees could avoid knowing what they manufactured as well as their power to refuse to accept the work they felt compelled to do, "because of secrecy, because of psychic numbing." And because, she meditated, the weapons they helped to make "are idols in the Old Testament sense—not golden calves, but golden nose cones." Aloud she wondered, "I don't understand how people can put their faith and trust in nuclear weapons and not trust the God who made this planet." Her voice, always low, thickened with intensity.

There was no guarantee that smashing a couple of reentry vehicles, taken from their boxes and set upon a workbench, would have any practical effect, Molly knew. But she had been faithful, she said. She had therefore been "freed from the myth of my own powerlessness. If I didn't end the arms race, I acted on behalf of life—and," she mused, "*connected* with a lot of people. We broke through the numbing."

Molly's intention on that hot September day, which began cool, was very simple. She intended to wreck as many warheads as possible. In her view, they violated Pennsylvania law, international law, and God's law merely by existing. She intended that those few warheads—she could not reasonably expect to dismantle the whole arsenal of around thirty thousand—would never be used. She did not make her plans by calculating backwards from the probable consequences. She did what she thought she had to do.

As she understood it, the nuclear arms race was her business—everyone's business. She knew she was expected to leave it to arms-control theorists to manage the risks of the weapons which were daily manufactured at plants like General Electric's Building Number 9. She was unwilling to do that. Therefore, she took it upon herself to begin to end what she saw as an overwhelming threat to herself, her family, and her community. She went to King of Prussia from her hometown of Pittsburgh on the western side of the state. She left her husband and her six children, who ranged in age from twenty-five to twelve, to commit the act that disrupted the day's work in Building Number 9 and left her, wearing the state's shoes, in jails away from home. In all, she spent seventy-eight days in five jails—four weeks in Berks County jail, two weeks in Lebanon County jail, five days in Mercer County jail, three and a half weeks in York County jail, two days in Delaware County jail, from which she was returned to York County jail. She was released just before Thanksgiving.

She knew something of the consternation she left in her wake: her husband, Bill, her children, her seven brothers and sisters, their husbands, wives, and children, and innumerable friends and associates were shocked and horrified. She had told members of her family that she was going to do something that might result in a long jail term but had shared no details, partly to prevent interference, partly to prevent conspiracy charges from being brought against them. Therefore, she had to explain and reassure.

"Dear Bill, and Gary, Linda and Bob [Linda's husband], Janine, Dan, Bob and Greg," she wrote on her first full day of imprisonment. "Missing you all." Meals, she said, were "pretty good." She was "sleeping in a dorm (curtains on the windows) with two bunk beds and one single. Downstairs is the recreation room and from there is the yard with grass and volleyball court. Anne and I did some yoga after dinner—she's teaching me. I'm reading Tolstoy short stories right now. He was a famous Russian novelist. He wrote *War and Peace*. Will be glad to get some books of my own. They have to be mailed in new. It may be O.K. to bring in my Bible. Otherwise, I can have a pair of jeans, two or three T-shirts, underpants, sox, shoes, nightgown and robe. The place is surrounded by trees, which I can see from the windows. Not bad." She might have been away on a trip or in the hospital having a baby.

"Please let everyone know," she wrote, "I'm feeling very good about the way things have gone. I feel very strongly that the Holy Spirit has been with us continually as we went about exposing the vulnerability of the powers that seem so strong."

She addressed the younger children. "Dan, Bob and Greg—I need you to be brave and strong and wise beyond your years. Please be good and help Daddy." And to Gary, Linda and Janine, the older ones, she said, "I'm counting on you—and on Dan—to be of help and to stay your own good selves." To her husband, Bill, who had done everything and said everything he could think of to prevent her from going to King of Prussia, she wrote, "I appreciate your love and support. I know I can count on you, and I know how rare it is to have that.

"This is a separation that may not be easy," she wrote, having no idea how long it would be, for in jail, all decisions are made by someone else and rarely explained, an inmate having almost no influence over what happens. Knowing how exposed and conspicuous her children must feel, with their mother in the news as a criminal, she wrote, "Maybe you're wishing right now that you had a normal mother instead of me. That's O.K. I understand. But don't think I'm a criminal because we tried to call others accountable. After seeing what I saw first hand, the precision and deep care that goes into producing something capable of 35 Hiroshimas in one small two- or three-foot cone—and that's all that those hundreds of workers in that one place do, forty hours a week—you know that it *has* to be stopped *soon* before it's too late."

She knew her family and community well and could predict what the common view would be: wives and mothers belong at home; families belong together. But she reminded them that "War breaks up families, while husbands, fathers, brothers, and sons go to fight and maybe be killed. People call it sacrificing for their country. And *no one* thinks it's strange or abnormal, even knowing that a war today can kill everyone."

Molly's hero was the Trappist monk Thomas Merton, who had written in 1963, "I believe we live in a time in which one cannot help making a decision for or against [people], for or against life, for or against justice, for or against truth. And all these decisions rolled into one (for they are inseparable) amount to a decision for or against God. Such an attitude," he went on, "implies no heroism, no extraordinary insight, no special moral qualities, and no unusual intelligence." As far as Molly was concerned, not to act was a decision *against* life, justice, and truth.

She tried to explain. Without being possessed of heroism, special insight, special morality, or special intelligence, she was a mother, and she had made her decision on that basis.

She felt deeply the deprivation of home, but she wrote, "It may be a good thing for you to have to fend for yourselves for a time. People who have everything done for them end up feeling helpless. People who learn to take care of themselves have a strength they'll never lose. I'm proud to see how Bobby and Greg have begun to pitch in more and more, doing things without being asked to do them." She offered practical, housewifely advice. "Dishes and laundry done two or three times a day don't pile up and seem impossible. Gary and Dan: please do your part to set the example and encourage the boys without bossing or hassling them."

More than her housewifery, she wanted to share some part of her sense of achievement. She and her seven companions had, after all, performed the first act of deliberate nuclear disarmament in thirty-five years, despite, as she commented wryly later, "the thousands of *man*-hours spent talking about it." She stressed the gender with raised eyebrows. She knew very well that even her supporters would be dazed, wondering what good it would do to make a grand gesture and end up in jail. While faithfulness rather than consequences had been on her mind, she was delighted with the consequences and wanted her delight understood. "I wish you could have seen the faces of the workers—at the time and later, when they brought us back to the scene," Molly wrote. "The impact was astonishing."

Molly kept up a lively correspondence. She wrote, "The mail is pouring in," and she was "very hungry for news." But "the best thing people can do for me is to step up the resistance to these crackpots who bring us Titan II[1], Directive #59[2], and now a radiation leak from [a] Nevada bomb test site."

Her imprisonment took place in one dreary county jail after another, each, she wrote, "stunningly like the military." What she had done seemed dwarfed by the consequences to some. "What good can she do in prison?" some of her friends wondered aloud. She wasn't trying to do any good in prison, she explained. Nor had she acted for publicity. She didn't want to go to jail. She had not pursued celebrity or martyrdom. Her object had been merely to act on what she believed. As a wife and mother, a citizen and a Christian, she felt called upon to do what was consistent with the survival of the people, the places, the ideas she loved. If she seemed buried in the avalanche of consequences that followed, well, that was something she couldn't control. She was, after all, only a tiny part of a number of systems and institutions—family, community, state and country.

To one reporter, she said, "This came to me as a gift, something I couldn't refuse, knowing what I know, loving my kids, hoping for grandchildren. I'm patient," she mused. "I've been working for a number of years. I haven't lost my patience. It's just that the situation demands more of all of us."

What seemed vandalism to General Electric employees and the Commonwealth of Pennsylvania and heroism to some of her supporters, was not so much civil *dis*obedience, she explained, as it was obedience to various legal or spiritual injunctions she felt were binding. Or not so much obedience—she disliked the authoritarian connotations—as it was an act of solidarity, bringing her religious faith and her sense of practical accountability together into one fabric without seams. "I think God works through people. Christ said, 'Love your enemy.' Well, you can't love your enemy with a nuclear weapon," she explained and went on, "Every mother ought to think about the threat that's hanging over her kids and ask what she's going to do about it."

Her children were the point of connection. What was right in this instance, obedience to Yahweh's unconditional injunction recorded in the Old Testament never to kill, suddenly—in the light of weapons technology— made good practical sense. Her children's lives were linked to the lives of the enemies' children. Hers could not survive unless theirs could too. To love one's enemy, the New Testament elucidation of the Old Testament absolute, was newly the condition of survival.

Montgomery County and the Commonwealth of Pennsylvania considered such a conclusion dangerous and illegal. Molly was a malefactor, to be kept in jail. And life in jail was something new in her experience.

"I ventured outside the walls without handcuffs today," she wrote from Lebanon County jail. She had been taken to a shopping center to get frames for her glasses, which had been broken in a volleyball game in the first prison, mended, and then broken again at the second. "Our time outdoors— for all of us—was interrupted so that the matron could take me. After I dressed in my own clothes, for the first time in a week, I had to wait nearly half an hour before we left," she wrote, and echoed the frustrated soldier's refrain, "Hurry up and wait."

She wrote that "Staff is proud of its shiny new building, strikingly similar in architecture to G.E.'s King of Prussia plant—brick, cinderblock, concrete, designed to squeeze out any humanity. Technology here, too, is master." To move anywhere, "you wait between double sets of remote-controlled doors for 'control' to wake up, check the T.V. monitor, and push the button for door number two. E—— says she once waited twenty minutes."

She rediscovered the helpless sense of childhood, the way in which being treated like children reinforced the inmates' irresponsibility and resentment. "The women feel this is like a kindergarten. A very boring one, not even finger paints and playdough, just a T.V., rug hooking kits and each other, all day, every day. For me, the advantage is having free access to my own private cell. I can read, write, pray, do yoga in relative privacy."

But common sense revolted. The warheads she had hammered were blessed by "national security," though they put all life in jeopardy. To protect the public from someone who meant to lessen that jeopardy, she was held in a "maximum security" prison with other dangerous people, "an eighteen-year-old paying off $600, plus fines, from a traffic accident at $10 per day; a twenty-year-old first offender who was with her boyfriend on an attempted armed robbery; a woman in for two months, charged with receiving stolen goods—the thieves are out on a lower bond, but she can't make bail. I told them *I* am the only dangerous criminal here." Absurdity governed the life of the prison. "We were just told to go to our cells for head count. We are six."

In the first jail, Berks County, Molly had written some reflections in her notebook. She imagined the wound she made in the lives of her family and friends, how it would close up during a prolonged absence, such as that she must contemplate. She thought it would be as if she had died and were mourned. She visualized "family and friends gathered at the house, bringing meat loaves and comfort to one another." The thought of the family gathered around food made her "want to return, to make roast chicken or spaghetti sauce, their favorites." She would miss more than a collective meal, though. "I want to watch Bob (14) and Greg (12) grow up, as I have the older ones."

She found the words and phrases at her disposal inadequate to explain "the suffering and loss I often feel," having given up—for an indefinite time—familiar patterns and relationships. "Today I feel my death to all that in its fullest, sledgehammer reality," says her notebook. "I saw the boys grow tall, begin to shave, remembering me with fondness, occasional visits or notes, and, perhaps, resentment.

"I've cracked their world open. As time goes on and the ragged edges heal, I'll be left out of their everyday reality." Her mother had died not long before, so she knew that loss. "If I were really dead, they might feel my presence as I do my mother's. Instead, they'll visit, and I'll wonder at the changes in them, no longer daily and imperceptible, but visible and startling. Talk won't be free and easy, but self-conscious.

"Perhaps I'll become a sort of myth. 'remember when she did this?' or 'we went there with Mom.' But my daily living reality has perished—at least for months, perhaps years."

Were the full sentences possible for each charge made against her to be imposed, she would spend the next sixty-four years in jail. She was just a month under forty-five years old at the time.

But, she reminded herself, rejecting self-pity as she wrote in her notebook, "It was my own decision to interfere with the production of nuclear weapons that could kill [her family], not understanding that they may experience the same guilt/anger reaction of a suicide by a close relative." Her syntax tied itself in revealing knots, indicating the complexity of her own emotions, the sense of her surprise, the sense of herself dead to those she loved (and perhaps of others dead at their own hands), a feeling shared by at least one friend, who declined to talk about Molly because "I couldn't talk about a relative who had just died, either."

"So now," wrote Molly, "I picture a lessening of grief as life goes on without me, as my presence is gradually forgotten, as new patterns of living emerge without my being a part. The pain will numb, then go away." She dreaded being "walled off from the world I love, a world of family and friends; my satisfying, frustrating work for peace and justice; of walks in the country; laughter over a beer; listening to good music; joking with my kids— all the things that bring joy into my life."

Her small fingernails, normally chipped and ragged, grew longer and pearly. "They've never been in such good shape," she laughed, but to trim and file them, she had to ask the matron if she might borrow a fingernail clipper and an old, soft emery board. "You could borrow a needle and thread if you wanted to mend something," she explained with a grimace. "Then the matron would call it right back."

"I've been allowed none of my books here—again," she wrote from Mercer County jail. She would collect a few books, sent in new from outside, and then be moved to another jail, her books taken away from her. "You don't have one belonging that hasn't carefully been gone over," she said.

From the outside, York County jail had the look of a cube made of sugar and Styrofoam, too white and glistening, set in the hills of central Pennsylvania, which were colored in early November like a threadbare Persian carpet. "This place is so disorienting," she wrote of it. "I'm *almost* grateful that Anne's finding it the same. Hard not to get lethargic. I did a couple of crossword puzzles and was glad to find that I can still do them. You begin to feel you've lost a few marbles. I would not like a long-term stay."

Each day—"another day of push-button conformity"—began with a greeting over the loudspeaker, a siren, the flickering on of fluorescent lights, and "the sound of our solid steel doors clanking open," a shower with a mechanically timed stream of warm water in a doorless, curtainless shower stall. The loudspeaker announced breakfast, to which each inmate carried her own used and washed throw-away plastic cup. Once, when she left her cup behind, she had to supply herself with one picked out of the trash.

To go to the bathroom, "You must press a button, and wait for the matron to activate the two-way speaker. 'I have to go.' The cell clanks open, then shuts behind the woman. Requests for toilet paper, Tampax, crochet hook, bring an unhurried response from one matron in particular, who smokes a cigarette before responding to the button." Eating, drinking, going to the bathroom—the mechanics of living—absorbed some of the too-plentiful time but drained energy. "I'd been too stubborn to ask the warden for my toothpaste, but yesterday, tired of brushing with water, I relented and asked for skin lotion, deodorant, toothpaste and shampoo, which are locked in a room, along with my jeans, shirt, sweater and some personal papers and letters which this place won't allow in."

By standing on her bunk—a breach of the rules—Molly could see a smidgen of the countryside out "through the strip of window." Her tiny view was some relief from the ruined lives of her sister inmates, whose faces "show the effects of drugs and jail," she noted. It amused her that, to pass the time, they played games like one called "Killer." "One young woman is in for homicide," she wrote, noting the irony that the real killer "plays it no better than the rest of us."

Weariness struggled with her attempt to define circumstances out of sight and out of mind for most of the people she knew. "Rehabilitation through sensory deprivation and infantilization—that's my description for this new maximum security jail. Designed to control every aspect of our lives and virtually to eliminate personal contact with the matrons, who themselves are controlled by rigid rules and paperwork, this place typifies the dehumanization of security-minded technology.

"The food is bad, but sufficient. The female pod is regularly cleaned by the women. Our laundry is washed daily. Our situation is like an infant's, whose bodily needs are met but whose curious nature is confined to a playpen."

She reported, "Fighting off deadly lethargy takes all my energy. My arms and legs get heavy and numb. If they came to release me today, I'd say, 'Come back tomorrow. I'm too tired right now.'"

And yet, she remarked a superiority she felt to her imprisonment. "My mind flies free," leaving the rest of her "to stand for count, remain on the cold, hard, metal seats after meals until it's time to scrape out our trays." Struggling with lassitude, tedium, and loneliness, she was discovering new resiliencies, using her imagination in new ways.

Her husband worried that she would be brutalized in jail. But "I haven't, in over two months, felt one moment of fear as I've lived among the 'hardened criminals,' awaiting trial, usually in here because they can't raise bail or pay fines." Rather, "it's the prison system that frightens me, the incredible arrogance of those who have interfered with my mail, even to the point of returning letters to my attorney and my co-defendants. I've been denied the right to call my attorney during my entire five-day stay in one jail (Mercer County), been transferred on minutes' notice. In here it's taken two days to be given my pen and my legal papers. In another jail, the matron read my outgoing mail. I refuse to be beaten down, but I will leave here angry."

But even in her outrage at the prison system's assumption that security derives from denying humanity, she noted, "The employees are more victimized than we are, sitting hour after hour in their glass cages, responding like robots to our press of a button or shouted request. Day follows boring day in this airless, sealed-off world. It's like living in a submarine. Robots or rebels are the only possible products."

She wrote pages of detail and fretted, "Still can't get it down right." There were times, she said, when "I was feeling such a sense of gratitude to be in here, sharing lives with the women here, some of whom struggle with tremendous odds." She reported having said to one woman, "To me the main message of scripture was to learn to love yourself. I think that's true: if we are to love neighbors as self, we must love ourselves enough to let God's love pour in."

Over and over again while she learned the separation and idleness of life in jail, she had to account for herself. Many people were bothered. They feared that anarchy might somehow be loosed by her act, for civil disobedience, unlike ordinary criminal acts, exposes how deeply the law depends on voluntary obedience. Molly had made the possibility of withdrawing that obedience real for others than herself, which made most people anxious. Though she was well known in Pittsburgh as a woman of perseverance in matters of peace, civil rights, workers' rights, women's rights, poor people's rights, human rights, she was also an ordinary person, a working-class mother and housewife.

Notes

[1] When a minor mishap caused a fuel tank to explode in Damascus, Arkansas, a nine-megaton Titan II missile was flung out of its silo and into the nearby woods.

[2] President Jimmy Carter's declaration of strategic policy, the aiming of United States missiles at Soviet missiles, commonly understood as a first-strike strategy, since there is little point in targeting empty silos. Therefore, they must be attacked before an enemy can fire the missiles therein.

CONTEMPORARY FEMINISM AND NONVIOLENCE

Maternal Nonviolence
A Truth in the Making

Sara Ruddick

. . . The defining activity of nonviolent activism is peacemaking, that sustained effort to create conditions of "peace" in which people can self-respectfully pursue their individual and collective projects free of the structural violences of poverty, tyranny, and bigotry. Nonviolent peacemaking is governed by four ideals: renunciation, resistance, reconciliation, and peacekeeping. Nonviolent activists renounce violent strategies and weapons. They resist, nonviolently, the violence of others, including their policies of bigotry, greed, and exploitation. The aim of nonviolent battle is responsible reconciliation in which crimes are named and responsibility for them is assigned. Peacekeepers find ways to avoid battles whenever possible and to halt necessary nonviolent battles as soon as aggression is turned back and the aims of justice are secured.

In examining maternal practice through the lens of nonviolence, I look for evidence of an ongoing attempt to renounce and resist violence, to reconcile opponents, and to keep a peace that is as free as possible from assaultive injustice. That is, I ask if there are principles in the practices of mothering that coincide with the four ideals of nonviolence. In attributing ideals of non-

Source: From *Maternal Thinking: Toward a Politics of Peace* by Sara Ruddick, pp. 161–76, 183–84. © 1989 by Sara Ruddick. Reprinted by permission of Beacon Press, Boston.

violence to peacemaking mothers, I speak about what they *aim* to teach children, but I say nothing about their pedagogical success. Mothers have little control over the decisions their draft-age children make about when or how to fight. Children are provoked to, encouraged in, and sometimes conscripted for violence by friends, public officials, and counselors, as well as by the frustrations and injustices of their lives. I do not intend to blame mothers once again for others' policies or their children's actions. In saying that mothers are governed by ideals of nonviolence, I am not talking primarily about mothers' effects on children but about the ideals that determine how mothers themselves think about anger, injury, conflict, and battle.

Those governed by an ideal can be identified by the efforts they make, by their shame, guilt, and determination to change when they fail to follow the ideal, and by their pleasure in their own and others' success. Mothers who beat and tyrannize their children or passively watch others do so and who show no signs of remorse or attempts to get help cannot be said to be governed by ideals of nonviolence. Nor is remorse sufficient to show such governance; indifferently abusive people can apologize many times over without seeking help or determining to change their violent ways. To say that an ideal governs is to say, at the least, that in an ordinary way, much of the time, the ideal is nearly fulfilled. Otherwise, ideals only mystify, as a sentimental mother-speech generally mystifies the realities of maternal life. In the peacemaking practices I describe, nonviolence is honored not in the exception but as the rule. . . .

. . . I aim to identify principles of maternal nonviolence that I believe could contribute to collective, public understandings of peacemaking. For my purpose, it is sufficient that there are *some* maternal practices actually governed by the ideals I articulate. Because I am not measuring statistical extent but rather articulating governing ideals, I refer only to those peacemaking maternal practices—atypical as they may be—that I have seen. When for stylistic ease I revert to the idiom of achievement—"mothers do . . . mothers say . . . mothers believe . . ."—I always mean only that what *some* mothers do, say, and believe is evidence of a maternal effort and that this effort is characteristic of at least some maternal practices of nonviolence. . . .

Ideals of Nonviolence

The most controversial and distinguishing ideal of nonviolent action is the renunciation of "violent" strategies and weapons. Simone Weil defined "force"—roughly her term for "violence"—as whatever "turned a person into a thing," treating that person as if he counted for nothing.[1] Gandhi spoke of "ahimsa," noninjury, a refusal to harm.[2] More prosaically, I take a violent act or policy as one that is either intended to damage or can predictably be expected to damage a person against whom it is wielded and for which there is no compensatory benefit for the person damaged. By damage, I mean serious and apparently long-lasting harm or injury. By compensatory benefit, I mean some good that the damaged person may expect from her injuries, as, for example, a patient hopes to benefit from assaultive chemotherapy.

Although damage is painful and harmful, not all pain and harm are violent. If I fall and break my arm I have not suffered violence. Violence is almost always coercive, inflicted without a person's consent, but people also inflict violence on themselves. The drug addict and anorexic are not, typically, coerced into the behavior that damages them. Someone violent to herself or cooperating in her own violence treats herself as a "thing" of no value, says to herself "I do not count." Damage can be psychological as well as physical and can be indirectly as well as directly visited on the violated person. A person whose loved one is killed or tortured is an indirect victim of violence. However, the clearest case of damage is physical injury or harm to the violated person. Other kinds of damage are understood by analogy to this central case, in which the human body becomes the place of pain and domination.

Whether in the midst of action or in moments of calm reflection, it is often very difficult to identify violence. The most elaborate definitions cannot substitute for judgment and indeed must be altered in its light. Who is to say whether damage could have been predicted? How serious is "serious," how long "long-lasting"? Who is to determine compensatory benefit? Although I worry over these questions in other discussions of nonviolence, for my purposes here I have clear enough cases of violence to anchor a definition. Torturing a person, burning her with napalm, destroying her home and provisions, killing her loved ones—all these routine acts of tyranny and war are clearly violent. So are painful and extensive beatings, sexual assault on vulnerable young people, and humiliating practices of shaming—the routine acts of domestic tyranny and violence.

In the renunciation of violent weapons and strategies, it is customary to distinguish those who are relatively weaponless and powerless from those who believe they could, if they chose, use violence effectively. Mothers, as we have seen, often feel powerless in respect to their children and, typically, are actually powerless in respect to men in their home and social group. Minority or poor mothers are also powerless in respect to men and women of governing classes and races.

Like other powerless people, mothers resort to nonviolent strategies because they do not have weapons—guns, legal clout, money, or any other tools with which to work one's will on others. Like the powerless everywhere, mothers are often enraged. Officials callously neglect or deliberately injure their children. Mothers feel as if they relinquish pleasures and ambitions to do important human work only to find that their work is taken for granted and their word for naught. Fantasies of revenge must thrive among mothers. Yet they are rarely capable of violent revenge on their own or their children's behalf. Officials—teachers, welfare workers, landlords, doctors and the like—can retaliate against the children as well as the mothers themselves at the hint of maternal violence. Even maternal anger is apt to be punished or trivialized (the "hysteria" of an "overinvolved" or "embittered" woman). Nor, ideally, can mothers turn against their children whom they are pledged to protect. To get their way, mothers engage in nonviolent techniques that are familiar from more public struggles: prayer, persuasion, appeasement, self-suffering, negotiation, bribery, invocation of authority, ridicule, and many other sorts of psychological manipulation. These techniques may go to the edge of violence—of real damage—without endangering either a mother, her children, or the people they fight against.

From the perspective of nonviolent activism, what is striking about mothers is their commitment to nonviolent action in precisely those situations where they are undeniably powerful, however powerless they may feel—namely, in their battles with children. Children are vulnerable creatures and as such elicit either aggression or care. Recalcitrance and anger tend to provoke aggression, and children can be angrily recalcitrant. Typically, the mother who confronts her children is herself young, hassled if not harassed by officials in an outside world, usually by her own employers, and often by adults she lives with. She brings to confrontations with her children psychological and physical strengths which are potentially lethal. Her ability to damage her children increases the more alone she is with them, the less others are available to go to the children's aid. Yet it is these same circumstances of frustration and loneliness that will tempt her to violence when faced with her children's recalcitrance. I can think of no other situation in which someone subject to resentments at her social powerlessness, under enormous pressures of time and anger, faces a recalcitrant but helpless combatant with so much restraint. This is the nonviolence of the powerful.

It might be thought that, like other powerful people, mothers only appear to renounce violence while actually maintaining control by the fear they inspire. It does not follow, however, that because mothers are fearsome, their control is typically and primarily a function of fear. Control by fear and threat is always fragile. Threats must be sufficiently frightening to deter but not so frightening to have undesired effects. When adults are frightened, they may react by deceiving those who frighten them, resenting and abandoning them, resisting them courageously out of self-respect, or becoming so terrified that they no longer can play or work. Young children, only barely able to distinguish the illusory from the legitimate fear, are still more likely to respond unpredictably and destructively when frightened. Although many mothers threaten, often ritualistically, their threats are often limited not only in number but, more important, by the context of protectiveness in which they occur. Those mothers who are governed by ideals of nonviolence know this and ensure that their threats occur amid effective, trustworthy means of nonviolent control.

Because they are powerful, mothers can also discipline a child by deliberately inflicting pain through measures that do not risk damaging a child, such as controlled "spanking," a deliberate use of pain quite distinct from damaging beatings or angry blows. Frequently, mothers who threaten or resort to the infliction of pain draw their children into the discipline, requiring them to pick a switch from the yard or to agree on and then count the number of strokes. I have heard such mothers defend their discipline as a measured expression of justice that prevents less worthy, capricious expressions of anger. Mothers (like me) who criticize the infliction of pain point out the danger that controlled violence will escalate into uncontrolled abuse, especially if a child becomes actively resistant. Moreover, both mothers and children can become sexually excited by the conjunction of pain, domination, and submission. Most generally, the social construction of a child's body as a vulnerable locus of pain seems a preparation for later public domination and submission, even if it does not humiliate or sexually confuse the young child.

Although I believe that the deliberate infliction of pain is predictably, though not invariably, damaging to a child, my point here is that it is within practices governed by ideals of nonviolence that mothers argue about pain in the ways I report. In my experience of maternal arguments, mothers do not advocate bullying, capriciousness, or any sort of physically damaging violence. Despite deeply felt generational, cultural, or temperamental differences among mothers, they seem to agree that a practice, *if damaging*, should be renounced and then go on to argue about damage. If my experience is at all typical, these maternal debates about the benefits and dangers of inflicting pain do not contradict but rather actually reflect an ongoing maternal effort to be governed by the ideal of renunciation, however differently the ideal is interpreted.

As their discussions about pain make clear, mothers who renounce violence must find some acceptable ways to train and control. This requires recognizing violence in its many forms. Beyond certain clear and visible acts of physical damage, the distinction of what actions seriously harm and injure varies from family to family and from culture to culture. There is a tendency among pacifist theorists to escalate the requirements for "ahimsa," or noninjury, considering even thoughts and wishes as damaging acts. Gandhi's description of ahimsa provides a striking example of such an inclusive definition:

> Not to hurt any living thing is no doubt a part of ahimsa. But it is its least expression. The principle of ahimsa is hurt by every evil thought, by undue haste, by lying, by hatred, by wishing ill to anybody.[3]

> Ahimsa really means that you may not offend anybody, you may not harbor an uncharitable thought even in connection with one who may consider himself to be your enemy.[4]

> Impatience is a phase of violence.[5]

Mothers who embrace the Gandhian ideal will be in for sleepless nights. It would be nearly impossible for mothers to renounce uncharitable thoughts and angers, let alone impatience. Rather, their task is to determine which hurts, hates, impatience, and lying are damaging and which strategies are effective and consonant with safety, development, and conscientiousness.

Maternal conversations, heard in a certain spirit, are as filled with controversy about the morality and effectiveness of strategies as are the meetings of war cabinets. By my definition, any strategy of fighting or resisting that does not actually damage an opponent is nonviolent. The trick is to distinguish permissible hurt from damaging harm, nonviolent coercion from damaging force. "Forcing" a child to go to bed or grabbing a knife from his hand is, in almost all contexts, nonviolent though coercive. An inoculation is a permissible hurt. But many bribes, threats, lures, reprimands, and other manipulative nonviolent techniques become questionable when development and conscientiousness are at stake.

Of the many controversial techniques of nonviolent manipulation, the uses of "self-suffering" are especially prominent because of the role they played in the public nonviolence associated with Gandhi and Martin Luther King, Jr. A self-sufferer takes upon herself the pain involved in fighting. Willingness to suffer is considered a condition of endurance and a testament to seriousness and courage. To assume rather than to inflict suffering is also, for both King and Gandhi, an expression of love. In the midst of the brutal violence of the civil rights movement, King promised:

> Send your hooded perpetrators of violence into our community at the midnight hour and beat us and leave us half dead, and we shall still love you.[6]

This echoes his mentor Gandhi:

> Love ever suffers, never resents, never revenges itself. . . . The test of love is *tapasya* and *tapasya* means self-suffering.[7]

Self-suffering is also a weapon that induces guilt and shame in the conscientious opponent and sympathy in the "whole world [that] watches." The famous nonviolent, unarmed assault on the salt mines in India, where Satyagrahi marched in unbroken ranks against soldiers who beat them, was an instance of self-suffering and, proleptically, a fulfillment of King's promise: "Be ye assured we will wear you down by our capacity to suffer."[8]

Whatever its public uses, in maternal nonviolence self-suffering is morally and practically limited. Self-suffering is sometimes a prominent maternal strategy. Mothers may manipulatively display the pain their children cause them, adeptly employing the tears and tones of suffering. Yet mothers often realize that children are not and cannot afford to be too long and deeply affected by maternal tears. The limits of self-suffering are part of a general limitation on provoking children's guilt and shame. A child's conscientiousness develops slowly and unpredictably. While the capacity for shame and guilt may be necessary for conscientiousness, excessive guilt leads to anger, indifference, or inhibition while humiliating shame damages a precariously developing self.

Like any other nonviolent strategy, techniques of self-suffering may be evaluated in terms of an insistence, central to pacifism, on the inseparability of means and end. Although Gandhi spoke of ahimsa as the means to truth, saying that "without Ahimsa it is not possible to seek and find Truth," he undermined this distinction conceptually and practically:

> Ahimsa and Truth are so intertwined that it is practically impossible to disentangle and separate them. They are like two sides of a coin, or rather a smooth, unstamped metallic disc. Who can say which is the obverse and which is the reverse.[9]

To paraphrase Gandhi, if the preservation and growth of children is truth, then a criterion of its realization is that it be achieved nonviolently. However closely an outcome resembles an original goal—a child asleep or in school—a method that damages a child has failed. Drugging a child to sleep or dragging her into a school room is not a means to but a perversion of the end they allegedly achieve.

Although the ends of mothering cannot be achieved violently and still remain maternal ends, nonviolence is not a mother's only goal. Mothers aim to nurture and train an adult capable of work and love. They also typically have aims for their children that are related to their religious, political, or intellectual groups. These long-range goals inform some intermediate choices and help a mother to make sense of her work as a whole. Nonetheless, they must be pursued flexibly, with attention to particular challenges and circumstances. Gandhi held on to the distant aim of home rule through years of actions, compromises, and settlement. Yet in the course of struggle, the long-range goal was too general to dictate strategy. Rather it was the nonviolence of ongoing struggle that gradually, over time, gave meaning to the goal. Similarly, a mother cannot decide what to do with a bullying or frightened child by appealing to models of adulthood. It is the nonviolence of daily life that is itself a goal to which longer-range aims must be adapted. Gandhi never gave up the goal of home rule. Mothers, by contrast, may be called on to relinquish religious or political aims that are dear to them. All the more important for mothers to learn to interpret long-range goals flexibly as they attend to the specific tasks at hand. As Gandhi would say, "The way is the truth"; or as feminists put it, "The process is the project."

There is nothing simple about a commitment to nonviolence. A mother often finds herself confronted with seemingly untenable choices. Either she gives her child sleeping pills or he will go sleepless and become increasingly unable to sleep; either she locks a child in her room or she continues to beat on her brother, all other means of prevention having failed; either she drags him sobbing into the classroom or reinforces his fear that school is indeed a dangerous place. Mothers have to do *something*—nighttimes and school days arrive, siblings must live together. Relief comes when a difficult day or phase has passed. The issue again is what counts as success. To the extent that a child is damaged, i.e., controlled violently, the ends of preservation and growth are compromised.

Partly because nonviolent fighting is exhausting and peace and quiet are such a relief, most mothers avoid battles when they can and end unavoidable battles quickly. To be sure, some mothers seem to thrive on battle with or among their children. The perception of a child's separateness, central to fostering growth and conscientiousness, is needed to prevent mothers from taking their children's part in battles with an inappropriate enthusiasm. Although she may be tempted to fight more often and with more fervor than children require, it is in a mother's self-interest to limit battles. Most of her children's "enemies" are members of her neighborhood and school community, often indeed children of close friends. Typically a mother will be held and will hold herself responsible for any damage her children cause or suffer if nonviolence turns to violence. In children's battles, as in adults', escalation can be swift—a shouting child stomps on the baby's stomach, an insulting taunt is met with a brick to the head. Moreover, even nonviolent battle has its cost. Hurting and being hurt are part of fighting. Scraped knees and feelings usually mend with astonishing speed, but they can also be stubbornly immune to aid; even the most nonviolent strategy can go awry and leave its scars.

Peace is the more secure, the fewer weapons at hand. In domestic as in public life, there is no substitute for disarmament. Ideally, a mother keeps her house and yard as weapon-free as possible, despite the advertising of toys far more lethal than play pistols and the increasing popularity in the United States of keeping real, dangerous guns at home. She also tries to disarm her neighbors' children. It would be unrealistic to leave weapons about, let alone to pile them up deliberately, and then to expect children not to use them when provoked. But as in public life, disarmament can never be complete. Even if real guns are banned, there are always weapons available to the weak as well as the strong—blocks, rocks, play trucks, and sewing needles, for example. Moreover, bigger children are often as physically capable of seriously injuring a smaller child as is a mother herself. Although weapons should be eliminated wherever possible, there is no substitute for the renunciation of violence. By example and precept a mother has to train children not to stamp on the baby, throw a rock at the head, push a toddler in the river, or squirt insecticide in an enemy's face.

To keep the peace, a peacemaking mother, as best she can, creates ways for children and adults to live together that both appear to be and are fair. She distributes goods and privileges, listens carefully to complaints, and respectfully explains the unavoidable differences in powers and rewards that are inevitable among adults and children of different ages. Faced with rivalry, tyranny or greed, nonviolent mothers do not sit passively by, letting a stronger or older child annex the possessions or exploit the smaller or more vulnerable one. Arbitrating and restraining, mothers appeal to interests the children share—or invent them. In reinforcing the fragile affections that survive rivalry and inevitable inequality, mothers who are guided by ideals of nonviolence work for the day that their children will come to prefer justice to the temporary pleasures of tyranny and exploitation.

A mother who aspires to nonviolence makes a peace worth keeping. But the best peace should not entirely prevent battle. Premature appeasement or totalitarian techniques of controlling conflict, though comforting, prevent children from learning how to recognize what they want, articulate their desire, and set out to achieve it. Such evasive techniques leave them unpracticed in victory or defeat and therefore unmindful of the necessity for and ways to achieve reconciliation. They encourage those who are treated unjustly to despair of change and allow those who dominate, either through strength or oppression, to remain oblivious to the cost their dominance exacts on themselves and others. To put the matter starkly, children whose conflict is always managed for them are trained both to submit to power and to exercise abusive power over others.

Mothers are often accused of appeasement and totalitarian control. They walk away from the scene, lie to make a child feel better, insist on the appearance of affection where there is none, bribe or threaten children into denying their anger and hurt, or create small rituals of disorder—shouts, slaps, and tears—that appear to express conflict while burying it in noise. Most mothers have sometimes done these things. The belief dies hard that children will be so good, or an order so artful, that fighting will disappear. Yet for the most part, mothers appreciative of nonviolence know that "peace and quiet" can mask many kinds of violence; some battles with and between children should and must take place.

Even more important than her attitude toward children's battles is a nonviolent mother's commitment to resist authorities and policies that are unjust or harmful. Like anyone else, in the face of superior power, mothers often succumb to fearfulness and despair. But they also often name and encourage, in themselves and their children, the duty to resist, and they recognize their lack of resistance as failure. Most striking is the courageous resistance, in the face of danger, against enormous odds, by mothers who live in poverty, tyranny, and slavery. In quieter times, more fortunate mothers exhibit their own barely visible courage as they get for their children what they need and learn to say no to those who hurt them. When they identify resistance as a virtue, mothers try to teach children to stand up for themselves and others, knowing that mothers themselves may be the first authority a child resists and that those around them, including other mothers, may criticize the spiritedness they have fostered. An unusually spunky mother, Grace Paley's Faith, the same character who took it to be part of her work to raise children "righteously up," faces the consequences of another mother's disapproval:

> How can you answer that boy?
> "You don't," says Mrs. Julius Finn. . . . "You answer too much, Faith Asbury, and it shows. Nobody fresher than Richard."
> "Mrs. Finn," I scream in order to be heard, for she's some distance away and doesn't pay attention the way I do. "What's so terrible about fresh. EVIL is bad, WICKED is bad. ROBBING, MURDER, and PUTTING HEROIN IN YOUR BLOOD is bad."
> "Blah, blah," she says, deaf to passion. "Blah to you."[10]

Peacekeeping is the art of avoiding battle; the challenge is to recognize when peacekeeping should end and battle begin. Resistance is the art of discerning, and then having the courage to fight, violences. The challenge is to recognize when fighting is no longer justified but is motivated by vengeance, battle pleasure, or inertia. In peace campaigns there is often a tension between those gifted in nonviolent fighting and those adept at peacekeeping. A peace politics must coordinate and reward the efforts of both kinds of work. Similarly, some mothers will be more adept at peacekeeping, others at resisting. In maternal conversations, mothers often help each other develop both gifts while using their special talents on behalf of each other's children.

Nonviolent battles are meant to end quickly, but not any end will do. People who have fought must be reconciled; harder, once nonviolent battle is won, people who have been abused must forgive. King's views are not atypical:

> Forgiveness does not mean ignoring what has been done or putting a false label on an evil act. It means rather that the evil act is no longer a barrier to the relationship. . . . The evil deed of the enemy-neighbor, the thing that hurts, never quite expresses all that he is. . . . We must not seek to hate or humiliate the enemy but to seek his understanding. . . . Hate multiplies hate, violence multiplies violence. . . . Hate scars the soul. . . . Like an unchecked cancer, hate corrodes the personality and eats away its vital unity.[11]

In public battles, where peoples and nations are hatefully and violently abused, to forgive is as intellectually confusing and morally controversial as is renunciation of violence at the outset. For mothers, by contrast, the ideal of responsible reconciliation is a routine aspect of training and education. Mothers name the evils that are done to or by their children. It is wrong (usually) to lie, bully, or humiliate, although children—and mothers—do these things. It is also wrong to suffer such insults in silence or to forgive perpetrators before the deed is named and the agent held responsible. Mothers, like children, are tempted to patch up prematurely, make do, and forget. After all, many "crimes" by and against children are trivial, and some cheerful forgetting is necessary to get through the day. But nonviolence is not simple. There is no rule for distinguishing the trivial "childish" escapade from more serious hurt. While moralism has its clear limits, cheery forgetfulness is no morality at all. Truthful, responsible reconciliation protects children from their own or others' hatred, which "scars the soul," and also from forgetful indifference to pain that they have inflicted or suffered and that, like hate, "corrodes the personality and eats away its vital unity."[12]

Assigning and taking responsibility comes fairly easily to mothers, even when they themselves have become violent. Maternal "forgiveness" is a more complicated phenomenon. Mothers often forgive their children even for serious crimes of violence and bigotry despite their clear harm. If a passionate loyalty overcomes her ability to name her child's crime and to urge upon him responsibility for it, then a mother has failed to live up to the ideal of responsible reconciliation. While mothers may forgive their children too easily, many find it difficult to forgive themselves. A responsible reconciliation would require of mothers a clear-sighted, resiliently cheerful appreciation of their own imperfections as well as their children's. It is probably most difficult for mothers to forgive people they perceive as their children's enemies—hard enough when opponents are children, almost impossible if the enemies are adults. Often children's "enemies" are also a mother's—Father, mate, grandparent, or friend who have treated both mother and child badly. In their harshness, mothers are not wrong. If mothers can name and take responsibility, it is much more likely that the peace that follows battle will be sturdy, Yet hatred does "scar the soul," frequently also imposing on the injured children a vengeance they no longer need. Often mothers realize this. After the bitterest divorce or most divisive neighborhood or school battle, there are mothers who let combatants and even outright offenders make amends and resume relationships in the interest of the active connectedness that is "peace."

The four ideals of nonviolence—renunciation, resistance, reconciliation, and peacekeeping—govern only some maternal practices of some mothers. Yet it is also true that to elucidate these ideals is to describe, from a particular perspective, maternal practice itself. Peacemaking mothers create arrangements that enable their children to live safely, develop happily, and act conscientiously; that is, they preserve, nurture, and train, exemplifying the commitments of maternal work. . . .

At its best, maternal nonviolence is a reality in the making, or, to borrow a phrase attributed to the French philosopher Maurice Merleau-Ponty, a *vérité-a-faire*, a truth-to-be-made.[13] The reality is only in the making because failures are many and the ideal marks a struggle that is often lost. Nonetheless there is a reality: there are maternal practices in which ideals of nonviolence actually govern. Mothers can, and often do, renounce the violence to which they are tempted, fight back against the violence done to them and their children, name and insist on responsibility for damages done, yet forswear a scarring hatred in favor of a peace in which they can love and work.

Peacemakers can learn from maternal nonviolence even when mothers themselves do not extend or publicize the nonviolence they imperfectly practice. Conversely, whether or not they take on public militarism, mothers should find it illuminating to look at the ordinary tasks and temptations of their work through the lens of nonviolence. Maternal struggles to achieve nonviolence parallel and illuminate the struggle to achieve a sturdy peace. Whatever their public antimilitarist commitments, nonviolent mothers offer an invigorating image of peace as an active connectedness. All participants resist others' violence and their own temptations to abandon or assault, persisting in relationships that include anger, disappointment, difference, conflict, and nonviolent battle.

Notes

[1] Simone Weil, *Iliad, Poem of Force*, p. 3 and passim.

[2] Gandhi's principal writings on nonviolence are collected in *Non-Violent Resistance* (New York: Schocken Books, 1981). A very useful book for understanding Gandhi's theory of non-

violence is Joan Bondurant, *The Conquest of Violence* (Berkeley: University of California Press, 1971). An excellent, brief, and secular discussion of nonviolence is Barbara Deming, "Revolution and Equilibrium," published, along with other essays on nonviolence, in *We Are All Part of One Another* (Philadelphia: New Society Publishers, 1984). The essay is also printed in pamphlet form published by the A. J. Muste Essay Series (New York: A. J. Muste Institute). The pamphlet is available from the War Resisters' League, 339 Lafayette St., New York, NY 10012. The political theorist Gene Sharp has written extensively on nonviolence, developing a strong tactical defense of its usefulness. See, for example, *Making Europe Unconquerable: The Potential of Civilian Based Deterrence and Defense* (New York: Ballinger Books, 1985). The War Resisters' League is a very helpful guide to the literature of nonviolence, and essays, journals, and books can be found in their small bookstore.*

Throughout this chapter I invoke the words of Gandhi and King as an aid of identifying maternal nonviolence. I do not, however, believe that there is any simple translation of domestic to public nonviolence.

[3] Gandhi, cited in Bondurant, p. 24.

[4] Gandhi, cited in Bondurant, p. 26.

[5] Gandhi, *Non-Violent Resistance*, p. 73.

[6] Martin Luther King, Jr., "Loving Your Enemies," sermon delivered Christmas 1957, Montgomery, Alabama, p. 11. King's writings have been collected in *A Testament of Hope: The Essential Writings of Martin Luther King, Jr.*, ed. James Melvin Washington (San Francisco: Harper & Row, 1986). Here I use pamphlet number 1 in the A. J. Muste Essay Series (New York: A. J. Muste Institute). This pamphlet, available from the War Resisters' League, includes "Loving Your Enemies," "Letter from the Birmingham Jail," and "Why We Are in Vietnam?"

[7] Gandhi, cited in Bondurant, p. 26.

[8] King, "Loving Your Enemies," p. 11.

[9] Gandhi, *Non-Violent Resistance*, p. 42. The march against the salt mines was led by Gandhi's followers and took place after Gandhi was arrested during his march to the sea to procure salt—a witty and effective protest against the salt tax. The event is depicted in the movie *Gandhi* and described in most accounts of Gandhi's campaigns. See, for example, Erik Erikson, *Gandhi's Truth* (New York: Norton, 1969).

[10] Grace Paley, "Faith in a Tree," in *Enormous Changes at the Last Minute* (New York: Farrar Straus and Giroux, 1987), p. 85. This passage was pointed out by Jane Lazarre, a mother of black sons who, along with her husband, was determined to raise her children to resist but also feared for their safety in a hostile world. She then had to steel herself to remain calm—though she was in fact both proud and frightened—when her adolescent sons were "fresh" not only to her but, more worrisome, to authorities on whose goodwill they depended.

[11] King, "Loving Your Enemies," pp. 4–8 and passim.

[12] King, "Loving Your Enemies," p. 8.

[13] Merleau-Ponty is cited in Raymond Geuss, *The Idea of a Critical Theory* (Cambridge: Cambridge University Press, 1981).

*Editor's note: The works by Bondurant, Deming, and Sharp mentioned in this note are included elsewhere in this anthology.

PART FOUR

PACIFISM

Preview

Richard Nixon, while he was president and the Vietnam War was still raging, characterized himself as a pacifist. This struck some pacifists as interesting, considering that he was in a position to end the war at any time after his election in 1968. United States involvement did not end until 1973, the war itself until 1975.

This raises the question of what pacifism actually is.

As William James (1842–1910) brings out in the first selection, pacifism is the conviction that war is wrong. Morally wrong. It is not the view that war is merely bad or even terrible. And to desire peace is not to be a pacifist; virtually everyone desires peace. Militarists desire peace. Politicians desire peace. Even Hitler desired peace (though not eternal peace, which he thought would bring about the downfall of humankind); it's just that what he desired was peace on his own terms. To be a pacifist is to believe that war is wrong and that it ought not be engaged in.

But just as the opposition to violence may take a variety of forms, so the opposition to war may take various forms.

Absolute pacifism holds that war is wrong under any conceivable circumstances, not merely under circumstances that exist in the world today or are likely to exist in the future. Probably few people are pacifists in this

173

sense. And it surely is unreasonable to expect that a conviction of the wrongness of war extends to this extreme. To insist that it must would be like saying that people are not vegetarians unless they are absolute vegetarians and would refuse to eat a single hamburger even if the fate of the universe hinged upon it. It is enough to be a vegetarian if one thinks eating meat is wrong in the world as we know it. And it is enough to be a pacifist if one thinks war is wrong in the world as we know it.

To be a conditional pacifist is precisely to hold this latter position: that war in the world as we know it is wrong. How we should live in the infinite number of worlds that science fiction might postulate may be of theoretical interest, but it has little bearing on the problems of war we actually face.

So-called "nuclear" pacifism, on the other hand, represents a serious qualification of the opposition to war. For nuclear pacifists are opposed only to nuclear war, not to war in general. Their opposition is not so much to war as it is to what they consider the excessive destructiveness of one type of war.

It is worth remembering also, as we noted in the introduction, that pacifism *per se* should not be confused with nonviolence. For it is opposition to the violence of war that makes one a pacifist; whether one opposes *all* violence is another matter. And, as we shall see in Part Five, Gene Sharp also distinguishes from pacifism the pragmatic nonviolence whose techniques he elaborates.

Pacifism, however, like nonviolence, may be espoused on various grounds, one of the most common of which is religious. But many pacifists oppose war on secular, moral grounds in the belief that it is too destructive to have any moral justification, or that, whatever its other consequences, it inevitably and unjustifiably kills innocent people.

In the opening article of this section, William James does not detail the reasons for his moral opposition to war. What is especially interesting about his discussion, however, is his attempt to find a practical way of doing away with war. It is a concept people could accept (assuming they accept his views of the function of war) whether or not they are convinced pacifists. He believes that there are certain tendencies in people that require outlets: the need for discipline, the need to confront demanding challenges, the need to exhibit hardihood and courage. These tendencies traditionally have found expression in the martial pursuits. Often war has been thought to be valuable to civilization expressly because it brings out such qualities.

This view is reduced to absurdity in the selection by A. A. Milne (1882–1956). Milne, reacting in part to the horror of World War I, blends history with his storytelling humor and finesse to point out the irrational logic of conducting wars because they "bring out some of people's best traits." He also illustrates various other absurdities of war.

Nonetheless, James's proposed solution to the problem of war is to find alternative outlets for these martial tendencies, particularly in the form of some sort of national service: a "moral equivalent" of war, as he puts it. At least some aspects of this reasoning are reflected in recent proposals to substitute national service for any possible future military draft.

Skeptics of pacifism commonly ask how one can refrain from using violence against those who would kill innocent people. "Doesn't pacifism amount to passivity?" they query. "How would a nation of pacifists respond to an aggressor?"

The first of these questions is addressed in the selection by Evelyn Wilcock, a Jew who asks the same question in the context of the Nazi atrocities of World War II and earlier. Her answer is the answer of all pacifists: nonviolence does not necessarily entail nonresistance. Wilcock documents the many nonviolent responses to the Holocaust undertaken by Jews and non-Jews alike.

Of course, such nonviolent resistance takes courage, perhaps courage of the highest kind. In a selection taken from his book *The Warriors: Reflections on Men in Battle*, J. Glenn Gray (1917–1977) begins with a quote from—of all philosophers—Nietzsche, in which Nietzsche gives strong voice to the moral perils of hating and fearing as well as to the moral perils of making oneself hated and feared. Gray argues that the horrors of modern war may make possible as well as necessary the cultivation of the great moral strength required to renounce all war.

Whether or not James is right that the abolition of war requires finding a substitute outlet for certain traits in human nature, it is surely the case that any realistic alternative to war must provide some accounting of how a people who have renounced war can hope to achieve the basic defensive objectives that they once believed justified going to war.

Liane Ellison Norman, who has served on the board of directors of the Civilian-Based Defense Association and is one of today's most effective writers on nonviolence and pacifism, confronts the critics of nonviolence on this issue and sets out what she sees as the bases of power that must be understood to make nonviolent defense work. Jessie Wallace Hughan (1876–1955), a leading pacifist and socialist who was active in the Fellowship of Reconciliation and the War Resisters League, leads readers through some of the steps of a possible nonviolent response to an invasion by a foreign power.

This question of how a pacifist responds to aggressive war is thus addressed directly in the essays at the end of this section. Further, they set the stage for the discussion of how nonviolence is best practiced, views that are taken up in Part Five.

The Moral Equivalent of War

William James

The war against war is going to be no holiday excursion or camping party. The military feelings are too deeply grounded to abdicate their place among our ideals until better substitutes are offered than the glory and shame that come to nations as well as to individuals from the ups and downs of politics and the vicissitudes of trade. There is something highly paradoxical in the modern man's relation to war. Ask all our millions, north and south, whether they would vote now (were such a thing possible) to have our war for the Union expunged from history, and the record of a peaceful transition to the present time substituted for that of its marches and battles, and probably hardly a handful of eccentrics would say yes. Those ancestors, those efforts, those memories and legends, are the most ideal part of what we now own together, a sacred spiritual possession worth more than all the blood poured out. Yet ask those same people whether they would be willing in cold blood to start another civil war now to gain another similar possession, and not one man or woman would vote for the proposition. In modern eyes, precious though wars may be, they must not be waged solely for the sake of the ideal harvest. Only when forced upon one, only when an enemy's injustice leaves us no alternative, is a war now thought permissible.

It was not thus in ancient times. The earlier men were hunting men, and to hunt a neighboring tribe, kill the males, loot the village and possess the females, was the most profitable, as well as the most exciting, way of living. Thus were the more martial tribes selected, and in chiefs and people a pure pugnacity and love of glory came to mingle with the more fundamental appetite for plunder.

Modern war is so expensive that we feel trade to be a better avenue to plunder; but modern man inherits all the innate pugnacity and all the love of glory of his ancestors. Showing war's irrationality and horror is of no effect upon him. The horrors make the fascination. War is the *strong* life; it is life *in extremis*; war-taxes are the only ones men never hesitate to pay, as the budgets of all nations show us.

History is a bath of blood. The *Iliad* is one long recital of how Diomedes and Ajax, Sarpedon and Hector *killed*. No detail of the wounds they made is

Source: *The Moral Equivalent of War*, by William James (The Association for International Conciliation).

spared us, and the Greek mind fed upon the story. Greek history is a panorama of jingoism and imperialism—war for war's sake, all the citizens being warriors. It is horrible reading, because of the irrationality of it all—save for the purpose of making "history"—and the history is that of the utter ruin of a civilization in intellectual respects perhaps the highest the earth has ever seen.

Those wars were purely piratical. Pride, gold, women, slaves, excitement, were their only motives. In the Peloponnesian war for example, the Athenians ask the inhabitants of Melos (the island where the "Venus of Milo" was found), hitherto neutral, to own their lordship. The envoys meet, and hold a debate which Thucydides gives in full, and which, for sweet reasonableness of form, would have satisfied Matthew Arnold. "The powerful exact what they can," said the Athenians, "and the weak grant what they must." When the Meleans say that sooner than be slaves they will appeal to the gods, the Athenians reply: "Of the gods we believe and of men we know that, by a law of their nature, wherever they can rule they will. This law was not made by us, and we are not the first to have acted upon it; we did but inherit it, and we know that you and all mankind, if you were as strong as we are, would do as we do. So much for the gods; we have told you why we expect to stand as high in their good opinion as you." Well, the Meleans still refused, and their town was taken. "The Athenians," Thucydides quietly says, "thereupon put to death all who were of military age and made slaves of the women and children. They then colonized the island, sending thither five hundred settlers of their own."

Alexander's career was piracy pure and simple, nothing but an orgy of power and plunder, made romantic by the character of the hero. There was no rational principle in it, and the moment he died his generals and governors attacked one another. The cruelty of those times is incredible. When Rome finally conquered Greece, Paulus Aemilius was told by the Roman Senate to reward his soldiers for their toil by "giving" them the old kingdom of Epirus. They sacked seventy cities and carried off a hundred and fifty thousand inhabitants as slaves. How many they killed I know not; but in Etolia they killed all the senators, five hundred and fifty in number. Brutus was "the noblest Roman of them all," but to reanimate his soldiers on the eve of Philippi he similarly promises to give them the cities of Sparta and Thessalonica to ravage, if they win the fight.

Such was the gory nurse that trained societies to cohesiveness. We inherit the warlike type; and for most of the capacities of heroism that the human race is full of we have to thank this cruel history. Dead men tell no tales, and if there were any tribes of other type than this they have left no survivors. Our ancestors have bred pugnacity into our bone and marrow, and thousands of years of peace won't breed it out of us. The popular imagination fairly fattens on the thought of wars. Let public opinion once reach a certain fighting pitch, and no ruler can withstand it. In the Boer war both governments began with bluff but couldn't stay there, the military tension was too much for them. In

1898 our people had read the word "war" in letters three inches high for three months in every newspaper. The pliant politician McKinley was swept away by their eagerness, and our squalid war with Spain became a necessity.

At the present day, civilized opinion is a curious mental mixture. The military instincts and ideals are as strong as ever, but are confronted by reflective criticisms which sorely curb their ancient freedom. Innumerable writers are showing up the bestial side of military service. Pure loot and mastery seem no longer morally avowable motives, and pretexts must be found for attributing them solely to the enemy. England and we, our army and navy authorities repeat without ceasing, arm solely for "peace," Germany and Japan it is who are bent on loot and glory. "Peace" in military mouths today is a synonym for "war expected." The word has become a pure provocative, and no government wishing peace sincerely should allow it ever to be printed in a newspaper. Every up-to-date dictionary should say that "peace" and "war" mean the same thing, now in *posse*, now *in actu*. It may even reasonably be said that the intensely sharp competitive *preparation* for war by the nations *is the real war*, permanent, unceasing; and that the battles are only a sort of public verification of the mastery gained during the "peace"-interval.

It is plain that on this subject civilized man has developed a sort of double personality. If we take European nations, no legitimate interest of any one of them would seem to justify the tremendous destructions which a war to compass it would necessarily entail. It would seem as though common sense and reason ought to find a way to reach agreement in every conflict of honest interests. I myself think it our bounden duty to believe in such international rationality as possible. But, as things stand, I see how desperately hard it is to bring the peace-party and the war-party together, and I believe that the difficulty is due to certain deficiencies in the program of pacificism which set the militarist imagination strongly, and to a certain extent justifiably, against it. In the whole discussion both sides are on imaginative and sentimental ground. It is but one utopia against another, and everything one says must be abstract and hypothetical. Subject to this criticism and caution, I will try to characterize in abstract strokes the opposite imaginative forces, and point out what to my own very fallible mind seems the best utopian hypothesis, the most promising line of conciliation.

In my remarks, pacificist though I am, I will refuse to speak of the bestial side of the war-*régime* (already done justice to by many writers) and consider only the higher aspects of militaristic sentiment. Patriotism no one thinks discreditable; nor does any one deny that war is the romance of history. But inordinate ambitions are the soul of every patriotism, and the possibility of violent death the soul of all romance. The militarily patriotic and romantic-minded everywhere, and especially the professional military class, refuse to admit for a moment that war may be a transitory phenomenon in social evolution. The notion of a sheep's paradise like that revolts, they say, our higher imagination. Where then would be the steeps of life? If war had ever stopped, we should have to re-invent it, on this view, to redeem life from flat degeneration.

Reflective apologists for war at the present day all take it religiously. It is a sort of sacrament. Its profits are to the vanquished as well as to the victor; and quite apart from any question of profit, it is an absolute good, we are told, for it is human nature at its highest dynamic. Its "horrors" are a cheap price to pay for rescue from the only alternative supposed, of a world of clerks and teachers, of coeducational and zo-ophily, of "consumer's leagues" and "associated charities," of industrialism unlimited, and feminism unabashed. No scorn, no hardness, no valor any more! Fie upon such a cattleyard of a planet!

So far as the central essence of this feeling goes, no healthy minded person, it seems to me, can help to some degree partaking of it. Militarism is the great preserver of our ideals of hardihood, and human life with no use for hardihood would be contemptible. Without risks or prizes for the darer, history would be insipid indeed; and there is a type of military character which every one feels that the race should never cease to breed, for every one is sensitive to its superiority. The duty is incumbent on mankind, of keeping military characters in stock—of keeping them, if not for use, then as ends in themselves and as pure pieces of perfection,—so that Roosevelt's weaklings and mollycoddles may not end by making everything else disappear from the face of nature.

This natural sort of feeling forms, I think, the innermost soul of army-writings. Without any exception known to me, militarist authors take a highly mystical view of their subject, and regard war as a biological or sociological necessity, uncontrolled by ordinary psychological checks and motives. When the time of development is ripe the war must come, reason or no reason, for the justifications pleaded are invariably fictitious. War is, in short, a permanent human *obligation*. General Homer Lea, in his recent book *The Valor of Ignorance*, plants himself squarely on this ground. Readiness for war is for him the essence of nationality, and ability in it the supreme measure of the health of nations.

Nations, General Lea says, are never stationary—they must necessarily expand or shrink, according to their vitality or decrepitude. Japan now is culminating; and by the fatal law in question it is impossible that her statesmen should not long since have entered, with extraordinary foresight, upon a vast policy of conquest—the game in which the first moves were her wars with China and Russia and her treaty with England, and of which the final objective is the capture of the Philippines, the Hawaiian Islands, Alaska, and the whole of our Coast west of the Sierra Passes. This will give Japan what her ineluctable vocation as a state absolute forces her to claim, the possession of the entire Pacific Ocean; and to oppose these deep designs we Americans have, according to our author, nothing but our conceit, our ignorance, our commercialism, our corruption, and our feminism. General Lea makes a minute technical comparison of the military strength which we at present could oppose to the strength of Japan, and concludes that the islands, Alaska, Oregon, and Southern California, would fall almost without resistance, that San Francisco must surrender in a fortnight to a Japanese investment, that in three or four months the war would be over, and our republic, unable to regain what it had heedlessly neglected to protect sufficiently, would then "disintegrate," until perhaps some Caesar should arise to weld us again into a nation.

A dismal forecast indeed! Yet not unplausible, if the mentality of Japan's statesmen be of the Caesarian type of which history shows so many examples, and which is all that General Lea seems able to imagine. But there is no reason to think that women can no longer be the mothers of Napoleonic or Alexandrian characters; and if these come in Japan and find their opportunity, just such surprises as *The Valor of Ignorance* paints may lurk in ambush for us. Ignorant as we still are of the innermost recesses of Japanese mentality, we may be foolhardy to disregard such possibilities.

Other militarists are more complex and more moral in their considerations. The *Philosophie des Krieges*, by S. R. Steinmetz is a good example. War, according to this author, is an ordeal instituted by God, who weighs the nations in its balance. It is the essential form of the State, and the only function in which peoples can employ all their powers at once and convergently. No victory is possible save as the resultant of a totality of virtues, no defeat for which some vice or weakness is not responsible. Fidelity, cohesiveness, tenacity, heroism, conscience, education, inventiveness, economy, wealth, physical health and vigor—there isn't a moral or intellectual point of superiority that doesn't tell, when God holds his assizes and hurls the peoples upon one another. *Die Weltgeschichte ist das Weltgericht*; and Dr. Steinmetz does not believe that in the long run chance and luck play any part in apportioning the issues.

The virtues that prevail, it must be noted, are virtues anyhow, superiorities that count in peaceful as well as in military competition; but the strain on them, being infinitely intenser in the latter case, makes war infinitely more searching as a trial. No ordeal is comparable to its winnowings. Its dread hammer is the welder of men into cohesive states, and nowhere but in such states can human nature adequately develop its capacity. The only alternative is "degeneration."

Dr. Steinmetz is a conscientious thinker, and his book, short as it is, takes much into account. Its upshot can, it seems to me, be summed up in Simon Patten's word, that mankind was nursed in pain and fear, and that the transition to a "pleasure-economy" may be fatal to a being wielding no powers of defence against its disintegrative influences. If we speak of the *fear of emancipation from the fear-régime*, we put the whole situation into a single phrase; fear regarding ourselves now taking the place of the ancient fear of the enemy.

Turn the fear over as I will in my mind, it all seems to lead back to two unwillingnesses of the imagination, one aesthetic, and the other moral; unwillingness, first to envisage a future in which army-life, with its many elements of charm, shall be forever impossible, and in which the destinies of peoples shall nevermore be decided quickly, thrillingly, and tragically, by force, but only gradually and insipidly by "evolution"; and, secondly, unwillingness to see the supreme theatre of human strenuousness closed, and the splendid military aptitudes of men doomed to keep always in a state of latency and never show themselves in action. These insistent unwillingnesses, no less than other aesthetic and ethical insistencies, have, it seems to me, to be listened to and respected. One cannot meet them effectively by mere counter-insistency on war's expensiveness and horror. The horror makes the thrill; and when the question is of getting the extremest and supremest out of human nature, talk of expense sounds ignominious. The weakness of so much merely negative criticism is evident—pacificism makes no converts from the military party. The military party denies neither the bestiality nor the horror, nor the expense; it only says that these things tell but half the story. It only says that war is *worth* them; that, taking human nature as a whole, its wars are its best protection against its weaker and more cowardly self, and that mankind cannot *afford* to adopt a peace-economy.

Pacificists ought to enter more deeply into the aesthetical and ethical point of view of their opponents. Do that first in any controversy, says J. J. Chapman, *then move the point*, and your opponent will follow. So long as anti-militarists propose no substitute for war's disciplinary function, no *moral equivalent* of war, analogous, as one might say, to the mechanical equivalent of heat, so long they fail to realize the full inwardness of the situation. And as a rule they do fail. The duties, penalties, and sanctions pictured in the utopias they paint are all too weak and tame to touch the military-minded. Tolstoi's pacificism is the only exception to this rule, for it is profoundly pessimistic as regards all this world's values, and makes the fear of the Lord furnish the moral spur provided elsewhere by the fear of the enemy. But our socialistic peace-advocates all believe absolutely in this world's values; and instead of the fear of the Lord and the fear of the enemy, the only fear they reckon with is the fear of poverty if one be lazy. This weakness pervades all the socialistic literature with which I am acquainted. Even in Lowes Dickinson's exquisite dialogue,[1] high wages and short hours are the only forces invoked for overcoming man's distaste for repulsive kinds of labor. Meanwhile men at large still live as they always have lived, under a pain-and-fear economy—for those of us who live in an ease-economy are but an island in the stormy ocean—and the whole atmosphere of present-day utopian literature tastes mawkish and dishwatery to people who still keep a sense for life's more bitter flavors. It suggests, in truth, ubiquitous inferiority.

Inferiority is always with us, and merciless scorn of it is the keynote of the military temper. "Dogs, would you live forever?" shouted Frederick the Great. "Yes," say our utopians, "let us live forever, and raise our level gradually." The best thing about our "inferiors" today is that they are as tough as nails, and physically and morally almost as insensitive. Utopianism would see them soft and squeamish, while militarism would keep their callousness, but transfigure it into a meritorious characteristic, needed by "the service," and redeemed by that from the suspicion of inferiority. All the qualities of a man acquire dignity when he knows that the service of the collectivity that owns him needs them. If proud of the collectivity, his own pride rises in proportion. No collectivity is like an army for nourishing such pride; but it has to be confessed that the only sentiment which the image of pacific cosmopolitan industrialism is capable of arousing in countless worthy breasts is shame at the idea of belonging to *such* a collectivity. It is obvious that the United States of America as they exist today impress a mind like General Lea's as so much human blubber. Where is the sharpness and precipitousness, the contempt for life, whether one's own, or another's? Where is the savage "yes" and "no," the unconditional duty? Where is the conscription? Where is the bloodtax? Where is anything that one feels honored by belonging to?

Having said thus much in preparation, I will now confess my own utopia. I devoutly believe in the reign of peace and in the gradual advent of some sort of a socialistic equilibrium. The fatalistic view of the war-function is to me nonsense, for I know that war-making is due to definite motives and subject to prudential checks and reasonable criticisms, just like any other form of enterprise. And when whole nations are the armies, and the science of destruction vies in intellectual refinement with the sciences of production, I see that war becomes absurd and impossible from its own monstrosity. Extravagant ambitions will have to be replaced by reasonable claims, and nations must make common cause against them. I see no reason why all this should not apply to yellow as well as to white countries, and I look forward to a future when acts of war shall be formally outlawed as between civilized peoples.

All these beliefs of mine put me squarely into the anti-militarist party. But I do not believe that peace either ought to be or will be permanent on this globe, unless the states pacifically organized preserve some of the old elements of army-discipline. A permanently successful peace-economy cannot be a simple pleasure-economy. In the more or less socialistic future towards which mankind seems drifting we must still subject ourselves collectively to those severities which answer to our real position upon this only partly hospitable globe. We must make new energies and hardihoods continue the manliness to which the military mind so faithfully clings. Martial virtues must be the enduring cement; intrepidity, contempt of softness, surrender of private interest, obedience to command, must still remain the rock upon which states are built—unless, indeed, we wish for dangerous reactions against commonwealths fit only for contempt, and liable to invite attack whenever a centre of crystallization for military-minded enterprise gets formed anywhere in their neighborhood.

The war-party is assuredly right in affirming and reaffirming that the martial virtues, although originally gained by the race through war, are absolute and permanent human goods. Patriotic pride and ambition in their military form are, after all, only specifications of a more general competitive passion. They are its first form, but that is no reason for supposing them to be its last form. Men now are proud of belonging to a conquering nation, and without a murmur they lay down their persons and their wealth, if by so doing they may fend off subjection. But who can be sure that *other aspects of one's country* may not, with time and education and suggestion enough, come to be regarded with similarly effective feelings of pride and shame? Why should men not some day feel that it is worth a blood-tax to belong to a collectivity superior in any ideal respect? Why should they not blush with indignant shame if the community that owns them is vile in any way whatsoever? Individuals, daily more numerous, now feel this civic passion. It is only a question of blowing on the spark till the whole population gets incandescent, and on the ruins of the old morals of military honor, a stable system of morals of civic honor builds itself up. What the whole community comes to believe in grasps the individual as in a vise. The war-function has grasped us so far; but constructive interests may some day seem no less imperative, and impose on the individual a hardly lighter burden.

Let me illustrate my idea more concretely. There is nothing to make one indignant in the mere fact that life is hard, that men should toil and suffer pain. The planetary conditions once for all are such, and we can stand it. But that so many men, by mere accidents of birth and opportunity, should have a life of *nothing else* but toil and pain and hardness and inferiority imposed upon them, should have no vacation, while others natively no more deserving never get any taste of this campaigning life at all,—*this* is capable of arousing indignation in reflective minds. It may end by seeming shameful to all of us that some of us have nothing but campaigning, and others nothing but unmanly ease. If now—and this is my idea—there were, instead of military conscription a conscription of the whole youthful population to form for a certain number of years a part of the army enlisted against *Nature*, the injustice would tend to be evened out, and numerous other goods to the commonwealth would follow. The military ideals of hardihood and discipline would be wrought into the growing fibre of the people; no one would remain blind as the luxurious classes now are blind, to man's relations to the globe he lives on, and to the permanently sour and hard foundations of his higher life. To coal and iron mines, to freight trains, to fishing fleets in December, to dishwashing, clothes-washing, and window-washing, to road-building and tunnel-making, to foundries and stoke-holes, and to the frames of skyscrapers, would our gilded youths be drafted off, according to their choice, to get the childishness knocked out of them, and to come back into society with healthier sympathies and soberer ideas. They would have paid their blood-tax, done their own part in the immemorial human warfare against nature; they would tread the earth more proudly, the women would value them more highly, they would be better fathers and teachers of the following generation.

Such a conscription, with the state of public opinion that would have required it, and the many moral fruits it would bear, would preserve in the midst of a pacific civilization the manly virtues which the military party is so afraid of seeing disappear in peace. We should get toughness without callousness, authority with as little criminal cruelty as possible, and painful work done cheerily because the duty is temporary, and threatens not, as now, to degrade the whole remainder of one's life. I spoke of the "moral equivalent" of war. So far, war has been the only force that can discipline a whole community, and until an equivalent discipline is organized, I believe that war must have its way. But I have no serious doubt that the ordinary prides and shames of social man, once developed to a certain intensity, are capable of organizing such a moral equivalent as I have sketched, or some other just as effective for preserving manliness of type. It is but a question of time, of skilful propagandism, and of opinion-making men seizing historic opportunities.

The martial type of character can be bred without war. Strenuous honor and disinterestedness abound elsewhere. Priests and medical men are in a fashion educated to it, and we should all feel some degree of it imperative if we were conscious of our work as an obligatory service to the state. We should be *owned*, as soldiers are by the army, and our pride would rise accordingly. We could be poor, then, without humiliation, as army officers now are. The only thing needed henceforward is to inflame the civic temper as past history has inflamed the military temper. H. G. Wells, as usual, sees the centre of the situation.

> In many ways, military organization is the most peaceful of activities. When the contemporary man steps from the street, of clamorous insincere advertisement, push, adulteration, underselling and intermittent employment into the barrack-yard, he steps on to a higher social plane, into an atmosphere of service and cooperation and of infinitely more honorable emulations. Here at least men are not flung out of employment to degenerate because there is no immediate work for them to do. They are fed and drilled and trained for better services. Here at least a man is supposed to win promotion by self-forgetfulness and not by self-seeking. And beside the feeble and irregular endowment of research by commercialism, its little short-sighted snatches at profit by innovation and scientific economy, see how remarkable is the steady and rapid development of method and appliances in naval and military affairs! Nothing is more striking than to compare the progress of civil conveniences which has been left almost entirely to the trader, to the progress in military apparatus during the last few decades. The house-appliances of today, for example, are little better than they were fifty years ago. A house of today is still almost as ill-ventilated, badly heated by wasteful fires, clumsily arranged and furnished as the house of 1858.
>
> Houses a couple of hundred years old are still satisfactory places of residence, so little have our standards risen. But the rifle or battleship of fifty years ago was beyond all comparison inferior to those we possess; in power, in speed, in convenience alike. No one has a use now for such superannuated things.[2]

Wells adds that he thinks that the conceptions of order and discipline, the tradition of service and devotion, of physical fitness, unstinted exertion, and universal responsibility, which universal military duty is now teaching European nations, will remain a permanent acquisition, when the last ammunition has been used in the fireworks that celebrate the final peace. I believe as he does. It would be simply preposterous if the only force that could work ideals of honor and standards of efficiency into English or American natures should be the fear of being killed by the Germans or Japanese. Great indeed is Fear; but it is not, as our military enthusiasts believe and try to make us believe, the only stimulus known for awakening the higher ranges of men's spiritual energy. The amount of alteration in public opinion which my utopia postulates is vastly less than the difference between the mentality of those black warriors who pursued Stanley's party on the Congo with their cannibal war-cry of "Meat! Meat!" and that of the "general staff" of any civilized nation. History has seen the latter interval bridged over: the former one can be bridged over much more easily.

Notes

[1] Lowes Dickinson, "Justice and Liberty," New York, 1909.
[2] H. G. Wells, *First and Last Things*, 1908.

The Pacifist Spirit

A. A. Milne

Pacifists All

If everybody in Europe thought as I do, there would be no more war in Europe. If a few important people thought as I do: if Ramsay MacDonald were Milne, and Mussolini were Milne, and Stalin were Milne, and Hitler were Milne, and anybody who might at any moment be in a French Cabinet were Milne, then, however intolerable the prospect in other ways, there would be no more war in Europe. If Beaverbrook were Milne, and Rothermere were Milne, and the proprietors of fifty chosen newspapers in Europe were Milne, there would be no more war in Europe. If only the Pope were Milne, and the Archbishop of Canterbury were Milne, then it is at least possible that there would be no more war in Europe.

This does not mean that there is an infallible Milne Plan for abolishing war; it is just a plain statement of fact. War is something of man's own fostering, and if all mankind renounces it, then it is no longer there. Equally, if those particular men who speak for, or order the voices of, the inarticulate were to renounce war, then war would no longer be there. Now when an articulate man feels deeply about anything, he tries, by writing or by preaching, to persuade others into his own way of thinking. In this book I am trying to persuade other people to feel as deeply as I do about war. If everybody reads the book (which is unlikely), and if everybody who reads it is persuaded by it (which is also unlikely), then the thing is done. There is an end of war. I can hope for no such immediate and gratifying response; but at least I can hope that, of the few who read it, a few will be persuaded by it, and will themselves try to persuade others. It is thus that ideas spread, and ultimately influence the world. St. Paul (with whom otherwise, however, I do not compare myself) was not deterred from writing a letter to a few friends at Corinth because he could not foresee the day when it would become the First Epistle to the Corinthians. . . .

At this point an Elder Statesman shows signs of impatience.

But, my dear Sir (he cries), what is this wonderful idea which you are hoping to spread? Whom are you trying to persuade, and to what? Except for a few fire-eaters here and there, we are all in agreement with you. We all know now what war is like, and none of us wants 1914 over again. The point which exercises us now is: *How are we going to prevent it?* If by Limitation of Armaments, then how shall we ensure that it is carried out? If by Pacts and Treaties, how shall we enforce them? We all know that modern war is disaster, but what are we going to put in its place? You talk about the Pope and the Archbishop as if you wanted to convert them. Convert them to what? Don't you think that *they* realize the horrors of war? Don't you think that they are just as ardent for Peace as you are? As we all are? Tell us what to *do*, not what to think. We have done our thinking; we are all of one mind as to what we want: Peace; and now the problem in front of us is how to obtain it.

I have typified this imaginary interrupter as an Elder Statesman, but his attitude of mind is common to people of various ages and varying professions. It exhibits the increasingly popular, but mistaken, belief that "We are all pacifists nowadays."

We are not.

Consider for a moment the Elder Statesman. For centuries he has been accustomed to think of war as the instrument of policy. Now he sees it suddenly as an instrument as fatal to himself, as fatal to civilisation, as to the enemy. Anxiously he wonders how to fashion, from this well-known, well-tried instrument, something less self-destructive. It is as if a mother saw her children playing with a live bomb, and instead of snatching it away from them, said kindly: "It would be nicer with your proper ball, wouldn't it, darlings? Just go on playing with that one, while Mummy tries to find it for you." This is not how people behave in their private lives. When a man sees poison in the glass which should have held a tonic, he throws it away. If, being all Pacifists nowadays, we thought that war was poison, we should throw it away. We should not roll it meditatively round the tongue, and wonder how to improve the taste. It is because I want everybody to think (as I do) that war is poison, and not (as so many think) an over-strong, extremely unpleasant medicine, that I am writing this book.

For alas! the Great and Good and Wise whom I have mentioned do not think as I do in this matter. The Prime Minister and Sir John Simon think that modern war is disastrous; I think that war is wrong. The Pope and the Archbishop of Canterbury think that modern war is horrible; I think that war is wrong. Lord Beaverbrook and Lord Rothermere think that modern war puts too great a burden on the tax-payer; I think that war is wrong. In short, I think that war is a Bad Thing, and all these gentlemen, and millions like them, think that war is now become Much too Much of a Good Thing.

It may be said that, since we all want to end war, it does not greatly matter that we condemn it in different degrees and from differing motives. I think that the realization of these differences is of the first importance to the cause of Peace.

For if there were no differences, if we all wanted the same thing, in the same way, for the same reasons, and with the same ardour, and if we found that we could not set about attaining it with any certainty of ultimate success, we could only conclude that we were striving against some Law of Nature, or of Civilisation, which was beyond human control. So, if we all want Peace, and think mistakenly that we want it for the same reasons and with the same ardour, our failure to visualize achievement will force us to the conclusion that the abolition of war is a task of superhuman difficulty.

One can imagine a genuine peace-lover expressing himself like this:

"Well, I've done my best. I always felt uneasy about war, and I only went into the last one because I was assured, and convinced, that it was a war to end war. It seems now that war has got too strong a hold on the world for us ever to end it. For fifteen years we have had all the greatest minds in Europe at work on the problem—and where are we? No nearer to the abolition of war than we were in 1913. In 1913, with a few exceptions, we all thought war was a natural and fine thing to happen, so long as we were well prepared for it and had no doubt about coming out the victor. Now, with a few exceptions, we have lost our illusions; we are agreed that war is neither natural nor fine, and that the victor suffers from it equally with the vanquished. Yet there seems to be no way of putting an end to it. So what is one to do? Nothing: except to see that one is as well prepared for the next war as one's neighbour; nothing: except pray that one will be finished with such a stupid world before Hell opens on it again."

It is not so hopeless as that. The greatest minds may have been at work, but they have not been single-minded. They have not been determined on Peace; they have merely been exploring the avenues of Peace with Honour, Peace with Security, Peace with—what you will.

If a man and his wife and his cook and his house-parlourmaid are all determined to have a refrigerator in the house, then in a very short time there is a refrigerator in the house. But if the husband wants a refrigerator, and thinks it ought to come out of the wife's allowance; and if the wife wants a refrigerator, and doesn't think they can afford it unless the husband gives up smoking; and if the cook wants it, and sees no place for it but the pantry; and the house-parlourmaid wants it, and sees no place for it but the kitchen; then, even if years elapse without a refrigerator coming into that house, it will still be a mistake to suppose that refrigerators are not obtainable. . . .

And if, after a lapse of years, it were discovered that, in fact, refrigerators cost nothing and took up no room, this prolonged household discussion about place and price would seem somewhat ironic.

So, to one who holds that without the abolition of War there can be neither Honour nor Security, these prolonged discussions about Peace with Honour and Peace with Security seem also somewhat ironic. . . .

The War Convention

I have called war "the conventional use of force" to attain an end. A Pacifist is generally assumed to be a poor-spirited creature who objects to any use of force in any circumstances whatever, and it is customary to ask him, by way of challenge, what he would do if England were invaded and a Storm Trooper tried to rape his mother. Why elderly mothers should have this special (and surely rather surprising) attraction for an invading soldiery, I do not know. Nor do I know what, in the circumstances, the passionate Militarist would do, nor why, in the midst of war's alarms, he should be by his mother's side to do it. Least of all do I know why this particular challenge is always issued to the Pacifist. I should have supposed that, since rape was so inevitably one of the accompaniments of war as to be almost the natural perquisite of the invading soldier; and since the passionate Militarist, in accepting war, accepts with complaisance the prospect of other people's mothers being raped; it is he rather than the Pacifist who should be asked the question. And asked it, not rhetorically, but with genuine interest. But assuming (as I think we may) that he makes a pious distinction between his own mother and other people's mothers, and that his acceptance of rape is general and patriotic rather than particular, then we may suppose that, instinctively and by the use of force, he would try to prevent the catastrophe. And one Pacifist, at least, would applaud him. . . .

It is difficult to work passionately for peace if, at the back of your mind, you feel that war is a gallant exercise, worthy to be sung by poets, which carries with it nothing for tears but an heroic death upon the battlefield. Ruskin, whose military experience must have included several drawing-room renderings of *The Charge of the Light Brigade,* is quoted proudly by an apologist for war as having said that "all the greatest qualities of man come out in armed conflict." One might be excused for thinking so after listening to that stirring ballad.

> Forward the Light Brigade!
> Was there a man dismayed?
> Not tho' the soldier knew
> Someone had blundered:
> Theirs not to make reply,
> Theirs not to reason why,
> Theirs but to do and die:
> Into the valley of Death
> Rode the six hundred.

Put like this, even the blundering (which comes out, so monotonously, in armed conflict) seems to earn its place among "the greatest qualities of man," for, if not heroic in itself, it is at least the cause of heroism in others. "Theirs not to reason why"—how finely *Homo Sapiens* exhibits his quality.

And yet . . .

If in the last four years 10,000 *Titanics* in succession had struck icebergs and gone to the bottom, each with a loss of a thousand lives, would any moderately sane person, in excuse for doing nothing but build more *Titanics* and crash into more icebergs, utter the complacent truth that all the greatest qualities of man come out in shipwreck?

And has the fact the greatest qualities of man undoubtedly came out in the Great Plague ever been advanced as an apology for bad sanitation?

And, looking on the bright side of earthquakes, can we not say that all the greatest qualities of man come out in earthquakes?

But most nobly, most gloriously, with a splendour which almost dazzles the sight, the greatest qualities of man have shone forth under religious persecution. Hail, then, rack! Hail, thumbscrew! Bring torches to the faggots, and let the brave fires of Smithfield burn merrily again. *Dulce et decorum est pro Christo mori.* . . .

Ten Million and Forty

It has been said that, if there were a law, made and enforced by all nations, that on the outbreak of war the Prime Minister and Foreign Secretary of the countries concerned were immediately hanged, then there would be no more war in Europe. This was said in the days when Parliamentary Government was more fashionable than it is now. But let us adapt and amplify the saying for modern use. Let us suppose that certain people were assured that, if ever there were another war in Europe on the scale of the last war, they themselves would be the first victims of it. What would happen?

First of all, we must select our victims, and for this purpose we will limit ourselves to the four Great Powers most likely to be concerned: England, France, Germany and Italy. From Italy we need only choose Mussolini; from Germany, Hitler, Goering and Goebbels. England being a democratic country, offers us a wider choice. I suggest the following:

Ramsay MacDonald, Stanley Baldwin, Sir John Simon. One unnamed Cabinet Minister, chosen by lot on the day that war is declared. The ministers responsible for the fighting services. Winston Churchill. Two unnamed Generals, two unnamed Admirals and two unnamed directors of armament firms, also chosen by lot. Lords Beaverbrook and Rothermere, and the Editors of *The Times* and *The Morning Post*.

France's politics being more fluid, it will be unprofitable to give names in advance, so let us decide merely that she furnishes a corresponding equality of victims with England.

Now here are forty people who are all going to die as a preliminary to the next war. Are the chances of another war lessened?

I can hear the Elder Statesman saying that "since the premiss is entirely outside the sphere of practical politics, any conclusion drawn from it is purely theoretical and therefore valueless." Theoretical, yes: but not valueless. On the contrary, it will be of the utmost value in helping us to appreciate the meaning of the war-convention. I beg my readers, therefore, to pretend, by a supreme exercise of the imagination, that my premiss is in actual practice.

I know that many people find it difficult to imagine the obviously impossible. It is, of course, impossible that on the outbreak of a war these forty important persons should die as for the purpose of this chapter they ought to die; that is, as men die in war: some with merciful quickness, some in slow agony. But it is not wholly impossible that they should be genuinely intent on peace; should believe that the certainty of their own deaths would keep them from ensuing war unnecessarily; should take a solemn oath to commit suicide on the outbreak of war; and (most unlikely supposition of all, but, I suppose, just conceivable) should keep their oath if war broke out. This being so, our premiss should be within the imagination of all of us. Assume, then, with confidence that these forty leaders are to be the first victims of the next war, and ask yourself whether the peace of Europe is the more assured.

Can there be any doubt? My own conviction is that, so long as these forty people exercised their present influence, any war between their countries would be "entirely outside the sphere of practical politics."

Now if this were indeed so; if it were the truth that these forty leaders would never in any circumstances condemn themselves to death; then the war-convention is definitely exposed as the ridiculous imposture which so many of us believe it to be. For the convention is that war is "a biological necessity"; an "inevitable outlet of human nature"; that it is "the extreme expression of Patriotism" (than which there is no higher religion); that it "stamps the mark of nobility upon nations"; that it provides opportunities (10,000,000 in the last war) of a "pleasant and fitting" death; in short, that it is ultimately the only way and the inevitable way and the noblest way of settling disputes between nations. But these forty people cannot seriously hold any of these beliefs if they are deterred from giving expression to them by such a trifle as their own forty pleasant and fitting deaths among ten million others. War is inevitable? Then they will not be able to avert it. War is human nature? But they also are subject to human impulses. War is the extreme expression of Patriotism? Well, who so patriotic as they? And so, if they showed (as I think they would show) that they *could* avert even the threat of war; if they affirmed (as I think they would affirm) that Patriotism and Peace were allies, not enemies; if, for the preservation of their own lives, they prevented (as I think they would prevent) ten million other people from dying gloriously for their country; then they would have given the lie to all the traditional theories which they have propagated about war. For war could not be less natural, less inevitable, less noble with 10,000,040 lives at stake than it was with 10,000,000.

To believe, then, that there would be no more war if the makers of it were always the first victims is to surrender all faith in war. It is to proclaim oneself as convinced a Pacifist as the writer of this book. If our rulers could keep us from war (without dimming the sacred lamp of Patriotism) when their own lives were at hazard, they can keep us from war now; they can always keep us from war; and the Millennium is within our reach. . . .

Now it is an interesting, if obvious, fact that nobody who talks bravely about war has ever been killed in war. Every word which has been uttered about the pleasantness of dying for one's country, every airy reference to death as a thing of minor importance, has been spoken by somebody who has not experienced death, but who could experience it at any moment if he really wished. Of the men and women who talk so gallantly to-day about war, ninety per cent have never encountered it, even though some of them may have worn uniforms. The remaining ten per cent (if, indeed, it be as many as ten per cent) survived the war. To be gallant and dashing and manly about an adventure which one has never had; to be brave about a danger which one has passed; this is not a courage whose badge the Pacifist is morbidly desirous of winning. When the young men of Oxford resolved never again to fight for "King and Country" a certain noble member of the Government called them in his graceful way "yellow-bellied." Whether he considered that those who opposed the motion were red-bellied (or possibly, like himself, blue-bellied) was not made public. But if he had been able to spare the time for thought, or had had anything to think with, he would have realized that it is not a habit of the young to be anxious about the morrow; and that, in regard to a danger which may or may not materialize some years hence, it is quite impossible to be either brave or cowardly.

We may agree, then, I think, that Pacifists are not necessarily cowards, nor Militarists brave. Dare we go farther and suggest that War is not necessarily manly, nor Peace effeminate?

Let us consider the suggestion by meeting our patriotic young women on their own ground: or what used to be their own ground: the domestic hearth.

Every cook nowadays has her "rights." Every young married woman has her "rights." From time to time what they think of as their rights will not be in accord. Suppose that when the rights of Cook and Mistress clash (on the point, say, of hot dinner on Sunday) war inevitably follows. China and cutlery is thrown, in a mild way at first, but soon more fiercely. Cook hurries from the house and returns with her male relations. Mistress drags her husband from his study, and telephones urgently for her brothers. The battle is then left to the men. There is a fierce set-to all over the house, the weapons of war being limited, by agreement, to fists, sticks and crockery. . . . By evening Peace is restored—or rather, dictated. Cook has won, and there are to be no hot dinners at all, not even on a week-day. Or Mistress has won, and Cook has no more evenings out, and pays for all the damage.

Now if the husband objects to living in a house like this, is anybody going to call him unmanly? Is it unmanly to think that this method of existence is all wrong and utterly silly? I don't mean just wrong and silly in our present ordered state, which gives us policemen and law-courts to meet these emergencies. I mean that, even in a community which lacked policemen, a sensitive, imaginative, intelligent man would feel that life lived like this was intolerable; that it ought not to be beyond human powers to evolve something more dignified; and that it was his duty to persuade his fellows to combine with him in search of that dignity. If he felt this, he could hardly be dismissed contemptuously as an effeminate creature who shirked being hit over the head with an umbrella.

In the last war ten million people were killed, and at least another ten million permanently affected, physically or mentally. If the manly Patriot contemplates this fact with an increased sense of virility, let him remember that this was not all that happened. Even had nobody been killed in the last war, the thought of its recurrence would still be intolerable to the sensitive and the intelligent. If a country is going to collect £7,000,000,000 from its people; if it is going to take three million men away from their ordinary occupation for four years; then it is possible to feel (without being unmanly) that there are more worthy ways of spending the time and money and employing the men than in sheer destruction. It is possible to feel that, sixteen years after the expenditure of that time and that money, one's country should have gained, rather than lost, in happiness, in dignity, and in beauty.

Impossible Pacifism
Jews, the Holocaust, and Nonviolence

Evelyn Wilcock

Long before other people asked me how a Jew could be a pacifist after the Holocaust, I put that question to myself. Pacifism and Jewishness after Hitler seemed to defy logic.

One story sticks in my mind. It was told to a teacher at my own school by a refugee boy newly arrived via the *Kindertransport* in December, 1938. He had been in Vienna; his mother had gone to Berlin to find out what had happened to his father, who had disappeared in Dachau:

> [Adolph] was shut up with other Jewish boys in a cellar for two days without food, and then as they were made to ascend one by one, a shot rang out as each one reached the top, and the boys began to cry. "And I was afraid too," says Dolphy—but it was only the Nazis having a little game by firing over each boy's head as he emerged.[1]

There is a moment of outrage; it becomes imperative to intervene with a stronger man, a larger gun. Hannah Arendt explained her attachment to Zionism after 1933: "When one is attacked as a Jew, one must defend oneself *as a Jew*. Not as a German, not as a world citizen, not as an upholder of the Rights of Man."[2] The idea is that if the roles were reversed, if the gun were in Jewish hands, that would be all right.

The propaganda image in the film *Triumph of the Will* is of a Nazi rally as a well-ordered camp, built by glowing, healthy young men and women. We have no comparable visual image to advertise the fortitude with which Jewish families withstood exclusion and disparagement. The view among many Israelis that Jews died without resistance during the Holocaust and that if we do something different next time around—fight, for instance—the outcome will be different, is widely prevalent.

Armed defense of Poland and France did not prevent the Holocaust. Jews participated fully in military operations during World War II, both in regular

Source: Reprinted with permission from *The Challenge of Shalom: The Jewish Tradition of Peace and Justice*, pp. 59–70, edited by Murray Polner and Naomi Goodman, © 1994 by the Jewish Peace Fellowship.

armies and armed resistance movements. A separate Jewish force would have been numerically insignificant. Soviet armies failed to prevent twenty million Soviet citizens dying in the war. Even after America entered the war, the Allies were not able to launch an immediate attack on Germany, which controlled the industry, raw materials, and manpower of all Europe. By 1945, foreign workers made up 30 percent of industrial labor in Germany, and 20 percent of the troops in German uniform were non-German.[3]

At some level we hanker after a Jewish community to match that image on the German film. On Purim, the children in Crakow Ghetto were allowed to dress up. Their teacher said, "Strangely, they want to play OD (Jewish Police) or SS men. They dressed for their parts as well as they could, using sticks for rubber truncheons. In their acting the little observers displayed all the cruelty the OD had inflicted on their siblings."[4] Yeshayahu Leibowitz argues that when Jews fight as Jews, for a Jewish nationalism, they cease to be Jews in a meaningful sense, and become like Nazis.[5] Few heeded Rabbi Weissmandel, rescuer of Jews in Slovakia, when he warned about the shrinking parameters of Judaism. "Because Rabbi Weissmandel was a religious man par excellence, he conceived Jewish nationalism as the great sin of assimilation in a national disguise, as a substitution for a universal religion, which, like all religions, has the purpose to give sense to one's life and solve the personal and collective dilemma of man in this world."[6]

Ever since biblical times, Jews have regarded defeat and natural disaster as God's punishment for their sins. It provided an explanation for suffering, and furnished hope that they could avert future catastrophe by mending their ways. We, too, want to feel we are in control and that it won't happen again. One is struck by the way the Holocaust literature—whether personal memoirs or academic analysis—is characterized by Jewish accusation and self-reproach.

We have internalized the German message that there was something deeply wrong with being a Jew at the time of the Holocaust, otherwise we would not have found ourselves in that predicament at all. A distinguished therapist who grew up in Germany confessed that when her darker-haired sister was singled out as a Jew, she failed to own up to the relationship. Still, we Jews are not to blame for having normal reactions in situations that are altogether not of our devising. A strictly observant teacher from the Beit Yakov community in Crakow was gnawed by pangs of guilt because she let slip a meeting with a Polish policeman who might have negotiated freedom for her family. "Did you do everything possible to save them; did you?" is a question we all ask.

The absence of certainty in the Holocaust means that it was not possible to take meaningful decisions and be sure of the outcome. In some situations going to a work camp meant death; but in others a work permit saved one. Some Jews resisted the Nazis by acquiring papers that would keep their families from the transports as long as they possibly could. But sometimes Jewish resistance meant volunteering to die in place of a wanted man: A young man from Wlodawa gave his life, unsuccessfully claiming to be the Rabbi from Radzyn.[7] People blamed themselves for leaving their families, or for staying with them, for not giving their lunch bread to beggars in the ghetto, or for refusing the offer of food.

Historians blame Jews who failed to escape from Paris or parents who prevented their children escaping from transports.[8] But in her diary, Etty Hillesum described Jews successfully hunting down a terrified young boy whose running away meant fifty extra victims were piled on the train as a deterrent. She wondered how the boy could live with the guilt.[9]

We cannot make free decisions for the future unless we get rid of the feeling that we did it wrong last time. Claude Lanzmann describes in *Shoah* how the victims were driven with unprecedented violence and beatings to the very door of the gas chambers, but without words, without any explanations.[10] We have no explanations either; we are not able to ensure that it will not happen again. Leibowitz says, "That may be the real horror of the Holocaust, that there is no lesson. . . . Atrocity is utterly senseless."[11]

In "Nonviolence in the Holocaust" in my book *Pacifism and the Jews*, I question the view that Jews complied with their own extermination and argued that, on the contrary, the prevailing Jewish nonviolence constituted a courageous assertion of Jewish difference that should be endorsed and admired.[12] I want to take the argument further and suggest that nonviolent minority dissent rescued Jews in the Holocaust and provides a model for effective practical resistance. The Final Solution was an emanation of state authority; the people most likely to challenge it were those who felt themselves governed by a higher authority than that of the state. For some this higher authority was a religious imperative; for others it was a question of individual conscience.

The Holocaust was not a military problem. It began with small difficulties in small towns and seemingly trivial relationships. Hannah Arendt described what *gleichschaltung* meant: "Cooperation (with the Nazis) meant that your friends cooperated. The problem, the personal problem, was not what our enemies might be doing, but what our friends were doing. This wave of cooperation—which was quite voluntary, or at least not compelled in the way it is during a reign of terror, made you feel surrounded by an empty space, isolated."[13]

Individuals became significant when they refused to go along with the majority. On the day of the boycott of Jewish enterprises on April 1, 1933, one headmistress, Frau Heinzmann, sent flowers to the mothers of all the Jewish pupils who had been excluded from her school.[14]

One should not naively suppose that a totalitarian society is established only as an armed camp, by arms; it recruits those whose cognition regulates society, those who engineer its physical, mental and spiritual health. The Holocaust began at that time when you could no longer confide in your doctor, or your child's teacher. Historians have recorded how German theologians, doctors, and psychoanalysts cooperated with the Nazi regime. The implications of such cooperation have to be agonized over on the personal level. The safest professional and personal relationships were unsafe. Break-down of social support could not be remedied with a gun.

Wolfgang Benz points out what nonviolent solidarity achieved when Jewish husbands in mixed marriages were arrested in the *FabrikAktion* of February–March, 1943: "When the non-Jewish spouses heard that their part-ners had been arrested and taken to the Assembly Point in Rosenstrasse, to be deported, they got together, besieged the Rosenstrasse and protested. 6,000 women shouted, screamed and howled for their husbands." It worked. The arrested were freed after a few days.[15]

Conscientious objection to military service involves refusing to go along with majority demands. Ten of the writers included in Wolfgang Benz's anthology of German pacifism from 1890 to 1939 were either Jews or of Jewish descent.[16] It is perhaps still not safe to say so. It might substantiate the Nazi accusation that Jews, particularly Jewish women in peace movements, had undermined the fighting spirit of young Germans in World War I. The idea that Jewish pacifism caused the Holocaust comes from Nazi ideology.

On the Allied side, Jews themselves became suspicious of pacifism. Pac-ifists were occasionally suspected of Nazi sympathies or, at best, regarded as bystanders who did nothing to save Jews. Doing nothing during the Holo-caust was the greatest reproach that Jews have leveled against themselves (and God). It was always the people of the next continent, the next country, or the next town, often helpless themselves, who were looked to for rescue. Pol-ish Jews in Auschwitz accosted the newly arrived Hungarian Jews, asking how they could have gone on living normally while their brothers and sisters from Poland were dying.

Few pacifists continue to live normally through a war or other humani-tarian crisis. It is not surprising that many of those who actively opposed the Holocaust were themselves objectors of conscience or linked to peace move-ments. The father of Hans and Sophie Scholl, the students who gave their lives for the nonviolent German resistance group the White Rose, had been a pacifist in World War I.

The Protestant minister at Le Chambon, in the Cévennes, André Rocmé, was a conscientious objector and his wife said:

> The Protestant church was not happy about it, because at the time consci-entious objectors were not admitted as ministers. But the parish wanted a man like my husband, not only because of his ideas about war and peace but on account of his general ideas about truth and justice.[17]

Rocmé was part of the Fellowship of Reconciliation. He was asked by Burns Chalmers, then working with Quaker Relief in camps in the south of France, to assist in rescuing Jews. Rocmé had warned his congregation about Nazism, preparing them for what might come to France; the village responded. Between 1942 and 1945 the five thousand people of the Le Chambon area sheltered between twenty-five hundred and five thousand Jews, at least one for every household. Rocmé narrowly escaped arrest when he refused to hand over a list of the Jews in his parish. His cousin Daniel was deported and died with the young Jews he had sheltered in the Youth Center.

In Le Chambon, Assistant Pastor Edouard Theis was also a pacifist. On the day of the French armistice with Nazi Germany, the two men preached that the responsibility of Christians was to resist through the weapons of the spirit the violence which is brought to bear on their consciences. Pierre Sauvage, whose parents were sheltered at Le Chambon, remarks that weapons of the spirit saved Jews, and so Jews should be interested in them.[18] If Jews allow the Holocaust to dictate a withdrawal from peace movements, our absence may carry its own message about what Judaism means.

Weapons of the spirit had always belonged to Jews. "By encouraging Torah study, one saves our nation physically as well as spiritually. Anyone who remains indifferent to a program [of Torah] obviously transgresses the passage, 'Do not idly stand by the blood of your brother.'"[19] The words match those of the priest in Janowka, near Tarnopol, who could not openly tell the congregation to save the Jews but would say in church, "Not one of you should take the blood of your brother." The villagers understood and left food for Jews sheltering in the nearby forest.

Jewish nonviolence is voiced at the margins by the observant Hasidim or ultra-Orthodox, whose views are discounted by academic intellectuals, and by American Reform rabbis, who work closely with non-Jews in welfare movements and whose theology has been suspected by some of syncretism.

Orthodox pacifism has been ignored, tainted with the idea that undermined all belief: namely, that the Holocaust was either God's punishment or God's negligence. Reb. Chasim dispensed with that argument. "My teachers, you heard, 'God destroys His people from off the face of the earth because of their sins.' Isn't it foolish to believe that? If this were a punishment from heaven because of our sins, why did all the rabbis, the pure and holy Tzadikim who were full of Torah and good deeds, why did they die?"[20]

Pacifists felt strongly that the conflict was the result of human behavior, the failure of modernity; some rabbis held Jews themselves at fault if they had identified with modern society. After *Kristallnacht*, Rabbi Wasserman wrote:

> The whole of mankind is seized with tension. . . . One country against another, within the country one people against another, and finally in the people itself one faction against another. All are ready to tear each other to pieces. This appearance, too, was foreseen from the very beginning for the days of the Epoch of the Messiah: 'I will set each man against his fellow' (Zechariah).[21]

Christian pacifist Evelyn Underhill wrote of pacifists as a tiny minority, strangers in a foreign land: "I think Hitler is a real 'scourge of God,' the permitted judgment on our civilization." Not a judgment on the Jews, one should notice; she held all responsible, including herself. By remaining pacifist, she abstained from the violence that marked the Nazi rise to power in so many German towns.[22] Rabbis did the same; like Underhill, they saw Hitler as a prelude to the messianic age, an Armageddon after which all would be judged. Only in that context should we understand those Orthodox believers who refused to participate in the war because it was a conflict belonging to God rather than to man.

Orthodox Jews had long seen through the hollow attraction of keeping peace through force. Jewish teaching already explained that relying on military force to prevent persecution in the end carries the message that might is right.

Jews were never the stronger community. Fighting served no moral purpose.

But renouncing war did not mean renouncing nonviolent defense. In his book on the Orthodox response to the Holocaust, David Kranzler dismisses the establishment view that the United States could do nothing to rescue the Jews beyond hastening the end of the war. He says that for Orthodox Jews it was a matter of morality and an urgent priority to prevent Jewish deaths.[23] Just as Quaker Relief and Service required action, so Torah also required that a "Jew should dedicate some of his time to fulfillment of the divine precepts and of good deeds to help others to the best of his ability. 'Be ye Holy'; the Jew must be Holy, his house must be Holy, and his whole heart must be holy."

"And I have separated you from the nations to be mine."[24]

It was that otherworldliness that sent the young Rabbi Solomon Schonfeld from London to the continent to gather Jewish children for the *Kindertransport* and that drove Rabbi Michoel Ber Weissmandel, son-in-law of Chief Rabbi Ungar, of the town of Nitra in Slovakia, to bargain for Jewish lives. When Weissmandel was at last arrested, he was persuaded by his followers to jump from the train on which his wife and children were being taken to their deaths.

One rabbi abandoned his family for the sake of the community; another died with them. Reb Yerahmiel Taub, a Hasidic rabbi in Warsaw, gave his followers permission to escape to the Russian forces even though it would involve eating forbidden food and not observing the Sabbath. But "he himself did not wish to leave the ghetto so he could remain with the other Jews. He was later sent to Treblinka (1942) where he died a martyr after his whole family had been exterminated by the Germans."[25] It was not the act itself which was specified by *halakhah* but the exercise of individual religious choice.

This was not a test in which there were right answers. One Jewish family deliberately ate on Yom Kippur to preserve their strength before a deportation. Other Orthodox Jews felt that their survival as Jews entailed conducting themselves as Jews even to the point of starvation—by observing dietary laws and fasts. Rabbi Wasserman was killed in Kovno while studying Tractate Niddah. If we think that it was his own fault, we do him an injustice. What he did determined only the character of his dying. Keeping religious law resisted Nazi law.

In the Holocaust, rigid ideas of what was legal and what was illegal could no longer be relied on. The food allowance for Jews in Warsaw was only 184 calories a day. The ghetto was kept alive illegally by child smugglers trading with peasants at subsistence level, or bringing gifts from the

"Aryan" side. Sometimes the soldiers and Jewish police turned a blind eye, or unpredictably they shot to kill. One of the children says it was hard to smuggle. They had been brought up to know that was a bad thing to do.

Jews had a problem with law. It was the custom to safeguard the community through self-regulation and adherence to local law. Questions certainly arose about the persistence of this policy beyond the point when it could produce the hoped-for benefit. Particularly problematic is the role of the Jewish police who, hostages themselves, facilitated selections for transports. It is hardly necessary to point out that few pacifists serve in police forces, most of whom carry arms, or that refusals to serve might have obstructed the Nazis. Officials, like Dr. Giuseppe Jona in Venice, died rather than hand over Jewish records. The Hasidic rabbi from Radomsko refused to cooperate in the arrangements to transport Jews from the Warsaw Ghetto. Rabbi Eliyahu Laskowsky refused to work with the ghetto *Judenrat* in Davart.[26]

Odette Meyers observed that geniuses were people who broke rules. She was saved from the Germans by Madame Marie Chotel, the concierge at the building where they lived in France. "I would say that one of the things that saved me was the fact that in thought, in action, even in her life-style, this woman broke rules, yet she was a genius at humanity."[27]

When the Jews of the Netherlands or of Paris were ordered to register, most obeyed. But at the age of sixteen, Paulette Szlifke disobeyed her mother by refusing to wear a yellow star. She had fair hair, could pass as non-Jewish, and became part of a Jewish resistance movement that distributed leaflets and engaged in industrial sabotage. Rule-breaking was perhaps taken to extremes by Major Julius Schmahling, the German occupation governor of Haute Loire, who (we are told) was the opposite of an "orders are orders" personality. It was he who diverted the attention of the SS from the Jews hidden in the village of Le Chambon.[28]

Recalling her solitary survival in the Netherlands, Marga Minco describes being delivered to the door of a day laborer who had to vacate his own bed so that she might sleep alongside his wife. The extra bed promised for her by the rescue organization never materialized, and the laborer who left daily for work at crack of dawn was always too exhausted by Sunday to make further inquiries. Asking whether the rest of the girl's family had all gone, her hostess stolidly remarked, "Not one ever comes back from there, they say."[29] The knowledge and courage of these people have, sadly, been underestimated.

Pacifists had always mitigated their isolation by forming support groups. People who hid Jewish children were also individualistic, but not isolated. A loose, informal network located homes for Jews while providing information and support to the rescuers. Group conformity has been unduly blamed in the Holocaust; social institutions also facilitated rescue. Priests and nuns were already dedicated to nonviolent service and to an authority higher than the state. Moreover, they had institutional buildings, local and regional contacts, and no families to be held for ransom. Trapped in occupied France, the Little Sisters of St. Vincent de Paul provided refuge in their school at the Chateau de Prèlefort. Local villagers managed to delay a German inspection. So when the officers arrived, the children were on their daily walk, and none of the staff was available. On another occasion twenty-eight adult fugitives were warned in time to leave, and the Germans discovered nuns and children assembled for a mass.[30]

Knowledge of the effectiveness of Christian nonviolent intervention in the Holocaust should prompt honest appreciation of Jewish organizational nonviolence as well. Blanket charges of conventionality and assimilation raised against European Jewish leaders ignore the benefits. The Danish Jewish community identified fully as Danes, and its leaders persuaded their members to exercise restraint and rely on Danish resistance to Nazism. Cooperation and, for the most part, nonviolence saved the majority of Danish Jews.[31] It was the same in Bulgaria. In both places there were popular demonstrations against the Nazi Jewish policy.

The orderly and nonconfrontational demeanor of Jewish groups working in other parts of Europe for rescue and relief was not as dramatic as the exploits of armed resistance but was the means of survival for many Jews. The Nazis deliberately deprived Jews of their social-support networks by uprooting families, ordering them to cities where they knew no one, or turning them into refugees. It has been suggested that Italian Jews survived because there was no centralized Jewish council, but the Committee to Assist Jewish Refugees (Comasebit) functioned throughout the Mussolini period and (reconstituted as Delasem) continued even after 1939, with the staunch involvement of senior clerics. Organizations became counterproductive only where they inculcated false confidence that the situation was under Jewish control, and thus stifled individual initiative. Part of the Nazi plan was to deflect criticism onto Jewish organizations. The Union Générale des Israélites de France (UGIF) has been accused of compliance. Raymond-Raoul Lambert in Marseilles did conduct quasi-legal negotiations with the Vichy authorities over the fate of foreign-born Jews, but recent research points out that UGIF was not monolithic. Lambert did not call central meetings, and outlying groups were left free to take what action they could.[32]

The saving of lives depended on French Jewish organizational liaison with Quaker and Christian relief societies. The head of the Protestant youth movement was asked to find homes for six hundred immigrant Jewish scouts. Partnership and the acceptance of shared objectives was worth more than militancy in a purely Jewish interest. Yvonne Nevejean, director of L'Oeuvre Nationale de l'Enfance, the Belgian child-welfare organization, responded to an approach by the Jewish Defense Committee and placed at least three thousand children in foster homes. In August, 1944, Marie Blum, one of the Jewish activists, telephoned everywhere—to convents, to all kinds of hostels, to homes for war orphans and prisoners' children—doggedly pleading the Jewish cause before influential people, and finally obtained shelter for the children in homes that were already overcrowded.[33] Contact and coordination between Jew and non-Jew were vital.

When we talk of networking between Jew and non-Jew, we must not forget that Jews were themselves members of ostensibly "non-Jewish" groups, insiders in sympathetic institutions ranging from the Italian Army to Danish scientific laboratories. Holocaust studies have had the effect of separating Jew from non-Jew, whereas our real experience is of ongoing integration and involvement with majority society. Some Christians saved Jews because they regarded Jews as special, God's people, the foundation of their own Bible and faith. We have to ask carefully of what that specialness consists. It was not Jewish descent, but that respect for life and that maintaining of human dignity that many survivors felt differentiated them as Jews from the Germans.

Far from providing a mandate for the use of war to settle ethnic conflict, the persecution of the Jews created a commitment to nonviolence. Fela Drybus survived the Lodz ghetto, and the camps of Auschwitz-Birkenau, Ravensbrück and Bergen-Belsen:

> I do confer trust. Life wouldn't be worth living if I couldn't do that. . . . The atrocities they committed, and the pleasure they took in torturing people, made me at least opposed to all kinds of violence. I've never hit my kids even, not once. And I am certainly a pacifist. The saddest thing is that we have learned nothing from the KZ [*Konzentrationslager*]. We go on persecuting people.[34]

Even in violent situations, some Jews refused to kill. Prisoners on a train from Auschwitz were mowed down by gunfire. One of them, Elli, a young girl, had the chance to pick up a rifle lying in the grass and shoot an SS soldier. Her injured brother urged her on. Her response was "Shoot? I can't. I can't kill anyone."

"Shoot him or I will!" He got up and reached for the rifle. She shrieked: "Bubi, don't." He was not able to lift it, and the rifle remained lying in the grass.[35]

What does it mean to leave the gun untouched? The war and the *Shoah* prompted such questions and so inspired a new Jewish literature of nonviolence. Watching an air raid as she lay in bed in Amsterdam, Etty Hillesum wrote,

> All disasters stem from us. Why is there a war? Perhaps because now and then I might be inclined to snap at my neighbor. Because I and my neighbor and everyone else do not have enough love. Yet we could fight war and all its excrescences by releasing each day the love that is inside us, and giving it a chance to live.[36]

The beliefs of Etty Hillesum or of Lily Montagu, a founder of British liberal Judaism and always an advocate of the pacifist ideal in Judaism, with their universal love and immediate concern for the pain of German women, make uncomfortable reading. We are right to be angry. We should never learn not to flinch, never treat as routine what happened in the Warsaw Ghetto.

Abraham Lewin described his anguish when his wife was taken and how his fifteen-year-old daughter cried out for her mother in her sleep. The technicians who made the death camps possible disowned responsibility. There should be none of that anonymity about being a Jew. Abraham Lewin and other members of the *Oneg Shabes* group deliberately left diaries hidden in the ghetto to demonstrate what being Jewish entailed. In Vilna, Zelig Kalmanovitsh argued against the armed uprising. In a powerful intellectual sermon, he declared that it had taken the Holocaust to show modern Jews what it meant to be Jewish: Jews instinctively chose Jewish identity with its nonviolent values, and rejected the identity of the ruler who did evil to them.[37] By so choosing, the Jews in the ghetto made the same choice as the non-Jews who elsewhere rescued them.

Judaism is not about being better than other people, but it is about being good. Anna Freud, secular, Jewish, and herself a refugee, wrote

> The value of being good is not as great as I thought for a long time. There has to be something else involved, which alone makes being good valuable for other people: perhaps it is to be without internal conflict, to be clear about oneself, but also to be able to endure something.[38]

I think of the little Jewish-Polish girls in Praszka near Breslau (Wroclav) who used to wave from the ghetto wall to the soldiers of the Wehrmacht as they drove east in their tanks, and of the soldiers waving back;[39] the current of common humanity flowing even in the Holocaust. We cannot absolve ourselves of the moral choices open to all people: to resist when necessary, our government and social pressure to conform.

1993

Notes

[1] *St. Felix Christmas* (Sussex, U.K.: Southwold Press, 1939).

[2] Elizabeth Young-Bruehl, *Hannah Arendt* (Princeton, N.J.: Yale University Press, 1982).

[3] David Cesarani, *Justice Delayed* (London: Heinemann, 1992), citing Mark Wyman, *DP: Europe's Displaced Persons, 1945–1951* (Philadelphia: Balch Institute Press, 1989) and Malcolm J. Proudfoot, *European Refugees: 1939–1952* (Evanston, Ill.: Northwestern University Press, 1957).

[4] Pearl Benisch, *To Vanquish the Dragon* (Spring Valley, N.Y.: Feldheim Publishers, 1991).

[5] Yeshayahu Leibowitz in Eyal Sivan, *Slave to Memory*, IMA Productions (1991), shown on BBC's Community Production's "Self-Exposure" (December, 1992).

[6] Asher Siegmund Forst in David Kranzler, *Thy Brother's Blood: The Orthodox Jewish Response during the Holocaust* (Brooklyn, N.Y.: ArtScroll, 1987).

[7] An episode celebrated by the Yiddish poet Yitshak Katznelson, cited in Abraham Lewin, *A Cup of Tears: A Diary of the Warsaw Ghetto*, ed. Antony Polonski (London: Basil Blackwell, 1988).

[8] Jeremy Josephs, *Swastika over Paris: The Fate of the French Jews* (London: Bloomsbury, 1989).

[9] Etty Hillesum, *Etty: A Diary, 1941–1943* (London: Jonathan Cape, 1983).

[10] Claude Lanzmann, *Shoah* (Paris: Editions Fayard, 1985).

[11] Leibowitz, in Sivan, *Slave to Memory*, op. cit.

[12] Evelyn Wilcock, "Nonviolence and the Holocaust: Conscience or Compliance?" in *Pacifism and the Jews*, ed. Evelyn Wilcock (Gloucestershire, U.K.: Hawthorn Press, 1993).

[13] Young-Bruehl, *Hannah Arendt*, op. cit.

[14] G. Elkan in Affidavit, p. III f. 109, Wiener Library, London, cited in H. D. Lerner, *When Compassion Was a Crime: Germany's Silent Heroes, 1933–1945* (London: Oswald Wolff, 1966).

[15] Ruth Andreas Friedrich, *Der Schattenman*, cited by Wolfgang Benz in *Juden in Deutschland, 1933–1945*, ed. Wolfgang Benz (Munich: C. H. Beck, 1988).

[16] Wolfgang Benz, ed., *Pacifismus in Deutschland* (Germany: Gustav Fischer Verlag, 1988).

[17] Carol Rittner and Sondra Myers, eds., *The Courage to Care* (New York: New York University Press, 1986).

[18] Rittner and Myers, *Courage to Care*, ibid.

[19] Shmuel Elchonon Brog, "Introduction to the Epoch of the Messiah: Letter to Young Israel, 1938," in *The Epoch of the Messiah*, ed. Elchanan Wasserman (Tel Aviv: Ohr, Elchonon Publications, 1964).

[20] Bernard Maza, *With Fury Poured Out: A Torah Perspective on the Holocaust* (Hoboken, N.J.: KTAV, 1986).

[21] Wasserman, *Epoch of the Messiah*, op. cit.

[22] Evelyn Underhill, "Letter to Mildred Bosanquet," quoted in Dana Greene, *Evelyn Underhill* (New York: Crossroads, 1990).

[23] Kranzler, *Thy Brother's Blood*, op. cit.

[24] Wasserman, *Epoch of the Messiah*, op. cit.

[25] H. J. Zimmels, *The Echo of the Nazi Holocaust in Rabbinic Literature* (no publisher given, 1975).

[26] Pesach Schindler, *Hasidic Responses to the Holocaust in the Light of Hasidic Thought* (Hoboken, N.J.: KTAV, 1990).

[27] Rittner and Myers, *Courage to Care*, op. cit.

[28] Rittner and Myers, *Courage to Care*, ibid.

[29] Marga Minco, *Bitter Herbs* (New York: Oxford University Press, 1960).

[30] Gérard Boutet, *Ils ont vécu l'Occupation* (Paris: Jean-Cyrille Godfroy, 1990).

[31] Leo Goldberger, ed., *The Rescue of the Danish Jews: Moral Courage under Stress* (New York: New York University Press, 1987).

[32] Richard I. Cohen, *The Burden of Conscience: French Jewish Leadership during the Holocaust* (Bloomington, Ind.: Indiana University Press, 1987).

[33] Quoted in Eric Silver, *The Book of the Just* (London: Weidenfeld and Nicolson, 1992).

[34] Anton Gill, *The Journey Back from Hell: Conversations with Concentration Camp Survivors* (London: Grafton Book, 1988).

[35] Livia E. Bitton Jackson, *Elli: Coming of Age in the Holocaust* (New York: Harper & Row, 1980).

[36] Hillesum, *Diary*, op. cit.

[37] Zelig Kalmanovitsh, "Three Sermons," in *The Literature of Destruction: Jewish Responses to Catastrophe*, ed. David G. Roskies (Philadelphia: Jewish Publication Society, 1988).

[38] Anna Freud, letter to Lou Andreas-Salome, 1924, quoted in Elizabeth Young-Bruehl, *Anna Freud* (New York: Summit Books, 1988/New York: Macmillan, 1989).

[39] Sonia Games, *Escape in Darkness* (New York: Shapolsky, 1991).

From *The Warriors: Reflections on Men in Battle*

J. Glenn Gray

. . . It was one of the most discouraged thinkers who wrote the most hopeful of all paragraphs about a future warless world. His prophecy ought to be regarded as recognition of man's power to alter the course of events by undergoing an inner change. I refer, curiously enough, to Friedrich Nietzsche and to the following paragraph from *The Wanderer and His Shadow:*

> And perhaps the great day will come when a people, distinguished by wars and victories and by the highest development of a military order and intelligence, and accustomed to make the heaviest sacrifice for these things, will exclaim of its own free will, "we break the sword," and will smash its military establishment down to its lowest foundations. *Rendering oneself unarmed when one has been the best armed*, out of a height of feeling—that is the means to real peace, which must always rest on a peace of mind; whereas the so-called armed peace, as it now exists in all countries, is the absence of peace of mind. One trusts neither oneself nor one's neighbor and, half from hatred, half from fear, does not lay down arms. Rather perish than hate and fear, and *twice rather perish than make oneself hated and feared*—this must someday become the highest maxim for every single commonwealth too.

This is surely one of the most remarkable prophecies in Western literature. Nietzsche rightly sees that war-making must be overcome through strength and voluntary decision of a strong nation or group of nations; peace will never occur as a consequence of weakness, exhaustion, or fear. Just as the destructive lusts within us require superior power for their containment, so does an institution as deeply rooted in our society as is war require strength for its eradication. A peace of the peoples is hardly something that will steal over us unawares. Prepared for by a gradual change in the disposition of dominant groups, the final stroke will come in consequence of a daring, voluntary, and decisive act of breaking the sword. That can happen only when strength

Source: From *The Warriors: Reflections on Men in Battle*, by J. Glenn Gray, pp. 225–40. © 1959 by J. Glenn Gray. © 1987 by Ursula A. Gray. Current edition: University of Nebraska Press, 1998. Used with permission.

of mind and resolution of will no longer feel the need of external supports like prestige and protocol. It can happen even then only when a nation "out of a height of feeling" takes the decision to risk everything for a supreme good.

This is the second point of importance that Nietzsche makes. In addition to moral strength, courage will be needed, and that of the rarest kind, if war is to be extirpated from our race. The strong are, unfortunately, not always the brave, particularly not when they must expose themselves to the threat of the less strong. How exceedingly unlikely that any of the world's stronger nations today would have the courage to disarm before their enemies! Only a few pacifists have the temerity to suggest such a thing. Who among our political leaders is strong enough to take the responsibility for an act like this? Many might say: "If I had myself alone to answer for, it would be worth the risk. But what right have I to jeopardize future generations of my people by so irrevocable an act as this? Individuals can afford to take their lives in their hands; rulers must tread the cautious path of security. As the people's representative, my duty is to guarantee their safety as best I can for the short time they are under my care. Dreamers and utopians are fit for writing books; they have no function in responsible political office."

This is the wisdom of the world today, and woe betide the ruler who does not follow it. The vast majority of our people want our "armed peace" no less than their representatives, or, more correctly, they see no alternative to a peace of armed might. The other path is too beset with risks, and the implicit rule appears to be: Better to perish through caution than through folly. Nevertheless, there have been, in rare moments of world history, intellectual and political leaders who have persuaded their people to take risks nearly as momentous as this would be. They have been all too few, of course, and of these few most have failed. Yet nearly all that is best in our cultural heritage is traceable to their courage and resolution.

One day in the ripeness of time new leaders may appear who will induce their peoples to take the irrevocable step, an act so bold it will be greatly contagious and compel imitation. Obviously such a deed will not be wholly the work of one man or a small group. The people as a whole must be ready to support the act. But even when large numbers have undergone that inner change of mind and heart described in earlier chapters, it will still require the most courageous of leaders to break the sword in their name and thus assume responsibility for possible failure. A man will be needed of great simplicity and profound conviction.

The most important point of all in Nietzsche's prophecy is necessary motivation for breaking the sword. If permanent peace is ever to come over the world, it will be made possible only by motives that are hardly yet operative in political life. "Rather perish than hate and fear, and twice rather perish than make oneself hated and feared." If the rank and file of a great nation could accept a statement of this kind, our future might be assured. Most of us do not enjoy hating and fearing political enemies, but we prefer it infinitely to perishing. We prefer it even when we realize that, indulged in to an extreme degree, hating and fearing destroy our humanity and make us little better than beasts.

If so many of us did not prefer life on almost any terms, we should recognize how intolerable are the burdens of fear and hate which oppress us in our time. They induce us to spend the greater part of our national substance on arms and armor, thereby depriving our people of much needed schools, hospitals, libraries, and a thousand other benefits of organized political life. Hate and fear impel us to propagandize our youth, to twist and torment the truth into national and provincial molds instead of allowing it the universal frame it requires. Hate and fear narrow our sympathies, choke back our generous impulses, make us caricatures of our possible selves. When one considers these things and many more that might be mentioned in any just indictment of hate and fear, there need be no surprise that any free spirit would prefer perishing to life under their dominion.

However, the more important reason for breaking the sword, says Nietzsche—and he is surely right—is that men ought to choose death twice in preference to being feared and hated. Until this becomes the highest maxim for a commonwealth, as it is now for exceptional individuals, we shall not have reached our goal. Such an impractical motive may on first hearing astonish us, so contrary to our natural impulses is it, and may occasion a contemptuous smile on the faces of so-called realistic men of the world. Why should a nation resolve to be no longer feared and hated and be willing to pay any price for such a resolution?

The answer is terribly hard to give to worldly minds who like to calculate advantages and measure motives as they measure materials. They will hardly comprehend a decision made by Socrates many hundred years ago to suffer injustice in preference to committing it because the former did less harm to the soul. The reason a nation that seeks to be just must abhor being hated and feared is not very different. To hate and fear are evil and damaging to our inner life, but being hated and feared are still more destructive of our higher impulses and potentialities. Nothing corrupts our soul more surely and more subtly than the consciousness of others who fear and hate us. Such is our human nature that we cannot possess power that others dread without becoming like the image of their fear and hate. To possess dread power does not corrupt us overnight; our features may remain benign for years. But inevitably the awareness that others tremble or grow enraged at sight of us poisons the mind and makes us, individuals or nations, in the end into aggressive pariahs, distrustful, capricious, and empty.

If nations ever reach the moral heights attained by exceptional individuals, they will shudder at the images of themselves their neighbors harbor. And they will do everything thinkable to change these images. The image of itself that a strong and gentle nation will one day find most intolerable is of a colossus, jealous of its prestige and alert to pounce upon any who challenge the established order. Conscious of its own intentions and motives, such a nation will not rest until others are aware of those intentions too. This can be accomplished only by deeds that cost something, not by words no matter how eloquent. Whatever the cost, the strong and gentle nation will bend every effort to close the gap between what it is and what it seems to others to be, for the cleft between seeming and being is a fatal one for the nation that is intent on reformation. A strong and gentle nation can only realize its aims when others are fully aware that power and gentleness can coexist and become the greatest benison for an unhappy world.

Nietzsche's prophecy declares that war must be ended suddenly, by a stroke that leaves no one in doubt about the significance of the deed. As the context of the paragraph quoted makes clear, Nietzsche believes that no gradualism can succeed here. On the contrary, men will have to make someday an absolute break with their past, as dope addicts must with their habit, if war is to pass away. The problem of war is no ordinary one, to be combated and resolved like other social issues. It demands an emotional reorientation of such a kind that men will thenceforth date their liberation from that day. In Biblical language, this transformation will be apocalyptic in kind, comparable to the ancient command of the Lord: Let there be light! Afterward, men will be unable to comprehend how it was they could have lived in darkness. "Let us break the sword," someone will declare, in effect, and out of a heightened feeling men will respond by destroying the engines of destruction and will resolve to learn the ways of war no longer.

There is no doubt that practical men will scoff at such a prophecy, contrary as it is to acceptable procedure of our time and to the course of most previous history. Moreover, the statesmen and internationalists who are laboring earnestly in the United Nations and elsewhere to forge little by little the fragile chains of peace are likely to consider the notion of a sudden end of war by an act of national will a foolish and dangerous dream.

To be sure, it would be an irresponsible man who would suggest that we give up the hard work of our international agencies in order to wait for something so uncertain and unreliable as a popular response of the sort Nietzsche suggests. What we need to do without fail is to redouble our efforts in international affairs, seeking the development of retarded areas, searching for legal justice in international disputes, and placating national resentments through resort to conferences and all the arts of compromise. If through these means we can extend one by one the years of our present uneasy peace, wars can be made to seem more outmoded sociologically, economically, and politically than they already do. Even if much of the effort of our international agencies does not directly promote the cause of world peace, it is desirable in its own right and must be done. Peace is, after all, not the only end that men legitimately pursue, and no one really knows in many instances what does contribute to peace in the long run.

Granting all this, I am nonetheless convinced that a transformation of a deep-going inner sort will have to come over men before war can be vanquished. All the machinery of international diplomacy and the highest standard of living for retarded peoples cannot bring about this change. It may be poetic exaggeration to assert that this conversion will happen suddenly; what is meant is that it will be a decisive change. In earlier chapters I have described it as an awakening, a coming to oneself, a discovery of friendship, a falling in love. Human nature, the ultimate source of all hostility, must be converted from its present state of hatred and fear in order to liberate powers within us the existence of which is suspected only by the tiny minority. Neither governments nor other institutions are able to combat at present the destructive forces latent within most of us. The leaders we need are not likely to spring from the earth; they, too, require for success a change in the populace of a fundamental kind.

How must we change, if there is ever to be opportunity to break the sword once and for all? The question is as difficult as it is suggestive and seductive. The temptation to forsake the bounds of the probable is great, but all of us are weary of socialist utopias which describe men who have unlearned customary pleasures, needs, and desires. Realistically, we should not expect men to alter their outer manner of life at all drastically, for changes can be thorough and revolutionary with comparatively little external reformation. The deepest changes of all are indeed likely to return us to the workaday world outwardly little affected, though our actions now proceed from a different motivation and eventually reshape the human environment.

The ancient Greek philosopher Heracleitus once wrote that "men are estranged from what is most familiar and they must seek out what is in itself evident." The sentence illuminates, as few others have done, much of my own war experience. The atmosphere of violence draws a veil over our eyes, preventing us from seeing the plainest facts of our daily existence. To an awakened conscience, everything about human actions becomes then strange and nearly inexplicable. Why men fight without anger and kill without compunction is understandable at all only to a certain point. A slight alteration in consciousness would be sufficient to put their deeds in a true light and turn them forever from destruction. It would require only a coming to themselves to transform killers into friends and lovers, for, paradoxical as it may seem, the impulses that make killers are not so different in kind from those that make lovers. I know no other explanation for the notorious linkage in war between the noblest and the basest deeds, the most execrable vices and the sublimest virtues.

The feeling of being at home in the world is likewise not much removed from the feeling of being exposed and hopelessly lost to all succor. And the sense of being thrown into being that existentialist thinkers describe is removed only by a line from the experience of man created in God's image that was painted by Michelangelo in the wonderful fresco "The Creation of Man." The change in us from the one state of being to the other is, of course, profound, but the psychological distance to traverse is slight. Most of us have known both extremes, often in an incredibly short span of time. It is as though a thin but impenetrable wall separated the two states. If at moments the wall seems easily torn away, usually it proves to be more durable than our lives.

Hence the search for that most familiar and evident of all truths, the belonging together of the human species, in religious terms, the brotherhood of man, is rarely attended with success. In World War II, I found myself separating those soldiers who were awakened and aware of their situation from those who were lost in it. The former were those I could communicate with and understand; the others were simply "the others," beyond my sympathy and concern. Yet in moments of clarity nothing is more apparent than the fact that the best and the worst of men are different in degree only, not in kind. The soldier who is moved by sentiments of friendship and preservative love can reject the soldier-killer, for example, but he cannot in justice deny common humanity with him. Nor should the soldier of conscience who acknowledges his guilt at every level fail to recognize the potentiality of similar awakening in the most reckless and ruthless of his comrades as well as in the enemy. There is too much evidence of such transformations for any of us to doubt.

The case is hardly otherwise in our present uneasy state of peace. To overcome this alienation from the evident and the familiar we need, above all, a genuine closeness to each other in contrast to the separation and isolation that now prevails so widely. It is evident that the overcoming of physical space is not bringing this nearness. As our planet becomes more and more overcrowded and problems of living space and food grow more pressing, the chances for conflict indeed become greater. Evidently there is little or no relationship between physical and psychical nearness, for it is possible to be alienated from one's own roommate and be near to someone a thousand miles removed in space.

So long as we are far from ourselves, it is impossible to be near to others. Well-meaning people often assume that what is required of us today is a wider set of relationships than is possible within the simple and natural unities of family, town, and province. The typical citizens of Kansas, Brittany, and Formosa can hardly become close to each other in any sense demanding intimate acquaintance with one another. What all of us need to gain is a closer relationship to those immediately about us. He who knows what genuine friendship is or the fullest type of erotic love cannot be as estranged from self or others as they are who have never experienced these things.

This nearness to each other, even if it be with one other human being, promotes greatly the development of reflection and self-awareness. Persons who know intimacy are driven to put the important questions: Who am I? Why am I? What is to be my function in life? The kind of knowledge they seek is not of a subtle kind, commonly miscalled philosophical, which an untutored man could not be expected to have. On the contrary, it is this knowledge that people of little formal learning are frequently pursuing more avidly than the falsely sophisticated. Because they are concerned with the important questions, they sometimes achieve the important gift of simplicity. I know of no better way to reach the familiar and the evident than by stripping away superfluities in our emotional, reflective, and social selves, and in our external environment as well. Simplicity manifests itself in directness of approach to other human beings, in the absence of dissembling and guile. Knowing himself, the simple man is conscious that the man he is addressing is, in essentials, not different from himself, and it is the human being in the other that he insists on speaking to.

A condition of this intimacy, all too rarely recognized by most of us, is a different attitude toward the objects of nature around us. A habit of intimacy with the things of nature can fan the creative sparks within us and strengthen the concern for preserving ourselves and others. It is not a misty sentimental feeling for nature writ large that we require; but, rather, a recognition of our dependence on the most humble objects of everyday use and of their importance and place in existence. Until we learn to experience more simply and directly our gardens and trees, the skies above us, and all the objects amid which we move and work, we will find it difficult to achieve closeness to neighbors and even to ourselves.

I have become convinced that the familiar and the evident are so remote because we moderns have increasingly separated ourselves from nature by replacing a primary artistic response to things with a technological mentality. Contrary to the will of many scientists, our science has become much too often an instrument for the exploitation of things and people. We have become so preoccupied with power and control over nature that we have lost an important dimension of our being, the disposition of thankfulness, of commemoration, of perceiving and enjoying something for its own sake. Instead of viewing these immediate objects of our environment in terms of their own being, we have come to regard them solely in terms of what they are for us. And to such an exploitative mentality, nature's voice becomes mute. Approached as material merely, to be worked up and pressed into the service of a self-styled lord of creation, she contains no revelation and no blessing.

To the man who is not interested in what a thing is in itself and for itself, no intimate relations are possible. Nature can be infinitely abused by such a one, but by no means understood. Only the cherishing, object-centered eye of the artist latent in all of us can make and keep us aware that nature does not exist only for us, but in her own right as well. The artistic gaze alone can discern those qualities in nature that are able to heal our restlessness and overcome our boredom, by enhancing the value of the commonplace. Art can reconcile us to our individual and collective fates as nothing else can, except perhaps religion. But art (I do not speak of the fine arts) has declined in our society as the narrow utilitarian ideal has grown, and the results are lamentable.

The effect on our religious traditions of this appropriative, ego-centered disposition of mind has been hardly less disastrous. Religion, like art, points to something greater and more worthy than the self and impels us to pay it homage. Religion relates man to his origins, aiding him thus in the search for a reason for existence. Modern man finds it hard indeed to discover anything in the universe worthy of worship. More often than not he conceives himself to be at the top of an unordered creation, able to survey the whole and to do with it what he will. But few are ready to worship him; he has demonstrated often enough that he is lacking in divine serenity and endurance.

Moreover, he himself knows full well that he can be no proper god, for he is filled with a longing for something or someone to whom to belong. In the face of an overpowering universe, he realizes, consciously or not, that his freedom and independence are relative and puny. What is missing so often in modern men is a basic piety, the recognition of dependence on the natural realm. And they feel the need of this piety without possessing it. There is no dearth of religions in our time, and they fulfill certain needs, but there is a general absence of religious passion for belonging to an order infinitely transcending the human. Separated from close association with nature and intimacy with her ways, we find it difficult to do homage to nature's god.

This separation of man from nature as a consequence of our too-exclusive interest in power is in part responsible for the total wars of our century. More than we ever realize, we have transferred our exploitative attitudes from nature to man. In total war, men become so much material, and civilian populations, like soldiers, have to be ravaged and subdued. Distinctions between innocent and guilty, the permissible and the prohibited, become extinguished. Men and machines approach each other more nearly. The most painful impressions of World War II for me, as I have said, were the ruthless trampling down of the works of nature and the innocent products of human art. Try as I might, I cannot but recoil, even in memory, from the destructive fury of a modern army directed upon the things of nature and her creatures, all untainted by any partisanship. The butchering of each other was almost easier to endure than the violation of animals, crops, farms, homes, bridges, and all the other things that bind man to his natural environment and help to provide him with a spiritual home.

Since that war, there has been no convincing evidence of change in this exploitative mentality. The fashioning of the atom bomb seems to me too dangerously typical of the modern mind, and the recent experiments with the hydrogen bomb an unrecognized blasphemy. Hardly anyone considers it possible that the poisoning of fish in the ocean by these experiments might be worthy of condemnation. Man can sin only against man, it seems, or possibly against God, not against nature. That the ocean should be violated, a region hitherto relatively immune from destructive lusts, seems to most, apparently, nothing else than a triumph of natural science.

In the desperate state of human relations in our day, one can understand the argument for testing weapons in order to keep national defenses strong. But I am objecting to the spirit in which it is done, involving, as it does, indifference to all that is not of human origin or use. This lack of concern stands, I believe, as a great barrier to the elimination of war. Before expecting man to spare his brother, we must persuade him to spare those things around him that contribute to his life as greatly as his brothers do. The growth of that preservative love and care which is in strongest opposition to destructive lusts involves an intimacy with things of which too many of us have as yet hardly an inkling.

The gift of nearness to the familiar and evident is happiness. Whatever else is true, we in the West will not learn to break the sword until we have happier populations. If there are any laws of psychology in this area at all, one must be that a happy people is a peaceful people. The capacity for happiness which most of us possess receives too rarely the sustenance it needs to become more than a capacity; more often it shrinks as we grow older. The longing for a paradise, which our hearts believe to be possible but which we cannot find, robs us of serenity; the large expectations of our youth remain unfulfilled. Though the components of happiness are no doubt many and not the same for all, emotional and intellectual intimacy with others is surely the one component essential to nearly all of us. For the few, association with the things of nature can of itself produce a happiness that suffices to fulfill the more solitary members of our species. But, for the majority, nearness to the things of daily existence can be a means for entering into closeness with other human beings, whether it be the comradeship of labor, the partnership of marriage, the friendship of kindred minds, or other associations.

More than anything else, happiness can provide a secure bottom to the world, sufficient to persuade us that we are no accidents on this planet. Happiness alone can transform the dull and colorless daily scene into an order pregnant with meaning and delight. When a person finds a friend to whom he can open his heart, when a woman finds a man she can love and to whom she can bear children, when any of us find a community we can love and serve, our little lives take on a significance we had not dreamed of. Far from being the restless ones who welcome war as a possible path to forbidden experience, we experience the threat of war as completely intolerable. Those who have a stake in peace realize too well that war can occasion the loss of all.

Nations containing genuinely happy citizens would shrink from exposing their great fortunes to the cruel chances of combat far more than wealthy nations now shun war from fear of loss. More than this, a nation with happy citizens would encounter greater difficulty in maintaining a hostile disposition in themselves or others, since happiness always presses toward universality. The people who one day break with their military past and declare that they no longer can endure to be hated and feared will not only be a happy people; their deed will be largely a result of their happiness. Having experienced closeness to each other, they will be eager to extend the experience to others. And for this they may be willing to take the greatest risks, more trustful and of larger faith than we. . . .

Peace Through Strength

Liane Ellison Norman

You want us to lie down and let the Russians trample over us, critics say of peace workers. There's some justice in this view: we've opposed particular wars or preparations for wars. But we've not sufficiently explored ways to *replace* warfare, which has historically been the principal *recorded*[1] means whereby nations, states, princes or parties within states have contended for both noble and ignoble ends—defense as well as conquest, liberty and justice as well as hegemony and despotism. In our hatred of war, we've ignored the needs it has satisfied.

War at its Old German linguistic roots means confusion, discord and strife. But war is also associated with splendid panoply and poetry. "Once more into the breach, dear friends," urges the warrior King Henry V, appealing to the tradition that burnishes the reputation of battle. Our culture tells us that though war is hell, it is honorable. It occasions solidarity, heroism, spectacle, comradeship, self-sacrifice and vitality.

War is thought to work, despite evidence that there's always at least one losing side, that each war concludes by making the next more likely. And when, for participants, experience tarnishes war, culture tells us there's no other way to pursue certain objectives.

Long-standing ambivalence about war has tightened like thumbscrews since 1945, when it became evident that nuclear weapons could do in seconds the damage it had taken decades—even centuries—to do in earlier times; could destroy not only populations and their works, but the very environment on which life depends. We who deplore violence have seized on each new piece of evidence that war is insupportable to make our point. But, say the dubious, so long as the world is not made up of saints, you cannot dismantle arms nor do away with war.

It's worth listening to our critics. History suggests it's realistic to be concerned about both conquest and tyranny. If we had neither weapons nor soldiers, what would we do if an enemy tried to conquer us? What would we do if our government suspended civil liberties, imprisoned, tortured and executed people like us? Women know that to accommodate bullying makes

Source: "Peace Through Strength," by Liane Ellison Norman, *Civilian-Based Defense*, Vol. 3, No. 2, March 1986. Reprinted by permission of the author and the Civilian-Based Defense Association.

them silent partners in violence. Peace, given such realities, smacks of weakness, cowardice, appeasement and submission.

Our language both reflects and shapes the problem. Peace means the absence or cessation of war, a negative definition. How can we have both peace *and* the power to stand up to conquerers and tyrants?

I ask my students to draw a picture of power, not an easy task, for while we use the term "power" with confidence, it's an elusive idea. One student draws God threatening a father who has his arm raised with a club to beat his son—my student. This picture crudely expresses a common notion about power: that in the nature of things, power resides at the top of some kind of hierarchy and that it involves the ability to hurt and/or humiliate. Those with high position have power *because* they can do violence. Parents, teachers, religious leaders and employers can make us do their bidding because they can punish us if we don't. This view of power is a wide-spread article of faith.

Looked at more closely, however, the power exercised by those in power is both *dependent* and *fragile*. No head of state governs singlehandedly. She[2] has aides and advisors to help formulate and transmit policy to bureaucracies; secretaries to answer the telephone, write letters and file records; tax collectors to provide revenues; experts of all varieties (planners, economists, engineers, construction crews, garbage collectors, mail deliverers, cooks, cleaners); police to enforce and courts to interpret the laws; and citizens, who by and large obey the laws, co-operate, submit to the general order.

The power to govern depends on the willingness of a multitude of people to be governed. If they withdraw their consent, even in significant part, no head of state can govern. In other words, citizens provide their leaders with power and can regulate its use. Those *in* power can use sanctions against the dissident and disobedient—or at least a representative sample—but even sanctions require obedience to carry out.[3]

For example, the federal government says Central American refugees are illegal aliens and requires that law-enforcement officials help catch and punish them. But a number of cities have declared themselves sanctuaries, which means that city employees will not assist the government in carrying out its policy. *The New York Times* (December 27, 1985) proclaims editorially that "Cities Can't Make Immigration Law." But cities, along with individual citizens, *make* law all the time when they *comply* with it. "If the law displeases them, let them petition Washington," scolds the *Times*, which nearly always reinforces the view that power rests only at the top. The cities, like the churches which have offered sanctuary, like those who once harbored runaway slaves en route to freedom or those who made white lightning during prohibition, refuse obedience to the federal government and laws they judge to be oppressive. Government is limited by the power of the people.

What really frightens power-at-the-top people is that citizens and localities may discover how powerful they are. However, with the discovery that they can resist the policies of their own government comes the insight that the same citizens and localities can formulate a defense that does not depend upon the kind of organized, legalized violence we call war.

To design a nonviolent defense requires thinking about conquest, victory and defeat. Though it seems to be about battlefields, war is really about *who* is to govern *what* and *how*. Conquest is meaningless unless the conqueror is able to govern: victory means that one or more of the contending parties acknowledges defeat, concedes the right of the victor to govern. One army may rout another, but unless the population represented by the defeated army permits itself to be governed by the conquerers, there is no conquest.

A conqueror can punish or kill those—or some of those—who resist, just as he does in battle. But conquerors do not bring with them whole regimes to govern, enforce and implement: even if they had the requisite human power, newcomers would not know *how* to make a conquered system operate. The conquerors, instead, have to persuade local people to run things for them by intimidation or reward. If the "conquered" refuse, braving threat or punishment, the "conquerors" are stymied. Increased oppression meant to persuade the population to obey may backfire: any regime that has to rely on excessive punishment to govern loses legitimacy and increases resistance. Precisely the same general principles apply to domestic tyranny as to foreign imposition: dictators, wherever they originate, rely on co-operation and consent, whether given with enthusiasm or fear.

Nonviolent defense strategy is to deny enemy objectives, to make the task of controlling a population and its institutions impossible. Historic instances—of the Danes and Norwegians in World War II, of the Czechs in 1968, of the Indians under Gandhi, of many others as documented by Gene Sharp[4]—are more suggestive than conclusive: they represent spontaneous rather than well-developed strategies, relying more on ingenuity and courage than preparation and discipline. But that very spontaneity, ingenuity and courage suggest that *with* preparation and discipline, with advance planning, with reinforcement by education and popular culture, nonviolent strategies can provide defense against both foreign conquest and domestic tyranny.

Nonviolent defense strategies cannot be used against nuclear weapons: but then, neither can violent defense strategies. But a country that ceases to menace others while maintaining its capacity to defend itself can afford to give up its nuclear weapons, which though expensive, undermine rather than provide security. While nuclear weapons provide a fundamentally incredible deterrent, nonviolent strategies *can* be used to deter an enemy by making clear in advance that the nonviolently-prepared country will make the task of conquest and governance costly, impossible and unpopular. But nonviolent defense *can not be perverted to offense*. While a country, region or people can protect themselves using nonviolent means, they *cannot* invade and intimidate using the same means.

A nonviolent defense strategy does not require that other nations relinquish violence: it can be used against violent, brutal and ruthless enemies. Nonviolent combatants need not be nice, cussedness being more to the point than saintliness. The effectiveness of their strategy does not require the moral conversion of the enemy. However, by depriving enemies of the arguments they rely on to justify otherwise outlawed acts of brutality, nonviolence undermines their conditioning. Recognizing that adversaries also have the power to withdraw their consent humanizes them, offering them options they may, as individuals, not have considered. This is what the advice to love one's enemies means in tactical terms.

Young men have to be *broken* of their humanity to be made soldiers. Nonviolent defense requires no such rupture of human inclinations, but rather a strengthening thereof. Nonviolent civilian, or popular defense, does not delegate society's dirty and dangerous work to adolescent boys, but relies on people to defend themselves—taking their share of casualties. Such strategies do not require temporarily setting aside civilian values, but fortify them. Violent revolutions habitually fail because the arts of war are ill suited to post-revolutionary order: violent revolution spawns counterrevolutionaries eager to avenge their losses, and those who win by violence can rarely be kind. Nonviolent defensive and revolutionary strategies are inherently democratic, for those doing the defending learn the skills, develop the stamina and support systems necessary to the withdrawal of consent not only from foreign tyrants and their agents but from tyrants closer to home as well. Thus nonviolent policies demand legitimacy now rather than eventually. Further, nonviolent strategies promote the continuous renewal of democratic principles, relying on the genius and knowhow of ordinary people and providing them with the means to rectify wrongs long before desperation makes them reckless.

Most societies teach people to be powerless. This is convenient for those who want to wield power *over* others, but is in the long run self-defeating because it prepares them to submit. The more powerless people think they are, the more easily they can be conquered. *The New York Times* sees no recourse but courteous petitions to those *in* power: the same habit of mind might well lead the *Times* to defer to a conqueror. The cities which defy the federal government in the matter of sanctuary are better prepared to resist foreign or domestic tyranny. Few parents, frustrated by a two-year-old resisting a snowsuit, teach the child to note and learn from that exercise of power. Few teachers, faced with students coughing in unison, use the occasion to teach the lesson of resistance and solidarity. It takes confident, secure adults and leaders to teach power and the discernment to use it well. However, violence springs from insecurity and the sense of weakness rather than security and strength: Rambo is a fantasy of power, not the real thing.

Some say there's no evidence that nonviolent strategies for defense would work. It's true that we haven't tested such strategies consciously enough to know for sure whether they would always do the trick: nor does warfare. It's also true, however, that we *have* tested organized violence, and while wars have won some gains, the price has been terrific. Part of that price has been the failure to develop other means of serious struggle.

And so we find ourselves in a corner: war has become too dangerous to use and we haven't as a civilization developed an alternative. But we have the opportunity, even this late in the day, to work together, hawks and doves, each with our partial understanding of the truth, to develop the means to make peace strong and strength peaceful.

Notes

[1] Recorded history and warfare developed at about the same time. The one has, not surprisingly, set down the story of the other.

[2] The feminine pronoun is used generically and does not exclude the masculine of the species.

[3] An army or police force must consent to carry out orders. Agammemnon could not prosecute the Trojan war without Achilles and his Myrmidons; commanders in Vietnam often could not get their troops to go into battle; at a certain point in Birmingham, police refused to turn fire hoses and dogs on civil rights activists when ordered to.

[4] *The Politics of Nonviolent Action*, 3 vols. Boston: Porter Sargent, 1973.

Pacifism and Invasion

Jessie Wallace Hughan

The pacifist proposal is a clear cut and serious one, and we must be ready to meet the challenge "If our nation should renounce war and the preparation for war, would this necessitate 'lying down' before a hypothetical invader?" The present pamphlet is an attempt to answer this question.

Now fear can be dealt with in only one way, through looking it straight in the face. We are going to imagine the United States completely disarmed and invaded by a foreign foe; we will indicate the available measures of defense, and then try to evaluate the chances of success as compared with the time honored military method.

Of course we can give no guarantee of victory, and no assurance against losses and casualty lists. We can promise only one thing, that while military defense, at its best, means breaking all the Ten Commandments, unarmed defense, at its worst, involves no such necessity. Shall we demand of the second method, then, a guarantee of success which the first is unable to give? Shall we not rather look into its possibilities with what objectivity we can, and if we find a reasonable prospect that nonviolent defense may accomplish its purpose with no greater loss and suffering than a war of corresponding magnitude, shall we not welcome the stern opportunity, just as decent individuals among us all would grasp at any dangers and hardships that might enable them to maintain their families without resort to manslaughter.

How Efficient Is Military Defense?

As the accounts of [World War II] are far from closed, let us take a look at the costs and efficiency of military defense as shown by a table of World War belligerents at the end of the war:

Source: From *The Quiet Battle: Writings on the Theory and Practice of Non-Violent Resistance*, edited by Mulford Q. Sibley (Garden City, NJ: Doubleday, 1963). Reprinted by permission of M. H. Sibley.

Country	Known Dead	Net Money Cost	Results
1. Great Britain	908,371	35 billions	Successful
2. Belgium	13,716		Unsuccessful
3. France	1,357,800	35 billions	Partially successful
4. Russia	1,700,000	22 billions	Unsuccessful
5. Germany	1,773,700	37 billions	Unsuccessful
6. Austro-Hungary	1,200,000	20 billions	Unsuccessful

Only two of the countries achieved even partial success. Failures meant the direct and indirect deaths of civilians, estimated as roughly equal to those in the armies, and a total of ten million refugees, one and a half million of these in Belgium and two million in France.

In considering the risks of military defense it is interesting to note that Belgium was well prepared against invasion in 1914. The peace strength of its army in 1913 was approximately 180,000 men, and the military estimates for that year amounted to 3,359,890 pounds sterling.

Belgium was protected also by ironclad treaties of alliance with Great Britain and France. Yet Belgium was as completely conquered by the German invaders as was Luxemburg, which possessed no army and put up no defense at all, both countries being eventually set free at the end of the war.

The tragedy of Czechoslovakia [in World War II] was an instance of unsuccessful defense through military preparedness, in the hope to avoid actual war. Fortified by the "second Maginot Line," supplied by the great Skoda munition works and relying, like Belgium, on the protection of two great powers, the Czech Republic, no more pacifist than Belgium, was forced to surrender without a battle.

The story of Poland, a traditionally belligerent nation with military forces of over a million, is even more tragic than that of Czechoslovakia, in so far as it declined to "lie down" before the aggressor until its men had been slaughtered and its cities bombed.

Finland, another heavily armed small country, succeeded for three months, aided by Arctic winter and difficult terrain, in beating back the Russian invasion. Its people were heroic; its defense included the famous Mannerheim Line; its Allies were Britain and France. Yet the terms forced upon it in March 1940, were even more severe than those it had scorned the previous December.

History contains no more tragic list of failures in defense than those of the years 1939–40. Six highly civilized nations, Norway, Denmark, Holland, Belgium, France and Greece have been invaded and conquered, leaving out of consideration countries such as Rumania and Hungary, which compromised with the aggressor as a ransom for survival.

Denmark, whose policy had been consistently anti-militarist though not pacifist, offered no resistance, but submitted without a struggle to German occupation.

Norway, Holland, Belgium, France and Greece put their trust in military defense and in the protection of their powerful ally, Britain. One by one they fell before the German blitzkrieg.

The Pacifist Proposal

In the light of this inadequacy of armed defense, the proposal is that . . . the United States take the first steps toward the goal of complete disarmament. In the event of an unprovoked invasion after this disarmament shall have taken place, we contend that the country will not be under the necessity of submitting to the invader, but will have at its command the tactics of non-violent noncooperation, in other words, by a general strike raised to the *n*th power. Under this plan resistance would be carried on, not by professional soldiers but by the people as a whole, by refusing to obey the invaders or to assist them through personal service or the furnishing of supplies.

Removal of Incentive to Invasion

It is, of course, true that the chance of an unarmed United States being invaded is about that of an unarmed citizen being shot as he walks up Fifth Avenue—possible, but improbable. The motivation of conquest in the present day world, unless such a conquest is undertaken for the sake of gaining military advantage in a larger war, is almost wholly economic, the desire for undeveloped raw materials or vast new fields for the investment of capital. The prizes of imperialism are countries like Ethiopia or China, with untapped resources and industrially unsophisticated people. Our own country is developed up to the hilt and so overflowing with goods and capital as to offer no temptations to conquest. Before it disarms it will, of course, have removed all trade restrictions on its own raw materials and will have completed the process of setting free its few imperialist possessions.

The policy of settling disputes through the World Court, arbitration and conciliation will be extended to questions of every type, and knotty problems such as tariffs and currency will be committed without reservation on our part to international boards of adjustment. By concrete instances we will prove to the world the readiness of American business to accept financial losses for the sake of peace as formerly for the sake of carrying on war.

The signal for total disarmament would doubtless consist of the passage by Congress of the Amendment to the Constitution already introduced several times into the Senate, taking from government the power to prepare for, to declare or to carry on war. As pacifist opinion gained in the United States, however, the army and navy would gradually have been reduced to such negligible proportions that the final passage of the amendment would form the culmination of a process whose goal was definitely foreseen. Foreign nations would then be formally notified of the unconditional adherence of the United States to the Kellogg Pact, and would not fail to assure us in the honeyed words of diplomacy of their wholehearted cooperation and devotion to the cause of world peace. The following up of this proclamation by actual disarmament might indeed tax the credulity of foreign governments. . . . All doubts would be removed, however, by the immediate throwing open to inspection of our former military and naval posts and munition centers.

By the time that disarmament goes through, therefore, we shall be endangered by none of the undeveloped territory which has rendered Great Britain and France as choice targets as Ethiopia and China, and by no bristling armaments such as rallied the world against Germany in 1914 and have again driven the terrified nations into war.

It is to be remembered also that the modification of the social mind which brings disarmament will have brought also a radical change in our own conceptions of patriotism and national honor. Patriotism is already becoming a very concrete matter, under the stress of civilian defense, and is expressing itself less in verbal protestations than in obedience to law and protecting love for one's fellow citizens—young men of military age as well as women and children. . . . As complete disarmament approaches reality, anti-militarism will *pari passu* have emerged as a sacred national ideal, for which patriots will freely sacrifice personal interest and if necessary life itself. Our state department, therefore, will be held strictly accountable for preserving friendly international relations and its efficiency will be measured by the skill with which it prevents disputes with other nations from approaching the danger line of war. To this department, rather than to the military, will be entrusted the lives and property of the country.

If asked how we know that these radical changes in social psychology and diplomacy will have entered into the situation, we reply that they are essential to the earlier stages of pacifist policy, and cannot fail to be accomplished facts before any nation is ready to take the final step of renunciation of all war.

Facing the Hypothesis

Once more we repeat our hypothesis, that of a country which has voluntarily renounced all war and done away with armament, this step having been prepared for by years of reliance upon policies of international justice and friendship rather than upon force or the growing threat of force, and of an unprovoked invasion by a foreign foe. Chimerical as may seem the idea of a foreign invasion under these conditions, the problem before us is confessedly a fantastic one, which we have promised to face in all seriousness. The imagination can call up certain possibilities. A government bankrupted through armament might hope to reimburse itself by tribute levied upon Wall Street; a dictator might seek to retain power through the prestige of foreign conquest or through the spreading of Fascist ideals by fire and sword.

Since there could be no mobilization on our part to make haste imperative, the foreign government would, of course, begin with negotiations of one kind or another—demands for tribute, territory, or complete surrender of political existence. These would be met by our government with diplomacy, with offers of arbitration and conciliation, and with formal recourse to the World Court. Only after deliberate defiance of world opinion could an enemy nation issue the ultimatum preliminary to invasion or proceed to a surprise attack without such notice.

We now have the United States faced with the alternative of resistance to the death or of "lying down" in submission. It is true that resistance is a lottery at best, and that even such absolute surrender as that of Germany in 1918 would have lost half its tragedy if it could have been put through in the summer of 1914, before a soldier had been mobilized. In the absence of revenge any tribute must be imposed by greed alone, and in that case might prove as stimulating to the surrendered country as the tribute paid by France after the Franco-Prussian war. Cultural ideas which run counter to group spirit can, of course, be enforced in name only, and there is evidence that a nation united in devotion to its traditions may maintain its own way of life even after nominal surrender.

How a Pacifist Nation Would "Prepare"

In the present discussion, however, we are disregarding the alternative of submission in any degree, and assuming a people firm in the determination to die rather than yield as individuals, or as a nation, to the demands of an invader. No surrender but resistance to the bitter end is the national policy.

The country is prepared for the conflict, having taken the bold step of disarmament, after years of mounting pacifism and in full anticipation of a possible test. Adventurous spirits have even looked forward to the chance of invasion as to the literal "war to end war" in which their nation might be the protagonist, with opportunities of heroism for every citizen undreamed of under the old regime.

The entire populace has been continually educated by all the resources of school, church and radio. Recognizing that its own country embodies liberty in such concrete forms as freedom of speech, freedom of assembly and freedom of conscience, it has centered its patriotism about these realities rather than such abstractions as empire and victory; accordingly it is alert to challenge any violation of civil liberty by friend or foe and to refuse even at serious sacrifice to submit to them. It has learned that while an individual can be restricted or punished, he can never be compelled to action against his will; its heroes have shifted from Caesar and Napoleon to such men as Socrates and Pastor Niemoeller. It has become a national ideal to despise anger and cruelty as pathological and to hold all human life sacred.

Most difficult of all, the masses have been trained in the exercise of individual courage, measured by the cool test of deliberate heroism rather than group recklessness. . . .

As pacifism gradually becomes the conviction of the majority of citizens, the soldier's task of killing the enemy will have lost the attraction it now holds, but the soldierly virtue of enduring hardship and death for one's country will have become the ideal, not of a single profession, but of an entire population. Government officials particularly, from the head of the state to the lowest civil servant, will realize themselves to be the successors of the army in its function of national defense, pledged, whatever their rank, to unswerving loyalty if crises should arise.

The present use of the word "defense" to designate services as far removed from the military as housing and teaching is an indication that the foundations for nonviolent resistance on a national scale are already being laid.

Exploration and surveys, soil reclamation, civilian aviation, prevention of flood and disease, relief of suffering from natural disasters at home and abroad, all these can afford increasing scope for the trained abilities now set apart for destructive purposes. The coast guard, enlarged to furnish protection throughout all coasts and inland waters, and the fire department, developed in forest and rural districts to the efficiency already achieved in cities, are amply able to provide physical equivalents for war, and can be made equally reputable by assigning to them the rank, pay and pensions now reserved for military defenders. A similar rise in honor and compensation can elevate the police force, both local and national, to the level of dignity where the army and navy now stand.

It is upon these various defense services, their officers high in the counsels of government and their privates in close touch with citizens everywhere, that the pacifist nation will rely in such hypothetical dangers as invasion by a foreign foe.

The propaganda and intelligence departments would carry even more responsibility under a pacifist government than at present. In time of peace their duty will be to inform the world of each concrete measure of disarmament and to interpret our policy of international friendliness to foreign peoples as well as to their governments. Radio and the screen will be utilized for this purpose, and our consulates abroad will circulate countless bulletins making clear the application of our "good neighbor" policy to the country in question. In case of invasion those departments will keep both friendly and hostile nations in touch with every measure and event. The foreign press will be given all facilities for news getting, and battalions of daring aviators will be ready to shower leaflets upon the enemy country if access to the press is closed. As observers abroad will have no discrepancies to reconcile between the protestations of our government and its known policies before the crisis, emergency propaganda of this type will be able to carry conviction impossible under the present regime.

Physical preparations for defense will of course be made, far less expensive than in the case of military resistance, but not less essential. The first of these is obviously the destruction of all firearms and other weapons of offense, with the machinery for producing them. This pledge of good faith to other nations is also a necessary defense measure to obviate "sniping" and other provocative incidents. Moreover, it will be important for an invading army to know that we possess no stores of war munitions which it may seize. For some time an exception may have to be made of the rifles of professional hunters and of small arms in the hands of the police, but, when private sale has once been abolished, only a negligible supply of the latter need be retained. As military "atrocities" chiefly occur under conditions of intoxication, one of the first war measures will be to destroy all distilleries and supplies of liquor throughout the country. Food and other necessities will have been stored at strategic points. Other defense plans will relate to methods of communication, of speedy evacuation, of rehabilitation, and of rendering various districts capable of maintaining themselves in possible isolation. The suggestions of the present article are the merest foreshadowings of the defense tactics which may be adopted. . . .

The Principles of Unarmed Defense

Though we cannot pretend to a complete blueprint of the working of unarmed defense, the four main principles are already established:

1. No services or supplies to be furnished to invaders.
2. No orders to be obeyed except those of the constitutional civil authorities.
3. No insult or injury to be offered the invaders.
4. All public officials to be pledged to die rather than surrender.

A Battle Without Arms

Let us now envisage the situation presented by the fantastic hypothesis of an invasion, fantastic in view of the years of friendly international policy which have preceded it, but yet a possibility. The potential enemy has ignored proposals of conciliation, and has either issued a humiliating ultimatum or opened hostilities by a surprise attack upon our coast. The world has its ear to the radio, and our government and people, morally and physically prepared, brace themselves for the conflict. As defense involves not only those of military age, but every man, woman and child in the community, there is immediate evacuation from threatened localities of all persons likely to be incapacitated through fear or physical weakness. Provision is quickly made for emergency supplies and communication, according to plans thought out beforehand. Civil officials, including directors of public utilities, as well as of government, have accepted the full responsibilities and dangers of leadership; succession to each important office has been provided for in the event of death or imprisonment, and citizens are well acquainted with the order in which those names on the long list of honor will take the place of those who have fallen.

Meeting with no opposition other than the ordinary traffic regulations, the enemy commander, with an escort picked for courage, enters the City Hall and is received with courtesy by the Mayor. After diplomatic preliminaries the Mayor, following the precedent of the heroic Mayor of Vienna in 1934, refuses the order to surrender and is taken prisoner. The first vice-mayor automatically succeeds, but the invaders exclude him from the City Hall, setting in his place a traitor or an officer of their own. Executives and clerks continue to perform their duties, however, until commands arrive from the enemy usurper, when they either ignore the orders or cease work altogether, quietly destroying combinations and documents if opportunity offers.

The city departments of fire and police, with the public utility services of telegraph, telephone and electricity, continue to function under their regular heads until these receive enemy orders. At this point they, too, will disregard specific commands or declare an instantaneous strike. Workers in garages, gas stations, airports and railroads will go on serving the civil population until interfered with, and resume work if and when pressure is removed. If their chief is arrested, the workers automatically transfer obedience to his successor on the list, failing to report to duty under an enemy appointee, but ready at a moment's notice to rally to their authorized head.

Food and strategic materials, if not already publicly owned, are controlled by trustworthy officials directed to refuse all supplies to the invaders, but to conserve and distribute them for the benefit of civilians.

The citizens in general follow the same rigid program of passive resistance as public employees. No one insults the interlopers, but no one sells to them or works for them. The usurping commander issues orders which are firmly ignored, but strict obedience is given to those legitimate officers who remain in authority. Civilian occupations go on as usual till the enemy touches them. In that case, work stops by magic and that particular unit of industry remains frozen till further notice.

Everywhere the invaders meet the same conditions—no battles, no opposing armies, no dangers, no chances for heroism. On the other hand, no surrenders to figure in the dispatches, no peasants offering food, no sullenly obedient populace, no technicians or workers to man the utilities. The soldiers have nothing to do but to serve themselves by routine labor, varied by assaults upon unarmed citizens and ignominious robbing of shops and hen-roosts.

Neither army morale nor war fever in the aggressor nation is likely to hold out long against this reversal of all that makes the spirit of a campaign. Our propaganda works havoc with the foreign soldiers and their own opposition politics with the foreign citizens. Before many weeks or months elapse, it is probable that the enemy government will hasten to cover up its blunder by recalling the inglorious and unprofitable expedition. [Nevertheless, let us face frankly]—

The Hypothesis of Ruthlessness

After the first skirmish with the people, the foreign general will consult his government as to the alternatives, terrorism or compromise. He has power to torture striking workers, execute disobedient citizens and deliberately starve the resisting community.

In the enemy country the first hysteria has died down, for civilian war spirit, like that of the army, requires battles and heroism for its sustenance. The opposition to the ruling group, always present whether open or suppressed, begins to gather strength.

Furthermore, the nation must save its face with other powers by at least the pretence of justifiability. Since a military dictatorship is even more dependent than a normal government upon the maintenance of an emergency situation, it cannot fail to find its popular support seriously undermined. Accordingly self-preservation will prescribe the more moderate course, to make the most of its nominal victory rather than risk political defeat through wantonly terroristic measures.

In this case the invaders, after a number of arrests and confiscations, will advance to their next objective, leaving behind them, in addition to the usual garrison, a complete corps of technicians and workers for essential services and communications. The citizens meanwhile will have returned more or less to normal life, hampered by the presence of the garrison, suffering occasional arrests and even executions when orders conflict, and subject to seizures of property when foraging necessity demands it. Their condition will be unenviable and even pitiable, but will differ more in degree than in kind from that of civilians under martial law in territory occupied by their own military defenders.

We are deliberately facing, however, the most fantastic hypothesis which can be devised, and must force our imaginations to a third possibility—that of extreme and gratuitous ruthlessness such as has never yet appeared in history. We are to envisage an implacable commander under an unscrupulous government, supported by a political party quite reckless of world or minority opinion. Conquest at all cost is the policy chosen; as civil officials refuse obedience they are one after the other arrested and executed, and recalcitrant workers are herded into concentration camps, their posts being filled by foreign soldiers. As enemy technicians are limited in number, only work necessary to the army will be performed and the public utilities will be largely cut off.

An actual battle is under way, between starvation and enemy violence on one hand and the will of a selected civilian population on the other. The food supply will of course constitute the chief point of strategy. Provisions for some days have been brought by the foreign transports, but these must be economized for an emergency while the army lives as far as possible upon the country. As part of its defense precautions the home government has avoided concentration of essential supplies where they may be seized, and the invaders proceed to the robbery of small stocks in the hands of retailers and individuals. Foraging parties break into homes and warehouses, carrying off what supplies they find, but the food industry, like other services, congeals into strikes as soon as interfered with. Dairy products, meat and fresh vegetables cannot be bought or requisitioned. The shop is closed, the dairy is uncared for, the crops are ungathered, and the stream of commodities which normally enters the city by train or truck is immediately cut off at its sources and turned by the government to other districts. A modern city is seldom distant more than a few days from famine, and in a very short time the limits of seizure have been reached. The army finds itself reduced to dependence upon imported supplies, in the midst of a populace kept from starvation only in so far as it is permitted to handle its own provisions unmolested.

At the first threat to the civilian food supply, on the other hand, the evacuation has begun of those persons who remained in the invaded region. By train and motor car until these are seized, and then on foot, they scatter over the country, destroying crops and stores as they go. . . .

Have there been casualties? There have—executions, imprisonments, deaths from exposure and starvation.

There is also the possibility that ruthlessness may do its worst, resorting to air and sea bombardment, high explosives and poison gas, to break the will of the people. Under military defense, on the other hand, attempts at bombardment are not a mere possibility but a certainty. . . .

As is now made clear to civilian defense groups, the government in war time aims first to protect things—factories and military supplies—and second to protect people,[1] but restriction of funds sets definite limits to those efforts. A pacifist government, on the other hand, would not be hampered in this way, but could direct its entire resources to the defense of civilian life and property.

It would be comparatively easy also to effect the evacuation of threatened towns. . . . Military governments are strictly limited in these matters, as the conventional defense requires the concentration of soldiers at danger points, with civilians for essential services, but the nonviolent state could arrange for the complete evacuation of danger zones, and would, of course, gain efficiency by being able to employ all its resources for the defense of civilians.

After making all allowances, the number of casualties is no easier to compute than in an old style conflict. . . . Is there any general sufficiently barbarous to decree even fifty per cent of this slaughter against unarmed civilians? It is possible, but improbable.

Between the two courses of nominal seizure of government and ruthless terrorism or bombardment there are of course countless degrees and modifications which would approach far more nearly a true forecast.

The Enemy Has Gained Nothing

Be the losses little or great, however, the important point is that the enemy has gained nothing by the engagement, whether in indemnity, supplies or capitulation. If an air force has been employed it will of course be unable to occupy the district, and an army attempting to follow up its advantage would meet in exaggerated form the conditions already indicated, a city stripped of supplies and of all inhabitants but an unyielding even if starving group of survivors.

In any case the invaders will proceed to press on into the interior, leaving a garrison behind them with workers for transport and communication.

Everywhere the invaders meet with communities of unyielding civilians, resolute in giving obedience to none but their own government; they receive no services of any kind from the population, and can secure supplies only from the forcible seizure of small stocks, which diminish and disappear in proportion to the degree of ruthlessness exerted.

The invading soldiers must depend upon imported supplies and as they advance into the interior transportation becomes a serious problem. In the World War, 100,000 men and 25,000 animals required the transportation of 780 to 2,100 tons daily, aside from ammunition. A present day authority, Major George Fielding Eliot, considers four tons of supplies necessary for every soldier, "plus eight tons for his equipment, etc.";[2] for an invading force of 100,000 this would require the transportation of 1,200,000 tons.

In order to avoid increasing the transportation problem by adding an immense force of laborers and technicians, invaders trust to the inhabitants for the bulk of their skilled and unskilled labor and since passive resistance by civilians has never constituted a feature of war, this has usually been practicable.

As unarmed defense . . . transfers resistance from the military to the civil population, the invaders of our hypothesis will have at their command no assistance of this type. Soldiers must not only attend personally to all their needs, but also man without native help all the railroads, telegraphs, and airports upon which the advance depends. At each stage, moreover, they must leave behind them a complete local government with garrison, technicians and workers, as the legitimate authorities will have new groups of defenders always ready to take the risks of restoring civil life at the rear of the invading forces.

It is, of course, unthinkable that the enemy would undertake the maintenance of public utilities and government upon any peace time scale. In 1935 the railroad employees of the United States numbered 1,013,000 and the federal civil service 824,259, amounting together to more than half the German or the Japanese army of that time, including reserves. Even the skeleton service required for military purposes would call for thousands of men, and we have taken in this estimate no account of garrisons, food, service and utilities other than the railroads. We cannot picture the advance of the invaders as anything but costly from a financial point of view, precarious as far as permanent results are concerned, and distasteful to the large proportion of the army who are compelled to exchange uniforms for overalls for an indefinite period.

Let us assume this advance of an invading force through a first class country to continue for, say a month. The enemy has cut a swath of nominal occupation on the one hand, or of devastation on the other, through the country. They may have reached the goal of our national capitol and burned it, as happened in 1813 (a war which was followed by a most successful peace). By landing several expeditions they may even have laid waste three or four broad paths into the interior. The effect upon the civil life of these localities has been that of a severe natural calamity; and persons and industry have been transferred after many casualties to districts as yet untouched.

The invaders, on the other hand, have achieved not one of the objectives for which the expedition has been launched. . . .

Any military advantages to the enemy must be only nominal. Naval and air bases have no meaning in the unarmed nation, and are worthless as stepping stones to new conquests when the territory is itself of great extent.

Most important of all, any efforts to engraft a foreign fascism will encounter, not a people weakened by the unquestioning obedience to the unified state which military defense requires, but a nation whose zeal for democracy has been sharpened and made effective by crisis after crisis of individual responsibility.

Plight of the Enemy Government

Meanwhile the prestige of conquest has turned into international ridicule as our people remain subdued and the invading forces encounter no perils upon which their heroism can feed. At the first indication that neither raw materials nor investment fields are to be gained, the business interests upon which the foreign government depends will criticize sharply the policy which has dislocated commerce by putting a former customer out of the running. As month after month conscript armies and wealth continue to be poured into the invaded territory the taxpayers become restive; self-interest, suppressed for a time under the passions of fear and hate, becomes once more articulate; and solid citizens lose their enthusiasm for financing the devastation of a country whose good faith in nonaggression has now been demonstrated. Within a few days, or weeks at the most, the invading soldiers themselves, bored with inaction and undermined by propaganda, will unfailingly sicken of order to kill and destroy and will lose their morale in the steady absence of opportunities to show courage and achieve distinction. Calls for new recruits bring response from few but the criminal classes, and unwilling conscripts cannot be depended upon to maintain the policy of ruthlessness.

Meanwhile, such countries as remain neutral at first, not sufficiently idealistic to protest at the threatened invasion, will soon be pressed by their own business interests to demand that ports be reopened and commerce with our people again made possible.

The invading government finds prestige and finances decreasing day by day, while the popular will to war, upon which military power depends for existence, has withered and died for lack of that upon which to feed. At home and abroad the expedition becomes the butt of ridicule. The opposition party, which openly or underground has long awaited the moment of weakness, stands ready to strike for control as soon as the bulletins of unsuccessful terrorism have had their effect upon workers and taxpayers. If some face-saving pretext is not speedily found to bring the recall of the mutinous forces, the military government will go down to defeat, carrying with it the hollow fabric of dictatorship in that country.

The Chances of Victory

But can this complete and speedy victory be guaranteed? It cannot. Pacifists are not endowed with omniscience, merely with common-sense, and nonviolence cannot claim immunity from those chances of war which have brought so many campaigns to naught.

The outcome indicated is inescapable, however, granted the two points of our hypothesis: first, that the invaded population is united in unarmed resistance, and second, that the enemy nation, though ruthless and unscrupulous under an artificial standard of ethics, is not a community of pathological fools. Nonviolent resistance is the only type of defense which, from beginning to end, yields to the enemy not even a prospect of any of the usual rewards of invasion: prestige, glory, indemnity, subject people, trade or military advantages, available territory, triumph of ideals. The pleasure of wanton destruction is the only satisfaction to be derived, and it is true that this impulse is to be reckoned with in dealing with children, with imbeciles, with intoxicated or desperate men. By no stretch of imagination, however, can the mere lust of killing strangers motivate the sane business men of an industrial nation to keep on financing armies indefinitely for unprofitable idleness overseas.

All victory consists in breaking down the will to war of the enemy people. Military defense tries to do this through fear, which frequently produces the opposite effect. Nonviolent defense works through self-interest, slower to arouse but more reliable in the long run.

It will be noted that the foregoing plans take absolutely no account of appeals to the compassion or ethics of the enemy. We have done this, not from a belief in the existence of nations or human beings completely callous to such an appeal, but in the desire to make our hypothesis as difficult as can be conceived. It would be unscientific, however, to shut our eyes to the existence of religion, humanity, and love of justice as elements in individual and group psychology. . . .

Under the old system, religion and ethics in the foreign country could usually be harnessed through fear to the military machine. Unarmed defense, however, prevents all clouding of the ethical issues, and cannot fail to enlist on the side of the invaded people all men of good will, wherever found.

Notes

[1] The British Defence Ministry's 1957 White Paper gives first priority to air bases and admits that British cities cannot really be defended.—Ed.

[2] *The Ramparts We Watch* (New York: Reynal, 1938).

PART FIVE

THE PRACTICE
OF NONVIOLENCE

Preview

The aim of practically all people is to better the world in some way, if only that small part of it occupied by them and their family and friends. This is as true of the egoist as of the altruist, of the yogi as of the commissar.

How best to do this? And with how large a portion of the world should we be concerned?

The second question can be put either of two ways: How wide in scope should our concerns be, or how narrow in scope may they conscionably be? Is there something in our makeup that prevents us from acting selflessly in the interests of all people, and perhaps other forms of life as well, or is it only our lack of perception and imagination that prevents most of us from extending our moral concerns? And if we can extend them, should we do so? The egoist says no, the altruist says yes. Those who regard all life as sacred extend those moral concerns further still.

These questions confront nonviolentists as well. Even those who insist that nonviolence must be brought to bear upon concrete social, political, and international issues, whether by way of principled commitment or simply as a tactic, and those who agree that we must have the wider concern, do not

233

always agree in their answer to the first of the above questions; that is, how best to go about producing nonviolent change.

One view holds that we must first seek to perfect, or at least to purify, ourselves either spiritually or morally as a precondition of being able to engage others nonviolently in an effective way. It is sometimes said, for example, that before we can love others we must first love ourselves, and many who have a principled commitment to nonviolence see love as central to that commitment.

A second view holds that although desirable from a moral or spiritual standpoint, such self-purification is unnecessary for the effective practice of nonviolence. This view is sometimes called *pragmatic nonviolence*. According to pragmatic nonviolence, nonviolent action requires only the concerted effort of large numbers of disciplined people. As Gene Sharp puts it with disarming simplicity: "In political terms nonviolent action is based on a very simple postulate: people do not always do what they are told to do, and sometimes they do things which have been forbidden to them." Any individual in a position to extend or withhold cooperation has potential power, and large numbers of people in such a position have enormous potential power. Tolstoy put this bluntly and perhaps a little uncharitably in a letter to Gandhi when he says of the British subjugation of India: "What does it mean that thirty thousand men . . . have subdued two hundred million vigorous, clever, capable, and freedom-loving people? Do not the figures make it clear that it is not the English who have enslaved the Indians but the Indians who have enslaved themselves?"

A third view, not always distinct from either of the two views already mentioned, holds that all nonviolent social and political action should be pure in its commitment to nonviolence. This view is sometimes called *principled nonviolence*. While some principled nonviolentists would also insist that one can not undertake to transform others until one has transformed oneself, others see a need for political and social change now. They see the transformation of self as an ongoing process that should not preclude efforts to transform others. But they would also insist that the means used to transform others must be pure. They would reject any tactics that aim to harm people, directly or indirectly through, say, the destruction of property. They take quite seriously Gandhi's assertion that "the means are to the end as the seed is to the tree."

The selections that follow are divided into four sets. The first set exemplifies the view that one must focus on self-purification and development of one's own character. The second set explains or illustrates the position that we have called pragmatic pacifism. The third set illustrates the position we have called principled nonviolence. The final set of articles speaks to the importance of extending moral concerns further still, to animals, to nature, and to Earth itself.

The first selection is written by Buddhist monk Thich Nhat Hanh, who participated in efforts to bring about a peaceful resolution of the Vietnam War when he lived in Vietnam and who has since sought to aid the children and boat people of his country. Hanh says that we must become peaceful and be nonviolent toward ourselves, and that only by so doing will we begin to acquire the understanding of social and economic states of affairs that will enable us to deal with their problems. "We have to perceive our political and economic systems correctly," he says, "in order to see what is going wrong." The next article, written by Sister Chân Không, shares fourteen Buddhist precepts that expand concretely upon the ideas put forward by Hanh.

Philosopher and beekeeper Richard Taylor (1919–2003) argues in the third selection that one must cultivate a sense of self-worth and promote self-worth in others through an abiding love for them. This abiding love, he says, is a constant awareness and attentiveness to the needs of others. Though Taylor speaks of pacifism, he reveals that he uses the term in a sense much broader than usual, a sense more closely akin to nonviolence.

Gene Sharp, on the other hand, the leading analyst of the techniques of nonviolent action, characterizes methods that facilitate the mobilization of the power in people, whether or not they have become peaceful within themselves in the way Hanh intends. Sharp's position is a form of political realism, not because it necessarily disavows the role of morality in social and political affairs, but because it emphasizes that the concern is with the practical implementation of nonviolence of a sort that anyone can understand, whether or not versed in the philosophical or spiritual aspects of nonviolence.

Jack DuVall's article applies Gene Sharp's principles to contemporary world politics, specifically addressing how nonviolence can be used to overthrow dictators. In recent years DuVall has worked to popularize and apply Gene Sharp's principles, helping to document the nonviolent overthrow of Slobodan Milosevic and Auguste Pinochet, for example. Prior to the U.S. military overthrow of Saddam Hussein's government, he worked to convince Washington officials that the overthrow could be accomplished nonviolently.

Principled nonviolentists are not averse to mass nonviolent movements like those advocated by DuVall, but they are somewhat more wary of them. Even Gandhi, when he saw the guiding principle of nonviolence becoming undermined by violent acts of disobedience, put an end to a nationwide general strike for Indian independence that might well have "succeeded." José-Antonio Orosco highlights this tension in his article on Cesar Chavez, where he contrasts Chavez's understanding of the dynamics of nonviolent political action with the understanding evinced by contemporary anti-globalization protesters, many of whom are closely aligned with what we have called pragmatic nonviolence.

In the final essay in this third set, Samdhong Losang Tenzin puts forth a plan for the liberation of Tibet from China, a plan that is an exemplary application of principled political nonviolence, integrating the Gandhian notion of truth with Buddhist notions of self-purification and nonviolence.

The essays in the fourth set apply the practice of nonviolence more broadly: to all animal life, to plant life, and in the case of one article, to Earth as a planet. In the first selection Albert Schweitzer explains his famous concept of reverence for life, which treats all life—animals and plants—as sacred. In the second selection Christopher Key Chapple uses the lens of Jainism, the religion with deep roots in nonviolence that was the subject of the first article in this book, to examine the Gaia hypothesis—the notion that the planet Earth is a living organism. Richard H. Schwartz argues for vegetarianism and concern for the environment on the basis of the religious texts of Judaism, which, as he points out, mandate kindness toward animals and stewardship of the environment.

All over the world peoples are being displaced by huge business and government projects in the name of "progress," "development," and "globalization." Arundhati Roy, perhaps the foremost of India's contemporary authors, addresses this issue by examining a nonviolent grassroots movement in India aimed at stopping the development of a dam and the displacement of the people who live where the dam is being built. This is a theme that has been repeated in the United States, with the building of the Kinzua dam and the displacement of the Senecas; and in Canada, with development by Hydro Quebec on Cree Indian land. Roy urges the support of such movements against this kind of development, calling such support "the real war against terror."

In "The Indian Way," Richard Deats recounts some of his childhood memories of growing up in West Texas. He compares cowboys' method of "breaking" a horse—an interesting expression in itself—with the Indians' method of befriending their ponies. As he puts it, the two methods "could not be in greater contrast."

Finally, this section's last selection offers excerpts from an interview with Gary L. Francione, a law professor who argues passionately that the fight today for animal rights is as morally sound as was the fight against slavery two hundred years ago. He bases his arguments ultimately on nonviolence, the rejection of violence as part of the repertoire of human behaviors.

PERSONAL PERFECTION

Feelings and Perceptions

Thich Nhat Hanh

Perceiving includes our ideas or concepts about reality. When you look at a pencil, you perceive it, but the pencil itself may be different from the pencil in your mind. If you look at me, the me in myself may be different from the me you perceive. In order to have a correct perception, we need to have a direct encounter.

When you look at the night sky, you might see a very beautiful star, and smile at it. But a scientist may tell you that the star is no longer there, that it was extinct ten million years ago. So our perception is not correct. When we see a very beautiful sunset, we are very happy, perceiving that the sun is there with us. In fact it was already behind the mountain eight minutes ago. It takes eight minutes for the sunshine to reach our planet. The hard fact is that we never see the sun in the present, we only see the sun of the past. Suppose while walking in the twilight, you see a snake, and you scream, but when you shine your flashlight on it, it turns out to be a rope. This is an error of perception. During our daily lives we have many misperceptions. If I don't understand you, I may be angry at you, all the time. We are not capable of understanding each other, and that is the main source of human suffering. . . .

The Buddha had a special way to help us understand the object of our perception. He said that in order to understand, you have to be one with what you want to understand. This is a way that is practice-able. About fifteen years ago, I used to help a committee for orphans, victims of the war in Vietnam. From Vietnam, they sent out applications, one sheet of paper with a

Source: *Being Peace*, by Thich Nhat Hanh (Berkeley: Parallax Press, 1987). Reprinted by permission of Parallax Press.

small picture of a child in the corner, telling the name, the age, and the conditions of the orphan. We were supposed to translate it from Vietnamese into French, English, Dutch, or German, in order to seek a sponsor, so that the child would have food to eat and books for school, and be put into the family of an aunt or an uncle or a grandparent. Then the committee could send the money to the family member to help take care of the child.

Each day I helped translate about 30 applications into French. The way I did it was to look at the picture of the child. I did not read the application, I just took time to look at the picture of the child. Usually after only 30 or 40 seconds, I became one with the child. I don't know how or why, but it's always like that. Then I would pick up the pen and translate the words from the application onto another sheet. Afterwards I realized that it was not me who had translated the application; it was the child and me, who had become one. Looking at his face or her face, I got motivated and I became him and he became me, and together we did the translation. It is very natural. You don't have to practice a lot of meditation to be able to do that. You just look, you allow yourself to be, and then you lose yourself in the child, and the child in you. This is one example which illustrates the way of perception recommended by Buddha. In order to understand some things, you have to be one with that something.

The French language has the word *comprendre*, which means to understand, to know, to comprehend. *Com* means to be one, to be together, and *prendre* means to take or to grasp. To understand something is to take that thing up and to be one with it. The Indians have a wonderful example. If a grain of salt would like to measure the degree of saltiness of the ocean, to have a perception of the saltiness of the ocean, it drops itself into the ocean and becomes one with it, and the perception is perfect.

Nowadays, nuclear physicists have begun to feel the same way. When they get deeply into the world of subatomic particles, they see their mind in it. An electron is first of all your concept of the electron. The object of your study is no longer separated from your mind. Your mind is very much in it. Modern physicists think that the word *observer* is no longer valid, because an observer is distinct from the object he observes. They have discovered that if you retain that kind of distinction, you cannot go very far in subatomic nuclear science. So they have proposed the word *participant*. You are not an observer, you are a participant. That is the way I always feel when I give a lecture. I don't want the audience to be outside, to observe, to listen only. I want them to be one with me, to practice, to breathe. The speaker and the people who listen must become one in order for right perception to take place. Non-duality means "not two," but "not two" also means "not one." That is why we say "non-dual" instead of "one." Because if there is one, there are two. If you want to avoid two, you have to avoid one also. . . .

If I have a feeling of anger, how would I meditate on that? How would I deal with it, as a Buddhist, or as an intelligent person? I would not look upon anger as something foreign to me that I have to fight, to have surgery in order to remove it. I know that anger is me, and I am anger. Non-duality, not two. I have to deal with my anger with care, with love, with tenderness, with nonviolence. Because anger is me, I have to tend my anger as I would tend a younger brother or sister, with love, with care, because I myself am anger, I am in it, I am it. In Buddhism we do not consider anger, hatred, greed as enemies we have to fight, to destroy, to annihilate. If we annihilate anger, we annihilate ourselves. Dealing with anger in that way would be like transforming yourself into a battlefield, tearing yourself into parts, one part taking the side of Buddha, and one part taking the side of Mara. If you struggle in that way, you do violence to yourself. If you cannot be compassionate to yourself, you will not be able to be compassionate to others. When we get angry, we have to produce awareness: "I am angry. Anger is in me. I am anger." That is the first thing to do.

In the case of a minor irritation, the recognition of the presence of the irritation, along with a smile and a few breaths will usually be enough to transform the irritation into something more positive, like forgiveness, understanding, and love. Irritation is a destructive energy. We cannot destroy the energy; we can only convert it into a more constructive energy. Forgiveness is a constructive energy. Understanding is a constructive energy. Suppose you are in the desert, and you only have one glass of muddy water. You have to transform the muddy water into clear water to drink, you cannot just throw it away. So you let it settle for a while, and clear water will appear. In the same way, we have to convert anger into some kind of energy that is more constructive, because anger is you. Without anger you have nothing left. That is the work of meditation. . . .

Perceptions are perceptions of our body, feelings, mind, nature, and society. We should have a good perception of the oak tree in order to see its Buddha nature, its function as a Dharma teacher. We have to perceive our political and economic systems correctly in order to see what is going wrong. Perception is very important for our well-being, for our peace. Perception should be free from emotions and ignorance, free from illusions.

In Buddhism, knowledge is regarded as an obstacle to understanding, like a block of ice that obstructs water from flowing. It is said that if we take one thing to be the truth and cling to it, even if truth itself comes in person and knocks at our door, we won't open it. For things to reveal themselves to us, we need to be ready to abandon our views about them.

The Buddha told a story about this. A young widower, who loved his five-year-old son very much, was away on business, and bandits came, burned down his whole village, and took his son away. When the man returned, he saw the ruins, and panicked. He took the charred corpse of an infant to be his own child, and he began to pull his hair and beat his chest, crying uncontrollably. He organized a cremation ceremony, collected the ashes and put them in a very beautiful velvet bag. Working, sleeping, eating, he always carried the bag of ashes with him.

One day his real son escaped from the robbers and found his way home. He arrived at his father's new cottage at midnight, and knocked at the door.

You can imagine at that time, the young father was still carrying the bag of ashes and crying. He asked, "Who is there?" And the child answered, "It's me Papa. Open the door, it's your son." In his agitated state of mind the father thought that some mischievous boy was making fun of him, and he shouted at the child to go away, and he continued to cry. The boy knocked again and again, but the father refused to let him in. Some time passed, and finally the child left. From that time on, father and son never saw one another. After telling this story, the Buddha said, "Sometime, somewhere you take something to be the truth. If you cling to it so much, when the truth comes in person and knocks at your door, you will not open it."

Guarding knowledge is not a good way to understand. Understanding means to throw away your knowledge. You have to be able to transcend your knowledge the way people climb a ladder. If you are on the fifth step of a ladder and think that you are very high, there is no hope for you to climb to the sixth. The technique is to release. The Buddhist way of understanding is always letting go of our views and knowledge in order to transcend. This is the most important teaching. That is why I use the image of water to talk about understanding. Knowledge is solid; it blocks the way of understanding. Water can flow, can penetrate.

Learning True Love

Sister Chân Không

On the fifth of February in 1966, a full moon day, Thây Nhat Hanh ordained the first six members of the Tiep Hien Order, the Order of Interbeing. This Order was created by Thây to help bring Buddhism directly into the arena of social concerns during a time when the war was escalating and the teachings of the Buddha were most sorely needed. Thây proposed that the Order be composed of monks, nuns, laymen, and laywomen, and said that the six of us first ordained were free to choose whether we preferred to live and practice as formal monastics or as laypersons. We three women chose to live celibate lives like nuns, although we didn't shave our heads, while the three men chose to marry and practice as lay Buddhists. Among the three women was Nhat Chi Mai, who immolated herself for peace just a year later.

It was a wonderful celebration! Each of us was given a lamp with a handmade shade on which Thây had calligraphed "Lamp of the World," "Lamp of the Full Moon," "Lamp of Wisdom," etc., in old-style Chinese. During the initiation ceremony, we six ordainees vowed to study, practice, and observe the Fourteen Precepts of the Order of Interbeing. Since that day, I have felt that these precepts are my primary teacher, especially when I have been under stress and do not know the best way to act. These are the Fourteen Precepts:

1. Do not be idolatrous about or bound to any doctrine, theory, or ideology, even Buddhist ones. Buddhist systems of thought are guiding means; they are not absolute truth.

2. Do not think the knowledge you presently possess is changeless, absolute truth. Avoid being narrow-minded and bound to present views. Learn and practice nonattachment from views in order to be open to receive others' viewpoints. Truth is found in life and not merely in conceptual knowledge. Be ready to learn throughout your entire life and to observe reality in yourself and in the world at all times.

3. Do not force others, including children, by any means whatsoever, to adopt your views, whether by authority, threat, money, propaganda,

Source: Reprinted from *Learning True Love* (1993), pp. 79–81, by Chân Không with permission of Parallax Press, Berkeley, California, www.parallax.org.

or even education. However, through compassionate dialogue, help others renounce fanaticism and narrowness.

4. Do not avoid contact with suffering or close your eyes before suffering. Do not lose awareness of the existence of suffering in the life of the world. Find ways to be with those who are suffering, including personal contact, images, and sound. By such means, awaken yourself and others to the reality of suffering in the world.

5. Do not accumulate wealth while millions are hungry. Do not take as the aim of your life fame, profit, wealth, or sensual pleasure. Live simply and share time, energy, and material resources with those who are in need.

6. Do not maintain anger or hatred. Learn to penetrate and transform them when they are still seeds in your consciousness. As soon as they arise, turn your attention to your breath in order to see and understand the nature of your anger and hatred and the nature of the persons who have caused your anger and hatred.

7. Do not lose yourself in dispersion and in your surroundings. Practice mindful breathing to come back to what is happening in the present moment. Be in touch with what is wondrous, refreshing, and healing both inside and around you. Plant seeds of joy, peace, and understanding in yourself in order to facilitate the work of transformation in the depths of your consciousness.

8. Do not utter words that can create discord and cause the community to break. Make every effort to reconcile and resolve all conflicts, however small.

9. Do not say untruthful things for the sake of personal interest or to impress people. Do not utter words that cause division and hatred. Do not spread news that you do not know to be certain. Do not criticize or condemn things of which you are not sure. Always speak truthfully and constructively. Have the courage to speak out about situations of injustice, even when doing so may threaten your own safety.

10. Do not use the Buddhist community for personal gain or profit, or transform your community into a political party. A religious community, however, should take a clear stand against oppression and injustice and should strive to change the situation without engaging in partisan conflict.

11. Do not live with a vocation that is harmful to humans and nature. Do not invest in companies that deprive others of their chance to live. Select a vocation that helps realize your ideal of compassion.

12. Do not kill. Do not let others kill. Find whatever means possible to protect life and prevent war.

13. Possess nothing that should belong to others. Respect the property of others, but prevent others from profiting from human suffering or the suffering of other species on Earth.

14. Do not mistreat your body. Learn to handle it with respect. Preserve vital energies (sexual, breath, spirit) for the realization of the Way. Be fully aware of the responsibility of bringing new lives into the world. Meditate on the world into which you are bringing new beings.

Pacifism As a Way of Life

Richard Taylor

For pacifism to be a guide to your personal life it must infuse all of your interactions with other persons and, perhaps, with living things generally. You cannot be a pacifist just when war looms, or on those days when you march and carry signs in peace parades, and then leave it behind you when you return to family and friends. You are required to be a pacifist always. That is what it means for it to be a guide to life.

To be a pacifist in this all-embracing sense is to be guided by love in all things, all the time. It would be hard, however, to find a more ambiguous term or misunderstood idea. Love is a word that is tossed around all the time, often little more than a buzz word or evocation of feelings, and endlessly trivialized.

Love is not the passionate attraction of the sexes, nor the protectiveness parents feel for their children, nor the devotion of the patriot to his country, nor the possessiveness of things owned and prized. It is, of course, all of these, and more, which illustrates its ambiguity and trivialization. These are not meanings that can serve as a guide to life, except in a perverse sense. Anyone who made the love of cars the very guide to his life, for example, would be simply unbalanced.

Love and the Universal Sense of Self-Worth

To get at its deeper meaning, and the only meaning it can have for a truly pacific life, we must first understand one of the most basic facts of human nature, and that is, the sense of self-worth.

Everyone experiences the whole of life through this prism. It directs everything we do and conditions all of our interactions with other people. Although we almost never give it a thought, it is always there, underlying everything.

This can be best seen through trivial examples. Thus, if you diminish, even slightly, a person's sense of self-worth, the hurt is lasting and often, indeed, never forgotten. The put-downs you received, even as a child, are remembered forever. If a parent or relative spoke slightingly of one of your

Source: Reprinted with permission of The Richard Taylor Revocable Living Trust.

achievements, however small, then it is likely never to be forgotten. A father who routinely belittles his son is simply cruel. The wounds never heal. You remember with discomfort the day your teacher humiliated you before your friends, and if you think of that teacher decades later that is the first thing that comes to your mind. If, in your first adolescent love, you were belittled, then again, you are scarred forever, even though you imagine that you have long since put it out of your mind. If she commented on your clumsiness as a dancer, or your ineptitude in your attempts at affection, or mocked some less than intelligent remark, then these otherwise insignificant things sting and the hurt remains, even though buried.

These seemingly banal observations, which in other contexts would border on triviality, are important for driving home something we almost never think about but which is the basis for the kind of love that has to be the foundation of pacifism, considered as a way of life.

Consider further, then, why high-powered executives are so driven, to the point sometimes of neglecting their health, their families, and what would seem to be the very ingredients of happiness. It is not for the resulting wealth, for that already exceeds their needs, and is, in any case, but another token of their self-worth. An author or poet craves glowing reviews and large audiences far more than the publisher's royalties. Scholars who never expect to reach large audiences are rewarded simply by seeing their works in print. Good politicians learn to speak in flattering terms to, though not always of, their political foes. A successful university president praises the achievements of his or her faculty, comparing them, for example, to those of other universities who may enjoy greater distinction.

Employers, too, are coming to appreciate the motivating force of this factor. They have not always. The assumption used to be, and to a large extent still is, that an employee's basic interest is compensation, when what they really want is recognition. Studies have shown that companies whose personnel policies recognize this consistently do better than others. Such a company encourages its employees—very likely called "associates"—to participate in planning, provides them with partial, though trivial, ownership, invites them to important meetings with management, where the highest officers of the company are outwardly indistinguishable from the rest. The focus, in short, is not on wages, but on what is far more important, the sense of self-worth.

Self-Worth and the Imperative to Love

In the light of all this we can begin to see that our obligations to other people are not derived from rules inherited by custom, nor are they, as philosophers have sometimes wanted to believe, deliverances of reason. Not all people are rational. Greed, malice, and plain stupidity are in constant competition with reason and they often win out. But while not all people are rational, all are possessed of the sense of self-worth that I have so tendentiously illustrated, and it is through this that we can give meaning to obligation. We must treat people with an awareness of that sense. And it is through this idea that pacifism is enlarged, from opposition to war to a love that is expressed in all of one's dealings with people, all of the time.

A man does not express love for his wife, for example, by leaving a tender note on the refrigerator for her to find, or by remembering to bring her a rose on Valentine's day. Behavior of this kind is prompted by all kinds of motives, often by nothing more than a desire to impress. A father does not express love for his son by trying to mold him to some preconceived model, such as that of a star athlete, but by constant awareness of whatever he has done well, whether it be large or small. So, too, with friends, associates, strangers, even those one dislikes. People whose lives and work may seem of little significance do not think of themselves that way. A man whose work consists of sorting and delivering mail takes pride in doing it well. He may envy the rich or powerful, but his sense of self-worth would not be increased were he to change places with them, for it is already the most powerful force in his life.

And there we find the real meaning of love. It is the constant awareness of the needs of others, most of them trivial. A man who loves his wife is aware every minute of her talents, her beauty, such as it is, and of any and all the things she does well, and he makes this known. He does not try to make himself look good by treating her as a possession or trophy. A man who loves his son notes all the things the boy does well, whether of small or lasting significance. And so, with all of your life's dealings. You know how to enrich a person's life just by being aware, and you also know how to wound, and you refrain, even when injury is "deserved." It accomplishes nothing. A push always produces a counter push, and violence always begets violence. Pacifism, in its minimal sense of opposition to war, is but a corollary of a life of love, as here described.

This is, certainly, the message of the Gospels, for the love that is described there, and by St. Paul, is not limited to opposition to war. In fact, nothing is explicitly said about war. The message has to do with personal relationships, considering as a neighbor anyone you encounter. Laying down arms is implicit in this. A person of limited understanding might interpret this as meekness, even weakness, but it is in fact the opposite, for it is an invocation of the most constant force in human relationships. To be a pacifist, in a philosophical sense, is to live by this knowledge.

NONVIOLENCE AS A POLITICAL TOOL

Nonviolent Action
An Active Technique of Struggle

Gene Sharp

In political terms nonviolent action is based on a very simple postulate: people do not always do what they are told to do, and sometimes they do things which have been forbidden to them. Subjects may disobey laws they reject. Workers may halt work, which may paralyze the economy. The bureaucracy may refuse to carry out instructions. Soldiers and police may become lax in inflicting repression; they may even mutiny. When all these events happen simultaneously, the man who has been "ruler" becomes just another man. This dissolution of power can happen in a wide variety of social and political conflicts. The factory manager's power dissolves when the workers no longer cooperate. Political power disintegrates when the people withdraw their obedience and support. Yet the ruler's military equipment may remain intact, his soldiers uninjured, the cities unscathed, the factories and transport systems in full operational capacity, and the government buildings undamaged. But everything is changed. The human assistance which created and supported the regime's political power has been withdrawn. Therefore, its power has disintegrated.

When people refuse their cooperation, withhold their help, and persist in their disobedience and defiance, they are denying their opponent the basic human assistance and cooperation which any government or hierarchical sys-

Source: Excerpt from Gene Sharp, *The Politics of Nonviolent Action*. Reprinted by permission of the author. The full text is available from Porter Sargent Publishers Inc., 11 Beacon Street, Suite 1400, Boston, Massachusetts 02108. Phone: 617-523-1670. Fax: 617-523-1021. info@portersargent.com.

tem requires. If they do this in sufficient numbers for long enough, that government or hierarchical system will no longer have power. This is the basic political assumption of nonviolent action.

Characteristics of Nonviolent Action

Nonviolent action is a generic term covering dozens of specific methods of protest, noncooperation and intervention, in all of which the actionists conduct the conflict by doing—or refusing to do—certain things without using physical violence. As a technique, therefore, nonviolent action is not passive. It is *not* inaction. It is *action* that is nonviolent.

The issue at stake will vary. Frequently it may be a political one—between political groups, for or against a government, or, on rare occasions, between governments (as in imposition of embargoes or resistance to occupation). It may also be economic or social or religious. The scale and level of the conflict will also vary. It may be limited to a neighborhood, a city, or a particular section of the society; it may at other times range over a large area of a country or convulse a whole nation. Less often, more than one country and government may be involved. Whatever the issue, however, and whatever the scale of the conflict, nonviolent action is a technique by which people who reject passivity and submission, and who see struggle as essential, can wage their conflict without violence. Nonviolent action is not an attempt to avoid or ignore conflict. It is *one* response to the problem of how to *act* effectively in politics, especially how to wield power effectively.

A Special Type of Action

It is widely assumed that all social and political behavior must be clearly either violent or nonviolent. This simple dualism leads only to serious distortions of reality, however, one of the main ones being that some people call "nonviolent" anything they regard as good, and "violent" anything they dislike. A second gross distortion occurs when people totally erroneously equate cringing passivity with nonviolent action because in neither case is there the use of physical violence.

Careful consideration of actual response to social and political conflict requires that all responses to conflict situations be initially divided into those of *action* and those of *inaction*, and not divided according to their violence or lack of violence. In such a division nonviolent action assumes its correct place as *one* type of *active* response. *Inaction*, which may include passivity, submission, cowardice and the like, will not detain us, for it has nothing to do with the nonviolent technique which is the subject of this book. By definition, nonviolent action cannot occur except by the replacement of passivity and submissiveness with activity, challenge and struggle.

Obviously, however, important distinctions must be made *within* the category of *action*. Here, too, a dichotomy into *violent* or *nonviolent* is too simple. Therefore, let us set up a rough typology of six major classes of the forms of action in conflicts, one of them nonviolent action, the technique with which we are concerned. This (rather crude) classification includes: 1) simple verbal persuasion and related behavior, such as conciliation; 2) peaceful institutional procedures backed by threat or use of sanctions; 3) physical violence against persons; 4) physical violence against persons plus material destruction; 5) material destruction only; and 6) the technique of nonviolent action. Obviously, each of these classes may itself be subclassified. People may shift back and forth between types of action, or back and forth between action and inaction. However, it is crucial to understand that the basic dichotomy of social and political behavior is between action and inaction, rather than between nonviolence and violence.

It is also important to see why and how nonviolent action as a technique differs from milder peaceful responses to conflicts, such as conciliation, verbal appeals to the opponent, compromise and negotiation. These responses may or may not be used with nonviolent action or with any of the other five kinds of action, but they should not be identified with the nonviolent technique as such. Conciliation and appeals are likely to consist of rational or emotional verbal efforts to bring about an opponent's agreement to something, while nonviolent action is not verbal—it consists of social, economic and political activity of special types. For example, asking an employer for a wage increase is an act of attempted simple verbal persuasion, but refusal to work until the wage increase is granted is a case of nonviolent action. Nor should nonviolent action be confused with compromise, which involves settling for part of one's objectives. Compromise is not a form of conflict or struggle, as is nonviolent action. As with violence, nonviolent action may or may not lead to a compromise settlement, depending on the issues, power relationships, and the actionists' own decision. Similarly, negotiation is not a form of nonviolent action. Negotiation is an attempt at verbal persuasion, perhaps utilizing established institutional procedures, but always involving an implied or explicit threat of some type of sanction if an acceptable agreement is not reached. Negotiation could, therefore, precede a strike or a civil disobedience campaign, as it can a war. But such negotiation is an approach which must be distinguished from a strike, civil disobedience, or other form of nonviolent action.

Nonviolent action is so different from these milder peaceful responses to conflicts that several writers have pointed to the general similarities of nonviolent action to military war. Nonviolent action is a means of combat, as is war. It involves the matching of forces and the waging of "battles," requires wise strategy and tactics, and demands of its "soldiers" courage, discipline, and sacrifice. This view of nonviolent action as a technique of active combat is diametrically opposed to the popular assumption that, at its strongest, nonviolent action relies on rational persuasion of the opponent, and that more commonly it consists simply of passive submission. Nonviolent action is just what it says: *action* which is nonviolent, not *inaction*. This technique consists, not simply of words, but of active protest, noncooperation and intervention. Overwhelmingly, it is group or mass action. Certain forms of nonviolent action may be regarded as efforts to persuade by action; others, given sufficient participants, may contain elements of coercion.

Another characteristic of nonviolent action which needs emphasis is that it is usually extraconstitutional; that is to say, it does not rely upon established institutional procedures of the State, whether parliamentary or nonparliamentary. However, it is possible to incorporate the technique into a constitutional system of government at various points, and it is also possible to use it in support of an established government under attack. Nonviolent action must not be confused with anarchism. That "no-State" philosophy has traditionally given inadequate thought to the practical problem of how to achieve such a society and to the need for realistic means of social struggle which differ in substance from those employed by the State.

Motives, Methods, and Leverages

The motives for using nonviolent action instead of some type of violent action differ widely. In some cases violence may have been rejected because of considerations of expediency, in others for religious, ethical, or moral reasons. Or there may be a mixture of motivations of various types.

Nonviolent action is thus not synonymous with "pacifism." Nor is it identical with religious or philosophical systems emphasizing nonviolence as a matter of moral principle. Adherents to some of these belief systems may see nonviolent action as compatible with their convictions and even as a fulfillment of them in conflicts. Adherents to certain other creeds which also emphasize nonviolence may, however, find this technique too "worldly" or "coercive" for them. Conversely, nonviolent action has often been practiced, and in a vast majority of the cases led, by nonpacifists who saw it only as an effective means of action. The popular idea that only pacifists can effectively practice nonviolent action—a view sometimes pressed with considerable conceit by pacifists themselves—is simply not true.

Furthermore, in many cases motivations for using nonviolent action have been mixed, practical considerations being combined with a *relative* moral preference for nonviolence (although violence was not rejected in principle). This type of mixed motivation is likely to become more frequent if nonviolent action is increasingly seen to have important practical advantages over violence.

It is frequently assumed that nonviolent actionists seek primarily to convert their opponent to a positive acceptance of their point of view. Actually, there is no standard pattern of priority for either changes in attitudes and beliefs, or policy and structural changes. Sometimes the nonviolent group may seek to change the opponent's attitudes and beliefs as a preliminary to changing his policies or institutions. Or the nonviolent action may be an expression of the determination of the members of the group not to allow the opponent to change their own attitudes or beliefs. Or the actions may be aimed primarily at changing policies or institutions or at thwarting the opponent's attempts to alter them, whether or not his attitudes and beliefs have first been changed (these cases appear to be in the majority). In still other cases, the nonviolent group may seek to change attitudes and policies simultaneously.

Nonviolent action may involve: 1) *acts of omission*—that is, people practicing it may refuse to perform acts which they usually perform, are expected by custom to perform, or are required by law or regulation to perform; 2) *acts of commission*—that is, the people may perform acts which they do not usually perform, are not expected by custom to perform, or are forbidden by law or regulation to perform; or 3) *a combination* of acts of omission and acts of commission.

There are in the technique three broad classes of methods. 1) Where the nonviolent group uses largely symbolic actions intended to help persuade the opponent or someone else, or to express the group's disapproval and dissent, the behavior may be called *nonviolent protest and persuasion*. In this class are such demonstrations as marches, parades and vigils. These particular methods may be used either in an attempt to change opinions or to express disagreement, or both. 2) Where the nonviolent group acts largely by withdrawal or the withholding of social, economic, or political cooperation, its behavior may be described as *noncooperation*. This class contains three subclasses which include *social* noncooperation, *economic* noncooperation (economic boycotts and strikes), and *political* noncooperation. 3) Where the nonviolent group acts largely by direct intervention its action may be referred to as *nonviolent intervention*. The nonviolent group in this class clearly takes the initiative by such means as sit-ins, nonviolent obstruction, nonviolent invasion and parallel government. The technique may be applied by individuals, by small or large groups, and by masses of people.

Just as there is diversity among the many specific methods which constitute this technique, so also wide variation exists in the intensities of pressures and the types of leverage exerted by this technique. When successful, nonviolent action produces change in one of three broad ways, which we call *mechanisms of change*. In *conversion* the opponent reacts to the actions of the nonviolent actionists by finally coming around to a new point of view in which he positively accepts their aims. In *accommodation* the opponent chooses to grant demands and to adjust to the new situation which has been produced without changing his viewpoint. Where *nonviolent coercion* operates, change is achieved against the opponent's will and without his agreement, the sources of his power having been so undercut by nonviolent means that he no longer has control. . . .

To a degree which has never been adequately appreciated, the nonviolent technique operates by producing power changes. Both the relative power and the absolute power of each of the contending groups are subject to constant and rapid alterations. This power variability can be more extreme and occur more rapidly than in situations where both sides are using violence. As may be expected, the actionists seek continually to increase their own strength and that of their supporters. They will usually seek and gain assistance and active participation also from among the wider group affected by the grievances. In addition, the nature of nonviolent struggle makes it possible for the actionists also to win considerable support even in the camp of the opponent and among third parties. This potential is much greater than with violence. The ability to gain these types of support gives the nonviolent group a capacity to influence—and at times to regulate—*their opponent's* power, by reducing or severing the power of the opponent at its sources. Usually the results of these complex changes in the relative power positions of the contenders will determine the struggle's final outcome.

Nonviolent discipline must be viewed in the context of the mechanisms of change of this technique and the ways in which these power shifts are produced. The maintenance of nonviolent discipline in face of repression is not an act of moralistic naïveté. Instead, it contributes to the operation of all three mechanisms and is a prerequisite for advantageous power changes. As a consequence, nonviolent discipline can only be compromised at the severe risk of contributing to defeat. Other factors are, of course, highly important too, and it should not be assumed that maintenance of nonviolence will alone inevitably produce victory.

The Technique of Nonviolent Action

Gene Sharp

Nonviolent action is a generic term: it includes the large class of phenomena variously called "nonviolent resistance," "satyagraha," "passive resistance," "positive action," and "nonviolent direct action." While it is not violent, it *is* action, and not inaction; passivity, submission and cowardice must be surmounted if it is to be used. It is a means of conducting conflicts and waging struggles, and is not to be equated with (though it may be accompanied by) purely verbal dissent or solely psychological influence. It is not "pacifism," and in fact has in the vast majority of cases been applied by nonpacifists. The motives for the adoption of nonviolent action may be religious or ethical, or they may be based on considerations of expediency. Nonviolent action is not an escapist approach to the problem of violence, for it can be applied in struggles against opponents relying on violent sanctions. The fact that in a conflict one side is nonviolent does not imply that the other side will also refrain from violence. Certain forms of nonviolent action may be regarded as efforts to persuade by action, while others are more coercive.

Methods of Nonviolent Action

There is a very wide range of methods, or forms, of nonviolent action, and at least 125 have been identified. They fall into three classes—nonviolent protest, noncooperation, and nonviolent intervention.

Generally speaking, the methods of *nonviolent protest* are symbolic in their effect and produce an awareness of the existence of dissent. Under tyrannical regimes, however, where opposition is stifled, their impact can in some circumstances be very great. Methods of nonviolent protest include marches, pilgrimages, picketing, vigils, "haunting" officials, public meetings, issuing and distributing protest literature, renouncing honours, voluntary emigration, and humorous pranks.

Source: "The Technique of Non-Violent Action," by Gene Sharp, in *The Strategy of Civilian Defence*, edited by Adam Roberts. Reprinted by permission of Faber and Faber, Ltd., London.

The methods of *nonviolent noncooperation*, if sufficient numbers take part, are likely to present the opponent with difficulties in maintaining the normal efficiency and operation of the system; and in extreme cases the system itself may be threatened. Methods of nonviolent noncooperation include various types of strike (such as general strike, sit-down strike, industry strike, go-slow, and work-to-rule); various types of boycott (such as economic boycott, consumers' boycott, traders' boycott, rent refusal, international economic embargo, and social boycott); and various types of political noncooperation (such as boycott of government employment, boycott of elections, revenue refusal, civil disobedience and mutiny).

The methods of *nonviolent intervention* have some features in common with the first two classes, but also challenge the opponent more directly; and, assuming that fearlessness and discipline are maintained, relatively small numbers may have a disproportionately large impact. Methods of nonviolent intervention include sit-ins, fasts, reverse strikes, nonviolent obstruction, nonviolent invasion, and parallel government.

The exact way in which methods from each of the three classes are combined varies considerably from one situation to another. Generally speaking, the risks to the actionists on the one hand, and to the system against which they take action on the other, are least in the case of nonviolent protest, and greatest in the case of nonviolent intervention. The methods of noncooperation tend to require the largest numbers, but not to demand a large degree of special training from all participants. The methods of nonviolent intervention are generally effective if the participants possess a high degree of internal discipline and are willing to accept severe repression; the tactics must also be selected and carried out with particular care and intelligence.

Several important factors need to be considered in the selection of the methods to be used in a given situation. These factors include the type of issue involved, the nature of the opponent, his aims and strength, the type of counter-action he is likely to use, the depth of feeling both among the general population and among the likely actionists, the degree of repression the actionists are likely to be able to take, the general strategy of the over-all campaign, and the amount of past experience and specific training the population and the actionists have had. Just as in military battle weapons are carefully selected, taking into account such factors as their range and effect, so also in nonviolent struggle the choice of specific methods is very important.

Mechanisms of Change

In nonviolent struggles there are, broadly speaking, three mechanisms by which change is brought about. Usually there is a combination of the three. They are conversion, accommodation, and nonviolent coercion.

George Lakey has described the *conversion* mechanism thus: "By conversion we mean that the opponent, as the result of the actions of the nonviolent person or group, comes around to a new point of view which embraces the ends of the nonviolent actor." This conversion can be influenced by reason or argument, but in nonviolent action it is also likely to be influenced by emotional and moral factors, which can in turn be stimulated by the suffering of the nonviolent actionists, who seek to achieve their goals without inflicting injury on other people.

Attempts at conversion, however, are not always successful, and may not even be made. *Accommodation* as a mechanism of nonviolent action falls in an intermediary position between conversion and nonviolent coercion, and elements of both of the other mechanisms are generally involved. In accommodation, the opponent, although not converted, decides to grant the demands of the nonviolent actionists in a situation where he still has a choice of action. The social situation within which he must operate has been altered enough by nonviolent action to compel a change in his own response to the conflict; perhaps because he has begun to doubt the rightness of his position, perhaps because he does not think the matter worth the trouble caused by the struggle, and perhaps because he anticipates coerced defeat and wishes to accede gracefully or with a minimum of losses.

Nonviolent coercion may take place in any of three circumstances. Defiance may become too widespread and massive for the ruler to be able to control it by repression; the social and political system may become paralysed; or the extent of defiance or disobedience among the ruler's own soldiers and other agents may undermine his capacity to apply repression. Nonviolent coercion becomes possible when those applying nonviolent action succeed in withholding, directly or indirectly, the necessary sources of the ruler's political power. His power then disintegrates and he is no longer able to control the situation, even though he still wishes to do so.

Liberation without War
Is There a Nonviolent Way to Overthrow Dictators and Achieve Democracy?

Jack DuVall

When the Romans imprisoned the apostle Paul and he was taken to be whipped, Paul asked his captors, "Is it lawful for you to whip a Roman citizen?" So a captain asked him: "Are you a Roman?" Paul answered, "Yes." The captain replied, "It took me a great deal of money to buy my freedom," showing skepticism that Paul—who probably looked like a penniless slave—was a Roman, and therefore free. Paul declared: "I was free born."

Represented in that exchange was a fundamental division in human thinking: between those who believe that only an external agency—money, personal influence, violence—can deliver people from oppression, and those who understand that each individual has the innate right to be free *and* the ability to become free.

Che Guevara, the violent revolutionary, once said: "I am not a liberator. Liberators do not exist. The people liberate themselves." Unfortunately, what the people can do to liberate themselves from tyranny or injustice has received far less attention than what terrorists, conquerors, or charismatic leaders have tried to do.

In many historical cases—such as the emancipation of American slaves during the Civil War, defeating Nazism in World War II, the Cold War with the Soviet Union—leaders saw no alternative to using or threatening military force against armed adversaries. When hostilities ended, relative freedom and peace ensued. And so armed might has been seen as the means of liberation.

When it became apparent in summer 2003 that stability in Iraq had not followed the military ouster of Saddam Hussein, some claimed that civil disorder always accompanied changes to democracy, citing the fall of Eastern European regimes in 1989. But no museums of antiquities were looted in Warsaw or Berlin when civilian-based movements brought down authoritar-

Source: Reprinted with permission from *Sojourners*, (800) 714-7474, www.sojo.net.

ian governments, nor did chaos reign in Manila when Filipinos chased out a dictator three years before.

When nonviolent movements mobilize people to use strikes, boycotts, civil disobedience, and other disruptive tactics—through a strategy to subvert an unjust regime's power—democracy ensues more often than when violence is used. If we disregard the costs of regime change through terror or war, by not comparing them to the risks and opportunities of nonviolent conflict, then we are issuing a blank check to the belief that liberation is always violent.

Terrorists believe that power comes from killing—they are attached to that belief as strongly as many are to their religious beliefs. But even though many people believe that weapons have power, most people who want to fight for their rights or justice are more interested in winning than in being killed—and they will listen to proof that violence is less effective than other methods of struggle.

The logic is this: those who threaten violence want something from those being threatened. That's a transaction, and each party to a transaction has leverage. If you refuse to give me what I want, even if I threaten you with violence, I cannot succeed unless I can pay the cost of ending your resistance. A civilian-based nonviolent movement succeeds when it drives up the cost of suppressing the people to the point that a regime's defenders are unwilling or unable to pay it.

This process is deliberate and systematic. First, a movement's members must set aside their partisan, ethnic, or ideological differences and unify behind the goal of liberating the country from its oppressors. Then the movement has to reduce civilians' fear of participating by first using nonviolent tactics entailing less physical risk, such as not paying taxes, work stay-aways, and commercial boycotts. This broadens a movement's base, as it recruits people who won't be violent but still want to act. Distributing the scope of resistance beyond the capital also strains the regime's outermost, least reliable agents.

The movement also has to challenge the regime's legitimacy. Tactics that tempt repression can force rulers to discredit themselves in the world's eyes. That takes nonviolent discipline, to crystallize the meaning of the choice between the regime and the opposition.

Then more disruptive actions—such as a general strike or larger demonstrations—can be sequenced to make it hard for an oppressor to maintain the semblance of control. When it's clear that nothing will be normal until the regime changes, even the military will begin to doubt the intelligence of endless obedience.

Finally, the movement has to anticipate repression and perhaps be ready to settle for intermediate goals, until its own strength is sufficient—it has to know when to buy time and when to reach for victory.

We are talking, of course, about staging a revolution. Thomas Jefferson believed that when a bad government could not be reformed, the people had a "right of revolution." He lived when nonviolent action was almost unknown as a political strategy, but he believed so strongly in the people's prerogatives that he countenanced the idea of violent revolt. Having no attachment to violence, Jefferson, if he lived today, would embrace this right of bloodless resistance. And he would see its relationship to producing government genuinely based on the people's consent.

Mohandas Gandhi often invoked the biblical maxim that "as you sow, so shall you reap"—that your achievement will reflect your methods. The history that Gandhi helped launch has confirmed that truth:

- In the 1960s, African-Americans used sit-ins and marches to pull apart racial segregation—yielding more tolerance and justice, imperfect as it is, than seemed possible beforehand.

- In Poland in 1980, workers used strikes to win the right to organize a free trade union, galvanizing the people to insist on fuller rights. When Solidarity took power, no one died.

- In South Africa in the 1980s, blacks in townships and factories used boycotts and strikes until apartheid lost the support of business and outside interests, compelling a new president to negotiate.

- In Serbia in 2000, a dictator was unseated after a nonviolent campaign liquefied the loyalty of the military—who refused his orders. Then a new, democratically chosen president took power.

"Nonviolence" may be a preferable form of behavior, but nonviolent action isn't effective unless it is driven by a strategy to take power. Gandhi did not want to make peace with the British. He incited a conflict in order to force them out of India.

Some think the Indians prevailed because the British were gentlemen (as if the Amritsar massacre hadn't happened). But that mistaken view reinforces another misconception: that violent oppressors can only be defeated with more violence. Yet there is no historical correlation between the degree of a regime's brutality and its hold on power. Everyone believed that Saddam Hussein was impregnable because he'd kill anyone who dissented. So most Iraqis were afraid to act. However, the fear of action does not mean that action, once taken, will fail.

In 2002, an Iraqi opponent of Saddam said he liked nonviolent resistance, but that Saddam was like Stalin—therefore it wasn't possible. He was asked what would happen if 5,000 people demonstrated in Baghdad. He said they'd all be shot. What if 20,000 should demonstrate? Same result, though much bloodier, he said. But what if 100,000 Iraqis should protest, demanding that Saddam go? He hesitated. Well, if that happened, he said, then things might go differently. Why? Because if that many Iraqis were determined to resist, the dictator's defenders would realize that fear as an instrument of power no longer worked—that Saddam had lost control of the country. Suddenly an impervious regime had been reduced in this Iraqi's mind to a strategic problem.

When American forces invaded, few Iraqi units were willing to defend Saddam. In a nation of 22 million, with hundreds of thousands in uniform, only an inner core of several thousand irregular fighters could be relied on. The very means by which Saddam had clung to power, his legendary savagery, had destroyed his internal support. If Iraqis had known how to organize and direct civilian-based resistance, and the same proportion of the population as joined movements elsewhere had participated, the regime likely would have collapsed almost as quickly as it did in the heat of war. As Bishop Desmond Tutu said, "When people decide they want to be free, there is nothing that can stop them"—not fear, not brutality, and not 5,000 *fedayeen*.

The continued presence of violent resisters in Iraq is a symptom of the present global crisis. Cadres of extreme fighters in terrorist and militant organizations have a proclivity for violence that evidence of its past futility cannot deter. There is no instance in the past century in which terror or violence created a society where political rights and prosperity resulted. So the promises behind violence are hollow. But new recruits are blind to its impotence—in part because the world's news and entertainment media keep recirculating the myth that violence is the ultimate form of power.

Yet while the failures of education and broadcasting magnify political violence, correcting them is only part of the cure. Terrorist networks that target civilians would destroy the new global society now taking shape, and suppressing them may take military action in some cases. But if a natural, worldwide peace is our goal, we must all do more, rejecting the operational premise of terrorists: that success in a great struggle requires violence.

On Sept. 11, civilians in North America were killed in the name of liberating civilians from certain rulers in the Middle East. But none of the reviled rulers has been weakened, and the reprisal of war has been hurled at terrorists everywhere. The choice of violence as a method of struggle is irrational because it generates a contest in which violent groups are inferior: they are not as well armed as the states they attack. And if they were to use a weapon of mass destruction against an innocent city, the massive retaliation and global revulsion would doom their cause. Political violence always exacts a fatal cost from those who embrace it.

The conflict with terrorists is not just about the evil of their tactics. It is also about the political conditions they exploit. Terrorist organizations have been given haven and help by some authoritarian regimes, even as they struggle to overthrow others. In both ways, political oppressors are at the heart of the global crisis.

There are 40 to 45 despotic regimes in the world. They include cult-of-personality dictatorships as in North Korea and Cuba; one-party states like China and Syria; and military strong-men, corrupt oligarchies, and clerical hierarchies that dominate weak democracies. If they all vanished tomorrow, the swamp of terrorism would be largely drained—because weapons and hideouts would be harder to acquire, and the local oppression that terrorists decry in order to motivate their base would disappear.

The world has a choice: we can wait until an odious regime or terrorist group is poised on the brink of a new, more sweeping atrocity, and then support or oppose military action to prevent or react to the crime. Or we can internationalize and expedite the removal of all political oppression, while undermining the appeal of violence as a strategy of liberation. Unless the world wishes to cede to Washington the responsibility to respond physically to global threats of violence, it must act to end the political oppression at the root of the problem.

Fortunately, there is a proven way to capsize murderous regimes: strategic, civilian-based resistance. But we can no longer afford to wait for indigenous movements to engage in the trial-and-error process of locally reinventing nonviolent struggle and overcoming their oppressors. We have to help them succeed.

They don't need enormous subsidies, and they don't need Americans parachuting in to tell them what to do. Only indigenous movements have the legitimacy necessary to rally popular support. But to outmaneuver tyrants, many need training in the strategies of nonviolent action as well as better information technology. A nongovernmental, international body—not serving any nation's interests, but pooling resources from many—should provide this help.

In the meantime, governments must ratchet up pressure on such regimes. For example, Burma's military junta, which imprisoned the Nobel Prize-winning leader of its nonviolent opposition, still gets help from India, China, other Asian nations, and Western corporations doing business with Burma. Other dictatorships are also fortified by our detachment and our trade. Political oppression anywhere is now everyone's business, because the violence it breeds can appear anywhere.

Just as St. Paul understood that his freedom was God-given, a natural right, the world is coming to acknowledge that rights are not conferred by states—they must be honored by states because they belong to individuals. Eventually it will be accepted everywhere that each person's rights come before any ruler's will and that no government is legitimate unless it is based on the people's consent.

The day when that becomes a universal fact will not arrive until the world realizes that rights are won more surely by the people than by terrorists or armies. To make nonviolent struggle the global boulevard to political liberation, we must relentlessly propagate the ideas and strategies that pave its way to victory. Former president Jimmy Carter has said that "nonviolent valor can end oppression." But not until we all enlist to help the valiant.

PRINCIPLED POLITICAL AND LABOR NONVIOLENCE

Cesar Chavez and Principled Nonviolent Strategy

José-Antonio Orosco

On August 1999, a small crowd in the French town of Millau descended upon a McDonald's restaurant under construction. Under the eyes of local police, the crowd proceeded to dismantle the pre-fabricated building, loading pieces of the walls, roofing, and electrical outlets into the backs of trucks. The crowd then paraded to the police headquarters in a festive mood. They unloaded the materials and then proceeded to the outdoor cafes. One of the leaders of the crowd, Jose Bove, claimed that the dismantling was in response to two issues (Bove and Dufour 2001, 3–18). First, the action was a protest against American tariffs levied against French cheese because of the European Union's refusal to allow entry to American beef with growth hormones. The tariffs had essentially priced Roquefort cheese out of the American market, adversely affecting French farmers. Second, the protest was directed at the globalization of "malbouffe," or bad food, as represented by the menu at McDonald's.

As a result of the protest, Bove was convicted of vandalism and gained international notoriety. He was invited to speak at the protests of the World Trade Organization in Seattle in November 1999. He gave his speech at a downtown McDonald's and then punctuated his visit by eating a Roquefort

Source: Used with permission of the author.

cheese sandwich in front of it. During the course of the rioting that marred the Seattle protests, that restaurant was vandalized. When he was later asked to reflect on his protest in Millau and the property damage in Seattle, Bove said that one must differentiate between different kinds of violence. He distinguishes between indiscriminate violence, which he criticizes, and an act of property destruction that "has a direct relationship to the problem" (Jeffress 2001). As an example of the latter, he mentions the case of French wine growers who destroyed a shipment of imported wine that they believed was eroding their market share. Bove claims that the destruction of the wine is appropriate as a form of civil disobedience, and points out that violence is sometimes needed for social change, citing the Boston Tea Party and the storming of the Bastille as examples.

Almost two years after Seattle, tens of thousands of anti-globalization activists gathered together in Genoa, Italy, in response to the meeting of the G-8 nations. At that meeting, small groups of protestors clashed with police, and Carlo Giuliani, a 23-year-old anarchist, was shot twice in the head at close range by police. Officials quickly cracked down on the protest leaders in order to quell any further violence. An investigation later revealed that the local police planted explosives in the headquarters of the protestors and lied about being attacked in order to justify the mass arrests (FAIR 2003).

Bove's responses and the events in Genoa raise important questions about the role of violence in modern civil disobedience: Are certain forms of violence legitimate as social protest today? If so, what kinds and what are their limits? Is violent civil disobedience strategically prudent for social movements today, given the kind of repression that they may unleash? This paper attempts to offer answers by drawing on Cesar Chavez's conception of nonviolent civil disobedience. I begin by examining several arguments that justify property destruction as a form of social protest against corporate economic globalization. These arguments stress that the question over the use of violence in social protest is not a moral one, but a strategic one; that is, about the most efficient means to achieve political goals. I then rely on Chavez's idea of nonviolence to demonstrate why these arguments about the strategic use of violence in social protest fundamentally misunderstand the dynamics of power and violence. Like Gandhi and Martin Luther King, Jr., Chavez adheres to absolute nonviolence. Yet for years, Chavez was a hardnosed community organizer before he founded the United Farm Workers union (Griswold Del Castillo and Garcia 1995, 22–40). Those experiences taught him that nonviolent civil disobedience is the best form of social protest, not only from a moral point of view, but strategy-wise as well, and that the costs of violent protest clearly outweigh the benefits for any movement dedicated to social justice.

Strategic Arguments for
Violent Civil Disobedience

Shortly after the WTO protests, Rachel Neumann criticized those nonviolent activists who disparaged the property damage in Seattle as merely an expression of "adolescent rage." Rage, she writes, is not an inappropriate emotional reaction toward institutional injustice. Part of the harm inflicted by institutional injustice, such as colonization, and in Neumann's view corporate globalization, is that it "refuses people their own emotions and natural reactions" by substituting foreign or artificial values and ideas that disrupt ways of life and belittle people's feelings of loss and injury (Neumann 2000, 89). Thus, to "condemn the rage by judging those who express it, without acknowledging the larger context of systematic state violence is to strengthen the opposition" (Neumann, 90). Instead of concentrating on the moral appropriateness of rage, she maintains, we ought to concern ourselves with developing political strategies for channeling it in progressive ways. Property destruction, in Neumann's view, need not be ruled out as a way to do this. Indeed, the emotional energy behind such anger can be used to develop more creative forms of civil disobedience beyond the usual rallies, sit-ins, and orchestrated mass arrests that have come to be the hallmarks of most instances of nonviolent protests today.

Proponents of absolute nonviolence usually dismiss property destruction, according to Neumann, because they rely on very broad and abstract definitions of violence and nonviolence. First, absolutists fail to make a distinction between *violence toward property* and *violence toward human beings* and, then, assume that the former almost always leads to the latter. However, there are historical examples that show this escalation does not always occur: "The Luddites smashed machinery, the Wobblies closed mills and mines, the English suffragists broke windows, and Earth First activists tinkered with engines and tires of logging trucks—all without injuring other human beings" (Neumann, 90). Second, proponents of nonviolence also fail to distinguish between different kinds of property. Here, Neumann cites from a communiqué of the ACME Collective, one of the anarchist groups in Seattle, that makes a distinction between personal property, "the things we own that have worth because they are dear to us (books, photos, the homes we have worked on)" and private/corporate property "that exists solely at the expense of others and with the purpose of generating more capital" (Neumann, 91). ACME believes that property destruction is not violence unless it kills or injures human beings in the process. They direct violence toward private/corporate property in order to "destroy the thin veneer of legitimacy that surrounds private property rights" and to "exorcise the set of violent and destructive social relationships which has been imbued in almost everything around us" (ACME Collective 1999). Thus, from the standpoint of Neumann and the anarchists, those who disparage property destruction as a form of civil disobedience fetishize property rights. Absolutists fail to appreciate how the production of private property in our world systematically violates human rights. Once we can recognize that violence toward things is not the same as violence toward people, and that not all property rights deserve respect, especially if it is property that is created and sustained through the exploitation of human beings, then property destruction can be classified as a form of civil disobedience rather than as a crime.

Such reflections, according to Neumann, move the issue of violent civil disobedience from morality into the realm of political strategy. Strategic issues deal with the question of command and control: When is it appropriate to engage in nonviolent protest and when is violence called for? Howard Zinn provides a set of criteria for the strategic use of violence (1968, 109). First, violent civil disobedience preferably ought to be directed at property rather than at human beings. Second, violent civil disobedience must be limited and not indiscriminate. Violence should be used "surgically" to remove injustice. Finally, violence must be aimed directly at the source of injustice—those officials or institutions perpetuating harm. Under these conditions, rampaging mobs randomly attacking people or property are not engaged in civil disobedience since they are not concerned with the "deliberate [and] organized use of power," that is, with ensuring that the violence they set free is controlled, directed at those people or places responsible for injustice, and in a manner that will inhibit the officials or institutions from harming the public (Zinn, 108).

Zinn offers these criteria as both moral and pragmatic regulative ideals. He recognizes that violence is an evil that should be used only as a last resort in order to defeat a greater evil. Moreover, indiscriminate violence on the part of protestors can turn the public against a cause. These considerations, however, are not enough to make the case for principled nonviolence. Like Neumann, Zinn finds absolutists politically foolish. It is morally appropriate to work to reduce violence in the world, in his view, but this does not entail that certain political circumstances will never arise that make it necessary to consider violence as a method of achieving some important social end. The proponent of absolute nonviolence refuses to acknowledge that there are values other than peace, such as justice, for instance, and that "it is possible to conceive of situations where a disturbance of the peace is justifiable if it results in some massive improvement of the human condition for large numbers of people" (Zinn, 106). His argument does not entail that violence is always the most appropriate response to injustice. Like Neumann, Zinn thinks that the use of violence ought to be guided by circumstances, not moral principle.

An absolutist might respond that there are very good strategic reasons for not engaging in violent forms of civil disobedience, namely, the possibility of massive state repression. Violent protest should be avoided because it invites retaliation and occasions official corruption. For Zinn, history does not establish that violence only begets violence. Shay's Rebellion, for example, deeply impacted the deliberations at the Constitutional Convention, violent union struggles in the 1930s brought about significant labor reform, and the urban uprisings of the 1960s drew attention to the conditions of the ghettos. He observes: "Independence, emancipation, labor unions—these basic elements in the development of American democracy all involved violent actions by aggrieved persons" (Zinn, 111). Thus, again, the question about the use of violence must be weighed and evaluated carefully by experience and circumstance. Zinn concludes: "I insist only that the question is so open, so complex, that it would be foolish to rule out at the start, for all times and conditions, all of the vast range of possible tactics beyond strict nonviolence" (Zinn, 111).

Chavez and the Pragmatics of Social Protest

Chavez, like other absolutists, would insist that the question about the use of violence in civil disobedience is not merely about strategy. Moral principles are always at the center of social struggles against injustice and it is misleading to think that one can completely abstract them away. Neumann, the ACME Collective, and Jose Bove hope that by making distinctions between different types of violence and property the moral arguments against material destruction will appear illegitimate. The absolutist will turn out to be backing the forces of injustice by valuing all property rights more so than human life and well-being. Yet, this argument is disingenuous; it too relies on a moral principle, namely, that one ought to value human life and well-being over things.

Chavez thinks that it is important for social justice movements to acknowledge such moral principles at their core. Otherwise, strategic thinking can foster habits that negatively transform the character of a movement. Chavez dedicated most of his adult life to the struggle against the dehumanization of farm workers by California agribusiness. He knew the history of farm worker struggles over the past century and understood all too well that growers were willing to rely on violence to maintain their power and keep farm workers in subordinate positions. The UFW was created to stop the misery of farm work and alleviate the workers' poverty by forcing agribusiness to respect their dignity as human beings. At the center of the UFW struggle, therefore, is a conception of human beings as autonomous and rational agents, capable of planning and making their own life choices. The growers commit injustice by maintaining a system that treats workers as "agricultural implements or rented slaves" instead of rational agents (Chavez 1969, 35). A violent response on the part of the workers would undermine the UFW struggle by weakening their commitment to this ethical ideal of humanity:

> If I were to tell the workers: "All right, we're going to be violent; we're going to burn the sheds and we're going to dynamite the grower's homes

and we're going to burn the vineyards," provided we could get away with it, the growers would sign a contract. But you see that that victory came at the expense of violence; it came at the expense of injuring. I think once that happens it has tremendous impact on us. We would lose our perspective and we would lose the regard we have for human beings—and then the struggle would become a mechanical thing." (Chavez 1970)

In this passage, Chavez worries that allowing any violence as an option leaves open the possibility that people could be injured or killed. This option permits a kind of utilitarian calculus to pervade the movement; one that weighs the cost of violence against the possible benefits for the movement. Such strategic thinking considers individual human beings as disposable pieces in the struggle toward a noble end.

Chavez is concerned about this kind of mentality seeping into the farm worker struggle precisely because it is the mindset with which the growers conceived of the farm workers. To agribusiness, farm workers were fungible resources that had to be accounted for in calculating profit, not individual human beings who deserved proper treatment and respect. Chavez constantly reminded both his supporters and detractors: "If to build our union require[s] the deliberate taking of life . . . then I choose not to see this union built," because it was the attitude that separated the UFW from agribusiness. Without this foundation, the UFW would simply become another business union, "mechanically" concerned with its own power, stability, and prestige, and not a movement dedicated to upholding the dignity of farm workers. Therefore, in Chavez's mind, acknowledging moral principles as limits to political strategy prevents instrumental thinking from compromising a social movement and corrupting its commitments into power politics.

Neumann and Zinn could concede that ethical evaluation might be called for when considering violence toward people, but still hold that ethical restrictions are inappropriate when dealing with the issue of property damage. Objects do not deserve moral treatment. The real issue is how best to target property and damage it in such a way to halt injustice. Chavez would respond that the idea of criteria for the use of property destruction is misleading because it fails to understand the dynamics of state power and violence. Violence is not a force that can be neatly controlled. Even if a group can limit their own violence and surgically apply it, they cannot control the wake of violent retaliation and repression that may follow. A group might control their own actions, but they cannot control the situation, which includes the reactions of other agents, that their actions engender.

Chavez believed that the use of violent protest by the farm workers in their struggle for collective bargaining contracts would only bring a backlash from the growers. Property destruction, in Chavez's view, would only perpetuate a cycle of violence that had been underway for decades rather than shift the balance of power in favor of the workers: "The important thing is that for poor people to be able to get a clean victory is something you don't often see.

If we get it through violence, then the employers will just wait long enough until they can get even with you—and then the workers will respond, and then . . ." (Chavez 1970). Indeed, even when the UFW was finally able to sign its first collective bargaining contracts in 1970, many growers quickly moved to thwart the farm workers by signing with the Teamsters instead (Dalton 2003, 16). This led to competition between the UFW and the Teamsters that frequently erupted into bloody confrontations between members of the two unions. While the two groups clashed in the fields, the growers were able to forestall making any real improvements for the farm workers. Chavez knew that any deliberate use of property destruction by the UFW would bring about an even more cruel backlash upon the farm workers than the one they were already experiencing with principled nonviolence.

Zinn acknowledges that violent protest may lead to backlash and repression. But, as he and Jose Bove suggest, history also shows that violence can sometimes shift the balance of power away from dominant groups. Nonviolence in the farm workers' struggle might very well be the appropriate tactic, given the willingness of the growers to react brutally. However, that judgment would be based on the conditions of that particular situation. Zinn would caution that we should not generalize from the farm worker experience and decide that violence is never appropriate, under any circumstances, because of the possibility of backlash.

Chavez thinks that, even from a strategic point of view, the likelihood of repression should make the call for use of violence by subordinate groups dubious. This is because, if and when the powerful do backlash, it is usually the poorest and most vulnerable members of the subordinate group that suffer. Chavez remarks:

> Examine history. Who gets killed in the case of violent revolution? The poor, the workers. The people of the land are the ones who give their bodies and don't really gain that much for it. . . . Those who espouse violence exploit people. To call men to arms with many promises, to ask them to give up their lives for a cause and then not produce for them afterwards, is the most vicious type of oppression. (Chavez 1978, 97)

Chavez cites the example of revolutions in Mexico and the rest of Latin America where the poorest members of society were the ones to suffer tremendous loss with little improvement in the institutions that directly affect their lives (Chavez 1970). Thus, for Chavez, the idea that such vulnerable groups are most likely the ones to endure the brunt of state retaliation should make activists who espouse violence question its effectiveness as means of social justice. If by social justice we mean a condition of respect, fairness, and equity for all members of society, especially the most disadvantaged, then a situation that provokes or encourages powerful groups to further harm, marginalize, or confine the disadvantaged is clearly not desirable as a tactic, and in fact, contributes to their oppression. We, therefore, ought to question the commitment to social justice of those groups that are cavalier about others caught in the web of repression, such as ACME, which brags about being able to escape the police while other demonstrators were pepper-sprayed, tear-gassed, and shot with rubber bullets (ACME Collective 1999).

Nonetheless, Chavez is willing to concede to Zinn that violence can sometimes alter society. Subordinate groups may be able to shift the balance of power in society using violence. However, such a change is not the same as creating more fair, democratic, or equitable conditions that will alleviate the suffering of the subordinate group. Indeed, Chavez maintains that victory won through violence validates the use of force and creates a precedent for its use in any new social arrangement that can hinder the development of stable democratic politics:

> If we were to become violent and we won the strike, as an example, then what would prevent us from turning violence against the opponents in the movement who wanted to displace us? Say they felt they had more leadership and they wanted to be leaders. What would prevent us from turning violence against them? Nothing. Because we had already experienced that violence awarded us victory. (Chavez 1970)

Violence, then, is not a substitute for the development of persuasive and reasonable leadership, or for the hard work of organizing people into self-managing groups that can protect their own interests in coalition with other communities. Violence can change the people in power, but it is not conducive to the formation of the kinds of social habits, political skills, and expectations that create a democratic civic space. In Chavez's estimation, only nonviolent organizing can rouse the disadvantaged and provide them the opportunity to become agents empowered to control the processes that directly affect their own lives:

> The burdens of generations of poverty and powerlessness lie heavy in the fields of America. If we fail, there are those who will see violence as the shortcut to change. It is precisely to overcome these frustrations that we have involved masses of people in their own struggle throughout the movement. Freedom is best experienced through participation and self-determination, and free men and women instinctively prefer democratic change to any other means. Thus, demonstrations and marches, strikes and boycotts are not only weapons against the growers, but our way of avoiding the senseless violence that brings no honor to any class or community. (Chavez 1978, 97)

Conclusion

In this paper, using Chavez's conceptions of nonviolence and organizing, I contend that arguments in favor of property destruction as a form of social protest fail to understand the dynamics of violence as a political tactic and how that failure mitigates the utility of violence as a strategy for achieving social justice. Violent civil disobedience, from Chavez's standpoint, threatens to compromise the politics of a social justice movement and to unleash repression from dominant groups that disproportionately affects the most poor and marginalized members of society. And while violence may occasionally alter power relationships in society, there is no guarantee that the new arrangement will benefit subordinate groups. Indeed, there is reason to think that social change brought about by violent means will have a harder time establishing a stable system of democratic will-formation. Chavez's experience reminds us that the struggle for social justice is about empowering and training the disadvantaged to be able to take control of their own lives and to have influence in the institutions that directly affect them. Violent protest, no matter how effective as a tactic in upsetting the balance of power in society, is not a substitute for this kind of training in democratic action. The extent to which violent civil disobedience attracts state repression is the extent to which it contributes to further oppression of the most disadvantaged members of our community.

Works Cited

ACME Collective. 1999. "ACME Collective Communiqué." http://www. nocompromise.org/news/99129a.html (July 14, 2003).

Bove, Jose, and Francois Dufour. 2001. *The World is Not for Sale: Farmers Against Junk Food*. Translated by Anna de Casparis. London: Verso.

Chavez, Cesar. 1969. "Good Friday Letter." In *The Words of César Chavez*, ed. Richard J. Jensen and John C. Hammerback, 34–36. College Station: Texas A&M University Press, 2002.

———. 1970. "César Chavez: Apostle of Nonviolence." *Observer.* http://www.sfsu.edu/%7Eceipp/cesar_chavez/apostle.htm (December 20, 2000).

———. 1978. "Martin Luther King, Jr.: He Showed Us the Way, April 1978." In *The Words of César Chavez*, ed. Richard J. Jensen and John C. Hammerback, 96–97. College Station: Texas A&M University Press, 2002.

Dalton, Frederick John. 2003. *The Moral Vision of César Chavez*. Maryknoll, NY: Orbis Books.

Fairness and Accuracy in Reporting (FAIR). "Media Missing New Evidence about Genoa Violence." http://www.fair.org/activism/genoa-update.html (August 19, 2003).

Griswold Del Castillo, Richard, and Richard Garcia. 1995. *César Chavez: A Triumph of Spirit*. Norman: Oklahoma University Press.

Jeffress, Lynn. 2001. "A World Struggle is Underway: An Interview with Jose Bove." *Z Magazine.* http://www.thirdworldtraveler.com/Reforming_System/World_Struggle_Underway.html (June 28, 2003).

Neumann, Rachel. 2000. "A Place for Rage." *Dissent*. Vol. 47, No. 2 (Spring), 89–92.

Zinn, Howard. 1968. "A Fallacy on Law and Order: That Civil Disobedience Must be Absolutely Nonviolent." In *Civil Disobedience and Violence*. Edited by Jeffrie G. Murphy, 103–111. Belmont, CA: Wadsworth,1971.

Satyagraha

Samdhong Losang Tenzin

Satyagraha is gentle, it never wounds. It must not be the result of anger
or malice. It is never fussy, never impatient, never vociferous. It is the
direct opposite of compulsion. It was conceived as a complete substitute
for violence.

—M. K. Gandhi, H, 15 April 1933

In every great cause it is not the number of fighters that counts but it is
the quality of which they are made that becomes the deciding factor. The
greatest men of the world have always stood alone.

—M. K. Gandhi, YI, 10 Oct. 1929

I. The Necessity of Restoring Tibet's Freedom

The idea that Tibet's freedom must be restored is not politically motivated, nor is it based upon some nation-state theory. Our struggle is not primarily an ethnic or political struggle. Rather, all people born in the spiritual
land of Tibet have a universal responsibility to all beings, and the fulfillment
of that responsibility is a duty that we all incur simply by the fact of our
births. If we do not live up to that birth-duty, then we are not worthy of being
Tibetans, and we are unable to act in a way that does justice to our heritage.
Not only is there nothing more rude and base than being unable to live up to
one's birth-duty, but even from a worldly point of view, one scarcely merits
the humanity that one enjoys. What is that responsibility about which I speak?
It is the preservation and dissemination of the unique inner sciences and cultural traditions that were preserved and enhanced over thousands of years by
the Tibetans of early generations, who considered them to be more precious
than their own lives. In these modern times, those traditions are closely linked
to the well being of all peoples. If the Tibetan people do not manage to preserve those cultural traditions and they then disappear as a result of Chinese
occupation, it will be a great loss not only for Tibetans, but for the whole
world. This heritage can not be protected if Tibet does not regain its freedom

Source: From *Satyagraha*, originally published by Satyagrahi Community (1997).

and if natural ecological balance without exploitation is not restored to Tibet. Therefore, the ultimate goal is not just political freedom for Tibet. Rather, our ultimate goal is the preservation, maintenance, and dissemination of the sublime cultural traditions of the unique inner sciences for the sake of the whole world. However, without the proper means and favourable conditions, it is not possible for us to fulfill that responsibility. We therefore must first undertake the spiritual practice of liberating Tibet without delay.

Even in strict political terms, Tibet is distinct from China in terms of ethnicity, language, philosophy, and literature. Indeed, every significant aspect of Tibetan culture is distinct from China. Historically, Tibet enjoyed complete independence until the Chinese invasion beginning in 1949. Even now no Tibetan wishes to remain under Chinese rule. For all these reasons, we have the right to regain our independent nation.

In addition, from an international perspective the presence of a buffer state between the two most populous Asian countries—India and China—would promote regional peace. Geographically, Tibet is the highest country in the world and the source of most of Asia's largest rivers; hence, Tibet's environment is of prime international importance. Tibet is also closely linked to the security and stability of neighboring nations such as India, Nepal, Bhutan and Myanmar. Indeed, Tibet's freedom would be extremely beneficial even for China. In short, if the international community felt that it could not allow Iraq to occupy Kuwait, then there is no reason whatsoever why China should be allowed to occupy Tibet. Until Tibet is freed from Chinese occupation, this stain on the development of modern civilization will not be removed, and the savage law of the jungle will undoubtedly persist into the twenty-first century.

Hence, the restoration of Tibet's freedom is important not just to Tibetans; it is also of great importance to the international community for the clear advantages that it offers. But unlike other countries' struggles for freedom, Tibet's freedom is not something for which we can wait for many generations; rather, we must act with great urgency. At this point, then, I will list some reasons why we must recognize that our extremely precious time is running out with each passing day.

1. If we are unable to quickly restore our freedom, Tibet will soon become the land of Chinese, and the Tibetan people will become a minority in their own country. The spiritual practice of liberating Tibet is undertaken for the sake of the philosophies and practices contained within Tibetan learning, culture and inner sciences. But if we do not act quickly, these things may well be irretrievably lost. Even should Tibet gain its freedom after that point, our only gain would be purely political freedom.

2. If we do not have the continued guidance of His Holiness the XIV Dalai Lama for some time after the restoration of our freedom, it is certain that we will be unable to build a new Tibet in accord with our

goals, and it is even possible that we would be unable to maintain our freedom.

3. If we do not restore Tibet's freedom within a few years, and if communist China continues to develop economically and strengthen itself politically, then within some ten years China may become a country of unchallengable strength. Even if China was to become democratic and peaceful, the restoration of Tibet's freedom might become even more difficult.

For the reasons listed above, the spiritual practice of restoring Tibet's freedom must have some clear result no later than 1997–1998, and with such a result as our immediate goal we must undertake a Satyagraha Movement.

II. The Characteristics of Free Tibet

In accord with the vision of His Holiness the Dalai Lama, after the restoration of freedom, Tibet will be a demilitarized zone of nonviolence—free of nuclear, chemical and biological weapons; it will be a centre of environmental protection, and it will follow Buddhist economic principles avoiding all extremes. Free Tibet will be a wellspring of the unique culture of the inner sciences, a country that will seek to alleviate the many sufferings inflicted upon the people by modern society. It will be a distinctive, spiritual, and authentically democratic nation, replete with those characteristics of old Tibet that stem from a world view based on love, and yet ornamented by the positive aspects of modernity that do not contradict those compassionate principles. Free Tibet will set a model political system, and it will help maintain peace and goodwill through out world, especially Asia. It is for this kind of future Tibet that we must now strive.

III. Methods

In our spiritual practice of restoring Tibet's freedom, our method is uniquely the nonviolent path of peace. Hence, all Tibetans, both at home and in exile, must strive to gain confidence in the nonviolent path of peace; they must likewise strive to put that path into practice. The nonviolent path of peace is a technique for particularly courageous people. Of course, the fainthearted and cowardly will find it difficult to imagine, but even those who have no confidence in the instructions of the inner sciences and the workings of karmic cause and effect will not easily understand the principles of this technique. Many simple-minded people think that if we earnestly practice the nonviolent path of peace, we do so simply because China's enormous population and military strength leave no other choice for us Tibetans, who are few in number and militarily weak. According to these people, if we had the capacity to wage war against China, it would be perfectly acceptable to restore our freedom through military operations. Many people do think this way, but it is a serious mistake. Indeed, it is an indication that they have no confidence in the nonviolent path of peace. Whether one has confidence in the principle of karmic causality—whereby virtue results in happiness and non-virtue results in suffering—or whether one views the situation from a purely political standpoint, the philosophical understanding here is that one cannot achieve faultless goals if one does not rely on faultless methods. It is with this philosophical understanding that one must practice the nonviolent path of peace, for it is only through this understanding that one can authentically refrain from all violence. If one were instead to practice nonviolence with some intent to deceive others, then it would be far better if one were not to participate at all. Despite the fact that violence could guarantee Tibet's freedom by tomorrow, we must firmly vow never to resort to it. Until we can make such a promise, our nonviolent path of peace will be neither perfected nor will be a powerful instrument to achieve our goal.

IV. Putting the Methods into Practice

Truth: In the Tibetan Context

There can be no authentic Nonviolent Peace Movement that is not based upon the truth. In a certain sense, truth and nonviolence are synonymous. One might wonder how we should use the nonviolent path of peace to perform the spiritual practice of liberating Tibet. The answer is that we must recognize that the truth is on our side, and with that recognition, we must engage ourselves in a Satyagraha campaign. With this in mind, I here briefly list some aspects of the truth to which we can lay claim.

1. It is true that Tibet is a spiritual land where the people earn their livelihoods in a spiritual and moral manner.

2. It is true that Tibet has enjoyed complete independence for the vast majority of the time since the earliest social formations until 1951.

3. It is true that the communist Chinese military invasion of 1949 and the subsequent forceful colonization of Tibet violates international law.

4. It is true that according to international law, the Seventeen Point Agreement that Tibetans were forced to sign under intense duress is not valid; not only is it not valid, but the Chinese themselves have failed to adhere even to a single point, and in doing so they have effectively annulled the agreement. Therefore, it is true that the Seventeen Point Agreement should not at all be considered a valid document as an evidence for the claim that Tibet is a part of China.

5. It is true that during the more than forty years since the Chinese invasion: the Tibetans have been deprived of their human rights; the reli-

gious and cultural traditions of Tibet have been devastated; Tibet's economy has been exploited; the Tibetan people have faced immeasurable oppression, torture and brutality; the Tibetan people have become less populous due to the deliberate population transfer of Chinese into Tibet; a deliberate attempt has been made to destroy our culture and our very identity; and Tibet's environment has been severely harmed. It is true that as a result of these and other atrocities, the Tibetan people have been wracked with suffering without even the least opportunity for happiness, and it is true that this way of governing Tibet has never accorded with the aspirations of the Tibetan people.

6. It is true that the vast majority of the Tibetan people object to the Chinese occupation and fervently yearn to restore Tibet's independence.

7. It is true that Tibet is not part of China, and except for China's illegal occupation of Tibet, neither the Tibetan head of state nor the Tibetan people themselves have ever legitimately agreed to accede to China. Therefore, it is true that a movement to free Tibet from an illegal rule is in no way a threat to China's territorial integrity.

8. It is true that we Tibetans are a distinct people with our own ethnicity, language, customary clothing, and cultural traditions. Hence, it is true that the Tibetan people have the right to self-determination, and this right has been clearly affirmed in: the United Nations resolutions of 1961 and 1965; the Verdict of the Permanent Tribunal of Peoples: Session on Tibet (Strasbourg, France, 1992); the proceedings of the Session on Issues Relating to Self-Determination and Independence for Tibet of the Conference of International Lawyers (London, 1993); the Statement of Action of the Conference of European Parliamentarians (Palace of Westminster, 1993); and the New Delhi Declaration of the World Parliamentarians Convention on Tibet (New Delhi, 1994). Not only was our right to self-determination affirmed in these contexts, but many scholars have made numerous clear and explicit statements about this matter. Based on their findings, it is true that we the Tibetan people meet all the definitions of a distinctive people according to international law, and we have the right to self-determination.

9. It is true that the Tibetan people have a responsibility to the world to protect, maintain, and disseminate our unique traditions of moral behavior and inner sciences.

10. It is true that this responsibility cannot be fully met if freedom is not restored to the Tibetan people.

11. Hence, it is an irrevocable truth that the restoration of our freedom is the birth-duty of every Tibetan.

The above-mentioned aspects of truth are not hypothetical, nor are they some form of political propaganda. Rather, they can be confirmed through either one's own senses or through indisputable evidence. Hence, as aspects of truth, they can neither be erased nor rendered untrue through irrational arguments and illegitimate force. This is the nature of truth. The Chinese continue to occupy Tibet by utter disregard and trampling on these aspects of truth, and the fact that they can do so stems either from our lack of faith in the truth of the aforementioned aspects, or from our lack of the courage needed to persevere in bringing them to their culmination. All the Tibetan people, both at home and in exile, must recognize these aspects of truth immediately, and with confidence in them, we must unhesitatingly and single-mindedly undertake a Satyagraha Movement in order to bring these aspects of truth to their culmination.

V. Plan for a Satyagraha Movement

Since His Holiness the Dalai Lama went into exile in India, much has been done in the attempt to restore Tibet's freedom. Accurate information has been disseminated throughout the world; frequent representations have been made to the United Nations; the Draft of the Constitution of Future Tibet has been formulated and disseminated; the Tibetan government in exile has been fully democratized, and numerous other activities have been undertaken. In addition, in 1979 the Chinese leader Deng Xiao Ping indicated that with the exception of complete independence, all other issues could be resolved through peaceful negotiations. Accordingly, many gestures, such as the repeated dispatch of delegations to Tibet and China, were made in an attempt to bring about a peacefully negotiated settlement between Tibet and China. In a continuation of these efforts, His Holiness drafted his Five-Point Peace Plan in 1987, and in 1988 he presented the Strasbourg Proposal before the European Parliament. Although he has made every possible effort to bring about a peaceful settlement, the Chinese have in no way acted in accordance with their earlier statements concerning their willingness to seek such a settlement.

Direct contacts and discussions with China have at this point of time been suspended, and an appeal has been made to persuade the Chinese through international pressure. In his March Tenth Message of 1994, His Holiness the Dalai Lama has publicly stated that if the appeal for international pressure does not lead to a satisfactory result within an acceptable period of time, then he will ask the Tibetan people for their opinion on the best way to proceed in the future.

Judging by the way that the Chinese tend to proceed, it seems rather unlikely that international pressure will actually bring the Chinese to the negotiating table at this point. As for the future, unless the Tibetan people, especially the Tibetans in Tibet, do not attempt to restore Tibet's freedom by undertaking a serious movement that will clearly indicate their aspirations, it seems unlikely that only international pressure and support will have much effect on its own. Hence we, the Tibetan people, must now prepare ourselves to submit a well ordered plan of action when the time comes for His Holiness the Dalai Lama to ask us for our opinion. This plan for a Satyagraha Movement is therefore submitted to the people for their consideration.

In short, the plan is as follows: if the Chinese authorities do not make progress that is satisfactory to the Tibetan people toward a peaceful settlement of the Tibetan issue through feasible and acceptable policies by the end of 1995, then from March 10, 1996, all of the Tibetan people, both at home and in exile, will with united hearts and minds begin a Total Nonviolent Satyagraha Movement. This is what we must decide to do.

VI. Required Qualifications of a Satyagraha Activist

1. Through unshakable faith and confidence in truth and the nonviolent path of peace, one must maintain proper ethical conduct (as is specified separately), which consists in part of never speaking falsehoods and never harming others. This conduct must have been maintained for not less than three months before entering the Movement.

2. One must have no anger, hatred, or intent to harm the objects of our resistance, the governmental officials and workers of communist China and all those siding with them.

3. When engaged in Satyagraha activism, one must have the courage never to respond to violence with violence, nor to use violence to protect oneself no matter how much one is beaten, imprisoned, tormented and tortured.

4. When undertaking the Satyagraha Movement to restore Tibet's independence, one should not consider it a political movement, nor some mundane activity, nor a campaign calculated to hurt the Chinese. Instead, one must recognize and believe that one is engaged in the spiritual practice of restoring Tibet's freedom for the sake of all sentient beings.

5. While participating in the Movement, one should in no way expect to gain fame, glory, political or economic profit, or recognition for one's notable accomplishments and the like.

6. One should not at any point remind others of one's contributions nor expect to receive credit, for one has abandoned all such notions. In particular, after the restoration of freedom one must have no expectation whatsoever of any political position, social status, financial support, or any other benefit for oneself or one's relations. And even if such an offer is made in free Tibet, one must firmly vow to decline it unless there is some clear and pressing need.

7. In all matters such as clothing, lodging, furnishings and so on, one must lead a life free of extremes; one must not participate in unethical ways of making a living, and one must have little desire for wealth.

8. One must never participate in any activities whatsoever, whether public or private, that are dishonest or untruthful.

9. One must see to it that one's family members, such as children and aged parents, are not dependent upon oneself for support; if they are dependent, then one must receive their permission.

10. One must have no outstanding loans, no accounts to be settled, no liabilities to manage, and no other such responsibilities to be met.

11. One must never break one's vow of truth and nonviolence, even at the cost of one's life.

12. One must not transgress those rules which from time to time are legitimately drafted by the leaders of the Satyagraha Movement.

VII. Decisions Required of a Satyagraha Activist

One must firmly make the following decisions:

1. From the moment that one enlists in the Satyagraha Movement, one must never abandon it until the Movement's announced goals have been met or every single activist has perished without exception.

2. No matter how much misery and hardship one faces in body and mind, one must persevere and never abandon one's activism as long as one lives.

3. Regardless of how much one is praised or reviled, if one's motivation is flawless, then one can never be dissuaded, no matter how many comments others make.

VIII. Points to Be Understood

A Satyagraha activist must clearly understand the following points.

1. One needs to understand from the very beginning that not only is it quite likely that one might well have to die soon after beginning one's activism, but it is possible that all of the members of the Movement will die, or that the goals of the Movement will not be achieved. But in any case, all members of the Movement will die within some seventy years. Hence, in as much as one must die either way, rather than dying a few years later without fulfilling one's birth-duty, it is clearly preferable to die a few years earlier while in the process of fulfilling

one's birth-duty. Even if one is not willing to die right now, how can one be guaranteed that one will live for any extended period of time?

2. Our goals might not be achieved even though everyone in the Movement has perished, but all the contemporary Tibetans will one day die even if we do not begin a Truth Movement. More importantly, whether the movement is unsuccessful or we fail to engage in a Movement, our culture and our ethnic identity will perish in either case. In as much as all would be lost one way or the other, rather than doing nothing and waiting for everything to be destroyed on its own, it is clearly preferable—no matter how one argues—that we lose everything while attempting to fulfill our birth-duty.

IX. Forms of Satyagraha

The Movement encompasses two forms of Satyagraha: personal and collective. From the day that a person who wishes to join the Movement has met all of the qualifications listed in topic 6, he or she can engage in any feasible form of Satyagraha suited to the time and place without depending on collective plans, and such a person may engage in Satyagraha whether inside or outside of Tibet. Many forms of personal Satyagraha are easy to perform, so everyone should continually engage in them; personal Satyagraha should be particularly emphasized when the time is not ripe for collective Satyagraha.

Collective Satyagraha should be undertaken by a group of at least five people, and it must be accompanied by a plan. The plan must be suitable to the time and place, and it must be adhered to when one engages in collective Satyagraha.

X. The Stages of the Movement

1. Personal Satyagraha can be undertaken at any time or place, and so it does not need to be regulated according to a specific sequence or stages of action.

2. Collective Satyagraha will begin from a specified date. From that date those Tibetans in exile who wish to participate in the Movement and who have met all of the qualifications will abandon all their property and assets for the duration of the Movement and return to Tibet to engage in Satyagraha.

3. From that same date, those people in Tibet who have enlisted in the Movement will collectively begin Satyagraha activism in their respective areas.

4. After assessing how many Satyagraha activists are available, they will be assigned to proportionally sized units. After the earlier activist

units of the Satyagraha Movement have been decimated through death, injury and imprisonment, a second unit should emerge after one or two days. The Movement will be sustained in this manner.

XI. Types of Satyagraha

The specific forms of Nonviolent Total Satyagraha must be determined in the context of the time and place of the intended activism; the current demands of the Movement must also be taken into account. Hence, it is not possible to fully describe all possible forms of activism at this point. In a rough sense, however, Satyagraha activism consists of Civil Disobedience, Non-Cooperation, and Peaceful Resistance. Listed below are some examples of such activism.

1. Activists will completely disregard all unacceptable orders and directives of the Chinese central government and the Chinese controlled regional and provincial governments in the Tibetan area.

2. Activists will neither cooperate with nor participate in any governmental or public work that forms part of a project initiated and/or controlled by the central, regional or local governments of communist China.

3. All activists who work in offices, schools, factories or other work places that are under the control of any department or office of the central, regional or local Chinese governments will resign forthwith from their respective place of work.

4. Activists will not purchase, sell, own, keep or use any item that has been produced by the Chinese government or by Chinese people.

5. Activists will not visit or patronize any restaurant, store, or hotel that is administered by the Chinese government or by Chinese people.

6. All activist students and teachers in any school will refuse to study or teach the Chinese language or any form of Chinese studies.

7. Activists will not employ any Chinese in any undertaking, whether at a construction site or even in a simple tailor or barber's shop.

8. Activists will not be partners with any Chinese in any undertaking, whether it be in retail, service, agriculture or industry.

9. In short, Activists will in no way associate or cooperate with any activity that is in any way related—whether directly, indirectly, or marginally—to the Chinese occupation of Tibet, the population transfer of Chinese into Tibet, or the destruction of the Tibetan environment. Through daily assemblies in the streets of each city, town and village, activists will peacefully resist without any violence whatsoever; activists will not even defend themselves with the poles of their flags and placards, let alone use actual weapons. Activists

will shout slogans of resistance and will ceaselessly make known their current demands both vocally and in writing.

10. One may engage in any other form of activism that is consistent with the principles of Satyagraha and its methods such as non-cooperation and passive resistance. When engaged in any such activity, one must do so according to plan and in a fashion that is suitable to the time and place. Although one will certainly have to endure stoically such hardships as enforced starvation, one must not deliberately sacrifice one's life through fasting, self-immolation, and so on.

XII. The Demands of Our Satyagraha Movement

The demands and the conditions that are to be initially made by the Satyagraha Movement should not be impossible to satisfy, nor should they even be particularly difficult to satisfy. Instead, it is crucial to begin the Movement with demands that are reasonably feasible. Below, then, are listed some demands that could be made at the outset of the Movement.

1. The population transfer of Chinese into Tibet must be ceased immediately.

2. Human rights must no longer be violated in Tibet and China.

3. Tibetan and Chinese political prisoners must be immediately released.

4. Tibet's environment must be protected, and in particular, the conducting of nuclear tests, construction of nuclear facilities, and dumping of nuclear waste must be immediately ceased.

5. The central and local political system must be immediately democratized.

If there is initially some acceptable result of the Satyagraha Movement due to one or more of the above demands being met, then in the second stage we should demand that the Tibetan people be given an opportunity to exercise their right to self-determination. What should be done after that point will follow naturally from the results of the previous operations.

XIII. Inevitable Obstacles to the Satyagraha Movement

The Satyagraha Movement is likely to face many possible impediments and obstacles, but most are little cause for concern. However, the two most serious obstacles could prove problematic. They are:

1. Satyagraha activists will face immeasurable torture and torment, and our tormentors will use every conceivable method to arouse our anger. In doing so, they will attempt to incite activists to employ violence

and falsehood, and it is possible that some will break their vow of nonviolence. Another possibility is that our opponents will recruit and infiltrate their agents into the Satyagraha Movement; these agents will then attempt to incite others to violence.

2. Through vague and false statements, and with the pretext of seeking some means of arriving at a settlement, time will be wasted in meaningless discussion that are intended to stop the Truth Movement.

We will need to face these two eventualities with great skill and vigilance.

XIV. Dissemination of Information Concerning the Satyagraha Movement

The Truth Movement does not seek publicity, nor is it a means to garner international support. It will be necessary to present statements that specify our demands to the governmental authorities of the pertinent regions as well as the officials of the Chinese central government. But except for such statements, one should not on one's own publicize the movement to the news media. Nevertheless, the movement need not be kept secret, so when requested one should promptly and clearly explain the situation to media representatives or any other genuinely interested person.

XV. Financial Support for the Movement

A mechanism needs to be established for the gathering of funds that have been properly accumulated by the activists themselves for the sake of the Movement. Such funds must not have been acquired through any unethical livelihood. The Movement may also accept donations that are not stained by unethical livelihood and are made without any expectation of return, including the expectation of fame or improved status.

XVI. Supporters of the Satyagraha Movement

Some people will wish to support the Movement without actually participating as activists. These people could perform duties such as the raising of funds, the maintenance of public relations, the gathering and dissemination of information, and the preparation of publications. Such duties could be performed either for the entire period of the Movement or for a specified time. Supporters may engage in such duties if they meet the following qualifications from topic VI: 1, 2, 4, 5, 6, 7, 11, and 12.

XVII. A Response to Skepticism about Satyagraha

There are many persons who remark that our Satyagraha Movement is entirely dissimilar to Gandhi's satyagraha, which was conducted while India was under British rule; nor is our Movement similar to movements that have been conducted in democratic countries. Instead, China is a country with a huge population and enormous military forces that has an immoral, unethical and shameless government with no rule of law nor any respect whatsoever for either human rights or the concerns of the international community. These skeptics go on to say that under such conditions, there is not only no way to begin a Satyagraha Movement, but were it somehow to begin, participating in it would be tantamount to suicide.

Although many people do think this way, the fact remains that if the path of truth and nonviolence is truly powerful, it must be capable of overcoming anything it faces. And if it is faced with lawless brutality, the path of truth and nonviolence will necessarily become even more potent. When truth confronts falsehood and nonviolence confronts violence, the stronger force will be the one that is more valid; the fact that one's opponents have more brute force does not mean that they will thereby have greater strength. When we say that Buddha Shakyamuni overwhelmed billions of demonic forces with a single meditation on love, we are not recounting a simple story; instead, I feel that we are speaking of a rationally supported symbol of the power of truth and nonviolence. Finally, even if participating in such a movement were to be tantamount to suicide, I have already remarked that we must die one way or the other. So rather than die having led an empty and meaningless life, it is far more meaningful and more in keeping with the demands of history to die while engaged in the spiritual practice of truth and nonviolence for the sake of our nation and its spiritual traditions.

NONVIOLENCE, NATURE, AND ANIMAL RIGHTS

Reverence for Life

Albert Schweitzer

The Meaning of Philosophy[*]

The purpose of all philosophy is to make us aware as thinking beings of the intelligent and intimate relationship with the universe in which we have to stand, and of the way in which we must behave in the presence of the stimuli that come from it.

One kind of philosophy is able to bring man and the universe together only by doing violence to nature and the world and by forcing the world into harmony with man's thought.

The other, the insignificant nature philosophy, leaves the world and nature as they are, and compels man to find himself and assert himself in them as a spiritually and creatively triumphant being. The first philosophy is ingenious, the second elementary. The first proceeds from one mighty manifestation of thought to another, as they appear in the great speculative systems of German philosophy, and we are carried away with admiration for them. This philosophy has its day and disappears. The second, the plain and simple nature philosophy, remains. An elementary philosophy, which first of all tried to find intelligent

*Source: Excerpt from *Goethe: Five Studies* by Albert Schweitzer, translated by Charles Joy, © 1948 Beacon Press.

283

expression in the Stoics and then perished with them because it failed to achieve an affirmative view of the world and of life, strives always to come into its own. This nature philosophy has come down to us in an imperfect form. It tried once again in Spinoza and in the eighteenth-century rationalism to think through to the affirmation of the world and life. When it was unable to do so, violence took the place of effort. The great speculative philosophy brought forth its systems of compulsion. At that time, when everyone was blinded by a world prostrate before thought, there was one man who was not blinded, who remained loyal to the elementary and humble nature philosophy, aware that it had not been able to think its way through to an affirmative conclusion in that eighteenth century in which he lived, but certain that it would have to do so; and he worked toward that end in the simple way which was his inner nature.

When I myself became aware of this and turned back to this nature philosophy—recognizing that it is our appointed task to bring it to an affirmative position in relation to the world and life, in so simple a fashion that all thoughtful people throughout the world would have to share in this thinking, and therein find peace with the infinite and incentive for creative activity—then I realized that Goethe was the man who had held out at the abandoned post where we were once more mounting guard and beginning to work again.

Human Awareness[†]

The fundamental fact of human awareness is this: "I am life that wants to live in the midst of other life that wants to live." A thinking man feels compelled to approach all life with the same reverence he has for his own. Thus, all life becomes part of his own experience. From such a point of view, "good" means to maintain life, to further life, to bring developing life to its highest value. "Evil" means to destroy life, to hurt life, to keep life from developing. This, then, is the rational, universal, and basic principle of ethics.

Ethics up to now had been incomplete because it had held that its chief concern was merely with the relationship of man to man. In reality, however, ethics must also be concerned with the way man behaves toward all life. In essence, then, man can be considered ethical only if life as such is sacred to him—both in people and in all creatures that inhabit the earth.

The actual living of this ethic, with its responsibilities extending toward all living things, is deeply rooted in universal thought. The ethical relationship of man to man is not something in and of itself, but part of a greater concept. The idea of reverence for life contains everything that expresses love, submission, compassion, the sharing of joy, and common striving for the good of all. We must free ourselves from thoughtless existence.

†Source: Excerpts from "Albert Schweitzer Speaks Out" A Year Book Special Report from the 1964 WORLD BOOK YEAR BOOK © 1964 Field Enterprises Educational Corporation. By permission of World Book, Inc. www.worldbook.com.

At the same time, we are all subject to the mysterious and cruel law by which we maintain human life at the cost of other life. It is by this very destruction and harm of other life that we develop feelings of guilt. As ethical human beings, we must constantly strive to escape from this need to destroy—as much as we possibly can. We must try to demonstrate the essential worth of life by doing all we can to alleviate suffering. Reverence for life, which grows out of a proper understanding of the will to live, contains life-affirmation. It acts to create values that serve the material, the spiritual, and ethical development of man.

The Goal of True Thought[†]

Whereas the thoughtless modern world walks aimlessly about in ideals of knowledge, skills, and power, the goal of true and profound thought is the spiritual and ethical perfection of man. This requires a new ethical civilization that seeks peace and renounces war. Only the kind of thinking dominated by reverence for life can bring lasting peace to our world. All lesser efforts for peace must forever remain unsuccessful.

A new renaissance must come, and it must be much greater than the one that lifted the world out of the Middle Ages. This new renaissance must help mankind to advance from the pathetic sense of reality in which it lives, toward the spirit of reverence for life. Only through a truly ethical civilization can life take on meaning. Only through it can mankind be saved from destruction, from its senseless and cruel wars. It alone can bring about peace in the world.

The Will to Live[††]

. . . The great fault of all ethics hitherto has been that they believed themselves to have to deal only with the relations of man to man. In reality, however, the question is what is his attitude to the world and all life that comes within his reach. A man is ethical only when life, as such, is sacred to him, that of plants and animals as that of his fellow men, and when he devotes himself helpfully to all life that is in need of help. Only the universal ethic of the feeling of responsibility in an ever-widening sphere for all that lives— only that ethic can be founded in thought. The ethic of the relation of man to man is not something apart by itself: it is only a particular relation which results from the universal one.

The ethic of Reverence for Life, therefore, comprehends within itself everything that can be described as love, devotion, and sympathy whether in suffering, joy, or effort. . . .

[††]Source: Excerpt from *Out of My Life and Thought* by Albert Schweitzer, translated by C. T. Campion, © 1949 Henry Holt.

Jaina Cosmology and Gaia Theory

Christopher Key Chapple

. . . Is it appropriate or useful to employ an ethical principle that arises from a specialized religious community of renouncers to address modern issues that arise from a radically different world view? We have seen that Jaina principles would strongly support an ecological ethic. However, to what extent would the Jaina perspective be useful for application to a problem that stems from an utterly foreign, scientific and technological world view?

If one is unwilling to question the presuppositions that have led to ecological demise, then the concepts underlying the theory and practice of *ahimsā* would be useless, and it would be meaningless to follow Jaina prohibitions against harming life forms. However, the environmental movement does in fact critique the premise that the earth was created for humans to exploit, as noted in the ground-breaking article by Lynn White.[1] The world view that created disturbances to the ecosystem has been called into question. Furthermore, proponents of the Gaia theory claim that the earth itself lives and breathes, rejecting the notion that the earth as we know it consists primarily of inert matter.

The Gaia theory is one of two new Western models proposed in response to this questioning of both the philosophical and the scientific presuppositions that allowed humankind to exploit nature mercilessly for its own purposes. Both this scientific model and the other, a theological model, can be readily adapted to support an ecological orthopraxy akin to that practiced by Jainas. The scientific model was first suggested under the title "biogeochemistry" by Vladimir I. Vernadsky, and later developed by James E. Lovelock, who dubbed it the Gaia theory, and Lynn Margulis, who is conducting research to help prove the hypothesis. The Gaia theory, as we will see, claims that many of the objects that in prior times were considered inanimate are in fact the by-products of biological processes. The theological model is known as panentheism, which literally means "everything in God." The term was first used by K. F. C. Krause in the nineteenth century, and has recently been reintroduced by process theologians. It emphasizes the presence of deity within each of its manifestations. Panentheism suggests that the world is a dynamic expression of God's creation, a "self-conscious Life within whom the unfoldings of the universe occur," and that human beings need to respect and protect the earth accordingly.[2] Although each of these differs significantly from Jainism, both give credence to the general Jaina claim that life extends beyond the obvious domains of plants and animals, and that steps need to be taken to assure that life systems are not unduly harmed.

Due to its similarities with the Jaina theory of life, we will briefly survey the history of the Gaia hypothesis and discuss its possible ethical implications in light of Jaina ethics. Vernadsky (1863–1945) is considered the father of a discipline known as biogeochemistry,[3] the predecessor of the Gaia hypothesis. Biogeochemistry posits a link between the formation of the earth and the processes of life. James Lovelock first formulated his version of the Gaia theory when NASA asked him in the 1960s to establish criteria by which life could be detected on other planets. He discovered that the atmosphere of earth differs radically from that of other planets in our solar system, and suggested that the best way to determine if life exists elsewhere in the universe is to determine the specific chemical composition of distant atmospheres. He then began to question what makes our atmosphere so different, and came to the conclusion that life itself produced our unusual array of gases. Specifically, millions of years ago, bacteria on earth ate and digested rocks. In the process, they removed carbon dioxide from the atmosphere, thereby producing new forms of limestone and releasing nitrogen and oxygen into the atmosphere. Without the presence of bacteria, none of the world as we know it could exist today.

Lovelock emphasizes that the many geological formations and in fact the air itself are not dead matter but part of the dynamic processes of a living system:

> Somehow both geologists and biologists have failed to note that their separate researches have clearly demonstrated that the world is massively affected by the presence of life. The air we breathe, the oceans and the rocks are all either direct products of living organisms [think of the chalk cliffs of Dover, just one gigantic pile of shells] or else they have been greatly modified by their presence, and this even includes the igneous rocks coming from volcanos. Indeed organisms are not just adapting to a dead world determined by physics and chemistry textbooks alone, they live with a world that is the breath and the bones and the blood of their ancestors and they themselves are now sustaining.[4]

He regards our planetary system to be like a living system. Each piece performs a particular function that allows other parts to flourish. One system's garbage provides food for another.[5]

In considering Gaia theory, certain similarities arise with the Jaina system. First, both see all life as interconnected. No single form of life can be considered without acknowledgment of an infinite web of life forms. The air we breathe, to which we owe our life, consists of gases that were produced by other life forms. Both systems emphasize recognition of interdependence. The Gaia hypothesis posits a relationship between the earth's atmosphere and the rocks that formed as the bacteria did their work. In turn, plants, animals, and humans need the atmosphere and each other to survive. Life forms cannot exist in isolation. The Jainas posit that the *jīvas*, or life forces, pervade the earth and its atmosphere. They undergo an unending process of transmutation, with the decay of one form giving birth to a new one.

Neither the Gaia hypothesis nor Jainism is apocalyptic. Jainism does not speak of the end of the world, only a rearrangement of its pieces and possible liberation for its most elevated monastic members. Proponents of the Gaia theory dismiss the notion that life on our planet will be obliterated by human interference. Rather, they claim that it might be severely mutated, but that some species, especially cockroaches and bacteria, will survive even the most horrid of environmental debacles.[6] Consequently, proponents of Gaia theory explicitly criticize as excessively anthropocentric the Teilhardian notion that humans are the pinnacle of the creation process, marching onward toward a final beatific state.[7] Lynn Margulis warns that if we do not take full responsibility for the production of all sorts of human wastes (including the chemicals that currently endanger the ozone layer) and if we do not curb our reproductive rate, the survival of human life as we know it is imperiled.

Both Gaia thought and Jainism raise issues of an ethical nature. Jainas, as we have seen, have developed nonviolent lifestyles stemming from their deep regard for all living beings and elements. By comparison, the ethics implied by Gaia is unformed, though an ethic that mandates reducing harm to the environment seems inescapable, as suggested by Margulis. Human beings share a development of conscience and a consciousness enriched by subtle emotions and deep memories; presumably these two qualities distinguish humans from the millions of other species that have taken birth on earth. According to Jaina philosophy, human persons can dissipate themselves in search of sensual gratification, but they can also reverse these tendencies, gain mastery over past karma, and actively pursue a life of nonviolence. In the process, they become nonspeciesistic and minimally intrusive on the environment.

The environmentalist lifestyle, advocated and practiced by many proponents of Gaia theory, is in many ways similar to the Jaina emphasis on recognizing the wider effects of one's activities. Both ancient Jainism and modern Gaia theory can be harnessed to support a contemporary environmentalist lifestyle. Individuals must account for the miles they drive and the garbage they consume in such a way that they are conscious of the extent and repercussions of their consumption of natural resources. Just as Jainas developed their sequence of five vows to prevent and reduce the destruction of living forms, so also vows not to pollute by minimizing purchases and recycling materials serve as approximate equivalents to Jaina monasticism.

Select vows of Jainism, interpreted with a bit of imagination, can easily be put to the service of ecologically sound living. The first vow, *ahimsā*, requires respect for and protection of all life forms, stemming from the premise that even a blade of grass is not different from oneself in its essential vitality. Advocates of vegetarianism claim that abstention from eating meat not only spares the lives of animals, but also helps contribute to a healthy ecosystem.[8] The third vow, not stealing, means that one abstains from taking what does not belong to oneself. This can be particularly instructive for peoples of the "developed world" who continue to consume the majority of the world's resources, spewing forth pollution as a primary by-product. The fourth vow, that of nonpossession, is tacitly environmental, as demonstrated by Acharya Tulsi. The less one owns, the less harm has been committed to one's ecosphere. On a practical level, the fifth vow, sexual restraint, can be seen as one way to hold down population growth. Psychologically, it can be used as an exercise in post-patriarchal interpersonal relations, in which regarding other bodies as potential objects for sexual gratification or the seeing of others as manipulable is transformed into seeing other people and other people's bodies as not different from oneself.

These examples suggest a few ways in which the ancient Asian nonviolent ethic can be reinterpreted in light of the contemporary environmental crisis. However, in order for people to be sufficiently motivated to change their lifestyles, they would have to respond to the environment in such a way that they would regard it as a living, breathing system, the balance of which is essential to their own health and well being. In short, they would have to respond to the Gaia concept, panentheism, or some reasonable equivalent with the same psychic responsiveness that has characterized the success of traditional mythological and symbolic systems. A new form of environmental orthopraxy, not unlike the Jewish system of Kosher food, is needed, wherein some goods are avoided or recycled. . . . Such actions can be seen as rituals that integrate a person into a wider ecosystem.

Thomas Berry has noted that much of the erosion of the earth's ecosystem is due to increasingly industrialized technology and expansion of transportation networks. Both of these take natural resources, convert them into "consumables," transport them across continents, and quickly process them into garbage.[9] Although the problem of environmental decay was not articulated during the time of Gandhi, the solutions that he proposed to counter the ills of colonialism can also be put into effect to redress this new and ultimately equally deleterious situation. The observance of nonviolence, coupled with a commitment to minimize consumption of natural resources, can contribute to restoring and maintaining an ecological balance.

Notes

[1] Lynn White, Jr., "The Historic Roots of Our Ecologic Crisis," Science, 155 (March 1967).
[2] For a discussion of ecological panentheism, see Jay B. McDaniel, *Of God and Pelicans: A Theology of Reverence For Life* (Louisville, Kentucky: Westminster/John Knox Press, 1989)

and his forthcoming contribution to *Ecological Prospects,* edited by Christopher Key Chapple (Albany: State University of New York Press).

[3] For a history of the development of this idea, see Jacques Grinevald, "Sketch for a History of the Idea of the Biosphere," in *Gaia, the Thesis, the Mechanisms and the Implications,* edited by Peter Bunyard and Edward Goldsmith (Cornwall: Wadebridge Ecological Centre, 1988), pp. 1–34.

[4] James Lovelock, "The Gaia Hypothesis," in *Gaia,* op. cit, p. 38.

[5] See James E. Lovelock, *Ages of Gaia* (New York: W. W. Norton, 1988).

[6] Lynn Margulis, talk delivered at "Ecological Prospects: Theory and Practice," conference at Loyola Marymount University, 1991.

[7] See Grinevald, op. cit, pp. 8–12.

[8] See Frances Moore Lappe, *Food First: Beyond the Myth of Scarcity* (Boston: Houghton-Mifflin, 1977).

[9] See Thomas Berry, *The Dream of the Earth* (San Francisco: Sierra Club Books, 1988).

Judaism, Animals Rights, and Vegetarianism

Richard H. Schwartz

Although it is not well known, Judaism has very powerful teachings about proper treatment of animals. If Jews took these teachings seriously, they would be among the strongest protesters of current practices related to animals.

According to Judaism, animals are part of God's creation and people have special responsibilities to them. The Jewish tradition clearly indicates in several places that it is forbidden to be cruel to animals, and that they should be treated with compassion. These concepts are summarized in the Hebrew phrase, *tsa'ar bal'alei hayim*—the mandate not to cause "sorrow to any living creature."

The 104th and 148th Psalms show God's close identification with the beasts of the field, creatures of the sea, and birds of the air. Sea animals and birds received the same blessing as people: "be fruitful and multiply" (Gen. 1:22). Animals were initially given a vegetarian diet, similar to that of people (Gen. 1:29–30). The important Hebrew term *nefesh chaya* (a "living being" or a "living soul") was applied in Genesis (1:21, 24) to animals as well as people. While the Torah clearly indicates that people are to have "dominion over the fish of the sea, and over the fowl of the air, and over every living thing that creepeth upon the earth" (Gen. 1:28), there is a basic relatedness, and the rights and privileges of animals are not to be neglected nor overlooked. Animals are also God's creatures, who possess sensitivity, and feel pain; hence they must be treated with compassion, justice, and protection.

God even made treaties and covenants with animals just as with humans (Gen. 9:9–10; Hosea 2.20). The Psalmist indicated God's concern for animals, for "His Tender mercies are over all His Creatures" (Ps. 145:9). They pictured God as "satisfying the desire of every living creature" (Ps. 145:16) and "providing food for the beasts and birds" (Ps. 147:9).

Perhaps the Jewish attitude toward animals is summarized by the statement in Proverbs 12:10: "The righteous person regards the life of his beast." This is the human counterpoint of "The Lord is good to all, and His tender

Source: Reprinted with permission from *The Challenge of Shalom: The Jewish Tradition of Peace and Justice*, pp. 132–36, edited by Murray Polner and Naomi Goodman, © 1994 by the Jewish Peace Fellowship.

mercies are over all his creatures" (Ps. 145:9). In Judaism, one who doesn't treat animals with compassion cannot be regarded as a righteous individual.

There are many Biblical laws involving compassion to animals. An ox was not to be muzzled when threshing in a field of corn (Deut. 25:4). A farmer was not to plow with an ox and an ass together so that the weaker animal would not suffer pain in trying to keep up with the stronger one (Deut. 22:10). Animals, as well as people, were to be permitted to rest on the Sabbath day (Exod. 20:8–10; 23:12). Based on the question of the angel of God to Balaam, "Wherefore hast thou smitten thine ass?" (Num. 22:32) the Talmud states that animals are to be treated humanely. Based on Deuteronomy 11:15, "And I will give grass in thy fields for thy cattle, and thou shalt eat and be satisfied," the Talmud teaches that a person should not eat or drink before first providing for his or her animals.

Many great Jewish heroes were chosen because they showed kindness to animals. Moses and King David were deemed worthy to be leaders of the Jewish people because they showed compassion to animals while working as shepherds. Rebecca was judged suitable to be Isaac's wife because of the kindness she showed to the camels of Eleazar, Abraham's servant. Rabbi Judah, a great scholar, was stricken with a toothache for thirteen years because he failed to show compassion to animals. The pain only stopped when he later prevented an act of cruelty to animals.

Given all this, one might wonder why Judaism doesn't advocate vegetarianism. Actually, the first Biblical dietary law was vegetarian.

Judaism and vegetarianism? Can the two be related? After all, what is a *simcha* (Jewish celebration) or holiday dinner without chopped liver, gefilte fish, chicken soup, and roast chicken? And what about those passages in the Torah referring to Temple sacrifices of animals and the consumption of meat?

Yet, a very strong case can be made that the Jewish tradition and Jewish values point to vegetarianism as the most desirable diet.

A case can be made that God's original intention was that people be vegetarian. In Genesis 1:29, God states, "Behold, I have given you every herb yielding seed, which is upon the face of all the earth, and every tree, in which is the fruit of a tree yielding seed—to you it shall be for food."

But in the time of Noah, when people had become depraved and would even eat a limb torn from a living animal, God gave permission to eat meat as a concession to human weakness.

A second vegetarian experiment was attempted when the Israelites left Egypt, when God provided manna for food. However, the people cried out for flesh. The Israelites' dissatisfaction with their simple diet angered Moses and God. Finally, flesh, in the form of quails, was provided. As the people chewed on the quails, a plague broke out and many people died. The place where this occurred is called "the graves of lust," perhaps providing an early warning of the many negative health effects of a non-vegetarian diet.

Later, the Israelites were again permitted to eat meat. Initially this could only be done when the animal was first used as a Temple sacrifice, a concession to the primitive universal practice in Biblical times. Finally, permission was given for the eating of meat without animal sacrifice, but with many restrictions (the dietary laws). Rabbi Abraham Isaac Kook, the first chief-rabbi of pre-state Israel and author of *A Vision of Vegetarianism and Peace*, stated that the many laws related to preparing and eating meat imply a scolding and are designed to keep alive reverence for life and to eventually lead people away from eating animals.

Rabbi Kook and others felt that in the future Messianic age, people would be vegetarians, as they were at the start of human history. They base this on the prophecy of Isaiah: "The wolf shall dwell with the lamb . . . the lion shall eat straw like the ox . . . and none shall hurt or destroy in all of God's holy mountain" (Isaiah 11:6–9).

Even so, while many Jews eat meat today, the diet most consistent with many basic Jewish concepts is vegetarianism. These concepts include the following:

The Jewish attitude toward animals can be summarized in the proverb, "The righteous man considers the life of his animal," the statement in Psalms, "God's tender mercies are over all of his creatures," and the Torah concept of *"Ts'ar Ba'alei Chaim,"* the mandate not to be cruel to any living creature.

Unfortunately, modern factory methods of raising animals are completely contrary to Torah values. Animals are raised in closed, confined spaces, fed a diet saturated with chemical additives, and denied fresh air, sunshine, exercise, or any emotional stimulation.

Judaism stresses preservation of health and life. This is so important that if it might save a life, a Jew *must* (not *may*) violate Jewish law such as those related to observing the Sabbath, eating Kosher foods, and fasting on Yom Kippur. Jews are to show greater care about dangers to health and life than about ritual matters.

Recent studies have documented many negative health effects relating to eating meat. A well-chosen vegetarian diet can sharply reduce the risk of heart attack, stroke, and several forms of cancer, which account for over half of the annual deaths in the United States.

Helping hungry people is a fundamental concept in Judaism. At the Passover Seder, Jews recite: "Let all who are hungry come and eat." *Ma'ot Chittim* is collected before the holiday so that poor people will be able to purchase matzos and other necessities. On Yom Kippur the words of Isaiah are read, indicating that one of the purposes of fasting is to sensitize us so that we will "share our bread with the hungry." In Biblical times the gleanings of harvests and the corners of the fields were to be left for needy people. The Talmud states that "aiding the poor and hungry weigh as heavily as all the other commandments of the Torah combined."

The earth belongs to God, but people are to be His co-workers in helping to preserve and protect the environment. Many laws in the Torah and Talmud stress the need to reduce pollution and avoid destruction of the earth.

Modern agricultural methods related to meat production are a prime cause of current environmental crises. The production and use of tremendous amounts of pesticides and chemical fertilizers to grow grain to feed animals causes extensive air and water pollution. Overgrazing has caused widespread erosion in many parts of the world. Mountains of manure produced by cattle raised in feedlots wash into and badly pollute lakes, rivers and streams.

Consistent with the concept that "the earth is the Lord's," the sages of the Talmud extended a commandment in Deuteronomy not to destroy fruit-bearing trees during a siege of a city to a prohibition of the waste or destruction of anything of value: "Whoever breaks vessels, or tears garments, or destroys a building, clogs a fountain or wastes food, violates the prohibition of *bal tashchit* (thou shalt not destroy)."

Meat-centered diets are extremely wasteful of grain, land, energy, water, and other resources. It requires about twenty pounds of grain protein to produce a pound of edible beef protein in a feedlot. Meat-centered diets require about eight times as much water and energy and up to seventeen times as much land as vegetarian diets.

Today, although enough food is grown to feed every person an adequate diet, 15 to 20 million people die annually due to hunger and its effects. Millions more, especially children, suffer from physical and mental retardation due to inadequate nourishment. Yet, 80 percent of grains grown in the U.S. and other wealthy countries are fed to animals destined for slaughter. In many poor countries, land which could grow nutritious crops for local inhabitants is used to raise cattle for export to wealthier countries.

In view of these important Jewish mandates to show kindness to animals, take care of one's health and life, feed the hungry, protect the environment, and conserve resources, and the negative effects flesh-centered diets have in each of these areas, many vegetarians wonder why Jews who take Jewish tradition and values seriously do not become vegetarians.

A switch to vegetarian diets would provide much help to a troubled world. It would free much agricultural land for nutritious crops at a time when there is so much hunger. Demand for scarce resources such as water, energy, and pesticides would be greatly reduced. There would be a great reduction in land, air, and water pollution. Medical expenses would be sharply reduced, freeing funds for other basic human needs. There would be a major decrease in cruelty to animals, which would perhaps lead to greater understanding and kindness among people, and hopefully a more peaceful world. An incidental advantage would be a revitalization of Judaism, since it would be applying its principles to help alleviate the world's problems.

The spirit of many Jewish vegetarians is summed up in the words of Nobel Prize winning author Isaac Bashevis Singer: "The longer I am a vegetarian the more I feel how wrong it is to kill animals and eat them. I think that eating meat or fish is a denial of all ideals, even of all religions. How can we pray to God for mercy, if we ourselves have no mercy? . . . As long as people will shed the blood of innocent creatures there can be no peace, no liberty, no harmony between people. Slaughter and justice can not dwell together."

1983 and 1985

Ahimsa

Arundhati Roy

While the rest of us are mesmerized by talk of war and terrorism and wars against terror, in the state of Madhya Pradesh in central India, a little liferaft has set sail into the wind. On a pavement in Bhopal, in an area called Tin Shed, a small group of people has embarked on a journey of faith and hope. There's nothing new in what they're doing. What's new is the climate in which they're doing it.

Today is the twenty-ninth day of the indefinite hunger strike by four activists of the Narmada Bachao Andolan (NBA), the Save the Narmada Movement.[1] They have fasted two days longer than Gandhi did on any of his fasts during the freedom struggle. Their demands are more modest than his ever were. They are protesting against the Madhya Pradesh government's forcible eviction of more than one thousand Adivasi (indigenous) families to make way for the Maan Dam. All they're asking is that the government of Madhya Pradesh implement its own policy of providing land to those being displaced by the Maan Dam.

There's no controversy here. The dam has been built. The displaced people must be resettled before the reservoir fills up in the monsoon and submerges their villages. The four activists on fast are Vinod Patwa, who was one of the one hundred and fourteen thousand people displaced in 1990 by the Bargi Dam (which now, twelve years later, irrigates less land than it submerged); Mangat Verma, who will be displaced by the Maheshwar Dam if it is ever completed; Chittaroopa Palit, who has worked with the NBA for almost fifteen years; and twenty-two-year-old Ram Kunwar, the youngest and frailest of the activists. Hers is the first village that will be submerged when the waters rise in the Maan reservoir. In the weeks since she began her fast, Ram Kunwar has lost twenty pounds—almost one-fourth of her original body weight.

Unlike the other large dams such as the Sardar Sarovar, Maheshwar, and Indira Sagar, where the resettlement of hundreds of thousands of displaced people is simply not possible (except on paper, in court documents), in the

Source: Copyright 2003 by Arundhati Roy. From Arundhati Roy, *War Talk* (Cambridge: South End Press, 2003), pp. 9–15. Used with permission. To request permission to reprint, please contact: arnove@igc.org.

case of Maan the total number of displaced people is about six thousand. People have even identified land that is available and could be bought and allotted to them by the government. And yet the government refuses.

Instead it's busy distributing paltry cash compensation, which is illegal and violates its own policy. It says quite openly that if it were to give in to the demands of the Maan "oustees" (that is, if it implemented its own policy), it would set a precedent for the hundreds of thousands of people, most of them Dalits (untouchables) and Adivasis, who are slated to be submerged (without rehabilitation) by the twenty-nine other big dams planned in the Narmada valley. And the state government's commitment to these projects remains absolute, regardless of the social and environmental costs.

As Vinod, Mangat, Chittaroopa, and Ram Kunwar gradually weaken, as their systems close down and the risk of irreversible organ failure and sudden death sets in, no government official has bothered to even pay them a visit.

Let me tell you a secret—it's not all unwavering resolve and steely determination on the burning pavement under the pitiless sun at Tin Shed. The jokes about slimming and weight loss are becoming a little poignant now. There are tears of anger and frustration. There is trepidation and real fear. But underneath all that, there's pure grit.

What will happen to them? Will they just go down in the ledgers as "the price of progress"? That phrase cleverly frames the whole argument as one between those who are pro-development versus those who are anti-development—and suggests the inevitability of the choice you have to make: pro-development, what else? It slyly suggests that movements like the NBA are antiquated and absurdly anti-electricity or anti-irrigation. This of course is nonsense.

The NBA believes that Big Dams are obsolete. It believes there are more democratic, more local, more economically viable and environmentally sustainable ways of generating electricity and managing water systems. It is demanding *more* modernity, not less. It is demanding *more* democracy, not less. And look at what's happening instead.

Even at the height of the war rhetoric, even as India and Pakistan threatened each other with nuclear annihilation, the question of reneging on the Indus Waters Treaty between the two countries did not arise.[2] Yet in Madhya Pradesh, the police and administration entered Adivasi villages with bulldozers. They sealed hand pumps, demolished school buildings, and clear-felled trees in order to force people from their homes. They *sealed* hand pumps. And so, the indefinite hunger strike.

Any government's condemnation of terrorism is only credible if it shows itself to be responsive to persistent, reasonable, closely argued, nonviolent dissent. And yet, what's happening is just the opposite. The world over, nonviolent resistance movements are being crushed and broken. If we do not respect and honor them, by default we privilege those who turn to violent means.

Across the world, when governments and the media lavish all their time, attention, funds, research, space, sophistication, and seriousness on war talk and terrorism, then the message that goes out is disturbing and dangerous: If you seek to air and redress a public grievance, violence is more effective than nonviolence. Unfortunately, if peaceful change is not given a chance, then violent change becomes inevitable. That violence will be (and already is) random, ugly, and unpredictable. What's happening in Kashmir, the northeastern states of India, and Andhra Pradesh is all part of this process.

Right now the NBA is not just fighting big dams. It's fighting for the survival of India's greatest gift to the world: nonviolent resistance. You could call it the Ahimsa Bachao Andolan (ahimsa means "nonviolent resistance"), or the Save Nonviolence Movement.

Over the years our government has shown nothing but contempt for the people of the Narmada valley. Contempt for their argument. Contempt for their movement.

In the twenty-first century the connection between religious fundamentalism, nuclear nationalism, and the pauperization of whole populations because of corporate globalization is becoming impossible to ignore. While the Madhya Pradesh government has categorically said it has no land for the rehabilitation of displaced people, reports say that it is preparing the ground (pardon the pun) to make huge tracts of land available for corporate agriculture. This in turn will set off another cycle of displacement and impoverishment.

Can we prevail on Digvijay Singh—the secular, "green" chief minister of Madhya Pradesh—to substitute some of his public relations with a *real* change in policy? If he did, he would go down in history as a man of vision and true political courage.

If the Congress Party wishes to be taken seriously as an alternative to the destructive right-wing religious fundamentalists who have brought us to the threshold of ruin, it will have to do more than condemn communalism and participate in empty nationalist rhetoric. It will have to do some real work and some real listening to the people it claims to represent.

As for the rest of us, concerned citizens, peace activists, and the like— it's not enough to sing songs about giving peace a chance. Doing everything we can to support movements like the Narmada Bachao Andolan is *how* we give peace a chance. *This* is the real war against terror.

Go to Bhopal. Just ask for Tin Shed.[3]

Notes

[1] The government of India plans to build thirty large, 135 medium, and 3,000 small dams on the Narmada to generate electricity, displacing 400,000 people in the process. For more information, see http://www.narmada.org.

[2] See http://www.jang.com.pk/thenews/spedition/pak-india/accord.htm.

[3] The activists ended their fast on June 18, 2002 after an independent committee was set up to look into the issue of resettlement. For more information, see http://www.narmada.org/nba-press-releases;jun-2002/ fast.ends.html.

The Indian Way

Richard Deats

When cowboys in the old West caught a wild horse, they saw it as a creature whose spirit had to be broken before it could be useful as a cow pony. An untamed horse was wily and dangerous, not to be approached by anyone but the traditional bronco buster. The method of breaking a wild horse was to tie him down in the chute of the corral so that a saddle could be put on. Then the bronco buster climbed on the pony's back and the chute gate opened. Released from his ropes, the shocked creature would take off into the corral, bucking furiously, his rider cheered on by a whooping crowd of onlookers. Sometimes the cowboy was able to stay on for only a few seconds before being thrown. But the process was repeated again and again until, finally, the horse no longer bucked. When the animal's spirit had been broken, it was ready to take its place among the other cow ponies on the ranch.

The Indian way of dealing with wild horses could not be in greater contrast. Native Americans saw the horse not as a wild beast to be subdued, but as a fellow creature and kindred spirit, worthy of respect and consideration. Instead of a hard-riding bronco buster, a gentle brave was given the task of making friends with the pony. Every day, he would bring food and water and spend time talking to the animal. In time, the pony became accustomed to visits from a two-legged creature and allowed the Indian to touch and stroke its body. As the horse learned to recognize the smell, movements and voice of a particular human being, its fear dissipated until, one day, the brave would know that he could put an arm around the pony's neck. Later, he would put one leg over his back. When the Indian finally slid his body onto the pony, without bit or saddle, training period was over. There was no bucking, ever. Horse and rider moved out of the corral as friends.

Source: *Fellowship* (March/April 1977). Reprinted with permission of The Fellowship of Reconciliation.

Nonviolence and Animal Rights

Gary L. Francione

... [A]ll sentient beings should have one right: the right not to be treated as our property—the right not to be valued exclusively as means to human ends. ... We all say that we take animal interests seriously, but in reality, our society treats animals in much the same way that it treats any other form of property. If, however, we did accord animals this one right not to be treated as property, we would be committed to abolishing and not merely regulating animal exploitation because our uses of animals for food, experiments, product testing, entertainment, and clothing all assume that animals are nothing but property. If we accepted that animals have the right not to be treated as our property, we would stop—completely—bringing domestic animals into existence.

... To bring about animal rights, it is essential to understand the basic legal and philosophical arguments for abolition. Logically, it is not possible to reform the system that exploits animals; we must abolish the exploitation. The abolitionist position is that the institution of animal property is morally unjustifiable, just as was the institution of human property that we called slavery.

Some who promote welfare reform maintain that it is acceptable for humans to use animals if they do so "humanely." Others seek welfare reforms because they believe reforms will eventually lead to abolition. I argue against these notions for two reasons.

First, as a theoretical matter, reform misses the primary moral point. It is, of course, always better to cause less suffering than more, but the real question is whether humans are justified in imposing any suffering at all on animals incidental to our use of animals as property. The nineteenth century reformers argued that it was better for a slave's owner to beat his slave four times a week rather than five. The abolitionists argued that all human beings had at least the right not to be the property of another; that to be property meant that a human had no value except that accorded the slave by the owner.

Source: Interview with Professor Gary L. Francione by Lee Hall, originally published in ActionLine, quarterly publication of Friends of Animals, Summer 2002. Used with permission.

The abolitionist position was that it was wrong to beat the slaves at all because the institution of slavery itself was morally unjustifiable and it did not matter how "humane" we made slavery. Putting a string quartet on the way to the gas chambers—as the Nazis did during the Holocaust—may make things more "humane" in some sense, but that misses the point, doesn't it?

If animals are morally significant at all, then we must abolish the institution of animal property. We must stop creating and owning domestic animals or using wild animals as means to our ends. My view is that we should abolish animal slavery and not seek to reform an inherently immoral institution.

The second reason for my rejection of welfarism is that, as a practical matter, it does not work. We have had animal welfare laws in most Western countries for well over a hundred years now, and they have done little to reduce animal suffering and they certainly have not resulted in the gradual abolition of any practices. . . .

As to why welfarism fails, this was the subject of my 1996 book, *Rain Without Thunder: The Ideology of the Animal Rights Movement*. In a nutshell, the reason has to do with the property status of animals. If animals are property, then they have no value beyond that which is accorded to them by their owners. Reform does not work because it seeks to force owners to value their property differently and to incur costs in order to respect animals' interests. Our legal and political systems are based on strong concepts of property rights. Thus, there is reluctance to impose the costs of reforms on owners when such costs will significantly decrease the value of animal property as far as the owner is concerned.

. . . I suggest that we need a new theory to replace the one that we have. I am not unrealistic. I recognize that even if we adopt an abolitionist theory, abolition will not occur immediately. Change will necessarily be incremental. But it is my view that the explicit goal must be abolition and that abolition must shape incremental change.

On the other hand, I can tell you what really is not realistic, and that is to expect that the industries who use animals to obtain profits will be able to police themselves. As I have often noted, "humane slaughter" laws are difficult to enforce, and the economic realities of the meat-packing business militate against conscientious self-enforcement of such standards. Moreover, such laws arguably increase overall suffering, because they make the general public feel better about eating meat or about any other regulated use of animals. This is the Catch-22 of animal welfare.

There will always be welfarists who promote longer chains for the slaves and call that incremental change. In *Rain Without Thunder*, I argued that the most important form of incremental change is educating the public about the need for abolition. We have not yet had that, for the U.S. movement has always been embarrassed about being "radical." We do not want to alienate the "mainstream." The problem is that the "mainstream" is polluted and we ought to stay far away from the "mainstream."

To those who claim that the abolitionist has no practical campaign to pursue right now, I have long argued that the contrary is true. Consider what would happen if the international animal movement had a sustained and unified campaign promoting a purely vegetarian diet. Imagine what could be done if a significant portion of our resources were channeled into making people aware of why they shouldn't eat animal products at all. At the end of five years, we would certainly not have achieved world veganism, but we'd probably have reduced the consumption of animal products considerably more than we have done with these "eat red veal" campaigns. . . .

When will we begin? I understand, of course, that many people in leadership positions aren't vegan. Therefore they find it difficult to embrace animal rights as a movement in which a vegetable-based diet is an axiom. Veganism, however, is the single most important issue in the movement. Veganism is the abolitionist principle implemented in one's own life. Anyone who maintains that she or he is an "animal rights" advocate but is not vegan cannot be taken seriously.

. . . Many advocates do claim that it is "elitist" to maintain that there are moral baselines, such as veganism. But that is like saying that it is "elitist" to say feminists must reject rape. It is simply inconsistent to maintain that you accept an animal rights position but continue to consume animals. Many advocates seem to think that veganism is optional and that it is only the "vegan police" who insist on veganism. That is no different from saying, in the context of advocacy for children's rights, that those who condemn all pedophilia are "pedophilia police." If a children's rights advocate is not a member of the "pedophilia police," she isn't an advocate for children's rights.

. . . Animal welfare—both as a moral theory and as a legal principle—requires in part that we balance human interests against nonhuman interests to determine whether a particular animal use or treatment is "necessary." If the human interest outweighs the nonhuman interest, the use or treatment is considered "necessary" and morally or legally justifiable. If the animal interest outweighs the human interest, then the use is considered "unnecessary" and morally and legally unjustifiable.

As my 1995 book *Animals, Property, and the Law* explains, the problem is that because animals are property, what we really balance is the interest of property owners against their property. And that is absurd. It makes no sense to talk about the interests of property which has only the value accorded to it by its owner. That is precisely why the laws that purported to regulate race-based slavery in the U.S. completely failed to protect the interests of slaves. It was simply not possible to balance the interests of a slave against those of a slave owner. The slave was a piece of property, a thing that was owned. As a matter of logic, we cannot balance nonhuman interests against ours, any more than we can balance our interests against those of our cars or wristwatches.

. . . Nonhumans will continue to be exploited until there is a revolution of the human spirit, and that will not happen without visionaries trying to change the paradigm that has become accustomed to and tolerant of patriarchal violence. . . .

Inasmuch as I maintain the necessity of revolution, let me make clear what I mean. I am absolutely and unequivocally opposed to any sort of violence directed toward humans or nonhuman. I am firmly committed to the principle of nonviolence. The revolution I seek is one from the heart: I try to get people—especially other men—to question and reject violence. I am interested in overthrowing patriarchy and the idea that some beings—whether white, rich males or white males or humans generally—have greater worth than other beings.

. . . There are at least two serious problems with the ape personhood campaign. First, the campaign reinforces the notion that some animals are better than others because they are more "like us." That is, instead of having humans at the top and all nonhuman on the bottom, we "allow" a few animals that are "like us" to come on over to "our" side. That leaves the vast majority of the "other" animals still on the bottom and without even a hope of moving "up" because they lack human-like characteristics that make "special" those animals given admission into the preferred category. In other words, the campaign for ape personhood threatens to substitute one hierarchy for another, and I am concerned that we eradicate the notion of hierarchy altogether.

Second, the "ape personhood" campaign is not only theoretically unsound, but has terrible practical consequences for animals. There is now an entire cottage industry of cognitive ethologists, inspired by Jane Goodall, who are urging that we must do more experiments in order to show how "like us" various apes are. I recently attended a conference at which various researchers were talking about the various experiments that they are presently doing and that should be done in the future to determine exactly how much "like us" apes are. How much more "research" will be necessary? How "like us" do these animals have to be before they get "promoted" in this hierarchy? I think that the "ape personhood" campaign has more to do with generating grants for researchers and certain "apes rights" lawyers than it has to do with animal liberation. Instead of insisting on liberation of animals from human constructs, a great deal of attention has focused on the idea, for example, of Koko the gorilla giving live chats on America Online. There is unprecedented interest in people who discuss intergenerational studies of language or some other form of cognition. Enough is enough. The focus ought to be a respect for their home environments, not circus-like parading of apes who have been carefully trained to act the way humans do. Does the fact that this is done under a scientific gloss make this any less of a circus? Does the fact that this is done in a courtroom by a bunch of lawyers make it any less of a circus? These antics show a lack of sensitivity about the past four decades of grotesque mistreatment endured by apes in human-created settings. We already know that the other apes have complex lives and share a notably similar genetic build. So why do we keep imposing human communication tests, self-recognition tests, and numerous human social interactions on them?

. . . We find animal advocates singing the praises of mathematically gifted parrots, perceptive rescue dogs, and other animals with impressive talents—particularly those whose intelligence can somehow be put to our use. . . . If we are serious about animal rights, we have a responsibility to stop bringing [seeing-eye dogs and other animals] into existence for our purposes. We would stop bringing all domestic animals into existence for human purposes.

. . . Many of us live with dogs, cats, or other animals and regard them as family members. Yet we stick dinner forks into other animals who are no different from the ones we consider family members. This is odd behavior when you think about it. And on the broader social level, nearly everyone would agree that it is immoral to impose unnecessary suffering on animals—which, by any definition of the term, means that it can't be right to impose suffering on them for human amusement, pleasure, or convenience. After all, a rule that says it is wrong to impose suffering on animals unless we find it pleasurable and amusing would sound silly. And yet, 99.9 percent of our use of other animals cannot be justified by any reason other than human amusement and convenience. It is 2002. No one maintains that we need to eat meat to lead an optimally healthy lifestyle. Indeed, an increasing number of health care professionals warn that eating meat and dairy is detrimental to human health. And animal agriculture is an ecological disaster. It takes between six and 12 pounds of plant protein to produce one pound of animal protein and it takes about 100 times more water to produce a pound of flesh than a pound of wheat. Our best justification for eating meat is that it tastes good. Our best justification for rodeos, circuses, zoos, hunting, and so forth is entertainment. In short, Western culture claims to take animal interests seriously, and we all claim to eschew unnecessary suffering; yet we impose suffering and death on animals in situations that cannot be described as involving necessity of any sort. That is what I call "moral schizophrenia."

When I first got into this, I believed that we should pursue improvements in the animals' living conditions. I thought that the emphasis on their conditions would lead to the abolition of the use industries. Over the years it has become entirely clear to me that animal welfare leads us only to more animal welfare. If we were protesting the establishment of a concentration camp, would it be appropriate to ask for improvements to the camp? No, because at some level one is undoubtedly conveying the message that the camp is okay. The only appropriate thing to do in this circumstance is to get rid of the camp, because the idea of the camp is the fundamental problem. The issue is not how it goes about its business, but its very existence. . . .

1. The animal rights position maintains that all sentient beings, humans or nonhuman, have one right: the basic right not to be treated as the property of others.
2. Our recognition of the one basic right means that we must abolish, and not merely regulate, institutionalized animal exploitation—because it assumes that animals are the property of humans.

3. Just as we reject racism, sexism, ageism, and homophobia, we reject speciesism. The species of a sentient being is no more reason to deny the protection of this basic right than race, sex, age, or sexual orientation is a reason to deny membership in the human moral community to other humans.

4. We recognize that we will not abolish overnight the property status of nonhumans, but we will support only those campaigns and positions that explicitly promote the abolitionist agenda. We will not support positions that call for supposedly "improved" regulation of animal exploitation. We reject any campaign that promotes sexism, racism, homophobia or other forms of discrimination against humans.

5. We recognize that the most important step that any of us can take toward abolition is to adopt the vegan lifestyle and to educate others about veganism. Veganism is the principle of abolition applied to one's personal life and the consumption of any meat, fowl, fish, or dairy product, or the wearing or use of animal products, is inconsistent with the abolitionist perspective.

6. We recognize the principle of nonviolence as the guiding principle of the animal rights movement.

PART SIX

EXAMPLES OF NONVIOLENCE

Preview

Just as those who are skeptical about whether nonviolence works often fail to see it working every day in their personal lives, nearly all of us fail to see important ways in which nonviolence has found expression (sometimes successfully, sometimes unsuccessfully, at least as measured by the attainment of its practical objectives) in the lives of other peoples and groups. The following selections highlight some of those ways.

The first selection shows the power of nonviolence embodied in an extraordinary individual, a towering, educated man born into wealth during British colonial rule of what was to become India and Pakistan. Abdul Ghaffar Khan (1889–1988), known by the honorific title "Badshah," meaning king of the khans, was a follower and close associate of Gandhi. A Moslem, he saw nonviolence flowing consistently from the basic teaching of Islam and brought that teaching to the fiercely warlike Pathan tribes of his homeland, the region of the Khyber Pass in what is now Pakistan. He there organized a "nonviolent army" of as many as 100,000 men seeking an end to British rule. For this he became known as the Frontier Gandhi. This end was achieved, even though the government of the emergent predominantly Moslem country of Pakistan subsequently repressed him and his movement. Upon his death in 1988 he was awarded India's highest civilian honor, the Jewel of India. His biographer, Eknath Easwaran, writes:

> Like Gandhi in Hinduism, like Martin Luther King, Jr., in Christianity, Badshah Khan and his "Servants of God" demonstrated conclusively that nonviolence—love in action—is deeply consonant with a vigorous, resurgent Islam. Khan's simplicity, deep faith, and selfless service represent the Islamic tradition at its purest and most enduring. (Easwaran, 1984: 188)

The next two selections focus on the Philippines. The first concerns the widely publicized revolution in the Philippines in which the dictatorial Marcos regime was overthrown in a basically nonviolent revolution led by Corazón Aquino, a woman with no previous experience in government, but a calm and radiant inner strength that inspired thousands. The second article, based upon an anthropologist's findings, reports on the institutionalized nonviolence of a primitive people on a Philippine Island—an account that at least casts doubt on the conventional wisdom that people are by nature violent and that it is naive to suppose that we can do away with violence without changing human nature. Whether the Buid remain nonviolent, and whether the Philippines remains faithful to its initial guiding values, is not the issue; the fact remains that in the first example nonviolence succeeded in achieving a major social and political objective, and in the second case nonviolence informed the social life of an entire people.

The next three selections highlight the role that nonviolence played in resisting or overcoming particularly repressive or brutal regimes, in one case the white South African apartheid government, in another the Nazis, and in the third case the Soviet Union. So often one hears it said that nonviolence might have worked for Gandhi against the British, but it would never have worked against the Nazis. As Ernst Schwarcz shows, it was used with some success against the Nazis in more than one instance. In recent years more research has expanded recognition of many more relatively successful instances of the use of nonviolence against the Nazis. Similarly, even the Soviet Union and South Africa were at a loss to know how to respond effectively against nonviolent opposition. As we saw in the previous section, the same bases of power underlie all governments, namely, the cooperation and acquiescence of those they control, and we see in these three selections the results in two historical contexts when a portion of that support is removed.

The next article focuses on Cesar Chavez (1927–1993), who began as a farm worker and eventually became a labor organizer. He was a five-foot-six Mexican American with little formal education, born in Arizona. His mother was a major influence in his life, and he is quoted as saying that "she *lived* her nonviolence. She prepared the way" (Hope and Young, 1979: 151). Committed to seeing that nonviolent action focus always on practical results, Chavez brought nonviolence to his tireless organizing leadership roles in promoting the cause of farm workers. "Our goal," he said, "is a national union of the poor dedicated to world peace and to serving the needs of all men who suffer."

The essays in the last section focus on the Middle East, on past use of nonviolence against Israel, and upon proposed nonviolent approaches to bringing healing to the existing conflict between Israel and the Palestinians.

In the first of these selections, R. Scott Kennedy, a founder of the Resource Center for Nonviolence in Santa Cruz, California, who visits the Middle East frequently and has written extensively about it, depicts the little-known story of the nonviolent resistance of the Druze of the Golan Heights against Israeli occupation and annexation. An Arab people adhering to an esoteric offshoot of Islam, the Druze have sought to maintain their identity as a people in the face of Israeli policies that they see as both dividing them from other Arabs and legitimizing Israeli control of the Golan Heights. Unlike the Palestinian Arabs in diaspora who seek a return to what they consider their homeland, and unlike those Palestinians of the occupied West Bank and Gaza who want independence, the Druze of the Golan think of themselves as Syrians and want a restoration of their status as such.

The next four selections consider Jewish and Arab views on the conflict between Israelis and Palestinians in the Middle East. Allan Solomonow, one of the most eloquent advocates of reconciliation in the Middle East, discusses Judaism's values of truth, justice, and peace as they apply to that region's problems. Mubarak Awad is a Palestinian and founder of the Palestine Center for the Study of Nonviolence, which he directed until his deportation by the Israeli government. He now directs the Washington, D.C.-based Nonviolence International. In this article he makes a case for the practicality of nonviolence as a means of promoting the Palestinian cause. Though an avowed pacifist himself (by which we take him to mean what we call a nonviolentist), the case he makes here does not preclude the use of violence by Palestinians at some time in the future, an aspect of his position that has been sharply attacked by his critics. In the next selection, Gila Svirsky, an Israeli co-founder of Women for Peace and former executive director of Bat Shalom (a Palestinian-Israeli women's peace organization), speaks to the effectiveness of the ongoing nonviolent activities in Israel that are so under-reported by the press. The final article is by Lucy Nusseibeh, a Palestinian woman who is founder and director of Middle East Nonviolence and Democracy. Nusseibeh also speaks of the ongoing and under-reported nonviolent activities of Palestinian women and of the hope and empowerment that such activities provide for Palestinians.

Those who believe in the use of violence as the ultimate means by which to attain objectives never conclude that, because violence took twelve long years to bring down the Third Reich, it is inefficient or does not work. By the same token, nonviolentists should not conclude that, because nonviolence has sometimes been inefficient or fallen short of immediate goals, it therefore does not work. Even though violence sometimes achieves certain tangible objectives, evidence also suggests that at deeper levels violence may not be effective. Nonviolence, on the other hand, fails sometimes to achieve immediate, tangible objectives, but here evidence also suggests that at deeper levels nonviolence may indeed be effective.

At the very least, the question remains open, and even where nonviolence was not undertaken as part of a planned commitment to nonviolence, as in some of the examples in this section, it represents a continuation of what Gandhi called an "experiment with truth": a continual putting to the test through social action of a way of getting along that all of us have seen work in various ways in our personal lives.

References

Easwaran, Eknath. 1984. *A Man to Match His Mountains: Bhadsha Khan, Nonviolent Soldier of Islam.* Petaluma, CA: Nilgiri Press.

Hope, Marjorie, and James Young. 1979. *The Struggle for Humanity: Agents of Nonviolent Change in a Violent World.* Maryknoll, NY: Orbis Books.

NONVIOLENCE IN ASIA

Nonviolent Soldier of Islam

Timothy Flinders/Eknath Easwaran

The Good Fight—
Badshah Khan, the Frontier Gandhi[*]

Nonviolent Muslims. Nonviolent Muslim *Pathans* in an "army of God" sworn to lay down their lives in the cause of freedom, without fighting back.

One could be forgiven a stir of doubt, some puzzlement.

Yet when Mahatma Gandhi first heard of the nonviolent resistance of Khan's Pathan tribesmen during the Salt Satyagraha of 1930, though he may well have been surprised, even awed, he would not have been puzzled. No doubt Pathans seemed to the rest of India like a kind of eastern Mafiosi—ruthless, clannish, vengeful, without scruple. But to Gandhi, who understood better than anyone else the inner dynamics of satyagraha, Khan's "miracle" was entirely consonant with his idea of nonviolence. In fact, Gandhi had been looking for a decade for the Pathans—or someone like them—in order to make a point.

Gandhi's search went back to the Kaira struggle of 1918, during which he had led Indian peasants in a nonviolent revolt against unfair taxes. The Kaira peasants won the struggle, but in the process they unmasked a truth about their nonviolence which Gandhi found disturbing. They had taken to nonviolence,

*Source: Timothy Flinders in an Afterword to *Nonviolent Soldier of Islam* by Eknath Easwaran, founder of the Blue Mountain Center of Meditation, copyright 1999; reprinted by permission of Nilgiri Press, P.O. Box 256, Tomales, CA, www.nilgiri.org.

they admitted, only because they lacked the courage to fight with violence. "With me alone and a few other co-workers," Gandhi reported, "[nonviolence] came out of our strength and was described as Satyagraha, but with the majority [of resisters] it was purely and simply passive resistance, which they resorted to because they were too weak to undertake the methods of violence."

This was not Gandhi's idea of nonviolence. True nonviolence did not issue from weakness but from strength. It was a matter of the powerful voluntarily withholding their power in a conflict, choosing to suffer for the sake of a principle rather than inflict suffering—even though they could. Gandhi called this the "nonviolence of the strong," as opposed to the "nonviolence of the weak" that he had found in his Kaira peasants. "My creed for nonviolence is an extremely active force," he insisted. "It has no room for cowardice or even weakness."

After much thought about the implications of the peasants' admission, Gandhi stunned his colleagues by starting a recruiting campaign in Kaira to raise an army of Indians to fight for the Empire in the First World War. If Indians were afraid of violence, he argued, then they should first learn to fight *so that they could renounce fighting.* "I do not infer from this that India must fight," he explained. "But I do say that India must know how to fight." To perplexed colleagues who thought he had lost his way, Gandhi gave a simple explanation: "A nation that is unfit to fight cannot from experience prove the virtue of not fighting." True satyagraha required fighters, fearless, impassioned, and dogged. If he could not find natural fighters, he decided, he would create them, even if it meant sending them to war.

Gandhi's recruitment campaign of 1918 proved a failure. The majority of Indians were not prepared to take up arms. "But do you know that not one man has yet objected [to recruitment] because he would not kill?" Gandhi wrote a colleague. "They object because they fear to die. The unnatural fear of death is ruining the nation."

When the war ended, so did his recruiting campaign. But Gandhi never stopped looking for those born fighters who would prove to the world that nonviolence was especially meant for the strong. "There is hope for a violent man to be some day nonviolent," he insisted, "but there is none for a coward."

In 1930 Gandhi heard about the heroics of Khan's Khudai Khidmatgars, and he must have known that he had found what he was looking for. Pathans *knew how to fight.* They were an unlikely lot, to be sure. But the Hindus' image of the menacing Pathans was incomplete: they were vengeful and they could be ruthless, but they were not without scruple. Honor was everything. They were capable of self-discipline and temperate in their habits. Raised with a Spartan abandon for comfort, they lived with a deep-running faith in God and legendary contempt for fear and cowardice: "The coward dies," we read, "but his shrieks live on. So [the Pathan boy] learns not to shriek." Gandhi could not have invented a people better fitted to his radical notion.

But he did not have to invent them. More than that, he did not even need to transform them: Khan had done it for him. Badshah Khan's genius, as

Easwaran has pointed out, was to sense the underlying nobility of the Pathan temperament—with its profound and compelling passion—and to tap it for a high purpose. "Being fighters," Khan explains, "they had learnt discipline already." All that he had to do was to give it "a nonviolent turn." And to everyone's amazement—except Gandhi's—it worked: Khan's Pathans became, we read, "the bravest and most enduring of India's [nonviolent] soldiers."

Even Khan was baffled at the extent of his success. "I started teaching the Pathans nonviolence only a short time ago," he told Gandhi once. "Yet, in comparison, the Pathans seem to have learned this lesson and grasped the idea of nonviolence much quicker and much better than the [Hindu] Indians. . . . How do you explain that?"

Gandhi, almost laconic in his self-assurance, told the Pathan leader: "Nonviolence is not for cowards. It is for the brave, the courageous. And the Pathans are more brave and courageous than the Hindus. That is the reason why the Pathans were able to remain nonviolent."

Thus the unique place of Khan's Khudai Khidmatgars in the history of nonviolence. They proved Gandhi's claim that nonviolence is meant for the strong—no insignificant matter in today's world, where violence is seen almost as a natural response to conflict and nonviolence is dismissed as a refuge of those who are too weak or too fearful to fight with guns.

But Gandhian nonviolence has another side to it: a side more personal than political, which aims at transformation. We can call this "transformative" nonviolence, to distinguish it from the more overt political forms. Here nonviolence is used as a tool to reform and regenerate human personality. The story of Khan's movement among the Pathans demonstrates the power of nonviolence to harness the negative forces in personality and use those same forces to transform an individual, a community, or even a society. Transformative nonviolence could find a special place in the regeneration of our own post-industrial democracies, wherever political tyranny has been replaced by subtler forms of oppression: meaninglessness, alienation, pervasive dissatisfaction, ennui.

Like Gandhi, Khan was essentially a reformer. He first seized upon nonviolence not as a political weapon—he was forced into politics by British suppression, he claimed—but as an antidote to the violence which had long paralyzed his vigorous but indiscriminate people. His first concern was not British repression, but the Pathan cult of violence and revenge. Khan found that Gandhi's nonviolence had the power to recast the Pathan temperament into a potent, positive force without diminishing its vigor.

"To me nonviolence has come to represent a panacea for all the evils that surround my people," Khan said. "Therefore I am devoting all my energies toward the establishment of a society that would be based on its principles of truth and peace." In his "Servants of God" Khan released a powerful, socially benign force equal but opposite to destructive forces embedded in the Pathan temperament and culture. In doing so, he was following almost to the letter the powerful dynamics of transformative nonviolence that Gandhi had discovered twenty-five years earlier in South Africa.

Dissatisfied with the hopeless inadequacy of the phrase "passive resistance" to describe the innate *power* of nonviolence, Gandhi coined his own term in 1906: *satyagraha. Satya* means truth in Sanskrit, and *agraha* comes from the Sanskrit root meaning "to hold on to," which Gandhi used as a synonym for "force." Thus *satyagraha* carries a double meaning: it signifies a determined holding on to, a *grappling* with truth; while at the same time it implies the force that arises from that grappling, what Gandhi called "soul-force." *Satyagraha* stands for both the means and the ends, the struggle and the force that is generated in that struggle.

As heat is generated by friction, Gandhi contended, power is released from within the depths of the human spirit in its struggle toward truth. The raw material for this power is passion. "I have learned through bitter experience," Gandhi explained, "the one supreme lesson to conserve my anger, and as heat conserved is transmuted into energy, even so our anger controlled can be transmuted into a power which can move the world." In this "truth-struggling" nothing is lost or repressed: energy is conserved and transmuted. Thus in its transformative aspect nonviolence is not *non*violence at all, but violence transmuted, harnessed, *used*. We could more properly call it *trans*violence, where the power of passions like anger, hatred, and fear is reshaped into a potent fighting force.

With his truculent, explosive Pathans, Khan had an abundance of raw material to work with. Because of their powerful tendencies toward violence, they had great potential for nonviolence. Their grappling toward nonviolent truths sometimes provoked excruciating suffering, and required a demanding physical and emotional about-face. A Khudai Khidmatgar who took Khan's oath renounced not just violence but the code of revenge itself, *badal*, the cornerstone of his value system and the cult of the heroic Pathan. "To bear this *zulum* [tyranny] without retaliation is hard indeed," we read one villager telling Verrier Elwin at the height of the British repression in 1932.

"But do you still believe in nonviolence?"

"With all our hearts."

Because of their demanding inner struggle, Pathans under Khan's leadership were able to invoke resources of courage and will that far exceeded their known limits, and came into possession of that inner-strength—"soul-force"—which Gandhi claimed we all possess but do not know about. It is a power released from within the depths of the human spirit. Gandhi called it the strength of God.

When he visited the Frontier in 1938, Gandhi made clear the profoundly spiritual nature of transformative nonviolence. "To realize nonviolence means to feel within you its strength—soul-force—to know God." At Utmanzai he told Khan's red-shirted officers, "If the Khudai Khidmatgars really felt within themselves an upsurge of soul-force as a sequel to their renouncing arms, they would have the strength of God behind them." Call it what you will, there is no denying the display of this power in the lives of both Gandhi and Badshah Khan, or in the collective force of Khan's Khudai Khidmatgars.

It is a tribute to the Pathans' capacity for faith, as much as to their bravery, that they could so genuinely accept such a foreign code of conduct and use it to work the reversals of thinking and action we read of here. Their transformations were not always complete or permanent, as in the case of the outlaw Murtaza Khan, but they were often profound, and even in Murtaza Khan's example they left permanent marks.

The full effect of Khan's movement on the progress of his people can never be measured. What remains unmistakable in the story of the Khudai Khidmatgars is that nonviolence, properly undertaken, recasts and empowers the human personality. Very little is known about this kind of transformation. While some attention has been given by scholars to nonviolence as a political weapon, virtually nothing exists in the literature regarding the effects of nonviolence upon those who practice it. Since we are dealing with such intangibles as "soul-force," faith, and "conscious suffering"—difficult qualities to quantify and observe—these dimensions of nonviolence may well lie outside the scope of traditional scholarship.

And perhaps this is as it should be. For in the last analysis, such nonviolence—this "truth-grappling"—is a private affair carried out mostly within the human mind and heart. To move it into a wider sphere of acceptance, what is needed is not study so much as committed individuals ready to undertake its disciplines.

The lack of work on this subject does not mean that we must proceed alone or unguided. There was Gandhi, after all, and now there is Badshah Khan to throw some light across the path. It is especially fitting in this regard that Khan's story is being presented to western audiences by Eknath Easwaran, for his primary interest in both Khan and Gandhi has been their personal transformations from flawed human personalities to permanent forces for good. This is not the place to enter into detail about the exact nature of the disciplines that nonviolence requires; Easwaran has done this exhaustively in other books. But to those who would follow in Khan's footsteps, the extraordinary story of his courage and doggedness in his fight against tyranny leaves no illusions about what is required. Nonviolence, whether political, social, or personal, is a battle, an unflagging engagement of the will against tyranny using the weapons of fearlessness, love, and faith. As Khan told his Khudai Khidmatgars, "You have to be against all tyrants, whoever they may be; whether individuals or nations . . . you will oppose them"—even, we can assume, if the tyranny is found to be those turbulent forces of the soul which tyrannize from within the recesses of one's own heart.

Those who would take up this call step into the stream of an ancient tradition of fighters that includes the Buddha and Jesus, continues through St. Francis, and is passed on today, among others, by Gandhi, Martin Luther King, Jr., Mother Teresa, and Badshah Khan. The fight, as Khan says, "is always noble," and those who make the attempt to enter its "holy edifice" will find their powers on the rise. The world needs such men and women. May they flourish—or as Badshah Khan himself might say to them, *Tre mash*: may they never grow tired.

Khan in Action[†]

. . . September of 1929 brought cooling winds to the Peshawar valley. Khan felt ready to do battle again—not with the British yet, but with his Pathans. He felt a great moment approaching and he was determined that his people would be fit for it.

At a boisterous gathering in Utmanzai one afternoon, Khan stood up and unveiled his feelings. He began by outlining the petty vices that had crippled his people. These hardy Pathans, whom no one could beat in an open, fair fight, were helpless before the clever British, he declared. And they had no one to blame but themselves.

"There are two ways to national progress," he told them:

> One is the path of religion, and the other is the road of patriotism. . . . You have all heard of America and Europe. The people in those countries may not be very religious, but they have a sense of patriotism, love for their nation, and social consciousness.
>
> And look at the progress that has been made there. Then take a look at ourselves! We have hardly learned to stand on our own feet yet. Look at their standard of living and then take a look at ours.

Thousands of proud Pathan eyes looked around—at the tattered rags, the hide-bare burros and thin goats browsing the stubble, the gaunt faces. . . .

> If we are on the road to ruin, it is because we have neither the true spirit of religion, nor the true spirit of patriotism nor love for our nation. . . . A great revolution is coming and you haven't even heard about it!
>
> During my recent visit to the subcontinent, I noticed that men and women were fully prepared to serve the nation. And here? Leave alone your women, even your men do not show any desire to serve. They hardly seem to understand the meaning of the word "nation"!

Khan looked around, his dark eyes blazing. The edge in his voice had brought the milling mass to silence. Bearded, turbaned heads did not move. Two goats scuffled behind the raised platform but no one noticed. Khan continued to hammer:

> A revolution is like a flood! A nation can prosper by it, and it can perish by it as well. A nation that is wide awake, that cultivates brotherhood and national spirit, is sure to benefit through revolution. If the people are vigilant they will be ready for the flood. When it comes the whole nation will move along with it.
>
> But if the people are asleep! If they are indifferent to each other and indifferent to the country, the whole nation will be swept away by the flood when the revolution comes.

†Source: From *Nonviolent Soldier of Islam*, pp. 108–13, by Eknath Easwaran, founder of the Blue Mountain Center of Meditation, copyright 1999; reprinted by permission of Nilgiri Press, P.O. Box 256, Tomales, CA 94971, www.nilgiri.org.

Khan paused again and took a deep breath. "O Pathans!" he thundered:

> Take a look at the developed countries of the world. Do you think their prosperity has just dropped from the sky? It has not, no more than our prosperity will drop from heaven!
>
> The secret of their prosperity is that they have men and women who sacrifice their luxuries, their pleasures, and their comfort for the sake of the prosperity of the nation.
>
> We do not have such men among us. We look only to our self-interest and let the country go to the devil! In other countries, people have learnt that no man is an island. But in our country everyone lives in a dream world of his own—like the animals. Any animal can find a place to live, find a mate, rear its young. Can we call ourselves the crown of creation if we do just that and nothing more?

Rarely had a Pathan spoken to fellow Pathans with words so plainspoken:

> Please remember this. If the nation prospers it will affect everyone. Every man, woman, and child will benefit. Do not think that by acquiring riches for yourselves your country will become prosperous. It will not. If you want your country and your people to prosper you must stop living for yourselves alone. You must start living for the community. That is the only way to prosperity and progress.

He had finished. Pathan vows filled the air, invoking the name of Allah and men spoke with steel in their voices. The badshah's words had cut their Pathan pride like a razor-sharp *tulwar*, but they were not bitter. They knew that the *tulwar* had been hurled from love—to rescue the honor of their nation.

For one young Pathan, Khan's words cut deep enough to keep him awake the whole night. The badshah had spoken nothing but the hard truth. Much had been promised by the gathering; a thousand oaths had been sworn. But was that enough? The flood was already near.

The next morning, before the muezzin *had called out the time for morning prayer, this young man was banging on the gate of Khan's courtyard, rattling a dozen chickens out of their roosts. He poured out his heart. Something had to be done. What about an organization, he argued, one whose members would swear on Allah's name to give their lives for their country? Not the Youth League—that was for organizers and social workers. What the country needed was men ready to die for it. It needed . . . soldiers!*

Khan liked the fire in this Pathan's voice. "Sit down. Let's talk."

Tea was brought, salted and hot, with a platter of fresh nan. *The sun was still below the horizon.*

Soldiers! Khan liked the idea. Plenty of Pathans were fighters, but those who actually went to join an army fought only for the Raj. Perhaps they did need soldiers—but certainly not more violence.

An idea slipped out, as formless at first as the faint shadows of the courtyard around them in the early rays of dawn. An army of nonviolent soldiers, drilled and disciplined, with officers, cadres, uniforms, a flag—perhaps even a drum and bagpipe corps like the Guides! And pledged to fight: not with guns but with their lives.

As far as Khan knew it had never been done. An army of trained professional nonviolent soldiers was something new.

The young man looked at the badshah. But Pathans? An army of unarmed *Pathans?*

"Who else?" Khan shot back. Who else but a Pathan would be reckless enough to try it? What could possibly take more bravado than facing an enemy in a righteous cause without weapons, neither retreating nor retaliating? It was the loftiest kind of honor.

Khan called for more tea. True, he admitted, Pathans would see it as a disfigurement of badal—*at first. The code of revenge seemed in their blood from birth. But then, hadn't Gandhi been talking for a decade about the "nonviolence of the strong"? He had argued that it was meant especially for the undaunted, for those who were not afraid to fight whatever the cost. A nation that was unfit to fight, he had said, could not prove the virtue of not fighting. Well, Pathans were far ahead there! All they needed was the understanding. If he could persuade half a dozen to try it. . . .*

They called themselves the Khudai Khidmatgars, "the Servants of God." Their motto was freedom, their aim, service. Since God himself needed no service, they would serve his people.

The Khudai Khidmatgars, under the leadership of Abdul Ghaffar Khan, became history's first professional nonviolent army—and its most improbable. Any Pathan could join, provided he took the army's oath:

> I am a Khudai Khidmatgar, and as God needs no service, but serving his creation is serving him, I promise to serve humanity in the name of God.
>
> I promise to refrain from violence and from taking revenge. I promise to forgive those who oppress me or treat me with cruelty.
>
> I promise to refrain from taking part in feuds and quarrels and from creating enmity.
>
> I promise to treat every Pathan as my brother and friend.
>
> I promise to refrain from antisocial customs and practices.
>
> I promise to live a simple life, to practice virtue and to refrain from evil.
>
> I promise to practice good manners and good behavior and not to lead a life of idleness. I promise to devote at least two hours a day to social work.

For a Pathan, an oath is not a small matter. He does not enter into a vow easily because once given, a Pathan's word cannot be broken. Even his enemy can count on him to keep his word at the risk of his own life. Nonviolence was the heart of the oath and of the organization. It was directed not only against the violence of British rule but against the pervasive violence of Pathan life. With it they could win their freedom and much more: prosperity, dignity, self-respect.

Khan drew his first recruits from the young men who had graduated from his schools. They flocked to him. Trained and uniformed, they snapped in behind their officers and filed out into the villages to seek recruits.

They began by wearing a simple white overshirt, but the white was soon dirtied. A couple of men had their shirts dyed at the local tannery, and the brick-red color proved a breakthrough. It did not dirty easily, the dye was cheap, and—best of luck—it had style. Villagers dropped their plows to see who these glowing figures were.

Recruits did not come easily, but Khan and his eager young volunteers persisted. Within a few months they had five hundred recruits—not enough for a Raj-shattering holy war, but a beginning. Volunteers who took the oath formed platoons with commanding officers and learned basic army discipline—everything that did not require the use of arms. They had drills, badges, a tricolor flag, the entire military hierarchy of rank—and a bagpipe corps.

Khan set up a network of committees called *jirgahs*, named and modeled after the traditional tribal councils that had maintained Pathan law for centuries. Villages were grouped into larger groups, responsible to district-wide committees. The Provincial Jirga was the ultimate authority. Since all the committees were filled by elected officers, the Provincial Jirga became a kind of unofficial parliament of Pathans.

Officers in the ranks were not elected, since Khan wanted to avoid infighting. He appointed a *salar-e-azam* or commander-in-chief, who in turn appointed officers to serve under him. The army was completely voluntary; even the officers gave their services free. Women were recruited too, and played an important role in the struggles to come.

Volunteers went to the villages and opened schools, helped on work projects, and maintained order at public gatherings. From time to time they drilled in work camps and took long military-style marches into the hills. As they marched, they sang.

> We are the army of God,
> By death or wealth unmoved.
> We march, our leader and we,
> Ready to die.
>
> We serve and we love
> Our people and our cause.
> Freedom is our goal,
> Our lives the price we pay.

Watching the narrow columns threading a curving mountain pass, one could easily imagine that some angry mullah was unleashing another holy war against the foreigners. But these Pathans, who for years had carried rifles and tucked small armories of revolvers and knives inside their waistbands, now carried only a stick for walking. They armed themselves only with their discipline, their faith, and their native mettle.

The Philippines
The Nonviolent Revolution That Surprised the World

Richard Deats

In mid-1985, when most interpreters of the Philippine situation were say-ing that the struggle against the Marcos dictatorship has passed the point of no return and was moving toward an inevitably violent showdown, Filipino Bishop Francisco Claver wrote:

> We choose nonviolence not merely as a strategy for the attaining of the ends of justice, casting it aside if it does not work. We choose it as an end in itself, or, more correctly, as part of the larger end of which justice itself is subordinate and prerequisite. We choose it because we believe it is the way Christ himself struggled for justice. In short, we equate it with the very Gospel of Christ. (*Fellowship*, June 1985)

While many, secular and religious alike, dismissed such sentiments as not only irrelevant but standing in the way of the coming revolution, only eight months later the mighty power of Marcos had collapsed before Filipino masses, armed only with their faith and their determination to be free.

One year after the "people power" revolution that swept Cory Aquino into the presidency, many still fail to grasp what was at the heart of those stunning events. For some, who believe that power grows out of the barrel of a gun, the defecting Philippine military under Enrile and Ramos was the key factor. Others, students of American imperialism, are convinced that the whole scenario—from the calling of the snap election by Marcos through the election and the revolt—was a plot carried out by the United States and its minions (even though the U.S. supported Marcos almost to the very end). Still others, proponents of the ideological analysis of the New People's Army, maintain that the February events (even though boycotted by the far left at the time) were the outcome of the many years of struggle by the masses against the Marcos dictatorship.

Source: *Fellowship*, Vol. 53, No. 3 (March 1987). Reprinted by permission of the Fellowship of Reconciliation.

Certainly each of these interpretations contains some element of truth. The defection of the Philippine military, behind the scenes efforts by the United States, and the cumulative effect of years of struggle against Marcos all played a part in his downfall. Great historical events are usually a combination of a whole series of factors. But what is missing from such interpretations is the recognition of the unique convergence of religious faith and active nonviolence. In the tumultuous election, during which over 100 persons were killed by armed goons of the Marcos forces, this nonviolent faith was at work, as unarmed Filipinos went to amazing lengths to insure a fair and free election. It was seen in Corazon Aquino's campaign and her tireless call for nonviolent resistance to the dictatorship. It was expressed by the Catholic bishops' pastoral letter urging "the way of nonviolent struggle for justice . . . [of] active resistance of evil by peaceful means—in the manner of Christ." It was prepared for in the numerous seminars in active nonviolence held in 1984 and 1985 with key leaders and grassroots activists. When it appeared that Marcos was determined to steal the election despite Cory Aquino's mandate, she brought together 250 people from various groups in a post-election strategy session, out of which came a seven point program of nonviolent action called the "People's Victory Campaign." The culmination of these manifestations of "people power" was seen in the millions of Filipinos who risked everything to bring about a "revolution of love" at a place, appropriately named, *Epifanio de los Santos* Avenue, the Avenue of the Epiphany of Saints.

This faith-based nonviolence is very different from nonviolence used only as a tactic, to be set aside in favor of "any means necessary" should it seem to fail. Filipino "people power" (*lakas ng bayan* in Tagalog) was an audacious expression of faith rarely seen on such a scale, and people power cannot be understood without reference to the faith that produced it.

Cory Aquino's insistence on nonviolence was authentically rooted in faith that had been tragically tested in her husband's martyrdom. In trying to decide whether or not to accept the growing insistence of the people that she run for the presidency against Marcos—by any rational calculations a Quixotic venture at best—Cory Aquino went to a convent of contemplative nuns for a full day of prayerful discernment. Afterward, she said, "When I was praying there, I asked the Lord to forgive Marcos, to forgive General Ver, so that I could forgive them, too. I asked only for forgiveness." Out of that act of forgiveness and the clarity it produced, she decided she would indeed run, saying simply, "The people will believe me . . . I am a victim; we are victims of this regime. We have suffered a lot. I can say I am with them in their sufferings. My sincerity will be real and will make people free from fear."

And free they were, as they rose up as never before, determined to be rid of their oppressor. Neither the clever plans of Marcos for subverting the election nor his ruthless armed forces proved capable of turning them back. The pillars of his support began to crumble, hastened by the defection of Defense Minister Enrile and Gen. Ramos. When this happened, Cardinal Jaime Sin made a nationwide broadcast calling on the people to place their unarmed bodies between the small band of defectors and the armed forces of the Philippines. But first he went to four orders of contemplative nuns: the Poor Clares, the Carmelites, the Sisters of the Holy Spirit, and the Pink Spirits. "Prostrate yourselves," he told them. "Pray and fast. The nation is in battle and you are the powerhouse of God."

It was not only the contemplatives who prayed. The faith of a people was aroused. All over the islands, as people gathered around their transistor radios and listened to the breathtaking events unfolding on the outskirts of Manila, many of them prayed for the deliverance of their nation from tyranny. Nuns, priests, pastors and lay people poured into the critical streets of their capital, following the incessant, detailed instructions from Radio Veritas. Fervent singing and praying arose from the crowd. The enemy soldiers were met with gifts and were addressed in a friendly manner. They were given food in a kind of spontaneous sacrament of the barricades. Nuns told them, "Pray with us. If you cannot say it aloud, you can do it through your heart and mind."

When air force planes appeared, people prayed for courage. As a column of tanks approached Channel 9, a girl brought a tiny statue of Mary and placed it in the road; two boys put their bikes next to it. An old woman sat in the road praying and the people began to sing "Ave Maria." When low-flying helicopters came over with guns pointed at the crowd, the people stood their ground and just sang louder. Throughout the crowds, all around the vital crossroads, masses were said and prayer meetings were held.

Soldiers loyal to Marcos were deeply affected by this unprecedented expression of courageous, nonviolent faith. Many remarked that for the first time they felt goodwill, rather than fear and disgust, from the people. In increasing numbers they defected, risking certain court-martial if Marcos prevailed. In the end, of course, he did not, and his regime toppled like a house of cards. Cory's nonviolent post-election strategy was projected for lasting months into the future, but the actual overthrow took only seventy-seven hours. (In fact, as AKKAPKA's Tess Ramiro said to me, "If it hadn't succeeded so quickly, we would have had more time to broaden and deepen the base of Cory's support and hence strengthen the potential of the new government.") Later, reflecting on what had happened, Fr. Jose Blanco, the Jesuit priest who heads AKKAPKA, the movement for peace and nonviolence, wrote this:

> People power is grounded and based on God's saving activity within us as a people. In the dictum of Augustine: God created us without us, but God will not save us without us. Our political liberation has been our work and struggle and sacrifice—but equally and internally it has been the work of God.
>
> Because we interpret the events in the light of faith and acknowledge God's saving activity in all that has happened, we must ask what God wants to communicate to us by his saving activity and presence. What does God wish us to proclaim to the world through our nonviolent revo-

lution? Simply this: the political problems of people can be solved without recourse to arms or violence.

The world's problems are best solved if we respect the humanity, the dignity of every human person concerned. The desire to be violent or to use violence can be tamed and diminished, if we show love, care, joy to those who are unjust. . . . Nonviolence searches out and addresses the humanity in the enemy or oppressor. When that common humanity is touched, then the other is helped to recognize the human person within and ceases to be inhuman, unjust and violent.

One does not have to be a Christian to reach out to the humanity in the other. Christian or not, believer or unbeliever, every single human being has been created as an image of God. To recognize that image and to respect it in an absolute way is to live the Gospel radically and in the nonviolent way.

The February revolution, for all its dramatic significance, was, of course, only the first giant step of the Filipinos out of bondage. The dictatorship was overthrown. Feudalism and imperialism were not. The Marcos era left a nation prostrate and bankrupt, with monumental problems, foremost being the concentration of wealth and land in the hands of a few powerful families; an enormous debt; widespread poverty and disease; and the efforts by the United States to exercise economic and military control over the islands for its own ends. The repeated upheavals of the first year are not surprising: desperate conditions foster an explosive situation. When thousands of farmers and activists demanding land reform marched on the presidential palace in late January 1987, the military panicked and opened fire, killing eighteen and wounding many. A grieving President Aquino, angered at the military's violation of her policy of reconciliation, immediately set up an inquiry. A few days later, when 15,000 demonstrators came again to protest their plight and the blatant slaughter of the previous march, Aquino ordered the barricades removed and told the police to step aside. Rejecting the military's advice, members of her Cabinet met with the surprised marchers, while nuns with rosaries prayed along the side of the route. The marchers were invited to send a delegation to meet with the president and set forth their grievances. Step by step, it seems, the people power revolution—led by a woman who is the opposite of macho politicians like Thatcher and Reagan—is demonstrating to the world something with enormous potential.

A month after the February revolution, the Philippine newsmagazine *Veritas* observed "Vestiges of the past regime remain, monstrous structures of injustice and oppression difficult to dismantle . . . we are called to continue working together to rebuild our country. Our vigilance cannot falter, lest the imperfect freedom we have won be stolen from us again. Liberation is a never-ending process on earth. But as our people grow in faith and political maturity there will be brighter Easters for those who continue to face the struggle."

In people power, the Filipinos have regained a deep sense of their own God-given dignity and potential, and a way of hope for the future. United and determined, armed with the power of truth and love, they can press on to continue their revolution to bring freedom, justice and peace to the land. If they are to have a fair chance in this effort, Americans must work to build a foreign policy that respects the sovereignty of the Philippines and allows the Filipinos to work out their own destiny in their own way.

Looked at in terms of historical significance, the people power revolution of the Philippines—regardless of what happens in the future—is of profound importance for humanity's ongoing struggle to find a way other than lethal violence for ending oppression and building what Martin Luther King, Jr. called "the beloved community." The increasingly destructive power of just wars and just revolutions have brought us to the brink of omnicide. Our global interconnectedness means that there is no longer any localized armed conflict; there is an ever present danger of such conflicts not only spreading to neighboring countries, but drawing in the superpowers as well, as we see in Central America, the Middle East and South Africa today. No one, no matter how young or old, is safe from the scourge of modern warfare. Even the earth, indeed all life, is threatened.

But there is another way! Ever so slowly we are learning to choose life, to discover means commensurate with our noble goals and our deepest professions of faith in the sacredness of life. In the Philippines, a bold "experiment with Truth" has provided new insights into the meaning of liberation struggle. The Filipinos stand alongside Gandhi's freedom struggle in India, the civil rights movement in the U.S., Solidarity in Poland and the growing worldwide nonviolent movement that seeks to live out the divine destiny to which we have been called, finding a way forward in history where justice, peace and freedom are inseparable.

Jungle Nonviolence

Stephen Braun

When Thomas Gibson first met members of a little-known tribe living deep in the steaming Philippine jungle, it was a case of mutual apprehension.

At 23 and fresh out of the London School of Economics where he studied anthropology, Gibson was nervous. He didn't know the group's language, this was his first experience with field work, and he couldn't be sure that this group's reputation for nonviolence was true.

He later learned that the members of the Buid (pronounced BOO-id) society he had come across were pretty nervous themselves. They considered people with pink skin to be cannibals and were afraid Thomas had culinary designs on their children.

It took many months, but gradually the fears on both sides waned and Thomas, now an assistant professor of anthropology at the University [of Rochester], was able to carry out the first close study of the Buid social, spiritual, and cultural systems. Despite personal hardships such as cases of malaria and dysentery, he ended up spending two years living with the Buid, from July 1979 to September 1981. He wrote a book about the experience and is continuing his research on the aspect of the Buid that had attracted him in the first place: their nonviolence.

In the Philippine Islands (and most of the rest of the world), the majority of the native peoples use violence to some extent, and in some, notably the headhunting tribes of the northern island of Luzon, violence plays a central role in the culture.

But the Buid are different. Faced with an aggressor, an individual Buid will run away if at all possible—and that is usually possible in the dense jungle forest. The Buid consider this honorable behavior, and Gibson says they have a variety of words to describe different types of retreat.

Within the Buid community, violent acts are not valued or rewarded. Buid individuals, like all humans, are capable of violence, but if a member does resort to violence, he is viewed as abnormal.

"They see violence as a form of insanity," Gibson says, "and they attribute it to being bitten by a kind of violent spirit."

Source: University of Rochester *Research Review*. Summer 1987.

Confrontation in Buid culture is avoided whenever possible. When two Buid speak, they often do so sitting with backs turned to each other and they try to avoid all eye contact. More often, Buid talk in groups, and, in such cases, the members generally sit facing the same direction—not each other. Disputes between members of a group are usually settled by a general meeting called a *tultulan*, in which both sides are heard and agreements are reached by consensus. In addition, the Buid do not feel compelled to argue or discuss an issue if they don't feel like it.

"It's not a culture in which questions have to be answered," Gibson says. "If they don't like a question or don't want to answer, they'll just ignore you. This makes confrontation and disagreement harder."

The question, of course, is why the Buid place such emphasis on nonviolence and how that value developed in their culture. After years of first-hand study and more years of thought and research on the matter, Gibson has some tentative answers, and they shed light on human behavior in general.

To understand the Buid's nonviolence, it's necessary to understand the other aspects of their life.

No one knows how long the Buid have lived on Mindoro, an island roughly the size of Massachusetts. Like other natives of the Philippines, they probably came by boat from mainland Asia thousands of years ago. Some Buid groups retain a form of writing that seems to be derived from South Asia languages, but the Buid do not use the characters for any but the most simple communication.

Buid life has been shaped largely by Mindoro's location midway between the capital city of Manila 150 miles to the north and Borneo to the south. The Islamic peoples of Borneo and the Spanish-occupied government in Manila fought for centuries over control of the islands between their respective centers of power. Mindoro was repeatedly raided for slaves and material, resulting in the depopulation of the coastal region. The Buid and other autonomous societies of the island's interior sought refuge in the interior and it was this, combined with the region's inherent inaccessibility, that has allowed the Buid to remain isolated for so long.

It wasn't until 1848 that the Spanish were able to gain a decisive advantage over their rivals and obtain firm control of Mindoro. Attempts to convert the native people to Christianity were tried many times both before and after the Spanish dominion, but missionaries could establish only a foothold on the island, and then only in the lowlands.

Since the second World War, however, economic pressures and increasing population have driven the Buid farther and farther into the jungle. Much of their former lands have been appropriated by Christian settlements, and much of the island's virgin forest has been razed for lumber and rattan vines. (In fact, the Philippines now has to import rattan—a commodity it formerly had in excess.)

The Buid have not been untouched by these pressures. They are not a so-called Stone Age tribe such as the Tasaday are alleged to have been. Like almost all Southeast Asian tribes, the Buid have used iron tools, primarily machetes and axes, for at least a thousand years, obtaining them by trade with lowland Christians and their predecessors. The Buid are excellent basket weavers and potters, and can build relatively sophisticated thatched-roof houses from bamboo.

They are also adept farmers, practicing a kind of slow-motion nomadic existence based on the "slash and burn" method of agriculture. They will clear a small portion of jungle and burn the vegetation so that the ashes enrich the nutrient-poor soil. They plant many crops simultaneously to prevent erosion and to use the soil most effectively. An elaborate system of crop rotation has been developed involving more than 100 species, including corn, sweet potatoes, beans, and a wide range of tropical fruits and vegetables.

Buid also hunt and fish and thus have a varied and ample diet. Gibson says he's tasted most Buid fare at least once, sampling such delights as green bananas (taste like chalk); fruit-eating bats (sweet); insect-eating bats (bitter); fat white insect grubs roasted over coals (crunchy and juicy); and monkey meat. The fare failed to captivate Gibson, who decided to buy rice from the lowland to supplement his Buid diet.

While Gibson lived with the Buid, he also lived *as* a Buid, dressing in a loin cloth and trying to participate in village life as best he could. He found it extremely difficult to learn the language because he couldn't "pay" anyone (in barter) to help him. The Buid have a very egalitarian society in which sharing of material goods is highly valued. The concept of paying for services rendered is foreign to them.

But Gibson was befriended by two Buid named Agaw and Gaynu, who slowly taught him the language and ways of their people. It took a year before Agaw, the leader of a settlement of approximately 70 Buid, trusted Gibson enough to invite him to eat with his family on a regular basis and to begin telling Gibson details of the Buid's elaborate religious and cultural life. The Buid opened even further to Gibson when he was joined in the jungle by his wife, Ruhi Maker, who, because she is short and relatively dark skinned, was accepted very quickly by the Buid.

Revealed to Gibson was a society with relatively fluid family patterns and a people whose lives are intimately entwined with a world of spirits and supernatural forces.

Buid men and women "marry" and "divorce" quite often. Gibson estimates that the average Buid man or woman will have five partners in his or her lifetime, though people with 10 partners are not uncommon. Indeed, it is the mediation and settlement of claims of splitting couples that occupies most of the village meeting time.

This fluid family structure has the effect of binding the Buid region together through the continuing movement of spouses between houses and settlements. The fragility of the marital bond ensures the primacy of the community as an object of allegiance. (Incest and very close intermarriages are frowned upon.)

Woven into the family structure and all other aspects of Buid life is a belief in a wide range of generally malevolent spirits, witches, and demons. These spirits must be repelled and avoided constantly, using chanting, animal sacrifice, and the help of Buid members called *fanlaian*, who have regular and controlled contact with the spirit world.

With this general picture of the Buid in mind, it is possible to attempt an explanation and understanding of their nonviolent ways.

Gibson attributes much of their nonviolence to negative associations with violence in the past. In light of the constant raids by strong and violent people from other islands, the Buid, Gibson speculates, have learned that avoidance is the key to survival. The avoidance of conflict has thus become synonymous with survival, assuming an appropriately strong value in their society.

The egalitarian nature of Buid society, with its emphasis on sharing and the avoidance of accumulated wealth, also tends to lessen the use of violence.

In trying to place the Buid within the larger context of Southeast Asian societies, Gibson has postulated four patterns of violence and nonviolence among cultures:

1. Societies, like the Buid, who reject violence and domination absolutely, associating them with evil outsiders. These societies exist on relatively small islands or narrow peninsulas, leaving them vulnerable to exploitation or domination.

2. Societies dwelling further inland, less involved with trade and less exposed to exploitation. Violence and competition occur between social groups, as when young men to prove courage, but a larger ethic of cooperation discourages mass violence.

3. Societies on large navigable rivers that allow members to maintain contact with and mobilize for war large numbers of fellow tribesmen. Maritime skills allow them to trade and raid other villages, and success with such violent tactics leads to wealth and prestige.

4. Societies which, like Type 2 societies, dwell inland, but which were less exposed to systematic pressure from state systems and so are relatively immobile and are organized into hereditary strata of aristocrats, commoners, and slaves. Slaves free the aristocrats to conduct long-distance trade, and provide the material for human sacrifice. Trading and violence serve to uphold the existing hierarchy.

Research into nonviolent societies such as the Buid, Gibson says, shows that facile generalizations about "innate" human violence and aggression are false. Gibson says everyone has a capacity for violence, just as they have the capacity to speak English. But to assume that this potential will always be expressed in terms of cultural values is wrong.

But the fact that a jungle society such as the Buid are nonviolent doesn't mean that people are "naturally" that way either. Gibson is careful to point out that the Buid have been influenced by outside forces for centuries and thus don't represent a window into some sort of pristine human nature.

In fact, he says, the Buid have been changing their attitude toward aggression lately in response to the threat posed by encroaching development and lowland missionaries. The Buid culture, like any culture, is not in equilibrium, he says, and is probably different today than it was five years ago when he was living there.

Gibson hopes to return to the Buid within a year or two, both to observe how the culture has responded to change, and to see again the friends he made among members of the tribe.

The Buid have thus far resisted wholesale incorporation into the modern world. They've taken such items as prove useful from technology, but have by and large preserved their semi-nomadic way of life. How much longer they'll be able to resist this—especially with their increasing reliance on cash crops and the outside economy—is uncertain.

"I'd like to see the Buid maintain as much autonomy as possible," Gibson says. "But it may be simply a matter of how much forest is left in which to hide."

NONVIOLENCE IN AFRICA

Nonviolence Plays a Role in Ending Apartheid in South Africa

The Center for the Study of Conflict

At the Center for the Study of Conflict, we study the combination of creative conflict resolution and nonviolence. Last year, using the negotiations in Norway between Israel and the P.L.O. as a model, we explained some of the techniques, dynamics, and power of creative conflict resolution. (The editor of *Foreign Policy* has just asked us to expand the article for his journal.) In this year's newsletter we will explain some of the techniques, dynamics, and power of active nonviolence, using the campaigns against apartheid in South Africa as a model. This nonviolent action was covered minimally by the American press, except for the international sanctions, which, however, proved to have less effect than is generally believed.

Violence also played a part in ending apartheid, 60% of the influence compared with 40% by nonviolence, according to an estimate by Dr. Nathan Shamuyara, the foreign minister of Zimbabwe. Whatever part violence played, it was never as severe as civil war, and the guerilla violence by the ANC was "totally ineffectual," according to David Ottaway, a reporter for the *Washington Post*. In 1985, one of the more violent years, South Africa suffered 136 terror incidents, according to the *Weekly Mail*, and in the worst

Source: *The Third Alternative*, Volume X. The Center for the Study of Conflict, Fall–Winter 1994. Used with permission.

years about 2,500 people were killed, few of whom were white. In 1966, Prime Minister Verwoerd was assassinated, but that did not stop his successors from brutally implementing apartheid.

The tradition of nonviolence in South Africa was strengthened by none other than Mohandas Gandhi. Starting in 1893, he organized civil disobedience and other protests there for twenty years, mainly among Indian immigrants. Some of his relatives are still in South Africa. In 1912, just before he left, blacks founded what became the African National Congress (ANC).

The Afrikaner's National Party gained control of the government in 1948 and imposed apartheid on the country. In 1952, the ANC held rallies and sit-ins against apartheid. The dynamic was to show blacks that there were a sufficient number of them willing to demonstrate. One result of the campaign was the enactment of new suppressive laws, but another result was that the ANC grew from approximately 7,000 to 100,000 members.

This campaign was a *protest*, which is one of the three general types of nonviolent action identified by Gene Sharp. *Noncooperation* and *intervention* are the others. In 1960, protesters demonstrated in Sharpville against the law requiring nonwhites to carry passes. The police killed sixty-seven blacks there, giving the nonviolence the dynamic of showing up the brutality of the government. In the short run, the campaign seemed like a failure. However, it was the first nonviolent action to bring international sanctions, and in the following thirty years, after seventeen *million* arrests for violations of the pass laws, blacks were still defying it. In 1976, in Soweto, police killed about 500 black school children who were peacefully protesting the imposition of the Afrikaans language as a requirement in their schools. Dene Smuts, a South African writer, believes that the shock this massacre gave to the white community may have begun the gradual moral shift that made President F. W. de Klerk's reforms possible. The shift reached the National Party by 1978, for in that year, Mr. de Klerk said, the Party began the self-analysis that led to his reforms.

Protests also occurred in less than massive and often clever ways. Walter Wink, an American theologian, has concluded that nonviolence in South Africa was "probably the largest eruption of diverse nonviolent strategies in a single struggle in human history." Shades of Gandhi. In 1986, protesters against conscription built sand castles in the shape of public buildings while wearing T-shirts protesting the draft. The police forbad the castle building, causing laughter even in Parliament over the ridiculousness of the action by the police. Walter Wink wrote in 1987, "The apartheid regime is, by the stupidity of its overreactions to funeral processions and minor harassments, helping to recreate a nonviolent movement among an oppressed people that had largely dismissed nonviolence as ineffectual." In 1989, many protestors who were detained in prison without trial went on a hunger strike. One dynamic was that they discomforted themselves, absorbing the hatred and surprising their tormentors rather than discomforting *them* by rioting. Another dynamic was that their death by starvation would have created martyrdom and emphasized the government's violation of the fundamental principle of the right to a trial. Some of the prisoners were released. A further result was that the mass use of detention without trial ended, possibly ushering in the final phase of the reversal of apartheid laws. After all, the leaders among the released prisoners could organize again. Another consequence was that, like many protest actions, the hunger strike raised questions about the fairness of apartheid.

Noncooperation took many forms. By 1979 strikes brought recognition of unions and of striking. After being displaced, seven million people squatted for shelter by 1988. Rent boycotts were undertaken by sixty percent of the black-township populations by 1986. Stayaways from school and work were performed by two million people in 1989—more than the number that voted in an election at about the same time. The dynamic was beyond the symbolic protests through nonviolent demonstrations; it was the withholding of goods and services from the white population, not only to register public opinion, as did nonviolent protests. The effect was to show the impossibility of enforcing apartheid.

Nonviolent intervention was exemplified by the international sanctions. These were prompted by the Sharpville massacre of 1960. They finally succeeded after 1985, when the International Monetary Fund and other sources stopped lending money to the South African government. In 1985, the financial sanctions were partly caused by the outrageousness of the South African government's declaration of a state of emergency, outlawing peaceful protests. However, in the main, sanctions did not succeed economically, according to our former intern Charles Green's research (which won the Robert W. Tucker Award at The Johns Hopkins University for the best undergraduate thesis on international relations in 1993). Green showed that the South Africans responded to the denial of goods by smuggling, manufacturing on their own, and improving their economy by selling gold, the price of which had increased. He notes that the sanctions did succeed in politically isolating and embarrassing South Africa.

Nonviolent actions are designed to pressure or convert the supporters of tyranny to change and to use nonviolence against it. In South Africa, white women wearing black sashes over their shoulders picketed Parliament against apartheid laws. In 1989, well-known whites including the mayor of Cape Town helped lead a march of 30,000 people (mostly blacks). Starting in 1984, even President P. W. Botha and later F. W. de Klerk performed civil disobedience by sending negotiators to meet with Nelson Rolililahla Mandela in prison at times when negotiating with the ANC was banned. The dynamic was to draw more and more South African whites into opposition to apartheid, 45% of them as early as 1986. President de Klerk said that 1986 was the year that the National Party decided to eventually incorporate the black majority into the political system. Pressure by whites was not the only reason. International financial sanctions had begun to take hold by then, and the banning of the ANC had been followed by 600 organizations joining together to continue its work, showing the government the futility of the banning. As well, violence against whites had increased.

The nonviolence movement in South Africa created an atmosphere favorable for the remarkable settlement that brought an end to apartheid, according to H. W. van der Merwe, director of the Center for Intergroup Studies in Cape Town. The writer James North noted the extent of this settlement when he said that the nation that "symbolized racial hatred has now become one of the world's greatest hopes for reconciliation." An interracial American couple who donate to the Center for the Study of Conflict has visited South Africa since the election of the Mandela government. They like the atmosphere so much that they are considering moving there if they can find work as physicians. Had more violence occurred, this amicable atmosphere would probably not have developed. One cause of the change in the atmosphere was some white church leaders' admission of the atrocities due to apartheid and the apology by F. W. de Klerk for them. Another cause was the repeated call by Archbishop Desmond Mpilo Tutu for reconciliation. Also, Nelson Mandela invoked Gandhi as his spiritual mentor and invited his jailers to his inauguration in a gesture that could be seen as forgiving the perpetrators of apartheid.

The nonviolent action South Africans used was not just moral suasion or power tactics; it covered all the domains of life. In the spiritual domain, Archbishop Tutu and others based some of the nonviolence on Christianity, the main religion of South African whites. Second, in the moral realm, blacks peacefully entered white beaches, demonstrating the injustice of whites' claiming such public places as exclusive. Intellectually, Nelson Mandela quieted the masses after an assassination because he used Lincolnesque phrases. In the social domain, the black-sashed white women brought whites into the struggle. School children undertook a demonstration at Soweto; all sentient people were emotionally shocked when the police killed 500 of these children. Politically, the campaigns stayed focused on forcing the government to negotiate. In economic terms, the sanctions and rent strikes denied money to the government and to whites in general. Physically, the squatters took spaces to live. And, in the aesthetic domain, songs kept up morale. Nonviolence is amazing, complicated, deep, pervasive, and very powerful.

NONVIOLENCE IN THE WEST

Nonviolent Resistance against the Nazis in Norway and Holland during World War II

Ernst Schwarcz

Opportunity arose in Norway . . . when that country was occupied by the Germans, to help in the victory of nonviolent resistance by concrete examples of patient endurance and of suffering in a forced labor camp. This was in the struggle of the Norwegian teachers against compulsory membership in the Nazi Union of Teachers in Norway. At least 98 per cent of all Norwegian teachers had refused to join the Nazi Union. Several schools were closed by the Quisling authorities; all teachers were threatened with arrest; and 300 teachers were sent to Kirkenes, in the north of Norway, to a forced labor camp. Some of the victims died as a result of the deprivations there, but not one gave in. The teachers appointed in place of those who had been arrested were only superficially trained, and could not fulfill their responsibilities. The government gave in and reinstated all the teachers.

Another example of nonviolent resistance is the struggle of the Church in Norway. After the German invasion of Norway in April, 1940, freedom of religion was assumed as a matter of principle, but only a few months later the

Source: *Paths to Freedom Through Nonviolence* by Ernst Schwarcz (Vienna: Sensen-Verlag, 1959). Reprinted by permission of Sensen-Verlag. Title provided by editor.

Quisling government began to interfere in Church affairs. The prayer for Parliament and the King was cut out of the official Church prayers. But when the clergy read the prayers, they paused for a long time at the appropriate place—and the congregation understood.

In December, 1940, the so-called Oxford Group Movement was banned. This is a movement for moral rearmament, and has no political aims. At the same time, the terrorist tactics of the "Hirden," the Nazi civil war organisation (similar to the S. A.), became unbearable; raids, physical violence and kidnappings in the approved gangster style were the order of the day. The activities of the Supreme Court were suspended simultaneously, and the clergy of the country were told to disregard their duty of silence. The Norwegian bishops then sent a pastoral letter to the congregations of the whole country, in which amongst other things, were these words: "Right, Truth and Goodness are a part of the Divine order, just as the Church sees them made possible in a constitutional state. It is useless to silence the Church here and accuse her of interfering in politics. Luther says 'The Church is not interfering in worldly matters when she warns the authorities to be obedient to God, the highest authority.' If the power of the State fails, and violence, lawlessness and repression of conscience are allowed by the authorities, then it is the task of the Church to be the guardian of conscience. The Bishops of the Church have therefore brought to the attention of members of the government those occurrences and official pronouncements which in the opinion of the Church are contrary to God's law. These occurrences and pronouncements give the impression that a revolution is taking place in the country, rather than an ordinary occupation in which the laws should be punctiliously respected as long as they are not in direct opposition to the occupation. Above us all is the One who has power over our souls. There is a ferment in the conscience of our people, and we regard it as our duty to let the statesmen hear the voice of the Church. . . ."

The authorities tried by every means in their power to prevent the publication and dissemination of the pastoral letter. But for this very reason the letter was read by many more people than usually read an official document. The letter was secretly duplicated, and read from the pulpit in many churches, in spite of the ban, while the spies of the Quisling government sat in the front pews. But no arrest followed since at the time the government wanted to avoid causing too much of a stir in connection with the Church and religion.

In February, 1941, a Nazi inspired Christian Unity Movement was founded. The Norwegian clergy were invited to join this movement, but only 20 out of 1139 complied. These 20 were so boycotted by their congregations that when services were held, their churches were empty except for a few followers of the "Hirden." Many of the clergy were subjected to police interrogations and arrested.

Then an attack on the rights of the church took place in Trondheim, and set the people of Norway in an uproar. On February 1, 1942, the pastor of the Cathedral Church was told to hand over the service, which was fixed for eleven o'clock, to a Nazi pastor. This service was to be broadcast. The Provost of the Cathedral postponed his service until two o'clock in the afternoon. A large number of people assembled, and about 1500 obtained seats. Thousands were still on the way to the church when an order from the Ministry for Church Affairs was received by the Trondheim police shortly before the beginning of the service. The order forbade the public entrance to this afternoon service. The service was held undisturbed, while the crowd in front of the church sang psalms and patriotic songs.

The Minister for Church Affairs had the pastor of Trondheim arrested, and after a preliminary hearing, deprived him of his office. The Bishops of Norway then each wrote identical letters of resignation to the Ministry. They stated that they would carry out their pastoral duties as before, but they could not work with a state which used violence against the Church. At first, only the resignation of Bishop Berggrav of Oslo was acknowledged, and soon afterwards that of Bishop Hille of Hamar. Both had to report twice daily to the police.

On February 5th, the Quisling government promulgated its first law. On February 1st, Quisling received new and wider powers from the occupation authorities, which amounted essentially to a complete "assumption of power." This law had to do with the education of children and young people. It became the focus of the entire nation's fixed resolve to resist Nazification.

On February 14th, the Bishops wrote a protest to the Minister for Church Affairs against the abolition of the right for parents to decide on their children's education. The contents of this protest were made public in most of the churches on February 22nd. Thereupon, the Ministry was so flooded with hundreds of protests from parents that the post boxes in Oslo had to be emptied by a constant procession of trucks.

At the end of February, all the Bishops resigned from office and several pastors were dismissed. Following this, a grand confession of faith was drawn up by two prominent churchmen. This document, called "The Foundation of the Church," was ready on Palm Sunday, and was immediately sent out to the entire country by underground channels. On Easter Sunday, April 5th, the dramatic moment arrived when this document was read from the pulpit after the sermon. The congregations were asked to show their agreement by rising to their feet. Fearlessly and as one man, the bands of the faithful rose in the crowded churches, while only tiny groups of Nazi sympathisers remained seated. At the same moment, the pastors laid down their offices (with the exception of the few who were friendly to the Nazis). The congregations stood by them. Soon after this, Bishop Berggrav was arrested. The laymen and theological students, who were appointed by the government to replace the pastors, were boycotted by the congregations. Not only the churches and schools offered nonviolent resistance to the Quisling government, the young athletes of Norway refused to take part in the sporting events officially organized by the Nazi "Sportfront."

Illegal sports meetings were held in the mountains and woods. On the King's birthday, many Norwegians went about the streets with red carnations in their buttonholes. They were arrested by the thousands, but released again after a short time.

The underground press and the distribution of secret news was wonderfully organized, and brought up-to-the-minute information on the latest events. When ten Norwegians were condemned to death for illegal activities, the English radio relayed the news two hours later. It raised an unheard storm of protest. To meet the sneer of the Germans that all Resistance workers were cowards, four of the men who had been sentenced to death volunteered as a bomb-disposal unit to remove a land mine in a bombed factory. After this, all ten were pardoned.

The Norwegian village of Televag, like the Czechoslovakian village of Lidice, was completely destroyed. In the later stages of the resistance movement, acts of violence were carried out against Gestapo and S. S. leaders who had acted with particular brutality in the persecution of resistance workers. But no German soldier was ever killed purely out of a feeling of hatred. On the contrary, German soldiers sometimes were treated with much friendliness by the Norwegians.

It is true that factories which worked for the German war machine were destroyed by bombing, but only at times when no human lives would be endangered. The greater part of the struggle was carried out by nonviolent means.

This spiritual resistance created an intolerable situation for the Germans, which tanks and canons could not help to solve. The decisive victory over the Germans was, of course, fought out on other fronts of war.

In another country, Holland, which also was occupied by the German army, doctors and artists called into being a resistance movement in which the majority of Dutch artists and medical men took an active part. Before everything else, the doctors refused to give up those patients who were being sought by the Germans. Protests were made and strikes took place in opposition to unjust laws which violated human rights. The doctors' resistance against German domination was based principally on the medical oath to preserve human life.

Encouraged by the example of the doctors and artists, resistance movements sprang up in other professions, among railway men for instance. The general strike of all railway workers practically paralyzed traffic between November, 1944, and the liberation of the country in May, 1945. Only a bare minimum of communications could be maintained by German personnel. In spite of the severe famine which ensued, the Dutch people supported the strike and held out all winter without heating and with dwindling supplies of food.

Lithuania's Nonviolent Struggle

Richard L. Deats

The astounding events of last August [1991] in the Soviet Union brought about the decisive defeat of hard-line communist, KGB and military elements that were determined to reverse that country's turn from totalitarianism to democracy. While the aftermath of the failed coup will continue far into the future, with many difficulties and dangers lying ahead, the extraordinary response of the people dramatically showed how deep the changes there have been. A once passive, subjugated people took charge of their own destiny and faced down tanks and armed troops, agents of the KGB and the brazen leaders of the coup. And they did it nonviolently, averting a bloodbath and revealing in the process the enormous power that resides in an unarmed but courageous people.

What transpired was the fruit of the past six years of the dismantling of totalitarianism through glasnost and perestroika. The ground for it was prepared by the emerging global consciousness working for democracy through nonviolent witness and struggle. Through the worldwide mass media, these struggles have leaped across boundaries and entered forbidden zones of silence.

Slowly but surely, this people power revolution has been building in the USSR. We can find it in virtually all of the fifteen republics. In this article, I will focus on only one of these republics, Lithuania, because of FOR's work there, and because Lithuania has been in the forefront of the struggle. [Editor's note: FOR is the Fellowship of Reconciliation.]

Following the lead of the "people power" revolutions of 1989 that swept out totalitarian governments across Eastern Europe, Lithuania began pursuing remarkable nonviolent policies, hoping to bring about a peaceful transition into a new, democratic future.

While there had long been talk, however muted, of independence in all of the fifteen republics in the USSR, the three Baltic republics—Lithuania, Estonia and Latvia (annexed by Stalin following the 1939 pact with Nazi Germany)—had the clearest case for independence of any, a fact that was even recognized by the Supreme Soviet, the national parliament of the USSR. Since 1989, each

Source: *Fellowship* (Oct./Nov. 1991). Reprinted with permission of The Fellowship of Reconciliation.

of the Baltic states took bold steps toward independence, resulting in a long drawn-out struggle with Moscow. Lithuania took the boldest steps, and the ensuing struggle there was the greatest, despite many similarities in the three states. Given the widely recognized illegality of the Stalin-Hitler pact, Lithuania declared that it was simply no longer willing to abide by Moscow's decisions.

Lithuania's "singing revolution" in the late 1980s began with a recovery of the long-suppressed sense of nationhood and the joyous restoration of the Lithuanian language, songs and traditions that had all been severely curtailed by Stalin's policy of Russification. Lithuania's red, green and yellow flag once again was raised throughout the country. A national government was elected that proclaimed the independence of Lithuania on March 11, 1990. Moscow retaliated with a blockade in April 1990 that embargoed 80 percent of Lithuania's natural gas and stopped many products from entering, such as tires, sugar and wood. Then on January 13, 1991, the Red Army moved in with tanks and troops and seized the national television tower in the capital of Vilnius. Facing unarmed demonstrators who had surrounded the tower and refused to leave, the troops took control, killing fourteen unarmed civilians.

Instead of surrendering or responding with a call to arms, the Lithuanian government called on people to "hold to principles of nonviolent insubordinate resistance and political and social noncooperation." In the ensuing months there was a standoff between the central government in Moscow and its troops and the government and people of Lithuania. Despite repeated provocations, including the killing of seven guards on the Lithuanian/ Byelorussian border last July 31, the Lithuanians have generally maintained an explicit policy of nonviolent resistance. In response to the August coup attempt, Lithuanian President Landsbergis urged the people to avoid actions that might provoke Soviet military units and to be "attentive and benevolent" toward Soviet soldiers and officers. He even urged people to provide shelter in their homes, if necessary, to military families being "terrorized" by reactionary "fanatics and secret services."

The Soviet army, like the Yugoslav army (or any other armed group for that matter), has been trained to deal with armed opponents. But a united, defiant and unarmed people—as the Philippines' Marcos and East Germany's Hoenecker discovered—are much more difficult to defeat. Building on this growing recognition of people power, the Lithuanian Ministry of Foreign Affairs has sought to develop a coherent and winning nonviolent strategy. Audrius Butkevicius, a physician who is now director general of the Department of National Defense, has consulted with counterparts in Austria, Sweden and Norway, nations that have incorporated aspects of nonviolence into their defense policies. Specialists in active nonviolence were invited to Lithuania to meet with governmental, academic and religious representatives (see the July 1991 Fellowship for the account of FOR's delegation of eight nonviolence teachers and trainers who went to Lithuania). Nonviolence materials have been translated into Lithuanian and a Center for Nonviolence is being established.

This has taken place under very difficult circumstances. Lithuania's great power, like Poland's under Solidarity, has been in the nonviolent, united will of its people. Its task, like that faced by Solidarity in the early 1980s, was to build a nonviolent strategy resting upon a broadly based people's movement. Lithuania needed to free itself from the internal evils (passivity that stifles initiative and violence that begets violence) and external evils (an occupying army and terrorism). From almost total isolation as one of the hardest republics to enter without a visa, it has emerged to build links with the nonviolent, human rights and religious communities in other countries and within the USSR.

At the heavily barricaded national parliament building in Vilnius, our FOR trainers met in May with the staff and commanders of the uniformed militia, or Volunteers as they are called. The Volunteers are typically thirty to thirty-five years old, married, college graduates who have been involved in the liberation struggle. Some of them are former athletes who are in a new situation where the government no longer financially supports athletes, so they need work. They have been a part of Lithuania's nonviolent struggle in the past months and have often acted with great courage and dignity. But they are still grappling with the meaning and full implications of active nonviolence. Some have the typical stereotypes of nonviolence that minimize its possibilities and romanticize the power of weaponry. In our workshop, we dealt with the theory and practice of nonviolence. Our participants had questions and concerns that grew out of the fear that the Red Army might move against the parliament. We drew historical parallels as we spoke of the accomplishments not only of the American civil rights struggle and the Gandhian movement, but also of Norwegian teachers against the Nazis in World War II and of Poland's Solidarity. We showed the film, "Where There is Hatred," that dramatized the Chilean resistance that overthrew Pinochet's dictatorship. (The film was later shown on Lithuania's alternate TV station.) The discussions were often sharp. Some wanted to combine a partially nonviolent, partially violent national defense. The great problem with that is that violence would likely undermine the credibility and strength of the nonviolence and provoke a strong attack in response. Some questioned the power of nonviolence in this kind of struggle; as one participant put it, "Communists are not human. You can't expect them to respond to nonviolence."

But what about what happened throughout much of Eastern Europe, where the nonviolent way ultimately prevailed over communism, we asked. Charles Alphin of our group, an African-American police captain from St. Louis whose work is with vice and narcotics, pointed out that in every struggle the temptation is to demonize the enemy, "just as some blacks think of white folks as animals." Brenda Carter, a member of our delegation from the New York State Institute of Nonviolence added, "We need to direct our anger toward creative solutions, not toward our adversaries." That was what we kept stressing: creative solutions, what Richard Gregg called "moral jiu jitsu," taking the enemy by surprise. A violent response to the army's attack on January 13 would have resulted not in fourteen deaths, but in hundreds, perhaps thousands more. And it would have been on the army's terms, with what it best understands: lethal force.

Believing it was important that we meet with "the other side," we talked with OMON, the feared "black berets" who occupied the former police academy, now a heavily armed bunker. The Soviet commander met us in his office, bedecked with the Soviet flag and a picture of Lenin. As he explained it, OMON saw itself as the protector of law and order, and breakaway Lithuania as illegal: a threat not only to Moscow but to the non-Lithuanian ethnic groups (such as Russians and Poles) living in Lithuania. In a tense but somewhat friendly dialogue, we urged the commander and his aides to refrain from violent acts, to open up lines of communication with Lithuanian leadership, and to be ready to accept third-party mediation. We had no illusions about what we may have accomplished, but we are certain that face-to-face meetings and dialogue are absolutely necessary in every conflict. Not long after our visit, following the failed coup in Moscow, the Soviet Interior Ministry disbanded the "black beret" troops.

We also heard that a number of non-Lithuanians in the republic feared that their rights would be ignored when independence finally came and that old fascist elements would re-emerge. This, at least, is an area where both sides need to listen to the concerns and fears of the other.

After our workshop at the parliament building, our delegation spent an evening in the beautiful old home of Maria and Vladas Viloziunas on the outskirts of Vilnius. Over steaming cups of tea, sandwiches and sweets, we listened to them and their adult children — several of whom are Volunteers—tell us of their hopes, apprehensions, and dreams of the future. Maria, homemaker and illustrator, spoke of Lithuania's Hill of Crosses where thousands and thousands of crosses stand. Though it has been repeatedly bulldozed by the country's oppressors, always the crosses reappear, a sign, she said, of the people's faith and determination. "Under the Tsars," she continued, "when our language was forbidden, Jews and Christians worked together, printing books and preserving our culture." And today, she reflected, "it seems that humanity is standing on the eve of great, momentous changes."

Vladas, sculptor and artist, shared with us his reflections about January 13. "The Communist Party and the KGB were well organized and planned each step in their attack. But they failed to calculate the spiritual energy we had. God loves these paradoxes! I came home that evening as the people sang before the troops and the Psalm I read spoke of the chariots being stopped: 'They will collapse and fall; but we shall stand upright. Give victory . . . O Lord; answer us when we call.' I'll remember that all my life."

The next day we went to the national cemetery in Vilnius to pay homage at the graves of the fourteen martyrs killed on January 13. Every grave was covered with flowers. The families of several of the victims were there, lighting candles, praying, planting flowers. In back of the graves was a traditional Lithuanian, hand-carved wooden crucifix. But this one was different. The fingers of the crucified Jesus were raised in a "V," the sign of victory. For me, that symbolized the ultimate power of powerlessness, of nonviolence overcoming violence, and of life over death.

Transforming Power in the Labor Movement— Cesar Chavez

Karen Eppler

Black Americans have been oppressed for centuries. Their struggle for civil rights is a dramatic example of the capacity of Transforming Power to illuminate social evils and to persuade citizens and leaders to eradicate those evils. The blacks relied on community ties and long, patient commitments to desegregation.

American farm workers are undeniably among the most oppressed groups in the nation. Unlike the blacks, they are a widely dispersed group. The necessity of finding seasonal work has made any real sense of community impossible to achieve. Racism divides white farm workers from blacks and Chicanos, language barriers make it difficult for Mexican Americans to work with their English-speaking neighbors, and poverty forces farm workers to worry about tonight's dinner rather than tomorrow's dreams. The task of organizing this divided, homeless and destitute group into a union of non-violent activists seemed impossible.

Cesar Chavez, born to a Chicano farm worker family, made this challenge his life work. Animosity and hostility were at the heart of most past labor actions. Violence and property damage were commonplace. The huge agribusinesses which employed migrant workers were certainly as cruel as any past employers on the American scene, except possibly slave owners. The life expectancy of farm workers is only two-thirds that of the average American. Violation of child labor laws and health requirements are commonplace, with some farms hiring one child for every two adults and others failing to install field toilets or supply plumbing for worker homes. Pesticide poisoning is the most prevalent cause of sickness among farm workers, but the companies did nothing to protect their workers from it. Perhaps most importantly, farm workers were not covered by Federal labor relations laws.

Source: *Transforming Power for Peace* by Lawrence S. Apsey, James Bristol, and Karen Eppler (Philadelphia: Religious Education Committee of Friends General Conference, 1986). Reprinted by permission of Lawrence S. Apsey.

Cesar Chavez worked to change these conditions. He chose as his tools the old weapons of labor, but under his leadership, strikes, pickets and boycotts were not characterized by violence and hatred but by compassion and good will. Chavez's dream was the creation of a union of agricultural laborers, capable of negotiating with growers and improving the lives of these migrant people. He began his campaign on foot, traveling from farm to farm explaining his goal and convincing others to become members of the United Farm Workers Union (UFW). At first he lived off his small savings, but when the money was gone, he begged as he went. The farm workers shared their food with him and, in sharing their poverty, they came to trust him. Despite the Union's growth, Chavez has continued to live the austere life of his people. He takes as his salary only five dollars a week. In a nonviolent campaign, the leader cannot exploit the workers. It is essential, Chavez insists, that the leader be one of the people:

> To come in a new car to organize a community of poor people—that doesn't work. And if you have money, but dress like they do, then it is phony. Professional hunger.[1]

Chavez had issued hundreds of union cards. The time had come to face the growers. The first objective was California vineyards. The wine grape growers refused to recognize the union and refused to hold a union election. The UFW called upon the nation to boycott California wines. The idea of a national boycott was important to Chavez because it would not only affect the wine grape growers but would also educate and mobilize many Americans. The boycott, and especially media coverage of cruel labor practices, convinced many vineyards to recognize the union. However, a few major vineyards continued to ignore UFW demands.

Strengthened by this partial success, the UFW decided to call a strike against the Giumaria Vineyards. It was hoped that successfully confronting these vineyards would convince other growers to accept union representation. Chavez spent many days preparing the workers for the strike. He taught them about Transforming Power, how to respond to threats and even blows without violence or surrender. But they were not prepared for what happened. The growers brought up truckloads of illegal aliens to pick the grapes. These poor Mexicans knew nothing about the strike or the UFW. They knew only that they were hungry and had been offered jobs. (The Giumaria Vineyards paid these immigrant laborers even less than they had been paying their usual workers.) Many of the strikers had no sympathy for these Mexicans. They saw only that these new workers were undermining the strike. They ambushed the strike breakers on their way back from the fields and beat then unmercifully. Chavez was hurt by this violence. He was not only saddened by this evil use of force against people who were only pawns of the oppressor, but he was also afraid that the strikers' behavior would alienate thousands of Americans who were boycotting Gallo wine.

With the view of cleansing himself and the union of violence, Cesar Chavez followed Gandhi's example and began a fast of penance. Fasting, he made a speech to the strikers, explaining that the UFW was not merely a union, it was a cause. "La Causa" promised a better world, a world where poverty and oppression would be replaced by equality and understanding. If the UFW was to help create this world, then it must itself become compassionate and peaceful. He told the strikers that he was fasting to purge the union of violence and that he would continue fasting until the violence was ended. The next day, no one was beaten and many of the strikers joined Chavez in his fast.

Buoyed by the UFW's growing faith in nonviolence, Chavez announced a table grape boycott directed at the same growers. By 1975, a Harris Poll indicated, 8% of the United States adult population was boycotting Gallo wines and 12% had stopped buying non-union grapes.[2]

As the UFW was gaining power in its action against the vineyard owners, a new and complex problem arose. Lettuce growers signed a contract with the Teamsters Union without a vote by their employees. A contract with a union that did not represent the workers was as meaningless as no contract at all. The Teamsters Union accepted terms which did not better existing working conditions. Outraged, the UFW called for a strike. Seven thousand out of the ten thousand pickers who worked for the lettuce growers walked off the fields. It was obvious that the UFW was the union preferred by the workers.

Because the pickers were too poor to maintain the strike, a lettuce boycott was added to the already successful grape and wine boycotts. This boycott was difficult to implement, since most lettuce heads were not marked with either the Teamster or the UFW insignia. The UFW convinced their growers to stamp lettuce heads and cartons with the eagle, the UFW emblem. Even so, it was difficult to measure the success of the boycott and supermarkets continued to sell non-union and Teamster lettuce.

Chavez decided on civil disobedience: to violate the law against secondary boycotts (boycotts against companies not party to the labor dispute, such as supermarkets in this instance). He began to organize a nation-wide boycott of all supermarkets that sold non-union or Teamster lettuce, grapes or wine. This boycott further organized the general public. UFW representatives travelled all over the country organizing groups of citizens to picket local supermarkets. The campaign became not merely a farm worker struggle, but a struggle which symbolized for the nation the oppressive nature of large corporate farming. With this secondary boycott, the UFW became a national political organization. Chavez went to speak about racism and the oppression of America's poor at rallies against the Vietnam war and civil rights meetings.

In 1975, California Governor Jerry Brown signed California's Agricultural Labor Relations Act, which guaranteed farm workers the right to petition for union representation and the right to vote for a union by secret ballot. In the elections which followed, the United Farm Workers Union won 113 elections while the Teamsters Union won only 24. The workers had voted for Chavez's dream.

UFW still faces enormous obstacles in its struggle to improve the living conditions of its members. But as they continue to use Transforming Power, to talk and to educate rather than to fight, there is good reason for optimism. The UFW has transformed the angry weapons of labor conflicts into nonviolent tools for justice.

Notes

[1] Peter Matthiessen, *Sal Si Puedes: Cesar Chavez and the New American Revolution* (New York: Random House, 1969) 84.

[2] Marjory Hope and James Young, *The Struggle for Humanity: Agents of Nonviolent Change in a Violent World* (New York: Orbis Books, 1977) 163.

NONVIOLENCE IN THE MIDDLE EAST

The Druze of the Golan
A Case of Nonviolent Resistance

R. Scott Kennedy

> Here is a modern day example of a nonviolent campaign, of a people very small in number, facing incredibly powerful odds militarily, saying "We don't have a military option. It doesn't pay for us to throw rocks or stones. We can never outviolence the Israeli army. But we can—through unity, cooperation and taking a principled stand, and accepting suffering—just refuse to cooperate and withhold our consent, and reasonably come to a solution that reserves and preserves our own rights and interests, at least in some measure."
>
> —Jonathan Kuttab, Palestinian lawyer.[1]

The Druze are a distinct Arab population in the Middle East whose tenets "developed in the eleventh century as an offshoot of the Isma'illiya, itself a radical fringe of Shi'ite Islam." Through their doctrine and practice, which synthesize Islam with influences from Christianity, Hellenism, neo-Platonism and other sources, the Druze have had a tenuous relationship to Islam. There is some dispute among members of the sect about its affiliation to Islam. "They uphold Muhammad as a prophet. But they do not revere him because they regard him as only one of several incarnations of Allah on earth, and not even the latest one."[2]

In face of centuries of persecution at the hands of both the orthodox Sunni Moslems and the more mystical Shi'ites, "they developed the concept

Source: "The Golani Druze: A Case of Non-Violent Resistance" by R. Scott Kennedy. *Journal of Palestine Studies*, Vol. XIII, No. 2 (Winter 1984), pp. 48-64. © 1984 by the Institute for Palestine Studies. All rights reserved. Used with permission. Footnotes edited.

of *taqiya*—camouflage—keeping their religious communal identity secret.[3] This communal secrecy is reinforced by a prohibition on marriage outside of the sect, insistence that one must be born a Druze and cannot through conversion become Druze, and restraint from proselytizing.

The Druze eventually settled on the slopes of the Mount Hermon mountain range in what is now Lebanon and Syria. They later spread through other mountainous areas in the southern parts of the Mount Lebanon range and elsewhere, such as the Carmel range in Palestine, where they located in easily defensible areas.

Today there are some 580,000 Druze throughout the world. Most live in the mountainous regions of Lebanon (the Chouf mountains), Syria (the Golan Heights), and Israel (Mount Carmel). Their mountain villages have historically afforded them some physical safety. According to Jamal Muadi, chairman of the Druze Initiative Committee, there are 50–60,000 Druze within the 1967 borders of Israel. Three hundred thousand Druze live in Lebanon. There are small groups in Jordan and even in India. And 27,000 Druze live in the United States, where they have formed an American Druze Public Affairs Committee.

The Druze have proven themselves a tight-knit, fiercely independent, politically flexible and pragmatic, and sometimes militant force in Middle Eastern politics—all important attributes for a minority religious sect in sometimes hostile host countries. According to Professor Moshe Sharon, the Druze "history as a small, persecuted sect within the world of Islam can be summed up in two enduring principles: the survival of the community and the exclusivity of territory. Over the centuries, the Druze have developed the military prowess to ensure both."[4]

Druze militancy has been demonstrated many times. They were among the leaders in the struggle in Syria against French colonial rule. In Israel, Druze have been conscripted into the Israel Defense Forces (IDF) since shortly after the creation of the Jewish state, the result of an accommodation reached between the Israeli authorities and traditional Druze community leadership. The Druze soldiers are known to be among the toughest of the IDF and often serve in the elite Border Patrol units.

For many people, first awareness of the Druze has come as the result of the recent fighting in Lebanon in wake of Israel's invasion of that country in June 1982. The Lebanese Druze are a key element in the coalition of leftist forces which make up the Lebanese National Movement (LNM). Walid Jumblatt, leader of the Druze in Lebanon, heads the progressive Socialist Party which has been battling right-wing Phalangist forces in the Chouf mountains for some months. He is the representative of both the Druze and the LNM in negotiations about the future political structure of Lebanon.

Much less publicized than those fighting in Lebanon are the Druze villagers in the Syrian Golan Heights who waged a courageous and effective nonviolent campaign against the Israeli occupation in 1982. In a region and a conflict sick with violence, the Golani Druze demonstrated the efficacy and power of nonviolence as a method of social struggle which can be utilized by unarmed civilians confronted by overwhelming police and military force.

The Golan Heights sit on Israel's northeast corner, bounded also by Lebanon to the northwest, Syria to the north and east, and Jordan to the south. During the 1967 Arab–Israeli war and soon thereafter, the bulk of the 110,000 Syrians of the Golan either fled or were forced out of their homes. Those few who remained included nearly 13,000 Druze, living in a handful of villages at the foot of Mount Hermon near the headwaters of the Jordan River. The Druze have farmed the region for decades, if not centuries, and are famous for olives and fruit, especially apples, grown within sight of Hermon's snowy heights and the ski-slopes opened there by Israel since 1967.

Israel considers the Golan strategically vital. From its heights above the Hula Valley Syrian soldiers from 1948 to 1967 fired on Israeli kibbutzim and towns (which had intruded in areas declared no-man's land in the 1948 ceasefire). Later, the slopes of Mount Hermon came to be called "Fatehland" as Palestinian *fedayeen* or guerrilla fighters took advantage of its mountain terrain to infiltrate into Israel.

The Golan, like the other occupied territories of the West Bank, Gaza Strip and East Jerusalem, has since 1967 undergone a continual and systematic process of annexation, not least in economic terms, to the State of Israel.[5] Many Druze now work as day-laborers in northern Israel's factories and agricultural settlements. Jewish settlements have been started in the Golan on lands confiscated from the Druze and other absentee Syrian landowners. More importantly, a major source of water in the Golan has been seized for exclusive use by the Jewish settlers, and other water sources are being partially diverted for use in Israel.

For more than ten years, the Golan was frozen in its status as militarily occupied land. (Israel insists on denoting the occupied territories "administered" territories, a device by which it seeks to avoid three dilemmas: proving the protection afforded to occupied lands by international law; extending the rights and privileges due to citizens of Israel in the event of annexation; risking even further isolation and disapprobation in the world community by the forced migration of Arabs from the territories seized in 1967.)

In the wake of Camp David accords signed by Israel and Egypt and brokered by the U.S. in 1979, the Israelis embarked on a policy of pressuring Syria either to join the Camp David peace process or risk losing the Golan Heights permanently. The U.S. offered tacit support for this maneuver by de-emphasizing, and eventually dropping, the Golan Heights from its list of subjects for discussion in negotiations about the return of occupied territories for a negotiated peace settlement with Israel.

The 1979 "Jerusalem Law" passed by the Israel Knesset moved Israel's capital city to Jerusalem. This action provoked widespread opposition by most countries in the world, including the United States. One aspect of this response was widespread opposition to the unilateral annexation of Arab land from beyond Israel's pre-1967 borders by the Jewish state. The governing circles in Israel had learned a lesson, at least for the time being: rather than formal annexation, a *de facto* process of assimilation would be pursued with the Golan Heights in order to avoid the harsh and nearly unanimous criticism of Israel's action on Jerusalem.

Some of the more extremely chauvinistic Israelis bridled under the international condemnation of further Israeli expansion, echoing David Ben-Gurion's comment that "it doesn't matter what the Gentiles say, what matters is what the Jews do." As a sop thrown to such parties which play a key role in the governing Likud coalition, it was made known that the Golani Druze would be allowed to ask for and receive Israeli citizenship. Implicit in this arrangement was the promise of favored treatment for those who made such a request. But to most Druze it was also a portent of the eventuality of annexation of the Golan Heights to the Jewish state.

If sufficient numbers of Druze requested Israeli identification cards and citizenship, the annexation of the Golan would be accomplished *de facto*. It would give the appearance of being a voluntary development, thereby anticipating and blunting criticism of Israel's gradual annexation of the occupied Golan.

According to Jonathan Kuttab, "The Israeli policy was to attempt to drive a wedge between them as Druze and between other Muslims or Arabs. 'You are Druze but not Arabs.'" This policy had proven quite successful within Israel itself, where a sharp distinction was drawn by the Israeli government between Druze and other Arabs. This "divide and rule" approach fits into a larger pattern of reinforcing divisions in the Arab world, setting them against one another as "Christian Arabs," "Muslims," Bedouin and Druze. In the 1950s, the Israelis had allegedly offered the Lebanese Druze leader Kamal Jumblatt assistance in setting up an independent Druze buffer-state between Israel and Lebanon and Syria. To some, the overtures to the Golani Druze implied attempts again to effect this process of "balkanization" meant to divide and weaken the Arab world.[6]

From passage of the Jerusalem Law in 1979 until the end of 1981, the Golani Druze were enticed to accept Israeli identification. Meanwhile, internal discussion progressed within the Druze community. Some Druze working in Israel lost their jobs or faced harassment for resisting the change in identification. But opposition to the Israeli move solidified and those who accepted Israeli identity cards were often shunned by the entire community. "They decided that anyone who accepts Israeli identity cards is really cutting themselves off from the community 'They are no longer one of us, no longer a Druze.'" (J. Kuttab)

A harsh reception greeted those who took Israeli identification: few would speak to them or enter their homes; they were not invited to community events, weddings or funerals; and they were not welcomed to religious gatherings. Their dead were denied the community's prayers. Such tremendous social pressure was exerted on them that all but a few diehard quislings returned their cards. Those who repented were required to recant publicly, or to go door-to-door to apologize to their neighbors, and to contribute money to support the families of those imprisoned.

There were of course other disincentives reinforcing the Druze resistance. Most have relatives living in Syria, some of whom are prominent officers in the Syrian army. They did not want to serve in the Israeli military like the Israeli Druze and end up fighting their kin and co-religionists. For most, their political sympathies clearly favored the Palestinian and the Arab cause. Many are confident that the Golan will eventually be returned to Syrian control. Some are mindful that Jordan recently declared that any Palestinians cooperating with the collaborationist Village Leagues in the West Bank would be considered "traitors." They could expect at least as harsh treatment by the Syrians.

In any case, for whatever reason, few Druze took advantage of the offer of Israeli identification. Inducements had failed.

In a sharp departure from parliamentary practice, Begin's ruling Likud coalition forced through the Israeli Knesset the requisite three readings and final passage of legislation formally annexing the Golan to Israel, on December 14, 1981. The unprecedented speed with which the legislation was passed prevented debate and disallowed any organized opposition. This was criticized by many members of the opposition Labor party as a further eroding of democratic practices in Israel. The annexation abrogated Syrian sovereignty over the region, denied the national self-identification of the people living there, and defied the declared American policy, if not its tacit support of Israeli actions, and the nearly unanimous opinion of other countries that Israel controls the occupied territories only temporarily as a trust.

With annexation formally accomplished, the Druze would be forced to accept Israeli identification, the irrefutable sign of Israeli citizenship. It was no longer a matter of choice; pressure would be applied to force compliance with the Knesset's action.

The Druze appealed to the Israeli government. They petitioned for a reversal of the decision. Their effort was to no avail. They finally publicly pronounced their intent not to cooperate with any attempt to convince, connive, or coerce the Druze into Israeli citizenship. "We're not fighting Israel, we cannot," they said. "We're not against Israel's security interests. Israel can do whatever it wants to us: they can confiscate our land. They can kill us. But they cannot tell us who we are. They cannot change our identity."[7]

Druze laborers refused to go to work, crippling industry in the North of Israel for several weeks. Many lost their jobs. Those who took Israeli identification continued to be ostracized. Nine village leaders, thought to be "ringleaders," were placed under administrative detention (imprisonment without trial).

Although the Israelis fabricated press reports to the effect that the Druze resistance had been abandoned, as more become known of their struggle, an astounding story of nonviolent resistance unfolded: the villages were cut off from one another by armed soldiers. When one village ran short of food, the villagers walked *en masse* to the neighboring village, overwhelming by sheer numbers the IDF soldiers positioned there to prevent it;

- the elderly and young violated curfew in order to harvest crops. Arrest of the elders created greater resolve among the villagers. When some of the children were arrested and carted off in helicopters, even more went out into the fields, hoping to get a free ride;

- a huge group of villagers once massed in the town square. An Israeli official in a helicopter hovering above the crowd ordered the soldiers to fire on the crowd to disperse them. The soldiers refused the direct order;

- groups of women surrounded Israeli soldiers, wrested at least sixteen weapons from their hands, and handed the guns over to army officers, suggesting the forces be removed. Guns sometimes were swapped in exchange for release of Druze in jail;

- a diversion resulted in several soldiers being locked inside a stable. Villagers took the keys to the commanding officer, told him where they were locked up, and suggested he let them out and send them home;

- one village took advantage of being home on strike to complete a major sewer project. They had been refused funds and permits for years by Israeli authorities. A "strike-in-reverse" resulted in trenches being dug and pipeline installed; and

- villagers began developing cooperative economic structures, such as sending the entire community out to spray trees with the understanding that the crops would be shared by all. They also began to set up their own schools.

Protracted negotiations continued between the village leaders and the Israeli government. Finally, after four months, Israel indicated that the efforts to force the Golani Druze to accept Israeli citizenship would be suspended. An apparent victory for civilian noncooperation seemed within grasp.

At one point there was talk that the Israelis would put a big fence around Majdal Shams, one of the Druze villages, and return it to Syrian control. According to Jonathan Kuttab, the Druze villagers joked, "If they do that, we will have succeeded in liberating Arab territory for the first time since 1948. Where all the Arab armies have failed, at least we might liberate this one little section of land. Why not?"

The Druze were led to believe that on April 1, 1982, the government effort to force citizenship upon them would end. Instead, the Israelis escalated from pressure to outright repression. An estimated 14–15,000 Israeli soldiers swarmed into the area. Seizing the village schools for military camps, they sealed off the Golan Heights from Israel and the other territories. The Israeli press, members of the Knesset, lawyers representing the Druze, and international observers were denied entry to the region. Israel imposed a state of siege which was to last 43 days. Electricity and water to the villages were cut off. Several homes were destroyed. In one demonstration nine people were wounded as it was broken up. At least two people died because ambulance service to nearby hospitals was denied Golani residents as part of the blockade. At least 150 people were arrested on each of several days. Fourteen received four-to-five-month sentences. Most received fines for failing to have Israeli identification in their possession.

During the siege, Israeli troops went door-to-door. They forced entry, confiscated the villagers' identification papers from the period of Syrian rule or military occupation, and left them Israeli identification papers instead.

The following morning the town squares of the various villages were littered with Israeli identity cards. The Druze had refused, even under direct and immediate threat of personal harm and communal suppression, to accept Israeli identification.

Partially as a result of the fierce resolve of the Golani Druze to resist Israeli force, and partially due to the intervention of Druze from within Israel on their behalf, the Israel government finally relented and lifted the siege. They diluted the strike's effectiveness by easing the pressure: withdrawing troops, taking away the checkpoints, and just leaving the Druze alone. The Israelis appeared ready to accommodate Druze sensitivities on the issue of their national identity. The strike continued, at a reduced level of intensity, until the Israelis invaded Lebanon in June 1982. The Druze first adopted a "wait and see" attitude, and later agreed to suspend the strike on July 19, 1982, "after Galilee Druze leaders said that the government [of Israel] would negotiate with the Druze community regarding their demands."[8]

According to the Palestinian English-language weekly *Al-Fajr* (Jerusalem), which covered the Golan situation at length, "The popular consensus in July 1982 was to accept the Israeli compromise formula put forth by the Druze *qadi* (judge) from the Galilee, which stated that the Israeli government will not interfere with the residents' basic civil, water and land rights, and will not impose army service on youths."[9]

Residents of the Golan were promised that identity cards would be specially designed to address their concerns—that the term "Arab" would be printed next to "nationality" (rather than "Druze"). This seemed to address the primary concern of the Golani Druze, such as Suleman Fahr Adin of Majdal Shams, who said "The Druze is one sect of the Islamic movement . . . not a nation. We are a religious sect, not more."[10]

But the agreement proved short-lived. According to Daoud Kuttab, a journalist writing in *Al-Fajr* (Jerusalem):

> The formula regarding the acceptance of Israeli ID cards failed because the Israeli government did not honor its promises to find an alternative solution for the identityless residents. . . . Forced by the lack of action on the Israeli government, most Golan residents have unwillingly taken ID cards, primarily in order to travel to their work.
>
> Most residents compare their situation to East Jerusalem, which, like the Golan, was annexed by Israel against the will of its residents. The Golanis point out that Palestinians of East Jerusalem [who] have not become Israeli citizens are not allowed to vote in the Israeli Knesset elections unless the residents make a separate application requesting citi-

zenship. Only 300 of Jerusalem's 120,000 residents have applied for and accepted it to date.[11]

Other conditions of the settlement have also not been fulfilled, including the commitment that the ownership of land is indisputable, that there will be no Israeli interference with the Golan water sources, that there will be open bridges to Syria and freedom to sell local produce to Syria, and assurances that there will be no transfer of land ownership in times of war or peace. While the Golani residents have been spared the income tax and "value added tax" which Israelis are obliged to pay, they are forced to pay a "Peace for Galilee" special war tax to offset the costs of the 1982 Israeli invasion of Lebanon.

It is difficult to speculate how the strike would have been resolved if the war in Lebanon had not intervened. At least one Druze villager suggested that the Druze suspended the strike rather than take unfair advantage of the Israelis fighting elsewhere. Most scoffed at this suggestion. Rather, they affirm, the Druze realized that they would not secure any satisfactory outcome from their strike while the Israelis remained preoccupied with a major military involvement in Lebanon. No further concessions could be won while the war was in progress. According to the *Jerusalem Post* (International Edition), "Operation Peace for Galilee put an end to the strike without further fuss. The government and the press no longer had time for Druze demands."[12]

Twelve Golani Druze who were arrested during the Spring 1982 strike filed a formal appeal before the Israeli High Court in Jerusalem, contesting the law requiring Israeli identification for the Golanis. The High Court ruled on May 22, 1983, against the appeal. The Court claimed the issuance of the identity cards to Golani residents is "a technical issue which is necessary to running the affairs of the local residents in the administered territories." This ruling again finessed the legal status of the residents of the Golan Heights, as it stopped short of ruling whether the territory has been legally annexed or is part of Israel. Thus, according to their legal counsel, the Israeli Court successfully avoided the key issue of addressing the Druze nationality.

Meanwhile, there is some continuity of the resistance still being carried on by the Druze. Many Druze have simply carried on their affairs without any kind of legal identification whatsoever, a particularly courageous posture given Israel's practice of harassing, imprisoning or deporting Arabs who do not possess proper identification.

According to Jonathan Kuttab who, as a West Bank lawyer, has carefully studied the use and abuse of law in the occupied territories:

> You cannot imagine what an identity card means under Israeli occupation. You have to carry it on you at all times. It is your only legal tie, the only legitimacy for me as a Palestinian living on the West Bank. My identity card is my most valuable possession in the world. I wouldn't trade it for anything. I could be an absentee. I would have no right to be here. I would be totally disenfranchised. Without identity cards you can-

not cash your checks at the bank, you cannot travel or move around. You cannot record or register births or marriages. You are legally a non-person. But these people were saying, "Throw in your identity card!"[13]

Other forms of resistance also continued. Five Druze were arrested for walking around without identity cards. They were taken to be tried in a local court run by the occupation authorities. The whole village turned up at the court, demanding that they too be tried. They loudly protested that they were not demonstrating, but only turning themselves in because they too were equally guilty.

The *Jerusalem Post* carried a news item claiming:

> The prolonged and bitter dispute within the Golan Druze community over the issue of Israeli identity cards ended unexpectedly at a modest ceremony earlier this month when Druze clergymen pledged to lift the religious and social ban imposed on those who had accepted Israeli identity cards. . . . It remains to be seen whether this step will be accompanied by a change in the government's attitudes to the local Druze population in the Golan.[14]

But other sources reported that the Druze community had not lifted its social and religious ban on Druze with Israeli citizenship. Druze leader Sheikh Ahmad Qadamani is quoted as saying, "Nothing has changed in the attitudes of Golan Heights residents against the Israeli occupation and the law annexing the Golan Heights. They still maintain their loyalty to their homeland, Syria."[15]

On September 23, 1983, "a unique and impressive memorial service" was held in the Golan Heights one week after the death of Kamal Kanj Abu Saleh, the spiritual head of the Golani Druze and a leader of the strike, jailed in 1982. A funeral procession from Majdal Shams turned into a large demonstration, involving an estimated 15,000 people on the Syrian side and 20,000 Golani Druze and supporters on the Israeli-occupied side of the cease-fire line. Lebanese Druze Leader Walid Jumblatt and Khaled Fahoum, Chair of the Palestine National Council, addressed the large crowd through loudspeakers, praising the Golani Druze for their 1982 strike. The Druze had convincingly demonstrated the power of concerted citizen nonviolent action in the face of tremendous odds and harsh and repressive military action.

There were of course unique factors contributing to the relative success of the Druze in the Golan Heights that could not necessarily be expected in other times or places. Few populations have so distinctive a community identity as the Druze, enabling them to act largely as a unit, as though by virtue of a group instinct. According to one Israeli scholar, "the Druze 'communal identity' guarantees the involvement of Israeli and Syrian Druze" in support of the Lebanese Druze in their effort to clear the Chouf mountains of Phalangist military forces. This scholar likens "their communal link to that which binds Jews throughout the world. . . . When it comes down to Druze survival, the communal bond cuts through national boundaries."[16]

Also, the strike was conducted on a relatively small scale: four villages of less than 13,000 people. Application of the same methods to a larger and less tightly-knit population would be an entirely different proposition.

The Golani Druze benefitted from the unique position of the Israeli Druze as well. In some respects, they enjoy certain privileges, but most importantly they serve in the Israeli army. The Israeli Druze raised public expressions of solidarity with their Golani coreligionists. At one point an annual military parade through the Israeli Druze villages on Mount Carmel near Haifa was cancelled because of planned boycotts in solidarity with the Druze of the Golan. As Israeli officials anticipated the invasion of Lebanon, involving Israeli Druze soldiers and certain to involve Lebanese Druze in some manner, pressure to defuse the crisis in the Golan would have grown stronger.

Israel clearly feared alienating the Israeli Druze. Even though some Israeli Druze think the support was sentimental and sectarian rather than political, there is concern in Israel about a growing tendency among Israeli Druze to identify with the Palestinian cause, even to the point of refusing military service.[17]

Another factor was the active support of a small but vocal sector of Israeli society which spoke out in defense of the Golani Druze civil and human rights and opposed the annexation.

Finally, the issue was one on which the Israelis could compromise without too great a cost. The Golanis were not demanding liberation from Israeli occupation. They simply asked for return to the *status quo ante.*

These unique aspects of the struggle may temper enthusiasm about the Druze's apparent success, or qualify applicability of their struggle to other situations. Nevertheless, a great deal can still be learned from their use of nonviolent resistance.

For one, they demonstrated the advantage and the power of organizing nonviolent struggle around realistic objectives. The strike was not an open-ended general strike demanding self-determination or an end to Israeli rule. It candidly assessed the political context in which it was raised and avoided ill-defined or hopelessly unrealistic objectives. Such piecemeal or incremental an approach may not satisfy the maximalist goals of revolutionary rhetoric or ideological dogmatism. Yet it gave the Golani Druze a concrete experience of their power in united action, and a tangible experience of success against a military occupier.

The Druze struggle suggests that effective nonviolent struggle may be the manifestation of a broad cultural cohesion, rather than a mechanistic means by which a new culture can be created. The Druze have a cultural cohesion which is rare, especially in the more highly developed countries.

Another factor contributing to their success was their frank assessment of the resources available to them. According to one Majdal Shams activist:

> We fight with hands and sticks against the Israelis. What can we do? We cannot wait for them to hit us and to fight us. They came to fight us in our villages and our homes. They attacked us for 16 years. And now also

they are attacking us. We reject it with our own rights. We have the specific conditions. We have to choose the place to put pressure and against
what. We have to choose correctly and to test correctly our methods and
our facts. Force must be met with counter-force, not passivity.[18]

George Lakey, one of the leading theoreticians and advocates of nonviolence as a force for social struggle, has commented, "Nonviolent struggle
doesn't just happen. It comes out of a social context, and people who actually
do the action are responding to a variety of things. They may be responding
to a change in conditions or changes in attitudes. They may see a glimmer of
hope where they didn't see it before. They may see a particularly brutal
event. Whatever the initial cause, what people are actually doing is casting
off submission and getting rid of their passivity.[19] Having thrown off submission and decided to engage in social struggle, the objective of nonviolent
action is, according to Professor Gene Sharp of Harvard's Center for International Affairs, "to make a society ungovernable by would-be oppressors."[20]
Despite difficulties encountered by the Golani Druze and short-comings in
terms of what they achieved, their 1982 general strike is a remarkable example of the action of which both Lakey and Sharp speak.

One chief cause for its effectiveness was that the strike was rooted in a
deep sense of the people's identity: their identity as Druze. The symbol of
their campaign was provided by the Israelis: the identity card. And the objective of their resistance was simple, attainable, and brought these elements
together in a compelling way: if you are a Syrian Druze, you cannot be an
Israeli, so don't accept the identity card! It was as simple as that.

The younger, secular and more politically radical and the older, religious
and more traditional leaderships were able to compromise on questions of
style, authority, political analysis and personal status. Decisions were arrived
at by a consensus process that, as one Palestinian remarked, rivalled the par-
ticipatory democracy of American's best town meetings. On five different
occasions as many as 2,500 people gathered together to make decisions. The
decision-making process for the villages was still largely intact because it
was centered within their religious practices and hence more immune to overt
Israeli interference. During the initial stages of the strike, Druze villagers
refused to work in their own fields or across the 1967 border inside Israel.
During the last two months of the strike, farmers returned to the fields but,
according to a Majdal Shams villager, "Everyone was deciding for the other
one. It means farmers cannot decide for themselves and workers cannot
decide for themselves."

Leaders may have helped to discern the advisability of various actions,
but they were primarily responding to what the community as a whole had
arrived at through consensus. This allowed for continuity in the campaign
and the building of momentum from one success to the next, even when leaders were placed under house arrest or in jail.

The Druze demonstrated the crucial contribution of a deeply-rooted collective morale and social solidarity as decisive factors in social struggle of

any sort. Druze villagers were prepared to undergo considerable personal sacrifice, including loss of jobs and crops, imprisonment and physical harm. Their willing acceptance of suffering inspired and encouraged others and rallied support.

One unexpected source of support came from within those soldiers sent to enforce edicts against the villagers' will. Villagers defied a strict curfew confining them to their homes to place tea and cookies outside their doors for the Israeli soldiers. They engaged them in conversation, and chose not to curse them. The early decision to talk with the Israeli soldiers resulted in villagers actively seeking soldiers out and speaking with them in their native Hebrew which they had been forced to learn in school. According to J. Kuttab, "The soldiers were really being torn apart, because they couldn't handle that type of nonviolence." The Druze began to expose the vulnerability of military force to nonviolent means of struggle.

Israeli soldiers generally function so effectively, at least in part, because of the widespread conviction that they are acting out of genuine security needs of their fellow Israelis and because so many of the situations in which they are stationed give them cause to fear for their own lives. In the face of a disciplined unarmed civilian population, which threatened neither Israeli security, nor the lives of the individual soldiers, the morale and discipline of Israeli soldiers began to break down. According to several reports, the division commander complained that the Golan situation was ruining some of his best soldiers.[21]

The nonviolent resistance campaign of the Golani Druze is not a definitive demonstration of the efficacy of nonviolence. But it is a provocative example of the power of a well-disciplined nonviolent campaign against tremendous military might. It proved to be difficult to manage by the Israelis, who depend ultimately on cooperation with their rule in all of the occupied territories in order to maintain it. But, perhaps most significantly, it has embodied an alternative for the Palestinians under occupation in the wake of the Lebanese war and PLO infighting which have destroyed their military capability.

Richard Falk, an expert on international law at Princeton University, has observed that the Palestinians may make a decisive contribution toward the peace process "by moving away from armed struggle as its central image of the politics of self-determination."[22] It is significant that Israeli Jews, active in movements in opposition to annexation of any of the occupied territories, are beginning to speak in similar terms. In a recent interview, Daniel Amit, Israeli physicist and co-founder of both the Committee for Solidarity with Bir Zeit and the Committee Against the War in Lebanon, commented, "My personal vision is that the (Israeli) peace movement has to develop nonviolent civil resistance tactics on a large scale. The human and numerical potential is there. If the Palestinians will come along, it will be like a forest fire."[23]

The potential impact of the Druze campaign on the Palestinians has not been lost on the Israelis. Several Palestinian activists and American service workers in the occupied territories noted that the Israeli military officials have devoted much more time to examining possible uses of nonviolence by the Palestinians than have the Palestinians themselves. The Israelis are actively developing means to reduce the potential impact of nonviolent struggle for the Palestinians. This is being done both through legal strictures drastically curtailing the ability to organize, and through harsh repression of any militant nonviolent action. A recent order by the Military Governor of the West Bank, for example, forbids demonstrations by Israelis. Political demonstrations by Palestinians have been outlawed since the beginning of the occupation in 1967. But the recent order is meant to nip in the bud a series of demonstrations by various Israeli peace and human right groups against Jewish settlements in the West Bank. It is telling that the Israeli military governor of the West Bank forced an American service organization to change the job description of one of its workers in the West Bank to delete "nonviolence education" as part of that person's work. Clearly nonviolence is perceived as a threat by the Israelis.

While the Druze campaign may not serve as a textbook for nonviolent struggle, or a clear direction for Druze in other geographical locales, perhaps other Palestinians will be able to hear the words of an Israeli anti-war activist who commented to a group of Majdal Shams villagers, "When you are able, competent and generous, you don't need arms."[24]

Notes

[1] The author met with Jonathan Kuttab in Jerusalem in January 1983. The direct quotations are excerpted from a tape recording of an interview with Kuttab and of a public workshop on Nonviolence and the Palestinian Struggle for justice led by Kuttab during a visit to California as guest of the Resource Center for Nonviolence on May 1, 1983.

[2] Joseph Berger, "Members of Druze Sect Guard Privacy, Keep Tenets of Faith Secret," in special to the Religious News Service, from *The United Methodist Reporter*, October 21, 1983, 5.

[3] Professor Moshe Sharon, "Why the Druze Are Formidable," *The Jerusalem Post* (International Edition), September 18–24, 1983, 14. Professor Sharon is Chairman of the Department of the History of Islamic People at Hebrew University and former Advisor on Arab Affairs to Prime Minister Menahem Begin.

[4] Sharon, 1.

[5] This process of economic assimilation of the occupied territories into the state of Israel has been graphically portrayed in the statistical studies of the former vice mayor of Jerusalem, Meron Benvenisti, in *The West Bank and Gaza Data Base Project: Pilot Study* Number 1, Meron Benvenisti, Jerusalem, 1982.

[6] Reports of the alleged Israeli offer to Kamal Jumblatt were heard in several conversations involving Golani Druze villagers during the author's visit to Majdal Shams on February 5, 1983. The apparent aim was to establish the Druze as an independent geographical national entity, closely allied to the state of Israel, and serving as a buffer between Israel and the surrounding Arab states. To these Druze villagers, Israel's actions in Lebanon, including the creation of the "Haddadland" buffer zone in Southern Lebanon during the 1978 invasion, and continued Israeli presence following the 1983 war illustrate Israel's efforts to divide and rule the Arab world.

[7] This paraphrase of Druze sentiment was reported by Jonathan Kuttab (Interview, May 1, 1983) who heard Golani villagers speak in these terms to an American journalist whom Kuttab accompanied in a visit to the Golan.

[8] "Golan Residents Must Carry IDs," *Al-Fajr* (Jerusalem) (International English Edition), May 27, 1983, 13.

[9] Daoud Kuttab, "Nationalism Flares," *Al-Fajr* (Jerusalem) (International English Edition), October 7, 1983. 7.

[10] Author's interview with Suleman Fahr Adin of Majdal Shams, February 5, 1983.

[11] D. Kuttab, 7.

[12] *Jerusalem Post*, August 21–27, 1983, 11.

[13] Interview, May 1, 1983.

[14] *Jerusalem Post* (International Edition), August 21-27, 1983.

[15] *Al-Fajr* (Jerusalem), August 19, 1983; also Israleft, August 15, 1983.

[16] M. Sharon, p. 1.

[17] During the February 7, 1983 visit and several previous visits, the author has met a dozen Druze who have either refused or avoided military conscription into the Israeli army. At one point, the Druze Initiative Committee claims to have garnered 600 signatures by Druze opposing such military service.

[18] Interview with Suleman Fahr Adin, Majdal Shams, February 5, 1983.

[19] Quoted in "Alternatives to Violence Video Forum," Section #2, produced by WTL/TV.

[20] Ibid.

[21] This report has not been independently confirmed, but it was mentioned by several sources, including Jonathan Kuttab, Druze villagers in the Golan and within Israel, and American nationals serving in various capacities in service organizations on the West Bank.

[22] Richard Falk, "Toward Arab-Israeli Peace," *CALC Report*, November–December, 1982, 34 (Clergy and Laity Concerned, 198 Broadway, New York, N.Y.). Falk is professor of International Law at Princeton University; he has traveled in the Middle East and written extensively about the Arab-Israeli and wider Middle Eastern conflicts.

[23] Quoted in Nat Hentoff, "Can Israel Create Its Own Gandhi, Muste or King?," *Village Voice*, June 28, 1983.

[24] Comment by Yeshya'ahu Toma Sik, of the World Service authority and War Resisters International/Israel Section, Tel Aviv, during the February 5, 1983, visit to Majdal Shams in the Golan Heights.

Living Truth
A Jewish Perspective

Allan Solomonow

Judaism boldly holds that it is not tenable to have any one of the three [truth, justice, peace] without the other two. In Zachariah we find the passage: "The world rests upon three things: on justice, on truth, and on peace." The interface of these three brings uncertainty to many of the West who regard truth as a more abstract quality separable from peace and justice.

Truth, justice and peace are the three tools with which to forge a life that reflects God's spirit; they are not merely standards for right action but literally the means for the preservation of the world.

> These are the things that you shall do: everyone shall speak the truth to their neighbor; fulfill the judgment of truth and peace in your gates; let none of you imagine evil in your hearts against your neighbor; and love no false oaths, for all these are things that I hate, declares the Lord. (Zachariah)

This decisiveness stands in deplorable contrast to a world in which the two "neighboring" superpowers, pitted against each other, send arms to their "friends" and "enemies" alike around the world. Even within the peace community stern debates consider whether justice is more important than peace or peace more important than justice—a concern others had resolved millennia ago.

While Judaism does not appear to require a commitment to nonviolence in order to fulfill its precepts, it so sharply curtails the use of violence that nonviolence becomes more often than not the only meaningful way to fulfill a life dedicated to truth, justice and peace. It is little wonder then that for centuries following the Jewish diaspora, the Jewish people endured through circumstances that would have absorbed most other peoples through assimilation.

The status of truth within Judaism is even clearer when the negative side is taken into account: What is the significance of the failure to act in a spirit of truth, peace and justice? It is said, "No deceit shall stand in the way of God." Neither untruth to God nor untruth to others is right. One of the prayers in the Sabbath service stresses: "Keep your tongue from speaking evil and your lips from speaking guile." It is not mere untruth but any departure from truth that is violative of a commitment to truth. This extends to any falsity or changing of one's word, slander, hypocrisy or speaking with an "evil tongue."

Satyagraha takes on deeper meaning within this Jewish context. The act of deviating from the truth is self-demanding and idolatrous. Deceit creates divisions and myths which conspire against the opening up into the fullness of God's universe. This is why believing truth must also mean living truth. The preservation of the universe is an active commitment requiring more than obliging intellectual platitudes. Truth presumes action even when it is far from clear that action is likely to yield results. After all, what matters is that the search for truth has been enjoined and must ultimately lead to justice and peace.

Conventional wisdom submits that "truth is the first casualty of war." It is probably closer to say that truth is the first casualty of oppression, injustice or, for that matter, any inhuman act. Truth is intolerable to those who seek to place their interests above those of others. One of the hallmarks of our modern age has become the centralization of mass modes of communication that tend to distort and sift through world events, preventing us from responding to these events in an appropriate manner. The profusion of disinformation has worked to disempower many who search for the truth, while fueling the conspiracy theories of others.

Today we Jews must ask ourselves: Is there any way in which we can do justice to truth/ peace/justice while supporting violence? This was a question we did not have to ask for the greater part of our history. Can we participate in military action without creating myths about an adversary? Can we work towards a more harmonious universe through armed intervention? Wouldn't we have avoided much of the Holocaust if Jews had undertaken more of the armed resistance such as the Warsaw Ghetto? Isn't it power that assures the State of Israel that it will not be destroyed by the surrounding Arab states? How are we to live in the truth when we believe we are in imminent danger of being destroyed? And how are we to take to heart our spiritual commitment when we tell ourselves that Muslims and Christians have perpetrated horrendous acts against us?

Paradoxically, the most immediate answer to these questions comes from a look at what is the most sensitive issue for Jews: namely, the survival of the State of Israel. Israel was established in the faith that there would be a place in the world where Jews could live as Jews in freedom and security. The creation of a state for Jews was meant to be a means to that end. Now, thirty-nine years following the establishment of Israel have not brought that freedom and security. The Middle East has become a cauldron of conflict that could easily erupt into nuclear conflict and superpower confrontation. Military responses by both Israel and the Arabs have become self-reinforcing.

The younger generation in each society has come to view the conflict as a natural and unavoidable state of affairs. Israel and the Arab nations are militarily stronger than we would have ever imagined, and one finds no peace, no justice and little truth in their confrontation.

The plight of the Middle East is a paradigm for the world. The history of Jew and Muslim was one of the more encouraging in history. From time immemorial Muslim and Jew lived together in relative peace within the Holy Land. The history depicted in our day is one of constant and undying hatred. Truth has been gradually dismembered to suit those who strive to see a different, divisive "truth." Arabs have become "terrorists" to many. Jews are seen as "settler-colonialist imperialists." Convenient labels have replaced the search for truth. Israel quite properly calls for peace. The Palestinian people understandably cry for justice. Each finds it hard to see that their aspirations are one and the same.

How is it possible for a people with such a remarkable spiritual heritage to lose sight of its wisdom? The ability of the Jewish people to live truth has been sharply challenged by the cumulative impact of anti-Semitism and the Holocaust. The immediate historical response to the Holocaust was one of denial, an unwillingness to deal with the immensity of the tragedy and its meaning. As we have emerged from that stage and begun to grasp its nature, we are moving towards the other extreme: to do whatever is necessary to assure that it will not happen again. The easiest response has been to do what other nations usually do: to become stronger yet. Israel and the Jewish People are now divided amongst those who harbour a vision of reconciliation and those who argue that "we have no alternative, we must stand and fight."

Judaism tells us that seeking truth *does not require us to choose between* Jew and Arab, Palestinian and Israeli. On the contrary, it tells us that the only life-affirming choice is to choose both. Israeli and Palestinian are no more separable than justice and peace. This is a hard lesson for each people to take to heart. Each has borne great suffering. One legacy of that historical suffering has been insecurity and a loss of faith. It has been a constant human temptation to seek the simpler and more "tangible" way in times of insecurity.

Despite the powerful forces at play there remain groups of Palestinians and Israelis who are in continuing dialogue for a mutual solution. Each works under threat of arrest, or worse. There are not only Israeli and Palestinian partisans of nonviolent action; in recent times, there have been joint nonviolent witnesses. If in this conflict Arab and Israeli can speak truth to power, the Jewish commitment to peace and justice may be freed to resume its prophetic message.

Nonviolent Resistance
A Strategy for the Occupied Territories

Mubarak E. Awad

Nonviolence is not an innovation in the struggle of the Palestinian people. Palestinians have used nonviolent methods since the beginning of the 1930s side by side with the armed struggle in their attempts to achieve their goals against Zionism. The six-month strike of 1936 and the Arab boycott of Israel are two prominent examples of the use of nonviolence in the service of the Palestinian cause. In the occupied territories today, the resistance against the occupation does not generally reflect violent methods. School and commercial strikes, petitions, protest telegrams, advertisements and condemnations in the daily papers, and the attempts to boycott Israeli goods are, in fact, manifestations of nonviolent struggle. Syrian citizens in the occupied Golan Heights are also conducting a powerful, concentrated and successful campaign of nonviolent resistance to the attempts of Israel to impose Israeli law on the Golan Heights. This campaign appears to be well organized and intelligent in its methods, ideas, and the execution of classic nonviolence tactics.

This study aims to discuss the issue of nonviolence as a serious and comprehensive strategy for resisting the Israeli occupation, and the means and tactical methods to implement this strategy as well as the problems and obstacles which it would face in the occupied West Bank and Gaza.

Present Conditions in the Occupied West Bank and Gaza Strip

The following important factors limit the nature and possibilities of the Palestinian struggle in those areas at the present time:

Source: "Nonviolent Resistance: A Strategy for the Occupied Territories" by Mubarak E. Awad, *Journal of Palestine Studies*, Vol. XIII, No. 4 (Summer 1984), pp. 22–36. © 1984 by the Institute for Palestine Studies. All rights reserved. Used with permission.

1. There are 1.3 million Palestinians living in the West Bank and Gaza Strip. They are unarmed, not trained militarily and not permitted to possess weapons either as individuals or collectively. Furthermore, they do not have the necessary lines of communication to receive military supplies in sufficient quantities to be able to carry on continuous military operations against the occupiers for any length of time.

2. Palestinian citizens endure the full authority of the power of the military government and its institutions. The military government exercises complete control over all aspects of the lives of the Palestinian people. This authority is exercised through a system for issuing or denying permits or licenses which are necessary for almost every activity. This structure operates as part of a policy aimed at controlling the population through segmenting the society and separating the citizens from one another, making citizens economically dependent on Israel, and utilizing certain sectors of the population and turning them into collaborators. These policies are designed to render the citizens incapable of effective opposition to the occupation authorities.

3. Palestinian citizens lack leadership, since they are separated from their accepted representatives on the outside. Local leadership is under strict scrutiny by the authorities. Attempts to form an organized local leadership like the National Guidance Committee, and attempts to unify their public activities so far have failed. The mayors, who are the more prominent local leaders, face considerable obstacles.

4. There is an Israeli plan for changing the character of the West Bank and the Gaza Strip by "Judaizing" it. The authorities impose themselves daily on the land, waters, institutions, and rights of the Palestinian people. A comprehensive structure has been set up for the Jewish settlements. The military government and Jewish extremists are proceeding relentlessly with this plan, and very little is being done to stop, delay, or hamper it.

5. The various methods used to implement this plan rarely depend on brute force. Rather, the Israelis exercise authority through slow, subtle, well-planned methods which are irresistible because they are built on the absolute authority of the military government and legislation that it creates, and economic and other pressures, as well as the existing departments of the established order. Behind these, of course, lies the power of the army, which intervenes to "maintain the peace" when the occupation faces any challenge. Thus, the plan of "Judaization" is being implemented under the very noses of the Palestinians, who feel utterly impotent to resist or delay these plans despite their awareness of them and appreciation of the danger they pose for them.

6. There are no immediate prospects for the liberation of the occupied territories. The hope that salvation may come from the outside no

longer exists. The military branches of the PLO are presently incapable of liberating the occupied territories by force and the Arab governments appear presently unable and uninterested in entering into a broad military confrontation with Israel aimed at liberating the occupied areas by force. Under these conditions, any attempt to halt or delay or obstruct "Judaization" must come from those Palestinians presently living in the occupied territory.

For the Palestinians who are living in the West Bank and Gaza during this period, the most effective strategy is one of nonviolence. This does not determine the methods open to Palestinians on the outside; nor does it constitute a rejection of the concept of armed struggle. It does not rule out the possibility that the struggle on the inside may turn into an armed struggle at a later stage. Simply put, the thesis is that during this particular historical period, and with regard only to the 1.3 million Palestinians living under the Israeli occupation, nonviolence is the most effective method to obstruct the policy of "Judaization." This struggle utilizes the largest possible amount of the potential and resources of Palestinians presently on the inside and offers all sectors of the Palestinian society an opportunity to engage actively in the struggle, instead of observing it passively, by listening to the radio, for example. It can neutralize to a large degree the destructive power of the Israeli war machine, and enlist in our service, or at least neutralize, important sectors of the Israeli society. Such a strategy focuses and increases any beneficial public international attention to our cause by revealing the racist and expansionist features of the Zionist movement and denying it the justifications built on its purported "security." It removes the irrational fear of "Arab violence," which presently cements Israeli society together. By removing this fear, it contributes to the disintegration of hostile Israeli society and helps to isolate Israel politically and morally.

The Assumptions

This approach is based on certain assumptions:

First, nonviolent struggle is a total and serious struggle, nothing short of a real war. There is no assurance that the enemy will be nonviolent. On the contrary, there are great sacrifices we should expect in the nonviolent struggle. Martyrs and wounded will fall, and Palestinians will suffer personal losses in terms of their interests, jobs, and possessions. Nonviolent struggle is a real war, not an easy alternative.

Second, nonviolent struggle is not negative or passive. It is an active, affirmative operation, a form of mobile warfare. It will require the enlistment of all resources and capabilities. It requires special training and a high degree of organization and discipline. Secrecy must be maintained in planning, organizing, and coordinating the different operations and campaigns. Most nonviolent activities will be illegal according to the laws and military orders presently imposed on the population.

The Israeli soldier is a human being, not a beast devoid of conscience and feeling. He has an understanding of right and wrong to which it is possible to appeal. Similarly, he can be demoralized. He constantly needs a reasonable justification for his activities. On the other hand, he has the potential for evil and oppression like any other person. He is often an intolerant racist and shares most of his government's evil assumptions.

At another level, the Israeli government is sensitive to public opinion, both local and international. It constantly needs international support and aid, and it has an image it wishes to project. At the same time, this sensitivity is limited: the Israeli government is willing to carry out its plans and maintain its oppression regardless of the views of the international community. Nonetheless, Israel does not possess the internal resources which will enable it to bear international isolation for a long time, as is the case with the racist government of South Africa, for example.

Suffering and pain can be useful in forging unity among the Palestinians to resist oppression. They also achieve for the Palestinians moral superiority over the occupiers and set in motion historical factors which insure the survival of the Palestinian people and their eventual victory. The Palestinian revolution was built on the blood of the martyrs and the suffering of our people. When a nonviolent person accepts this suffering voluntarily in defense of his principles instead of having this suffering imposed upon him involuntarily, he or she increases and accentuates these benefits.

Of course, there is no more assurance that a nonviolent struggle will be victorious than there is an assurance that armed struggle will achieve its end. Victory and success in a nonviolent struggle cannot be measured by easily observable, external, objective criteria. Nonviolent struggle achieves its goals and effect upon the hearts and minds of the Israeli soldiers, for example. It can manifest itself in a higher rate of Israeli emigration, by a loss of fighting spirit for the Israeli soldier, by their complaints and protest against the actions of the Israeli government. Similarly, the increasing moral and political isolation of Israel abroad is difficult to measure, but it can be a real and important phenomenon with definite consequences.

The Political Positions of the Nonviolent Movement

The strategy of nonviolence does not impose a particular political position. It is not necessary that a nonviolent strategy be politically moderate. The nonviolent movement need not prefer a solution based on a two-state solution over a secular democratic state in all of Palestine. Nonetheless, all participants in the nonviolent struggle must share minimal common political beliefs, must stay within the consensus of the Palestinian people and must work toward the goal of self-determination for the Palestinian people. It must certainly ratify the legitimacy and singleness of the representation of the Palestinian people through the PLO, the popular national positions toward settlement, land expropriation, control over land and water resources, and the unified Palestinian goal of the return of the refugees to their homeland.

Points of Contact

One of the most important aims of any nonviolent movement is to find points of contact between the citizens and authorities which highlight the evil and oppression on the one hand, and which lead to a useful and meaningful confrontation on the other hand. The importance of finding such points of contact becomes clear when we observe two common phenomena:

First, there are the constant attempts of the authorities to distance themselves from the citizens and to interpose Arab intermediaries or "civilian employees" whenever they carry out their most insidious practices, economic or otherwise. This is coupled with the policy of calling in the army, as another face of the occupation, which only acts "to preserve security" when the population rejects these practices.

Second, there is the instinctive need of demonstrators to draw the Israeli army into a confrontation with them. The method most commonly used presently is to burn tires, throw stones, or set up roadblocks. In some cases, demonstrators have called up the army by telephone. Some Israeli politicians (such as Moshe Dayan) realized the wisdom of reducing these confrontations by minimizing the military presence, particularly in the cities. Such a wise policy (from their point of view) does, in fact, reduce the points of contact and confrontation, without improving the position of the Palestinians. Therefore, it is necessary for any nonviolent movement to seek points of contact and to select among them the useful points which can lead to fruitful and successful confrontations.

Methods of Nonviolent Resistance

The most complete list of methods that have been used in nonviolent resistance is found in Gene Sharp's *The Politics of Nonviolent Action* (Boston: Porter-Sargent, 1973). I will mention here a few of these methods as they have been used in the occupied territories.

Demonstrations

This has been the most commonly used method in the occupied territories. The aim of demonstrating is usually to educate, express positions, indicate solidarity and support, protest, and make demands. It is, in other words, a means of expressing a point of view. The most successful demonstration is one where the organizers have asked, and answered in advance, the following queries: What is the message that we wish to get across? Who is our target audience: the international press, local Palestinians, the military government, the Israeli public? It may be necessary for us to try to reach the common Israeli soldier with our message as well. It goes without saying that we must attempt to understand the psychology of the target audience and to use this understanding in formulating the content and method of the demonstration.

In developing demonstrations, creativity and innovation are important. Gathering large numbers of people for marches and raising the Palestinian flag is excellent, but after 16 years of occupation we need creative ideas for demonstrations. Some tactics can include protest prayers, fasts, silent demonstrations, using powerful symbols such as yellow armbands (which the Nazis forced the Jews to wear), concentration camp costumes, commemoration services for martyrs, guerrilla theater, as well as affirmative and constructive activities such as giving gifts to commemorate national occasions, giving prizes to honor fallen martyrs, and the like. One of the more successful demonstrations was the clean up campaign which the youth of al-Bireh and Ramallah undertook to protest the dismissal of the mayors and the closure of the municipalities. A demonstration can be creative, or even humorous, as long as it succeeds in delivering its message. An example of this type is blowing whistles and carhorns in Ramallah to protest the closure of Bir Zeit University. That demonstration frustrated the Israeli army in Ramallah. The authorities pursued the demonstrators and the whistlers with the same vigor that they use to pursue stone-throwers, but without the explanations and the justifications which soldiers used in the past to beat them and humiliate them.

Obstruction

The goals of the occupation authorities are generally opposite from those of the population. This is very clear in the cases of building settlements, opening roads, and land confiscations. These operations, however, can be obstructed and effectively prevented. It has happened before that Palestinians have thrown their bodies before bulldozers in order to prevent them from carrying out their functions. The reader may consider this foolhardy, but it has, in fact, accomplished something in the past and may indeed be extremely successful. Palestinians on the inside can attempt to block roads, prevent communications, cut electricity, telephone, and water lines, prevent the movement of equipment, and in other ways obstruct the government in carrying out its unjust plans. If this obstruction occurs violently (such as by throwing stones or closing the road with a roadblock without staying in its vicinity), the reaction of the authorities will also be violent and the authorities will find a ready excuse to redouble its efforts. Soldiers will shoot, claiming self-defense. New forces will be called in under the pretense of "protecting" the innocent civilian plans from troublemakers and attackers, and other such justifications. If the obstruction occurs in a non-violent fashion, and the obstructors openly declare that they do not wish to injure anyone, but that they are merely obstructing a plan which injures them and their interests, then repression will also follow and soldiers will shoot in this case as well. But the situation will be entirely different. Palestinians in this case will be accepting and suffering the sacrifices, and even the martyrdoms, as a price they are willing to pay to preserve their land, and as a sign of their love for that land and their resistance to injustice and oppression. This message will also be very clear to the Israelis. They cannot, in such a case, accuse anyone of anti-Semitism or hatred for Jews. Neither will they be able to use the excuse of "terrorism," or to claim that the disturbances are the creation of a small, hateful minority of troublemakers, cowards, and provocators who inflame the rest of the population. All these myths will be revealed for the lies that they are. Instead, these self-sacrifices will achieve their maximum effect. Their influence will not only fall on public opinion, but will also touch concerned Israelis and Palestinians. Attention will center on the immediate issue—the particular parcel of land being confiscated, the specific settlement which is being built, the family which is being deprived of its home, the building which is being destroyed. At the very least, the Palestinians will in this fashion be able to record in an unequivocal manner their steadfast position, for which position they are willing to sacrifice and suffer consequences.

Refusal to Cooperate

This method is similar to the method of obstruction described above, but it is based on the fact that Israel cannot govern the West Bank and the Gaza Strip without the cooperation of the subject people. This cooperation is usually obtained by force, threats, violence, and punishments (individual and collective). Yet, in spite of all this, the oppressed people always have the option of refusing to cooperate if they are willing to pay the price.

The Syrians in the Golan Heights have taken such a decision. They have clearly indicated that their identity is an internal matter and no amount of external force or persecution can force them to be anything other than what they are—an occupied Syrian people. In the West Bank and the Gaza Strip, refusal to cooperate can take several forms, each with its own potential and its own problems. I will list them here briefly as an example of the possibilities, not a comprehensive list. It must be borne in mind that conditions may not presently be suitable for carrying out some or all of them, and that each requires thorough study and planning before it is attempted.

1. Refusal to work in building Israeli settlements or opening roads or any of the other "Judaization" construction projects;

2. Refusal to work in Israeli factories;

3. Refusal to fill out any forms, give any information, or give any cooperation to the authorities (the police or the army);

4. Refusal to carry or produce identity cards;

5. Refusal to pay fines, thereby filling the already overcrowded jails and disrupting the entire judicial and "security" apparatus;

6. Refusal to submit requests for the many licenses and permits which are required under different laws or military orders;

7. Refusal to appear, when summoned, to the offices of the police, the civilian administration, or the military government;

8. Refusal to cooperate with or contact the officers or employees of the military government or the civilian administration that operate in the fields of health, education, agriculture, or others;

9. Refusal to sign or fill out any forms or documents that are printed or written in Hebrew;

10. Refusal to participate in any celebrations or activities initiated by the military government, the civilian administration, or known collaborators, or activities in which such people participate;

11. Refusal to work as employee of the military government or the civilian administration;

12. Refusal to pay income taxes;

13. Refusal to pay the value-added tax or any other tax;

14. Refusal to abide by house arrest orders or restrictions on travel, or orders declaring an area to be closed, or curfew orders;

15. Collective social boycotts of traitors and collaborators.

All these activities are within our power to execute. They are, in the first place, based on refusal or rejection. It is elementary that Palestinians can only carry out such activities selectively, one or several for a limited or permanent period based on the objective conditions prevailing at each particular stage. The existence of broad mass support for any activity reduces the dangers and sacrifices that any one individual would have to make in order for that activity to succeed. This method of resistance, at a minimum, forces the authorities to utilize a very large number of employees and soldiers to rule the occupied territories. Similarly, this refusal to cooperate overburdens the governing system and may even paralyze it.

It is also obvious that some of the activities listed above are impractical or unwise at the present stage, and must await a later stage in the struggle.

Harassment

This is different from the methods of obstruction or refusal to cooperate, in that it concentrates on the psychological aspects of harassing the Israelis, their employees and collaborators as they carry out their duties in the occupation system.

Since this method is a form of psychological warfare, it must be exercised after a thorough understanding of the Israeli mentality, and after carefully selecting the suitable tactics at each stage. Persistence is a basic element in the method of harassment. Hot/cold tactics may be utilized. This means a quick switching between protest and denunciation on the one hand, and appeals and affirmation of good will, on the other hand. It is possible under this method to use the telephone, letters, whistling, calling, provocations (but avoid curses and unjustified humiliations), slogans, hand gestures, body motions, and the like. The idea is never to allow the existence of any quiet or calm that may be interpreted as an acceptance of the prevailing situation. The person being harassed must be constantly reminded of the role that he plays in the injustice from which we are suffering and against which we are demonstrating. It is possible that this harassment may increase until it reaches the level of obstruction, or negatively, until it reaches the level of noncooperation. However, the distinctive feature of this method is that it is constantly active, affirmative, always taking the initiative, and aimed against the morale, the psychology and the mentality of the oppressor.

Boycotts

One of the major themes of the occupation is the subjugation of the economy of the West Bank and Gaza to the Israeli economy. These occupied areas have become a large market for Israeli goods and services. During the past 16 years Israeli goods have flooded the Arab markets and have even taken the place of the traditional production and consumption. Tnuva dairy goods, for example, are found everywhere, and the government bus company, Egged, runs its buses on several Arab lines. "Elite" chocolates, Israeli cigarettes, soft drinks, soaps, and many other Israeli goods are commonly found in Arab homes and markets. The initial call for a boycott of all Israeli goods and services which was made at the beginning of the occupation was unorganized and impractical. Today, however, it is possible to boycott one particular product or company, and to link the boycott to a single goal or demand which is reasonable. Such a limited boycott will be very effective and can accomplish intermediary goals upon which it is possible to build, and proceed to further gains.

Resources must also be aimed at creating alternatives to Israeli goods, and toward a return to natural foods in home consumption, for example. At any rate, natural foods are tastier and more nutritional than the prepackaged and canned products of Tnuva.

The importance of boycotting Israeli goods and services is well known. What is required is organizing limited, partial boycotts against some of these goods, linking them to specific demands, creating reasonable alternatives for these products and improving the Arab goods and services, for example, making the buses run on time.

Boycotts are very effective since there is no law—and can be no law— which forces Palestinians to buy or use Israeli goods and services, particularly if the Palestinians are willing to sacrifice by giving up such goods totally (assuming there are no alternatives). It is important to note that the residents of the Golan Heights did, in fact, boycott all Israeli goods and foods which they found it possible to do without, and have returned to reliance on local goods, plants, herbs, and other popular foods.

Strikes

Strikes are a form of refusal to cooperate (see above) which have long been used by the Palestinians. This method must be improved, particularly with respect to the period and length of the strike, when and how it is utilized, and how it can be used for attainable intermediary goals. Declaring an open strike calling for "the end of the occupation," for example, is a serious error.

Support and Solidarity

Acts of support and solidarity are important to demonstrate and deepen unity and cooperation among Palestinians; to reduce the impact of Israeli oppression and penalties by distributing it among a large number of people, and to escalate the confrontation with the authorities and create "points of contact" (see above) in a manner that helps the Palestinian struggle.

The Israeli policy of punishments and suppression is built on the principle of isolating anyone who opposes its laws or policies, labelling such an individual a "troublemaker" or an "inciting element," then punishing him or her severely as a "lesson" to others. Therefore, all activities of solidarity and support for such an individual defeat the aims of this policy.

One example of this was the rebuilding of five homes in Beit Sahur which were destroyed on the grounds that the owners' children had thrown rocks at an Israeli army vehicle.

Another instance occurred when an Israeli court attempted to try six Syrian Druze in the Golan Heights for failure to possess and produce an identity card. Several thousand Druze congregated outside the court to hand themselves in, insisting that they were all guilty of the same "crime" since they also refused to carry Israeli identity cards.

It is clear that in both these, and in many other examples of support and solidarity the authorities were prevented from achieving their aims. On the contrary, they created a strong sense of solidarity, a deeper unity and a more stubborn rejection of the Israeli practices.

Alternative Institutions

Perhaps one of the most important methods of nonviolent resistance to the occupation is the creation of alternative institutions and methods to replace the present unjust institutions of the occupation. This can occur in three separate ways.

First, the building of an entire infrastructure independently of Israel (universities, factories, institutions, libraries, hospitals, schools, etc.). This infrastructure becomes the necessary nucleus for the future Palestinian state. The creation of these institutions obstructs the process of annexation and "Judaization," and makes possible a political solution built upon Israeli withdrawal and the creation of an independent Palestinian state. It is also, in the long run, the best guarantee for the continued steadfastness and survival of Palestinian nationalism and the Palestinian people upon their land.

Second, the process of creating alternative social institutions for solving problems or offering services for which the population must presently turn to Israeli-run institutions, or for which permits and licenses issued by the military authorities are necessary. An example of this is the corrupt court system. Here it may be possible to create an alternative by strengthening and developing the process of arbitration or traditional law, after removing the backward aspects of that system. Similarly, it is possible to create alternatives for the health insurance *(Kopat Holim)* and other services.

Third, making plans, enlisting resources and setting up committees to provide for the needs of the population in case individual or collective punishments are imposed during the struggle. An example of this is taking care of the needy families of detainees. Another is to create alternative curriculi and programs for study in case schools and universities are closed, make arrangements to meet in homes, store food, water, fuel, and candles to be used during prolonged curfews and economic sieges. In addition, we need to arrange alternative methods of contacting the foreign press and the outside world, or receiving and transmitting news in the eventuality that a certain area is closed off. Finally, we need to set up popular committees to carry out the functions of the municipalities when they are closed, or when they are turned over to Israeli officers or collaborators, in order that the population will continue to receive the necessary services during that period.

Here, it is important to note that new methods of channeling funds (other than the bridges and the joint Jordanian-Palestinian Committee) must be found, and better utilization of local resources must be made to fund projects in case the authorities prohibit or delay the entry of monies from the outside.

In pursuing this method, we must make every effort to utilize existing loopholes and legal opportunities in creating new institutions. We should utilize existing licensed institutions and develop them as well as create unofficial bodies, such as *ad hoc* popular committees, which meet to coordinate a project, but then proceed to act separately without a recognized legal structure. The Arabs in East Jerusalem could set up societies, or companies under the more liberal Israeli law could be utilized. Such bodies could then proceed to operate in the West Bank and Gaza as if they were "Israeli" bodies.

Civil Disobedience

Civil disobedience usually comes at a much later and developed point in the nonviolent struggle. It involves the conscious and deliberate commission of illegal acts and violation of known military orders and laws. This form of direct action must be carefully contemplated. A nonviolent person utilizing this method must be willing to take the full legal consequences of his or her actions. This could be done by prominent individuals deliberately accepting punishment to highlight the injustice of the law in question, or it could be a mass movement aimed at paralyzing the particular law and showing that it cannot work without the consent of the population.

In embarking upon civil disobedience, the planners must anticipate different responses by the authorities. These may range from ignoring the protest to selective enforcement against leaders or prominent individuals or massive and brutal repression. During civil disobedience, nationalist leaders may choose to declare that one of their goals is to fill up all the jails. This would be relatively simple to achieve since the jails are already crowded. Such a declaration, if acted upon, could prove extremely effective. It would rob the jails of their effectiveness in frightening the population and in ensuring compliance, since every additional person jailed would bring the leaders one step closer toward achieving their goals. Secondly, pursuit of this goal would strengthen solidarity among the Palestinians and make jail a symbol of victory and success rather than a feared punishment. Thirdly, if there were mass support for this goal, the law in question could easily be rendered ineffective, since the authorities cannot afford to use up all the jail space simply to enforce one military order or law.

One aspect of nonviolence that is worth emphasizing in this respect is that the Palestinians would be voluntarily accepting and rejoicing in the persecution and suffering inflicted on them. Bravely and steadfastly to accept persecution for one's beliefs brings one very close to the power of nonviolence. It neutralizes the effectiveness of the instruments of repression and improves the internal steadfastness and power of the resister. The greatest enemy to the people and the most powerful weapon in the hands of the authorities is fear. Palestinians who can liberate themselves from fear and who will boldly accept suffering and persecution without fear or bitterness or striking back have managed to achieve the greatest victory of all. They have conquered themselves, and all the rest will be much easier to accomplish.

Nonviolence is the most effective method of resisting the Israeli occupation in the West Bank and Gaza today. The methods, tactics, and strategy of classic nonviolence must, of course, be modified to meet the present circumstances, but they have considerable applicability in this situation. Moreover, these methods can be successfully utilized, at least in part, by individuals who are not necessarily committed to nonviolence and who may choose, at a different stage, to engage in armed struggle. Meanwhile, nonviolent struggle continues to offer Palestinians in the West Bank and Gaza an excellent opportunity to struggle toward liberation.

Nonviolence in the Israeli Women's Peace Movement

Gila Svirsky

Nonviolence as a strategy has been practiced throughout the Israeli women's peace movement since the founding of Women in Black in early 1988, one month after the first Palestinian Intifada broke out. The Women in Black movement began as a small group of Israeli women carrying out a simple form of protest: Once a week at the same hour and in the same location—a major traffic intersection in Jerusalem—they donned black clothing and raised a black sign in the shape of a hand with white lettering that read "End the Occupation."

From this modest beginning, women throughout Israel heard of this protest, and launched similar vigils. Throughout the north of Israel, where many Palestinian citizens of Israel reside, the vigils had Arab and Jewish women standing side by side. From Israel, it spread to dozens of other countries. The strength of this movement is its clear and unchanging message presented in a nonviolent manner: End the Occupation. The target audience for this message is the Israeli public and leadership, the international public and leadership, and the Palestinian people. The intent is to magnify the voice of those who object to the occupation, but do not have political clout as individuals. Because of the persistence of these women and the growing number of vigils, this movement seems to have had widespread impact.

When the al-Aqsa Intifada broke out in late September 2000, nine Israeli women's peace organizations joined together as the Coalition of Women for Peace and launched a series of nonviolent actions. Some of these involved civil disobedience, such as lying down on the street to block the entrance to the Israeli Ministry of Defense, as a way to protest 'closure' in the territories. Subsequent actions, often in cooperation with mixed-gender peace organizations, involved other nonviolent but illegal acts—the rebuilding of demolished homes or the removal of blockades and filling in of trenches intended to enforce the closure. In other actions, individual women stood in front of army bulldozers or chained themselves to olive trees in an effort to prevent

Source: *Going Places*, Vol. IV, No. 213 (September 5, 2003). Used with permission.

further destruction of Palestinian homes and property. Some of these actions ended in arrests.

This coalition of women's peace organizations has also staged mass actions of nonviolence that are legal. A year and a half ago (December 2001), 5,000 Israeli and Palestinian women marched together from the Israeli to the Palestinian side of Jerusalem under the twin banners, "The Occupation is Killing Us All" and "We Refuse to be Enemies." This June, Israeli women staged a mass 'lie-in' in Tel Aviv, with 1,000 women wearing black, stretched out on the pavement as a sign of mourning for the victims of the occupation.

Some of the member organizations of the Coalition engage in other forms of nonviolent resistance. The presence at checkpoints of the women in Machsom [checkpoint] Watch is often enough to prevent particularly cruel harassment of Palestinians. Recently these women prevented a soldier from firing at a child by deflecting his gun, leading to their arrest for "interfering with the IDF." The organization New Profile supports conscientious objection to army service, and last year launched a "Women Refuse" campaign. What do they refuse? "To raise our children for war, to ignore war crimes committed in our name, to support the occupation, to continue our normal lives while another nation is suffering because of us." This is a profound use of nonviolence—an attempt to change the militaristic culture of Israeli society and to instill the values of nonviolence in Israeli children.

The most successful case in Israel of the use of nonviolence in the service of peace is the Four Mothers Movement. This group, founded in 1997 by four women whose sons were serving in the Israeli army, sought to mobilize the Israeli public to demand that Israel withdraw its troops from Lebanon, based on the argument that Israel's prolonged presence there serves no security purpose, but jeopardizes the lives of soldiers. The movement was initially met with scorn from senior military officers ("What do women know about security?" they mocked). But at the heart of the Four Mothers' strategy was leveraging their status as mothers. This was effective in a society that may disrespect professional women but honors its mothers.

The Four Mothers Movement never used civil disobedience, but held small demonstrations and vigils that highlighted the sincerity of their plea as law-abiding women, not politicians. Their status as mothers who had sons serving in combat units gave them the right, in the eyes of the public, to challenge Israeli policy in Lebanon. They demanded—and were accorded—meetings with the highest government officials, whose inadequate answers were then magnified through the well-run media work of this group. The "authentic," mother-oriented nature of this movement, and its dissociation from partisan politics, struck an empathetic nerve among the Israeli public. The deaths of Israeli soldiers were on the increase in Lebanon, and the message of the Four Mothers fell on attentive ears, feeding public dismay over the seemingly endless body bags. Within three years of the start of the movement, the Israeli army withdrew from Lebanon.

The women's peace movement in Israel has used nonviolence in varied and creative ways. While the most dramatic actions have had civil disobedience and risk-taking at the core, a large array of lawful actions has also been used, and no less effectively. Women demonstrators sometimes feel "protected" in the belief that the police and army will not harm women, although that belief has proven to be unjustified. But the strategy of nonviolence clearly provides a greater moral strength and persuasiveness than violent strategies. The practice of nonviolence has also been empowering to those who feel otherwise helpless, and results seem to confirm its effectiveness.

Nonviolence
Ordinary Palestinians Fight for Their Freedom

Lucy Nusseibeh

The essence of Palestinian resistance is nonviolence: the steadfastness, the resilience, the dignity, and the humanity in the face of the unrelenting humiliations and brutality of the Israeli occupation. Such nonviolent resistance is much more the norm than the violent acts that grab headlines. As daily life for Palestinians becomes increasingly less livable from every point of view, there is growing interest in finding ways to get life back on track and, therefore, in using nonviolence as perhaps the best way to do this.

With or without the glimmer of hope afforded by the road map [the 2003 U.S. plan for a comprehensive settlement to the Israel-Palestinian conflict], Palestinian nonviolence needs to be appreciated and strengthened. Violence is only in the interest of those who would dominate and exercise control through fear. If the Middle East situation is allowed to deteriorate, there will be no guarantee that it will not suck the rest of the world into a vortex of violence and fear. Civil society, both at the local and the international levels, can and must help at this crucial juncture if the cycle of violence is to be stopped in our fragile and interconnected world. Now is the time for the world to understand the centrality of nonviolent action for Palestinians, and to act and speak out in support and solidarity of all those working with it.

Nonviolence is the assertion of one's rights without using violence. Often it involves withholding or withdrawing support from illegitimate sources of power. It is based on the courage and humanity of ordinary people and their determination to live in dignity and decency. It is not surrender, and it is not necessarily even compromise; rather, it is a means to achieve justice and change without using violence,

Nonviolence is also empowerment. It grows from the development of potential, and, therefore, it helps develop long-term democratic solutions to problems and injustices. Violence, on the other hand, even if it brings victory through sheer force in the short term, ultimately only disempowers, not only

Source: *Going Places*, Vol. IV, No. 214 (September 12, 2003). Used with permission.

those who it oppresses and "beats," but those who use it, because it inevitably reduces their humanity.

Nonviolence tends to be associated with certain situations and names, such as Gandhi, Martin Luther King, and others, and is seen as something specific: a march, a strike, preferably an event that will touch the hearts of the oppressors and transform the conflict. This is a major part of active nonviolence, which the Palestinians have used throughout their struggle, from the early protests against Jewish/Zionist immigration in the 1920s, and especially during the intifada of the 1980s.

That intifada was organized around noncooperation with the occupying power, such as refusing to pay taxes. There were battles over which hours shops would be open or shut (with the Israelis sealing the locks of those who would not comply and arresting the shop owners), and over the right to organize committees to teach children during periods when schools were closed.

There was tremendous power in the unity of Palestinian civil society at that time—across factions, age groups, social divisions, and (the less formidable, but still traditional) geographical divisions—as everyone joined in to get the Israeli occupation off their backs and out of their daily lives.

The deliberate use of nonviolence helped to unite, and build trust throughout the Palestinian community, as Palestinians sensed the power of their refusal to cooperate with the occupier's system, and felt liberated as a result. They also felt empowered by the directives that came only from the "underground leadership" rather than from the top. This unity culminated in the unilateral declaration of independence for the state of Palestine in November 1988—a nonviolent beginning.

There is also a determination by Palestinians to refuse to allow the Israelis to crush them, their identity or their determination to be free. This is an equally valid form of nonviolence, and it is perhaps more long-term and far-reaching than orchestrated actions, which have continued throughout all the years of occupation. Care and respect for essential human needs—with or without a government structure—are forms of active nonviolence as well.

We saw this, for example, when the streets of Nablus were filled with children being taught classes in defiance of the interminable curfew, or when the population of Ramallah simply defied the curfew, whether to visit friends and relatives or to announce their presence by beating on pots and pans. Yet the simple daily acts of survival also represent Palestinian active nonviolence, even if not recognized as such by those doing them.

Examples of this daily form of nonviolent action include the groups of women who visit the most remote villages to meet with women unable to leave their communities in order to hear their pain and find ways to help them and their children; the drivers of the shared "Ford" taxis (the only way left for most people to get around at all), who persist in finding ways of getting from one place to another despite roads that have been dug up or blocked off; the teachers who make their way to work and patiently help and care for children even when they themselves have spent the night in fear; and the many people who not only keep going but who develop initiatives like summer camps and other activities for children, such as the Palestinian children's opera or the riding stable in Jericho.

These actions belie the cruel and unfair stereotype of the Palestinians as all, without exception, potential terrorists. Moreover they are the hope for the future of the democratic Palestinian state, which will succeed based on the active participation and long-standing nonviolence of its citizens.

Selected Bibliography

Ackerman, Peter, and Jack DuVall. 2000. *A Force More Powerful.* New York: St. Martin's Press.

Addams, Jane. 1907. *New Ideals of Peace.* New York: Macmillan.

Ansbro, John J. 1984. *Martin Luther King, Jr., The Making of a Mind.* Maryknoll, NY: Orbis Books.

Apsey, Lawrence S., James Bristol, and Karen Eppler. 1986. *Transforming Power for Peace.* Philadelphia: Religious Education Committee of Friends General Conference.

Arnett, Ronald C. 1989. *Dwell in Peace: Applying Nonviolence to Everyday Relationships.* Elgin, IL: The Brethren Press.

Bacon, Margaret Hope. 1980. *Valiant Friend: The Life of Lucretia Mott.* New York: Walker and Company.

Bainton, Roland. 1960. *Christian Attitudes Toward War and Peace: A Historical Survey and Critical Re-Evaluation.* New York: Abingdon Press.

Ballou, Adin. 1846. *Christian Non Resistance in All Its Important Bearings, Illustrated and Defended.* Edited by William S. Heywood. Philadelphia: J. Miller M'Kim.

Bedau, Hugo Adam, ed. 1969. *Civil Disobedience: Theory and Practice.* New York: Pegasus.

Bok, Sissela. 1989. *A Strategy for Peace: Human Values and the Threat of War.* New York: Pantheon Books.

Bondurant, Joan V. 1988. *Conquest of Violence: The Gandhian Philosophy of Conflict.* Princeton, NJ: Princeton University Press.

Brock, Peter. 1968. *Pacifism in the U.S. from the Colonial Era to the First World War.* Princeton, NJ: Princeton University Press.

———. 1970. *Twentieth Century Pacifism.* New York: Van Nostrand Reinhold.

Brooks, Thomas R. 1974. *Walls Come Tumbling Down: A History of the Civil Rights Movement: 1940–1970.* Englewood Cliffs, NJ: Prentice Hall.

Chavez, Cesar. April 1969. "Letter from Delano," *Christian Century* 23, 539–540.

———. April 1969. "Nonviolence Still Works," *Look* 1, 52–57.

Cooney, Robert, and Helen Michalowski. 1987. *The Power of the People: Active Nonviolence in the United States.* Philadelphia: New Society Publishers.

Day, Dorothy. 1972. *On Pilgrimage: The Sixties.* Garden City, NY: Curtis Books.

Dellinger, David. 1970. *Revolutionary Nonviolence.* New York: Bobbs-Merrill.

Deming, Barbara. 1958. *Prison Notes.* New York: Monthly Review Press.

———. 1974. *We Cannot Live Without Our Lives.* New York: Grossman.

———. 1984. *We Are All Part of One Another: A Barbara Deming Reader.* Edited by Jane Meyerding. Philadelphia: New Society Publishers.

Easwaran, Eknath. 1984. *A Man to Match His Mountains: Badshah Khan, Nonviolent Soldier of Islam.* Petaluma, CA: Nilgiri Press.

Estey, George F., and Doris A. Hunter. 1971. *Nonviolence: A Reader in the Ethics of Action.* Waltham, MA: Xerox College Publishing.

Freund, Norman C. 1987. *Nonviolent National Defense: A Philosophical Inquiry into Applied Nonviolence.* Lanham, MD: University Press of America.

Gandhi, Mohandas K. 1963. *Non-Violent Resistance.* New York: Schocken Books.

———. 1986. *The Moral and Political Writings of Mahatma Gandhi.* Vols. 1–3. Edited by Raghavan Iyer. Oxford: Oxford University Press.

———. 1993. *Autobiography: The Story of My Experiments with Truth.* Boston: Beacon Press.

———. 1999. *Vows and Observances.* Berkeley, CA: Berkeley Hills Books.

———. 2002. *The Essential Gandhi: An Anthology.* Edited by Louis Fischer. New York: Vintage.

Gioseffi, Daniela. 1988. *Women On War: Essential Voices for the Nuclear Age.* New York: Simon & Schuster.

Gluck, Sherna, ed. 1976. *From Parlor to Prison: Five American Suffragists Talk About Their Lives.* New York: Vintage Books.

Gregg, Richard B. 1966. *The Power of Nonviolence.* New York: Schocken Books.

Hanh, Thich Nhat. 1967. *Vietnam: Lotus In a Sea of Fire.* New York: Hill & Wang.

Hanigan, James P. 1984. *Martin Luther King, Jr. and the Foundations of Nonviolence.* Lanham, MD: University Press of America.

Holmes, Robert L. 1989. *On War and Morality.* Princeton, NJ: Princeton University Press.

Juergensmeyer, Mark. 1986. *Fighting Fair: A Non-Violent Strategy for Resolving Everyday Conflicts.* San Francisco: Harper & Row.

King, Martin Luther, Jr. 1958. *Stride Toward Freedom.* New York: Harper & Brothers.

———. 1963. *Strength to Love.* New York: Harper & Row.

———. 1964. *Why We Can't Wait.* New York: A Signet Book.

———. 1967. *Where Do We Go From Here: Chaos or Community?* New York: Bantam Books.

Lakey, George. Winter 1968. "Technique and Ethos in Nonviolent Action: The Woman Suffrage Case," *Sociological Inquiry*, 37–42.

———. 1987. *Powerful Peacemaking: Strategy for a Living Revolution.* Philadelphia: New Society Publishers.

Lynd, Staughton, ed. 1966. *Nonviolence in America: A Documentary History.* Indianapolis: Bobbs-Merrill.

Mabee, Carlton. 1970. *Black Freedom: The Nonviolent Abolitionists from 1830 through the Civil War.* New York: Macmillan.

McAllister, Pam, ed. 1982. *Reweaving the Web of Life: Feminism and Nonviolence.* Philadelphia: New Society Publishers.

Mehta, Ved. 1977. *Mahatma Gandhi and His Apostles.* New York: Viking.

Merton, Thomas. 1980. *The Nonviolent Alternative.* Edited by Gordon Zahn. New York: Farrar, Strauss and Giroux.

Miller, William Robert. 1966. *Nonviolence: A Christian Interpretation.* New York: Schocken Books.

Muste, A. J. 1940. *Nonviolence in an Aggressive World.* New York: Harper & Bros.

———. 1967. *The Essays of A. J. Muste.* Edited by Nat Hentoff. New York: Simon & Schuster.

Nagler, Michael. 2001. *Is There No Other Way: The Search for a Nonviolent Future.* Berkeley, CA: Berkeley Hills Books.

Nagler, Michael, Richard Deats, and Melinda Moore. 1999. *The Steps of Nonviolence.* Fellowship Publications.

Narveson, Jan. 1965. "Pacifism: A Philosophical Analysis." *Ethics*, Vol. 75, 259–271.

Norman, Liane Ellison. 1989. *Hammer of Justice: Molly Rush and the Plowshares Eight.* Pittsburgh, PA: The Pittsburgh Peace Institute.

Robinson, JoAnn Gibson. 1987. *The Montgomery Bus Boycott and the Women Who Started It.* Knoxville: University of Tennessee Press.

Ryan, Cheyney C. "Self-Defense, Pacifism, and the Possibility of Killing." *Ethics*, Vol. 93, No. 3, 1983, 508–524.

Sharma, I. C. 1965. *Ethical Philosophies of India.* Edited and revised by Stanley M. Daugert. Lincoln, NE: Johnsen Publishing.

Sharp, Gene. 1970. *Exploring Nonviolent Alternatives.* Boston: Porter Sargent.

———. 1973. *The Politics of Nonviolent Action.* Boston: Porter Sargent.

———. 1980. *Social Power and Political Freedom.* Boston: Porter Sargent.

Sibley, Mulford A., ed. 1963. *The Quiet Battle: Writings on the Theory and Practice of Non-Violent Resistance.* Garden City, NJ: Doubleday.

Solomonow, Allan, ed. 1985. *Roots of Jewish Nonviolence.* Nyack, NY: Jewish Peace Fellowship.

Taylor, Ronald. 1975. *Chavez and the Farmworkers.* Boston: Beacon Press.

Tolstoy, Leo. 1961. *A Confession, The Gospel in Brief, What I Believe.* New York: Oxford University Press.

———. 1961. *The Kingdom of God Is Within You.* New York: Noonday Press.

———. 1970. *The Law of Love and the Law of Violence.* New York: Holt, Rinehart and Winston.

Wells, Donald A. 1967. *The War Myth.* Indianapolis: Bobbs-Merrill.

Wink, Walter. 1987. *Violence and Nonviolence in South Africa: Jesus's Third Way.* Philadelphia: New Society Publishers.

Zunes, Stephen, Lester Kurtz, and Sarah Beth Asher, eds. 1999. *Nonviolent Social Movements: A Geographical Perspective.* Oxford: Blackwell.

Selected Web Sites of Interest

The Albert Einstein Institution
The institution begun by Gene Sharp to promote the study and use of strategic nonviolence.
http://www.aeinstein.org

Civilian-Based Defense
A compilation of Web sites related to civilian-based defense.
http://www.blancmange.net/tmh/cbd1.html

Conflict Resolution and Peacebuilding
An excellent bibliography by Catherine Morris, with many additional links.
http://www.peacemakers.ca/bibliography/bib37nonviolentdirect.html

The Fellowship of Reconciliation
The Web site for the oldest and largest interfaith nonprofit organization dedicated to peace and nonviolence.
http://www.forusa.org

Ghandi
Site maintained by various nonprofit organizations in India; offers a variety of information about Gandhi.
http://www.mkgandhi.org

The International Center on Nonviolent Conflict
Jack DuVall's organization for education about nonviolence and training political practitioners of nonviolence.
http://www.nonviolent-conflict.org/resources.shtml

The King Center
http://thekingcenter.com/

The Martin Luther King, Jr. Papers Project
http://www.stanford.edu/group/King/

The M. K. Gandhi Institute for Nonviolence
The institute founded by Arun Gandhi and his wife Sunanda to promote and teach the philosophy and practice of nonviolence.
http://www.mkgandhi.org

Nonviolence International
The nonprofit organization begun by Mubarak Awad to extend the practice and understanding of nonviolence throughout the world.
www.members.tripod.com/nviusa

Nonviolence USA
A Web site with many links related to nonviolence.
http://pages.prodigy.net/gmoses/nvusa/index.htm